INFLUENCERS & CREATORS

INFLUENCERS & CREATORS

Business, Culture and Practice

ROBERT V KOZINETS, ULRIKE GRETZEL & ROSSELLA GAMBETTI

Los Angeles | London | New Delhi
Singapore | Washington DC | Melbourne

Los Angeles I London I New Delhi
Singapore I Washington DC I Melbourne

SAGE Publications Ltd
1 Oliver's Yard
55 City Road
London EC1Y 1SP

SAGE Publications Inc.
2455 Teller Road
Thousand Oaks, California 91320

SAGE Publications India Pvt Ltd
B 1/I 1 Mohan Cooperative Industrial Area
Mathura Road
New Delhi 110 044

SAGE Publications Asia-Pacific Pte Ltd
3 Church Street
#10-04 Samsung Hub
Singapore 049483

Library of Congress Control Number: 2022946099

British Library Cataloguing in Publication data

A catalogue record for this book is available from the British Library

Editor: Natalie Aguilera
Editorial assistant: Rhoda Ola-Said
Production editor: Vijayakumar
Copyeditor: Christobel Colleen Hopman
Proofreader: Benny Willy Stephen
Indexer: TNQ Technologies
Marketing manager: Ruslana Khatagova
Cover design: Francis Kenney
Typeset by: TNQ Technologies
Printed in the UK by Bell & Bain Ltd, Glasgow
BB0347322

ISBN 978-1-5297-6865-7
ISBN 978-1-5297-6864-0 (pbk)

At SAGE we take sustainability seriously. Most of our products are printed in the UK using responsibly sourced papers and boards. When we print overseas we ensure sustainable papers are used as measured by the PREPS grading system. We undertake an annual audit to monitor our sustainability.

TABLE OF CONTENTS

List of Tables   vii
List of Figures   ix
Author Bios and Affiliations   xi

1 Influencers and Creators   1

2 A Macrosocial Perspective   27

3 Business and Social Media Marketing Concepts   53

4 Influencer and Creator Ecosystem   83

5 Principles of Influence   109

6 Diversity, Equity, and Inclusion   135

7 Cultural Effects   155

8 Ethics and Regulation   185

9 The Business of Influence   213

10 Partnering with Influencers and Creators   241

11 Running Campaigns   271

12 Measuring and Assessing Campaigns   291

13 Trajectories, Technologies, and Transformations   315

References   341
Index   365

LIST OF TABLES

Table 1.1 Some video game streamers and their unique style and content———————————————————— 5

Table 1.2 A sampling of definitions of influencers ————————— 8

Table 3.1 Examples and characteristics of PESO media types ——— 60

Table 5.1 Sources of social influence ————————————— 114

Table 5.2 Cialdini's principles of persuasion ———————————— 130

Table 9.1 Budget categories for influencer marketing campaigns—— 228

Table 10.1 Key elements of influencer and creator contracts ——— 264

LIST OF FIGURES

Figure 1.1 Differences and similarities between influencers and creators —————— 16

Figure 1.2 Winkelmann's 'Gigachad' —————— 18

Figure 1.3 Influencers and other related concepts —————— 19

Figure 1.4 Influencer marketing, influencer advertising, and influencer relations —————— 23

Figure 2.1 Base and superstructure in the influencer system —————— 31

Figure 3.1 Influencer marketing within the PESO model —————— 60

Figure 3.2 The marketing funnel —————— 66

Figure 3.3 Quang Tran's eating ritual to elicit consumers' desire —————— 69

Figure 3.4 Brand desire spiral —————— 70

Figure 4.1 The influencer and creator ecosystem —————— 89

Figure 5.1 The influencer communication process —————— 122

Figure 5.2 Ohanian's model of source credibility —————— 126

Figure 6.1 Types of diversity —————— 140

Figure 6.2 Visual representation of White versus Black pay gap —————— 143

Figure 6.3 Self-empowering discourse of inclusivity on Blair Imani's Instagram pages —————— 151

Figure 7.1 Forces and effects of influencer culture —————— 159

Figure 7.2 James Charles' intensified dramas on YouTube —————— 162

Figure 9.1 Influencer marketing campaign process —————— 220

Figure 9.2 Categories of influencer marketing campaign goals —————— 223

Figure 9.3 Influencer marketing campaign classifiers —————— 231

Figure 10.1 #Ogniversionedite campaign by Lierac Italia, 1 —————— 245

Figure 10.2 #Ogniversionedite campaign by Lierac Italia, 2 —————— 246

Figure 10.3 A sample influencer outreach email ——————— 258

Figure 10.4 Finding the right balance in an influencer brief ———— 261

Figure 10.5 Processes involved in the partnering phase———— 267

Figure 11.1 UNICEF campaign with Halima Aden ——————— 276

Figure 11.2 Influencer campaign promotion by Bretman Rock ——— 279

Figure 11.3 The key phases of influencer campaign execution ——— 284

Figure 11.4 The dos and don'ts of influencer campaign
execution——————————————————— 288

Figure 12.1 The formula for influencer marketing return on
investment (ROI)————————————————— 301

Figure 12.2 Key performance indicators for measuring influencer
marketing objectives ————————————— 305

Figure 13.1 New product adoption curve———————————— 321

Figure 13.2 Cottagecore aesthetics———————————————— 323

Figure 13.3 The virtual Vocaloid and influencer Hatsune Miku ——— 328

AUTHOR BIOS AND AFFILIATIONS

Robert V. Kozinets

Robert V. Kozinets has been researching and consulting in the world of social media marketing for almost 30 years. He advises companies and organisations, develops methods and theories, educates and serves as an expert witness on topics relating to influencers and social media. His work has been published in books, peer-reviewed articles, blogs, Tweets and as research videos (on YouTube), research music (as Kozmic-X on Spotify), research art (on Pixels.com) and poetry. Netnography, one of his innovations, transformed research practices in industry and the social sciences. His websites at kozinets.net and netnografica.com contain many resources from his work and his up-to-date blog. He has taught and conducted research at some of the world's top universities, including in Australia, Brazil, Ecuador, Peru, Italy, Norway, France, Ireland, New Zealand, the United Kingdom and Israel, as well as in his home base of USC in Los Angeles, California.

Ulrike Gretzel

Ulrike Gretzel is Director of Research at Netnografica and a Senior Research Fellow at the Center for Public Relations, University of Southern California. She received her PhD in Communications from the University of Illinois at Urbana-Champaign. Her research spans the design, use and implications of emerging technologies, ranging from mobile applications and social media to smart cities, robots and the metaverse. She has over 20 years of experience conducting academic and practice-focused research. Her research has been funded by national science foundations and businesses around the globe. She is frequently acknowledged as one of the most cited authors in the fields of tourism and persuasion and is an elected fellow of the International Academy for the Study of Tourism. Her work has been quoted in major news outlets such as *The New York Times* and *The Australian*.

Rossella Gambetti

Rossella Gambetti, PhD, is Professor of Branding and Consumer Culture at the Università Cattolica del Sacro Cuore in Milan, where she is Director of LABCOM (Research Lab on Business Communication). She is also a research fellow of the Jayne and Hans Hufschmid Chair of Strategic Public Relations and Business Communication at the Annenberg School for Communication and Journalism, University of Southern California (LA). Rossella is an interpretive scholar whose research is focused on the interplays between consumer culture, branding and technology and how these are shaping consumption, communication and society. Rossella has been a visiting scholar at universities in the United States and in Japan and has published her works in journals such as *Marketing Theory, Journal of Business Research, California Management Review, Business Ethics Quarterly* and *Management Decision*.

1

INFLUENCERS AND CREATORS

CHAPTER OVERVIEW AND OBJECTIVES

Using examples and illustrations, this chapter will introduce the key focus of the book – influencers and creators – and set the conceptual groundwork for distinguishing them from other concepts such as celebrities, brand ambassadors, and opinion leaders. Beginning with a look at the world of influencers and the general changes in the media landscape, the chapter will overview the fundamental qualities of influencers and creators. Although the activities of both creators and influencers are centred on social media, they are valued for different reasons. Readers will learn the essential qualities that influencers and creators possess, and also the elements that are common but not essential. The chapter will close with a discussion of the differences between influencer marketing and influencer relations.

PROVOCATION: Are content creators and influencers the same thing? Do influencers have to make money? Can people be influencers and not be on social media?

KEYWORDS: content creator, influencer, opinion leader, celebrity, brand ambassador, digital marketer, personal branding, influencer advertising, influencer marketing, influencer relations

RICHARD TYLER BLEVINS ON TWITCH

You may not know who Richard Tyler Blevins is. But chances are that if you play video games, you almost certainly know his online alias, Ninja. Blevins, who was born in 1991, is a professional gamer who began his career playing e-sports with Halo 3. But his success playing e-sports pales to his success as a content streamer on Twitch. His fame as a game streamer spread to the mainstream media in 2018 when he streamed his Fortnite play together with the rap icons Drake and Travis Scott, as well as the football wide receiver JuJu Smith-Schuster, setting a record for viewers on Twitch. Currently, Ninja has the most followed channel on Twitch, with over 18 million followers, as well as almost 24 million followers on YouTube.

There are many people who produce their own video game-related material and share it on social media, and they each have their own unique personas, styles, and content focus. Blevins/Ninja is a creator of engaging streamed content who is widely followed and recognised for his fun-loving, goofy, and wildly energetic personality. Not only is he an excellent game player, he also makes watching his play highly amusing and exciting. As Table 1.1 shows, there are numerous other video game influencers who each have their own personal style and focus, from Jelly and his child-friendly video game reviews to Markiplier and his sarcastic focus on the horror genre to Syndicate and his helpful tutorials and how-to guides. Each of these gamers has developed what marketers would clearly recognise as a personal brand and they have also applied it to branding their social media channel or content stream. The question is whether these gamers are influencers, creators, or both, and this chapter will discuss just that.

What has happened to the world of media and marketing? Numerous trust-based surveys such as the Nielsen Report (Global Trust in Advertising Report, 2019), Gallup (Marketing Charts, 2021a), and Edelman (2021) have all charted the widespread and global erosion of faith and interest in traditional advertising. This long history of research tells us that, for decades, people have been tired of the unrealistic promises and fantasy imagery of traditional advertising. And this mistrust is well earned! In 2019, Chevron advertising claimed that it was 'part of the solution' to climate change. However, the company was widely criticized because its plans for carbon capture and storage covered less than 1% of its 2019 carbon emissions. And not only are fossil fuel companies like Chevron untrusted, advertising practitioners in general are considered only marginally better than car salespeople (Marketing Charts, 2021a). Only one in ten Americans who were surveyed considered advertising professionals to have

Table 1.1 Some video game streamers and their unique style and content

Stream's real name	Pseudonym or streamer channel brand	Unique voice/image
Richard Tyler Blevins	Ninja	Fun-loving, goofy, and wildly energetic personality
Sean William McLaughlin	Jacksepticeye	Extremely detailed video game reviews, nit-picking, and a wide genre range
Alia Marie Shelesh	SSSniperWolf	Humorous, quirky, Call of Duty and first-person shooter games
Tom Cassell	Syndicate	Informative tutorials and videos; how-to-play or get unstuck from particular video games
Mark Fishbach	Markiplier	Horror genre mixed with comedy narration, lots of jokes, and sarcastic comments
Jess Bravura	Aphmau	Imaginative, whimsical, storytelling; 'Minecraft diaries'
Jelle Van Vucht	Jelly	Family content; child-friendly video games reviews

honesty and ethical standards that are 'high' or 'very high'. Besides mistrust, there is also incredible advertising fatigue. Experts estimate that the average American is overwhelmed by between 6,000 and 10,000 pieces of advertising every day (Carr, 2021).

It is little wonder that people have been trying to ignore and evade commercials and use technologies or even pay fees to escape from this bombardment. People have developed psychological strategies to deal with the profusion of advertising and marketing in their lives. An important precursor to advertising avoidance is being able to recognise advertising and similar persuasion attempts.

PERSUASION KNOWLEDGE AND SCHEMER'S SCHEMA

The fact that people resist traditional advertising has been widely studied. Advertising theorists Marian Friestad and Peter Wright coined the term 'schemer's schema' to recognize that, over their lifetimes, people build up knowledge about the persuasion attempts of marketers, salespeople, and advertisers to help them resist and cope with the barrage of commercial information that comes their way (Friestad & Wright, 1994).

One of the important outcomes of this mistrust and need to cope with advertising has been the steadily increasing appeal of more authentic types of recommendations, such as customer reviews by actual users. When social media began to offer a range of voices of 'real people', this was widely seen as a welcome relief to the outpouring of untrusted professional salespeople and potentially biased reviewers who previously populated most of the mass media channels. Beginning with the blogging movement of the late 1990s and early 2000s, people reacted favourably to brand and product reviews by social media content makers who seemed to be (1) similar to themselves, (2) knowledgeable about niche topics, (3) not commercially motivated, and/or (4) engaged and directly communicating with the members of their audience.

It did not take long for marketers to notice. Before long, brand managers and other communication professionals started building blogger-based strategies into their marketing plans, trying to make sure that those 'real life' voices were engaging with their brands in ways that they could try to control. For instance, when one of the authors of this book was studying a blogging nurse influencer in 2006 (Kozinets et al., 2010), a pay-per-post company was already offering her money to post favourable reviews of their products. Contemporary efforts to take advantage of the persuasive power of influencers directly evolved from these early attempts to manipulate electronic word-of-mouth. There is no doubt today that influencer marketing is a big-money industry. With his gaming streams, Richard Tyler Blevins creates highly engaging content for his audiences – for which he earns impressive amounts of money. In an unconfirmed rumour, Electronic Arts (EA) paid him $1 million to play their 'Apex Legends' game in his video stream. Altogether, Ninja makes an estimated $10 million per year.

The world of social media is currently poised between that past reality where people considered it to be a more trustworthy alternative to traditional media and advertising, and a current reality where its many commercial operations are openly being acknowledged and sceptically questioned. There is no doubt that the massive success of influencers like Richard Tyler Blevins illustrates that something dramatic has already happened not only to the world of video games but also to comedy, fashion, travel, fitness, parenting, pet ownership, education, sports, dating, collecting, work, and almost every other aspect of human behaviour and interest. Through their knowledge, their expertise, and their entertainment value, influencers have become a vitally important part of our culture – and this has happened around the world. Over the last decade, they have also become an increasingly integral part of the business ecosystem. One of the most apparent ways we can measure this importance is in terms of economic value. Globally, the market value of influencer-related outputs was estimated at $13.8 billion in 2021 (Statista, 2021a) – and we consider this estimate to be low because the revenue streams of influencers are diverse.

During the social media intense COVID-19 pandemic, the influencer and creator industry grew rapidly because people were home and spending more time on social media and shopping online. Research suggests that the influencer marketing industry grew at the remarkable rate of 33.6% between 2020 and 2021 (eMarketer, 2021). The pandemic also halted the traditional advertising industry by putting restrictions on filming. In addition, the industry itself changed as influencers were driven to improve their business strategies, content creation tactics, and engagement mechanisms (Femenia-Serra, Gretzel, & Alzua-Sorzabal, 2022). Social media industry players introduced new platforms (most notably TikTok), altered existing platforms, changed algorithms, and focused on measurement techniques in a way that made directly communicating with audiences more challenging and expensive for brands. On top of this, a considerable portion of Generation Z became of age during the pandemic, leaving marketers struggling to find ways to reach this new target market.

In just a couple of decades, influencers and creators have transformed the way people learn, communicate, vote, shop, travel, eat, and much more. And they have changed and continue to change the way business, marketing, and advertising are conducted. As social media influencers like Logan Paul and Danielle Bernstein rack up tens of thousands per sponsored post, people begin to question whether they can trust these attractively persuasive voices, or whether they are just the same old snake oil salespeople dressed in new influencers' clothing. With consumer tracking, coupon code promotions, and sophisticated platform algorithms becoming ubiquitous, we live in a far more complex media environment than the one we had even ten years ago. The old schemer's schema now needs to adapt to the constantly evolving schemes of new media creators.

These facts mean that we need a specialised understanding of the way influencers and creators work today. Social media and digital marketing, public relations, and digital advertising are included in broad academic disciplines. But these fields struggle to stay current and to deal in sufficient depth with rapid developments in the world. Social media as a serious topic of study has largely passed 'under the radar' because its rise has been so swift. Social media, as well as the culture and business that surround them, are already an incredibly important part of our society and economy. Learning about how the influencer and creator industry works is important if we want to understand the greater impact of social media on our lives and our world. We will begin in the next section by clearly defining influencers and creators and distinguishing them from related terms like celebrities, opinion leaders, and brand ambassadors.

DEFINING INFLUENCERS

The world of influencers and creators is still relatively new and keeps evolving. As a consequence, researchers and communication managers have not yet settled on definitions for influencers and creators. Still, most of us use these terms all the time, without being able to define them. In order to go deeper into the topic, however, it is going to be necessary to be very specific about the characteristics of influencers and other related concepts, such as creators and opinion leaders.

Even before social media came into the world, influencer was a word. It simply means someone who exerts influence over other people. However, the word has come to mean a lot more than that when used in the context of social media. We have collected some important definitions of influencers in Table 1.2, which you should consult before reading the remainder of this chapter.

Table 1.2 A sampling of definitions of influencers

Definition: An influencer is...	Source
'One who exerts influence: a person who inspires or guides the actions of others; often, specifically, a person who is able to generate interest in something (such as a consumer product) by posting about it on social media'.	Merriam-Webster dictionary (2021)
'A new type of independent third party endorser who shapes audience attitudes through blogs, tweets, and the use of other social media'.	Freberg, Graham, McGaughey and Freberg (2011: 90)
'Individuals who post to their social media accounts in exchange for compensation'.	Campbell and Grimm (2019: 110)
'Individuals who are in a consumer's social graph and have direct impact on the behavior of that consumer'.	Ge and Gretzel (2018: 1273)
'Everyday, ordinary Internet users who accumulate a relatively large following on blogs and social media through the textual and visual narration of their personal lives and lifestyles, engage with their following in "digital" and "physical" spaces, and monetize their following by integrating "advertorials" into their blog or social media posts and making physical appearances at events'.	Abidin (2015: para. 1)
'Someone in your niche or industry who wields influence. Influencers have specialized knowledge, authority, or insight into a specific subject'.	Influencer Marketing Hub (2022a)
'A content generator, one who has the status of expertise in a specific area, who has cultivated a sizable number of captive followers – who are of marketing value to brands – by regularly producing valuable content via social media'.	Lou and Yuan (2019: 59)
'A third-party actor that has established a significant number of relevant relationships with a specific quality to and influence on organizational stakeholders through content production, content distribution, interaction, and personal appearance on the social web'.	Enke and Borchers (2019: 267)
'A type of "microcelebrity" – a style of online performance in which individuals attempt to gain attention and popularity by employing digital media technologies, such as webcams, blogs and social media'.	Drenten, Gurrieri and Tyler (2020: 42)

Table 1.2 A sampling of definitions of influencers *(Continued)*

Definition: An influencer is...	Source
'A type of micro-celebrity who has accrued a large number of followers on social media and frequently uses this social capital to gain access to financial resources'.	Cotter (2019: 896)
'Social media influencers are referred to as people who have built a sizeable social network of people following them. In addition, they are seen as a regard for being a trusted tastemaker in one or several niches'.	de Veirman, Cauberghe and Hudders (2017: 798)

The Core Qualities of Influencers

In order to understand what an influencer is, and to be able to compare it with and distinguish it from the term 'creator' and other related concepts, we need to establish the core qualities of influencers. First, our definition needs to acknowledge the connection between influencers and social media. Influencers as we know them could not exist without social media and digital content delivery platforms such as Instagram, YouTube, Facebook, TikTok, Douyin, Twitch, LinkedIn, Pinterest, Twitter, Spotify, and others. Podcasts would also be included, which accounts for our listing of Spotify. The world of influencers is a world of social media posts and followers, likes and shares, content created and consumed, and comments and replies. Although the influencer types vary on different social media (e.g., fashion influencers on Instagram versus video game influencers on Twitch), influencers must utilise at least one social medium – and many of them use several.

What these influencers have in common is that they (1) build relationships with people through (2) a consistent and distinctive voice and image expressed through their (3) social media content. Influencers build relationships by leveraging some quality, virtue, or talent of their own and putting it out there on social media. It could be knowledge, skill, expertise, talent, a social position, a profession, a beautiful or handsome appearance, a likeable personality, a fun attitude, an amazing or interesting life experience or ongoing experiences, a great sense of humour, a willingness to perform crazy stunts, or something else. The varied gamer profiles presented at the beginning of the chapter illustrate this diversity. Whatever it is, influencers provide people who tune into their content something that social media users enjoy, find interesting, useful, or valuable.

Many of these qualities or virtues can appear together in a single influencer. For example, Charli D'Amelio has a fun personality and is attractive, as well as being a talented dancer and someone who has gone through and can share the experience of having an eating disorder. An important aspect of influencers is that they strategically position and market themselves by engaging in personal branding.

PERSONAL BRANDING

'Personal branding is a strategic process of creating, positioning, and maintaining a positive impression of oneself, based in a unique combination of individual characteristics, which signal a certain promise to the target audience through a differentiated narrative and imagery' (Gorbatov, Khapova, & Lysova, 2018: 6). There are three distinct and measurable characteristics of personal branding: brand appeal, brand differentiation, and brand recognition (Gorbatov et al., 2021).

Content, combined with the name and personal brand of the influencer, creates a recognizable influencer 'channel' or program, regardless of whether it is featured in a blog, on YouTube, or in a podcast. In Charli's case, many of her followers admire her amazing skills as a dancer (she has been dancing since she was three and is a trained competitive dancer). An influencer's qualities, talents, and skills are expressed consistently through a regular stream of social media posts and perhaps other follow-up communications (e.g., replies to comments). It is through these posts that the influencer builds an image and a reputation for consistent performance (in other words, a brand) amongst those who audience the material, and in the wider world. The relationship between an influencer and their audience is based on regular content sharing by the influencer and engagement by the audience that ideally turns into dedicated following. Indeed, attracting, curating, engaging with, understanding, and retaining their audience through content and communication becomes the focus of an influencer's social media activity.

INFLUENCER

The term 'influencer' refers to personal brands that build relationships with an engaged audience through a regular flow of consistent, authentic, and distinctive content posted on at least one social media platform.

Our definition of an influencer applies equally to people with different sizes of audiences, from those who attract millions of online followers like Kendall Jenner to those who have a few thousand, such as travel nano-influencer Julie Rose. Our definition includes individual people who post on social media, but it also would encompass a family influencer like The Bucket List Family (which is a group of people, not an individual), a pet influencer like Doug the Pug, a virtual influencer like Guggimon, or a non-human influencer like Eugene the

Egg. Each of these influencers has a unique and distinctive voice and image. But what they have in common is that each of them builds relationships with people who become interested followers based on the unique spin and content of their social media posts. This audience gathering is the core of what an influencer is.

Influencers typically present themselves as real people. They frequently use their real names. And, whether they're broadcasting from their bedroom or introducing you to their friends, family, and pets, they typically try to appear authentic. They invite their audience 'behind the scenes'. The sincerity with which they perform is an important aspect of our definition of an influencer. Influencers are authentic when their performances are consistent and their actions match what they say and are compatible with the beliefs they promote through their personal brands.

Authentic influencers remain true to their own values and character in the face of external pressure. In this way, they are genuine: they stand for something and are not afraid to tell you what it is. And they are frequently enthusiastic about their beliefs. Moreover, they are consistent in their performance. Even when a character's behaviour is scripted, such as with the Brazilian virtual influencer Lu do Magalu, it is consistent. Lu do Magalu has an ethos, a storyline, and a personality that she expresses and acts upon. In the world of influencers, being a 'real' person or showing one's 'real life' can be beneficial, but what is most important is an authentic *performance*. That authentic performance is a type of personal branding in which influencers consistently perform the voice, tone, and image that makes their persona appealing to a specific audience and renders their social media content distinct and appealing.

What an Influencer Is Not. . .

To provide definitional clarity, it is important to establish boundary conditions. We acknowledge that these boundaries can be rather fuzzy in the influencer world.

An influencer is not necessarily a profit-oriented professional. As we are defining the core of what an influencer is, it is also vital to consider what is not necessary to include in that definition. Many of the definitions of influencers in Table 1.2 emphasise that influencers have the power to influence other people, especially their purchase decisions. But brand deals and contracts to endorse products are not essential to the definition of influencers. Although many influencers deal with topics that may impact purchase decisions, others might not. Yes, influencers can influence purchase decisions. But they can also inform people about how to be kinder to their family members, how to study more effectively, or how to pet their cats – so, we could also call them informers. They can inform people about causes and charities, social movements and political candidates, and personal matters such as living a fuller life or having better relationships. How about Kristina Carrillo-Bucaram, an Ecuadorian Lebanese social media influencer who follows a fully raw food and vegan diet? A lot of her content is about living more simply. Greta Thunberg has over 12 million Instagram followers and does not do brand deals. Amy Ratcliffe is a devoted Star Wars fan who also gathers an audience through her editorship of The Nerdist. There are many people who gather smaller audiences ('nano-influencers' and 'micro-influencers') who have not monetised them. Influencers can perform, inspire, and entertain rather than sell.

So why would a definition emphasise only the potential economic impact aspect of the influencer, and not the informer, performer, inspirer, and entertainer aspect? Monetisation, whether in the form of gifting (free products to influencers) or paid brand deals, is a very important part of the social media marketing industry today. Historically, much of the coverage of the social media phenomenon has been written by journalists and media people with ties to the advertising industry and so it reflects their business perspectives. As we all know, money makes the world go round and it also pays the bills for a lot of social media personalities. But many influencers with devoted followings realise that they and their personal brand – and not some other company's brand – is ultimately the most important thing they must manage. By gathering an audience for their content, they can influence people's lives and decisions in ways that may not directly involve promoting brands and convincing their audience to buy things. Focusing only on a social media poster's direct impacts on purchase decisions seems to be a limiting thing to include in a definition of what makes an influencer. So, the definition of influencers does not necessarily need to include financial or other forms of compensation.

Another thing we eliminate is the emphasis on size. An influencer does not need to have millions of followers. Some of the definitions in Table 1.2 emphasise the large size of an influencer's audience or following, casting a big group of followers as essential to being an influencer. This follows a colloquial use of the term 'influencer' that may confuse it with celebrities or media personalities. This is perfectly understandable, since some of the biggest and most recognised influencers in the world, people like Kim Kardashian and her half-sister Kylie Jenner, Cristiano Ronaldo, and Ariana Grande, are celebrities from the worlds of television, professional sports, and music. Although some major celebrities such as Justin Bieber and Calvin Harris began their careers as people who posted their original material on social media and built audiences, many other celebrities found quick followings on social media because they were already famous. In these cases, they may have already had a strong personal brand, and they may not even have created or managed their own social media accounts. So, while it is certainly true that celebrities can be or become social media influencers, it is not the case that every influencer is necessarily a celebrity.

CELEBRITY

A celebrity has fame or a large degree of public recognition, along with command of significant attention in the mass media.

An influencer can talk to business audiences, not just to consumers. It is important to realise that not all influencers are business-to-consumer (or B2C) influencers, such as top fitness and fashion influencers Jen Selters and Chiara Ferragni. Instead, businesspeople might follow Sheri Hinish, the 'SupplyChainQueen', who informs businesspeople about current issues and solutions in global supply chain management. The size of the following is basically irrelevant in this case. Industry practitioners already acknowledge that there are business-to-business influencers who might speak to very small and specialised audiences. For example, there may only be a dozen people in the world who specialise in purchasing the steel used to manufacture ships. Yet, if they all listen to the same influencer, that person may have the attention of a very important audience worth tens of millions of dollars a year.

Distinguishing Influencers From Brand Ambassadors

In order to distinguish influencers from brand ambassadors, it is important to recognize that influencers usually are independent third parties in relation to the brands and products that they might endorse. The personal brand of an influencer is always in the foreground. Influencers usually author and almost always own their own social media content. None of these things are true for brand ambassadors.

BRAND AMBASSADOR

A brand ambassador is someone who retains a year-round and exclusive contract with a brand to appear in advertising and attend public relations events.

An influencer would not have an exclusive contract with just one brand – although they might give exclusivity to a brand within a certain type of product category for a limited amount of time. Influencer contracts are also usually shorter than those of brand ambassadors. Brand ambassadors often do not write their own content because they are not generally building and promoting their own personal brand. Brand ambassadors do not own the brand content that they post but are contractually obligated to give brands the right to use their likeness for brand-related purposes. Most importantly of all, influencers are hired by brands because of their unique style, ideas, and personality that they bring to the material they create for their audience. Alternatively, a brand dealing with a brand ambassador would generally insist that the ambassador adopt the brand's style. The Canadian fitness fashion brand Lululemon's appointment of the non-binary and transgender professional runner Nikki Hiltz as one of their brand ambassadors is an example of the kind of longer term and contractual relationships brands have with brand ambassadors.

Distinguishing Influencers From Opinion Leaders

OPINION LEADER

An opinion leader is a figure who interprets the meaning of media content or messages or curates information for a larger or more public audience of media users.

According to the two-step flow theory of communication of Katz and Lazarsfeld (1955), information flows from the mass media to opinion leaders (step one) and then from opinion leaders to the mass public (step two). Opinion leaders do not actively generate messages themselves. Rather, they digest, interpret, and modify messages from others (Bennett & Manheim, 2006). Influencers engage in a more complex and diverse set of actions than those required of opinion leaders. Influencers create their own content, and also strategically curate and manage both their personal brands and their audiences (Femenia-Serra, Gretzel, & Alzua-Sorzabal, 2022). Opinion leaders do not do any of these acts. Instead, they are valued for their opinion based on their knowledge/expertise, taste, or social position. Individuals look to them for guidance in terms of what messages to consume.

However, it is important to note that in the Chinese social media ecosystem, the term 'key opinion leader' (KOL) is commonly used to describe influencers. Chinese KOLs often have larger audiences and a greater commercial focus than influencers outside of China. They also typically need verified accounts to maintain authenticity and gain trust. In contrast, key opinion customers (KOCs) are individuals who spread word-of-mouth within smaller circles and with a more personal touch.

Distinguishing Influencers From Digital Marketers

DIGITAL MARKETER

A digital marketer is a person or organisation that uses digital technologies to connect with potential customers to promote products and brands.

Digital marketers use digital channels such as search engines, websites, mobile apps, and social media to reach customers, build brand awareness, gather market intelligence, and promote and sell brands, products, and services. Although some influencers might promote brands, this is not their primary function and, in fact, there are many influencers who do not promote brands or act as marketers. Furthermore, digital marketers do not engage in the same personal branding and authentic performances as influencers.

However, when influencers create their own brands, some of their efforts might be directed towards marketing their products or services. For instance, Madeleine Darya Alizadeh (@dariadaria) is an Austrian fashion and lifestyle influencer who promotes her own fashion label dariadéh as a sustainable and ethical product line that supports social and ecological projects and offers comfort for sizes XXS to XXXL. Similarly, Meg Jerrard, an Australian journalist and travel influencer frequently features travel destinations and brands in her Instagram feed alongside her own solo female travel-related services (tours, seminars, etc.).

Distinguishing Influencers From Content Creators

CONTENT CREATOR

A creator or content creator produces professional content that is recognised for its quality, uniqueness, aesthetics, or style. They post this content on their own social media channels or grant others the right to use it, often for a fee.

There is a lot of confusion in the social media marketing industry around the connection between influencers and content creators. Many people use the term synonymously. Some believe that the term 'creator' or 'content creator' is a more attractive term than influencer because it does not suggest manipulation or a persuasive sales orientation.

The media and advertising industries have an insatiable appetite for high-quality and timely content, such as well-written product reviews, beautifully staged brand photographs, and vibrant videos. Marketers who want this high-quality content may not want the audience gathering and authentic performance that influencers provide. Content creators are those whose primary goal is to create high-quality, even distinctive content. Photographers, illustrators, writers, graphic designers, videographers, video editors, podcast producers, and other professionals are examples of creators. Sometimes, creators' work will be posted on the social media accounts of those who commission their works, rather than on their own account. Michael Joseph

Winkelmann is a content creator who uses the Instagram handle Beeple-Crap (see vignette box).

As Winkelmann's work demonstrates, there is considerable skill involved in content creation that not all influencers will demonstrate (some influencers are amateurish in their content production). Many content creators will have a distinct aesthetic or style that audiences and marketers recognize and value. Every day, many professional content creators, such as journalists and professional reviewers, create and post things online. Not all content creators attempt to build personal brands or perspectives.

The diagram in Figure 1.1 illustrates the similarities and differences between influencers and creators. Consider influence and content creation to be activities, with influencers and content creators acting in specific roles. When we think of them as activities and roles, it becomes clear that a single person can do both. Just as one person can walk and chew gum at the same time, one person can also be a content creator as well as a source and gatherer of targeted public influence. The area where the two concepts overlap is depicted in Figure 1.1 as the intersection of the two Venn diagram circles.

The difference between influencers and creators is one of emphasis. Generally, when we refer to creators or content creators, we are emphasising

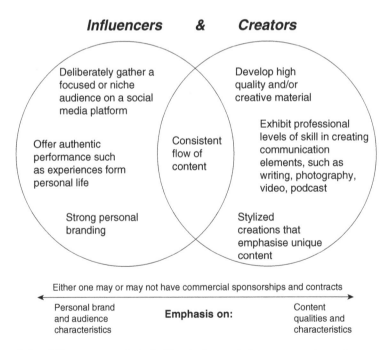

Figure 1.1 Differences and similarities between influencers and creators

those who are responsible for producing uniquely styled, professional, or otherwise valuable content and then share it on social media. Creators create professional content which is recognised for its exceptional and one-of-a-kind quality. They are usually skilled in working with social media, and they understand how social platforms interact with their particular areas of expertise in content creation. Influencers emphasise interaction with an audience and relationship building activities rather than the production of stylish content. While influencers engage in personal branding, content creators focus on social media content branding.

SOCIAL MEDIA CONTENT BRANDING

Social media content branding is a process of creating and maintaining a consistent and differentiated style in a social media channel, stream, or other regular sources of identifiable content.

BEEPLE-CRAP: PORTRAIT OF A CONTENT CREATOR

Michael Joseph Winkelmann is a content creator. Winkelmann is an American digital artist who creates and posts darkly fantastic, satirical, science fictional works on social media that combine popular culture references and news with sociopolitical commentary. Although he is creating content that builds an audience, his Instagram brand, Beeple-Crap, is more of a gallery for his unique and provocative digital art to be displayed than it serves as a place where he builds trusted relationships with an audience who cares about his opinion. As a result, his work has been central in commercialising his social media activity, rather than his opinion or his ability to reach a particular audience. His bizarre 3D images were featured in concert visuals for Childish Gambino, Imagine Dragons, Nicki Minaj, Zedd, Skrillex, deadmau5, and others, and his artwork was featured on Louis Vuitton's Women's Spring 2019 ready-to-wear collection as well as in window displays at their flagship stores around the globe. We can see from Figure 1.2 that Winkelmann's work is distinctive and professional. The question of whether it is valuable is something that depends upon the question: 'valuable to whom'? Although, for many years, Winkelmann simply gave away his art images online, occasionally selling a print of his work for $100 or less, artists like Nicki Minaj and brands like Louis Vuitton eventually found it valuable.

Figure 1.2   Winkelmann's 'Gigachad'

Source: Creative Commons License.

sWooZie: AN ANIMATED YOUTUBE CONTENT CREATOR

The work of YouTube personality Adande Thorne is another good example of content creation. Thorne, also known as 'sWooZie', is perhaps best known for the humorously narrated animated autobiographical videos he releases as his key content. Although Thorne might have some endorsement deals with brands, the main revenue he makes is from the advertising fees he earns from the viewership of his content – over one billion cumulative views on YouTube. As a television show does, the audience's attention to his animated videos is monetised by showing advertising before and during the content. As the creator of this content, Adande gets a cut of this revenue.

Influencer Characteristics and Roles

Influencers are frequently confused with many other related concepts, including celebrities, opinion leaders, digital marketers, brand ambassadors, and creators.

This confusion occurs because influencers can take on a variety of communicative roles from creating, curating, spreading, and amplifying commercial and non-commercial messages to managing conversations with followers. Although there are areas where influencers and these other concepts overlap, as illustrated in Figure 1.3, the concept of an influencer is distinct. The preceding definitions and discussions show that each of these concepts has distinct characteristics that it does not share with the concept of an influencer, and vice versa. However, in practice, many influencers exhibit characteristics and engage in activities that overlap with these various concepts. This makes the influencer world diverse and exciting, but it can also lead to confusion when researching and working with influencers.

Influencers are often labelled and categorised to make it easier for audiences to find them or to identify them for specific commercial purposes. Influencer categories can be based on demographic characteristics (e.g., Silver Influencer for older individuals or momfluencer for women with children), ethnicity (e.g., Black influencer), the size of their following (from celebrity to nano-influencer), the platform on which they communicate (e.g., YouTuber), the topic they focus on (e.g., plantfluencer), the type of audience they attract (B2C vs. B2B influencer), the type of content they produce (e.g., vlogger or livestreamer), whether they are human or not (e.g., virtual or computer-generated imagery (CGI) influencer), their geographic location (e.g., Italian influencer), or the language they speak (e.g., Spanish-speaking influencer). No matter what these specific labels are, the definition of an influencer applies across all these categories.

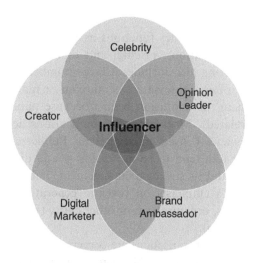

Figure 1.3 Influencers and other related concepts

In summary, an influencer builds meaningful relationships with an audience through consistently providing social media content featuring authentic performance and a distinctive voice and image, all reflecting and contributing to their personal brand. They do not necessarily have brand deals, large audiences, or an emphasis on their 'real lives' – although they certainly might. They do not even have to be human or individual people. Ours is not intended to be a universal definition. Instead, it comes from a specific perspective. We do not focus exclusively upon the commercial roles of creators and influencers – but we certainly do not exclude them, either. Making money is essential to understanding influencers not only as an industry but also as an impactful cultural and social phenomenon. We have defined the various influencer-related terms so that they can be useful for people who are trying to understand what influencers are in a social and cultural sense, what they do from a communication perspective, as well as how to work with them from a marketing and public relations perspective.

INFLUENCER MARKETING AND INFLUENCER RELATIONS

Does influencer marketing include public relations functions? What distinguishes public relations from marketing? Is influencer relations the same as public relations? By answering these questions, this section seeks to shed light on the more or less strategic ways in which influencers can be used to achieve diverse communication goals.

Marketing Versus Public Relations

Marketing includes all the sales functions as well as new product development, supply chain operations, pricing, and market and consumer-related data analysis. Marketing also includes a large number of different communications activities, often abbreviated as marcom or marketing communications (which is where the confusion begins because public relations is also communications related). Marketing communications activities tend to be related to revenues and focused on campaigns. Public relations responsibilities, on the other hand, tend to be more closely and directly related to the world of reputation and its strategic management. Public relations activities transcend marketing's emphasis on revenue generation and focus on the longevity of a business, organisation, or other entity (which could be a public official or even a nation).

Both marketing and public relations are concerned with brands and branding. Companies market their brands to differentiate them from competitors so that consumers will think that they are superior, choose them, and generate revenue for the firm. Companies use public relations to bolster their corporate brands so that people will believe the company is legitimate, trustworthy, and a good citizen. A company like Unilever will use public relations to build its corporate brand, but it will use marketing to sell its Dove and Axe brands of body wash.

From Influencer Advertising to Influencer Relations

Collaborations with influencers can span across all marketing functions and often include public relations goals. However, they can be more or less strategic and shorter- or longer-term in orientation. Depending on this orientation, influencer-based communication efforts can be divided into three categories: (1) influencer advertising, (2) influencer marketing, and (3) influencer relations.

INFLUENCER ADVERTISING

The short-term and tactical use of influencers or creators in campaigns to prompt sales is known as influencer advertising.

Influencer advertising reflects the desire for marketers to seek short-run or even immediate results. Influencer advertising involves using an influencer's channel to post commercial messages that the marketers have composed for them or asked them to share with minimal, if any, additional creative input on the part of the influencer. The placement of pre-composed or partially composed marketing messages in the feeds of social media influencers is similar to viral marketing or the use of advertising in other paid media. As with a paid advertising purchase in a television show or radio program's commercial break, the advertiser is buying access to the influencer's audience. Influencer advertising can also involve the purchase of creator content so that it can be repurposed for brand campaigns.

INFLUENCER MARKETING

The shorter-to-medium term and tactical involvement of influencers and creators in marketing communication campaigns designed primarily for revenue generation is known as influencer marketing.

Ultimately focused on revenue generation, and also using campaigns, influencer marketing reflects a more medium-term time orientation. Influencer marketing uses the talents of influencers and content creators to create original and authentic brand material (or brand 'assets') that the brand can repurpose for promotional purposes. Unlike influencer advertising, influencer marketing leverages the unique voice or style, intricate understanding of social media platforms, and ability to effectively reach desirable target audiences of individual influencers who are usually chosen for single campaigns. Similar to influencer advertising, it is generally focused on discrete campaigns with specific communication or revenue-based performance goals.

INFLUENCER RELATIONS

Longer-term and more strategic partnerships with influencers and creators, which emphasise organisational-influencer fit and future performance, are known as influencer relations.

Influencer relations activities are longer term, more strategic, and more focused on a good fit between the image of the influencer or creator and the brand than either influencer advertising or influencer marketing. Influencer relations are still campaign-based, but generally involve cultivating relationships between the brand and the influencer or creator by working together over longer time periods that extend beyond single campaigns. Influencer relations campaigns and professionals rely more extensively upon the creative input and audience insights of influencers than either influencer advertising or influencer marketing. Over time, influencers who work on influencer relations campaigns become like spokespeople who are, in effect, an extension of the company and brand.

Influencer relations should be considered a type of public relations function. It is a relatively longer-term in orientation and more reputationally concerned approach to using influencers and creators than influencer marketing or influencer advertising. We express these relationships in Figure 1.4.

In the real and fast-moving world of social media marketing, there can be a lot of overlap between these neat clean categories. In practice, and when done well, influencer advertising can turn into influencer marketing, and influencer marketing can shade into influencer relations. The differences between the three activities represent different perspectives on the appropriate use of influencers and creators. This is why Figure 1.4 is drawn as a continuum. Influencer relations is a strategic, investment-oriented, and long-term approach to working with influencers or creators, while influencer advertising is more tactical, extractive, short-term and mostly ignores the many things influencers and creators can bring to the table beyond simple access to content or a target audience. Most organisations will find

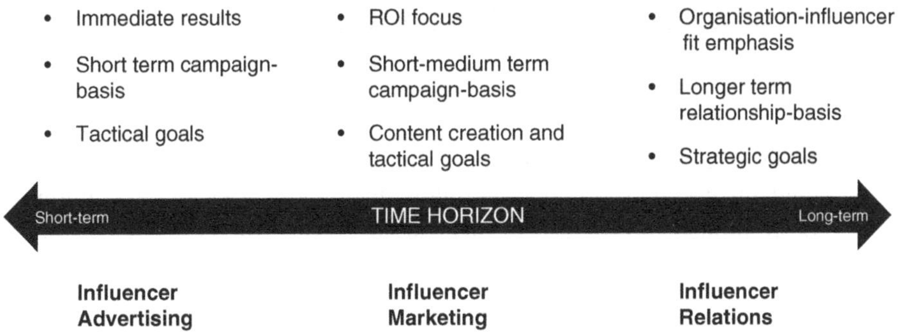

- Immediate results
- Short term campaign-basis
- Tactical goals

- ROI focus
- Short-medium term campaign-basis
- Content creation and tactical goals

- Organisation-influencer fit emphasis
- Longer term relationship-basis
- Strategic goals

| Short-term | TIME HORIZON | Long-term |

Influencer Advertising

Influencer Marketing

Influencer Relations

Figure 1.4 Influencer marketing, influencer advertising, and influencer relations

themselves engaging with influencers or creators somewhere between the two polar extremes. However, as marketers are realising, with the high cost of finding and vetting influencers and creators and the high risk involved in single-campaign approaches, there is a clear trend towards influencer relations.

CHAPTER SUMMARY

Communication technology and its applications have altered our cultural landscape. Social media influencers and creators have emerged as popular and trusted voices, attracting large audiences and gaining significant cultural, social, and economic importance. Influencers are people who build relationships with their audiences by delivering consistent, authentic, and distinct performances that are linked to a personal brand and shared on social media. They may or may not have brand deals, large audiences, or a focus on their 'real lives'. They are not even required to be human. Celebrities, opinion leaders, digital marketers, brand ambassadors, and creators are not the same as influencers. They are roles that sometimes overlap with influencer activities. Brands and other communicators can use influencers and creators in three ways: influencer advertising, influencer marketing, and influencer relations. Influencers and creators are used in campaigns in all of these activities, but the emphasis is different. Influencer relations is the most long-term, interactional, strategic, and concerned with the fit between the image of the influencer or creator and that of the brand or company.

EXERCISES AND QUESTIONS

Exercises

1. Identify three different influencers and familiarize yourself with their contents if you do not already follow them. Now, apply the definition of an influencer provided in this chapter to each one. Do they fit the definition well?

2. Check out the Instagram account of Eric Rubens (https://www.instagram.com/erubes1/). Would you describe him as an influencer or a content creator?

3. Find an example of an influencer marketing campaign, an influencer advertising campaign, and influencer relations campaign online.

Questions

1. Why did influencers gain popularity in business as a way to promote brands?

2. What are some of the key similarities between the following related concepts:
   a. Creators and influencers?

   b. Brand ambassadors and digital marketers?

   c. Celebrities and opinion leaders?

3. What are some of the key differences between the following related concepts:
   a. Creators and opinion leaders?

   b. Brand ambassadors and digital marketers?

   c. Celebrities and influencers?

4. A focus on influencer relations is better than influencer marketing. Do you agree?

ANNOTATED READINGS

Bloomstein, M. (2021). *Trustworthy: How the smartest brands beat cynicism and bridge the trust gap*. Page Two: Vancouver.

Content strategy guru Margot Bloomstein captures a net of experiences of copy-writers, designers, creative directors, and CMOs to offer an understanding of how these business experts navigate the challenges of building trust in an era of consumer cynicism through imagery, editorial style, storytelling, and retail design.

Hearn, A. (2008). Meat, mask, burden: Probing the contours of the branded self. *Journal of Consumer Culture, 8*(2), 197–217.

An erudite, insightful, and historical account of the roots of personal branding in popular media and consumer culture.

2

A MACROSOCIAL PERSPECTIVE

CHAPTER OVERVIEW AND OBJECTIVES

This chapter will present a macro perspective on the environment in which influencer and creator content is created and commercialised. Brands and platforms are key elements in a combination of techno-logical, social, and economic resources that create the productive ability that enables influencers and creators to work and their content to propagate. These resources also structure the influencer and creator experience in important ways. In their work and content, influencers and creators draw on and are affected by the attention economy, gig economy, reputation economy, algorithmic culture, and surveillance capitalism, which each create their own sets of demands. Holding these different elements together in a dialectical relationship is the governing ideology of neoliberalism. The chapter will introduce and explain these structural and ideological factors, setting the stage for a deeper understanding of the influencer ecosystem.

PROVOCATION: What social forces influence the world of influencers? How does the world of influencers fit into the wider social and economic world they labour within?

KEYWORDS: affordance, algorithm, data, fan labour, attention economy, gig economy, reputation economy, algorithmic culture, neoliberalism, surveillance capitalism

---

THE TIME TRAVELLING MOMFLUENCER

Influencers and creators do not operate in a vacuum. They are the product of a society and economic system that values, enables, and promotes certain things while discouraging others. They are also highly dependent on technologies that allow them to create and distribute their contents. Imagine a time-travelling momfluencer who ends up in Russia in the 1950s. What opportunities would she have to create and spread messages and build and interact with an audience? Would she be able to derive income from her efforts? Now fast forward to North Korea in 2020. Do you think there are many thriving North Korean momfluencers? Why not?

To help you answer some of the questions raised in our opening vignette, this chapter will dive into some of the driving forces behind the influencer and creator economy to explain why it has become so prominent over the last decade, although not in all countries or at least not to the same extent.

BASE AND SUPERSTRUCTURE

Although influencers and creators are a relatively recent phenomenon, they developed in a global context with a long, varied, and rich socioeconomic history. One of the founders of sociology, Karl Marx, devised notions of base and superstructure, which can help us better understand the environment in which influencer and creator content production and commercialisation take place. Figure 2.1 illustrates the way that these central sociological ideas relate to the world of influencers and creators in our digital economy today.

The productive forces, or the materials and resources that create the different commodities and services that society's members require to function, are referred to as society's base. In an information economy like ours, which some would call 'post-industrial' (Bell, 1976), many products and services might be informational or digital – for example, online access to a word processing application or the usage of a new set of animated emojis. Despite how informational our electronic exchanges might be, they are still industrial in that societies build industries around and with them, such as the technology industry or the influencer industry. For influencers and creators to be able to produce content that has the potential to be industrialised, they need access to technological devices such as phones and computers, things like ring lights and editing software applications, as well as networks and platforms.

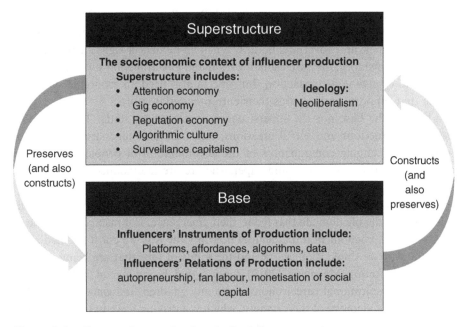

Figure 2.1   Base and superstructure in the influencer system

SOCIETAL BASE

The productive forces or the materials and resources that create the different products and services required for a given society to function.

SOCIETAL SUPERSTRUCTURE

All other parts of a given society besides the means of production, including people's education, culture, philosophy, conventions, and identities, which shape and are shaped by the societal base.

As the name suggests, the base supports the development of a particular superstructure. The superstructure encompasses all other parts of society, including people's education, culture, philosophy, conventions, and identities. Influencers depend on their education and technical skills, as well as proficiencies with things like fitness routines or cooking, to create interesting content for their audience. Beyond these types of personal skills, influencers depend on a society's administrative system, which includes its social institutions, political system, legal authorities, and governing bodies. When an influencer signs a contract with a brand, for instance, they are using the legal and governmental superstructure of society to engage in a transaction. Influencers also need an economic system in place that supports and rewards their entrepreneurial efforts.

Neither the base nor the superstructure is natural or static. They are both social constructions and social creations, and base and superstructure are the constantly changing consequences of the accumulation of people's continuous social interactions. The base and superstructure are interconnected in complex ways. Both construct and preserve each other. To a large extent, influencers reflect the social, economic, and cultural environment in which they work, while also fuelling the phenomena that led to their emergence. For instance, influencers are a cultural phenomenon that shapes not only the way we consume media but also the way we think about work and the kinds of jobs that are being created. Mobile Marketing Magazine (2019) reports that becoming an influencer has become an aspirational career choice for many children. Influencers also reflect the governing ideology of their society, which is a driving force in the continuous development of base and superstructure.

IDEOLOGY

A set of beliefs, norms, and values, especially the political beliefs on which people, parties, or nations base their actions. Although the term has acquired negative connotations, its true meaning is simply to signify this set of impactful beliefs (not whether you think they are good or bad).

Different nations represent different ideologies. In China, for instance, the political ideology that serves as a natural context for the actions of influencers and creators is very different than it is in Australia. However, worldwide there are many similarities in the ways that the base and the superstructure interact in the world of influencers and creators. In the superstructure, ideology is utilised to rationalise what happens in the base. It establishes conditions in which the current production relations appear fair and natural, even though they may be unfair and structured to benefit only the ruling class. This general role of ideology is true regardless of what the ruling political system or party calls itself, or the way it chooses to govern. Some societies, for example, may employ religious ideology to persuade individuals to obey authority and strive hard for salvation. Others may believe that everyone has an equal opportunity to become wealthy if they work hard enough. Societies might enforce loyalty to a political party or leader. Regardless of the focus, the core premise of Marxian sociology is that a society's intellectual underpinning, including its governance and political machinery, often serves to preserve the interests of those who control the means of production that power the society. In the world of influencers and creators, these underpinnings can assume very interesting digital forms because one of the most important tools for the production and distribution of content is the social media platform.

POWER AT THE BASE: INSTRUMENTS AND RELATIONS OF PRODUCTION

To understand the importance of the base to the activities of actual or potential influencers and creators, we must understand how the societal base relates to concepts of power. Power can work through social systems in both visible and invisible ways. Although influencers may seem to be individuals making decisions of their own accord, there are many technological, institutional, and social factors that guide their actions.

POWER

The capacity to influence the actions, beliefs, or conduct (behaviour) of others.

One of the key requirements guiding influencers is their need to gather an active and engaged audience on a recognised social media platform. This is what allows them to turn their content into financial or other resources. To attract this substantial, interested, and active audience, influencers need access to resources that are controlled by other parties. We therefore adopt a resource-based conceptualization of power to guide the discussion.

A RESOURCE-BASED THEORY OF POWER

'Power is a property of the social relation; it is not an attribute of the actor' (Emerson, 1962: 32). According to resource dependency theory (Pfeffer & Salancik, 2003), actor A has power over actor B to the extent that A has resources that B depends upon, and to the extent that there are no other actors or sources of the same resources. When B depends heavily on A for resources it cannot obtain anywhere else, there is said to be a power imbalance favouring actor A (Casciaro & Piskorski, 2005).

Instruments of Production

Platforms as Instruments of Production

SOCIAL MEDIA PLATFORM POWER

Social media platforms as 'sociotechnical and performative infrastructures' generate shifting networks of relationships and shape the ability to act and to interact (van Dijck, 2013: 26).

Social media platforms such as YouTube, Instagram, and LinkedIn are the means by which influencers produce, distribute, and gain financial benefit from their content. Today, these platforms give influencers and potential influencers access to the almost 4 billion people around the world who use social media platforms to gain information and communicate for personal and business purposes (BroadbandSearch, 2022). One of the main uses of social media platforms is for commercial purposes and, in fact, advertising revenue is a major source of revenue for many platforms (Statista, 2021b). Facebook is the most popular platform among marketers globally, followed by Instagram, LinkedIn, YouTube, Twitter, and Pinterest. Commercial interest in platforms is not only dependent on the size and type of audience a platform can attract but also increasingly on the ways in which brands can engage with desirable platform audiences. Thus, commercial interest in a platform now often goes hand-in-hand with the opportunities these platforms offer for influencers and creators.

Platforms are not just technology-based communication channels but they also mediate the relationships among audiences, influencers, and marketers in fundamental ways. As Gillespie (2010: 351) contends, social media sites are platforms 'not necessarily because they allow code to be written or run, but because they afford an opportunity to communicate, interact, or "sell".' Hence, platforms are sociotechnical infrastructures inasmuch as they capture the interrelatedness between people and technology. Platforms are social because they enable social connections among people. They are also technical because they are based on the interweaving of material technology, procedures, and related knowledge. Finally, platforms are performative insofar as they act as 'mediators of social acts' (van Dijck, 2013: 29). That means that platforms, or aspects of them, can act just as other actors do, having an impact on other actors such as brands, influencers and content creators, and their audiences.

The digital economist Nick Srnicek states that 'platforms are a newly predominant type of business model premised upon bringing different groups together' (2017a: 254–55). Srnicek recognises that 'by providing the infrastructure and intermediation between different groups, platforms can monitor, extract and monetise all the interactions between these groups' (*ibid*). The ability to monetise social interactions such as that arising from an engaged audience who cares about an influencer's fitness advice is an important capacity supported by platforms. It highlights platforms as the key enabling actors of a new form of capitalism that Srnicek (2017b) terms 'platform capitalism'. This form of capitalism is supported by a platform's affordances (Postigo, 2016).

Affordances and Platform Power

Think about Gretzel's (2017a: 1) definition of social media as applications, websites, and other online technologies that enable users 'without technical expertise to easily produce and publish content'. A platform's affordances are what make this easy production and publishing possible. Instagram's smooth interface and useful filters made editing and sharing beautiful photographs effortless and attracted a lot of non-professional creators who engaged in extensive content creation as a result. Platforms decide what user actions they enable based on their business models in conjunction with the goals of the particular users they want to attract or engage. For instance, recent developments in platforms make it increasingly straightforward to shop for products without having to leave the application, creating new affordances for consumers, marketers, and influencers that help generate revenue for the platform.

AFFORDANCE

An affordance is 'what material artifacts such as media technologies allow people to do' (Bucher & Helmond, 2018: 235).

Affordance theory was originally developed in the field of ecological psychology to refer to a specific kind of relationship between a bird and the aspects of its environment that looked like good possibilities to the bird for achieving its nest-building goals (Gibson, 1979). Later the concept of an affordance became used to refer to 'the perceived and actual properties' of something (Norman, 1988: 9), for example, a platform like Reddit or Weibo, and how it provides people with opportunities to do something that they want to do.

What exactly do platform affordances allow influencers and creators to do? There are many different technology tools that platforms provide to help influencers measure and understand how audiences engage with their content. Having these tools helps influencers and creators create content that can assist them to achieve their goals, whether those might be expanding the size of their audience, increasing the reach of specific pieces of content, or eliciting responses to posted content. For example, YouTube's affordances include a variety of formats (e.g., YouTube Shorts) through which vloggers, for example, promote new beauty techniques, trends, and goods (Gannon & Prothero, 2016; Mardon, Molesworth, & Grigore, 2018). YouTube also offers a variety of advertising types, including display advertisements and skippable and non-skippable video advertisements. Similar monetisation affordances are present on many social media platforms that are popular with influencers, such as Twitch.tv (Johnson & Woodcock, 2019) and Instagram (Drenten, Gurrieri, & Tyler, 2020).

These affordances give the influencer the ability to attract and engage sizeable audiences, and ultimately allow them to turn their efforts and ingenuity into money. But they also give the platform power over the influencer. Because platforms are the actor who controls the instruments needed for production in the influencer and creator economy, there is often a significant power imbalance in favour of the social media platform. Evolutions in social media platforms – including updates to their affordances – shape the behaviours of influencers and creators. Notably, when platforms introduce changes to improve their commercial viability, influencers and creators have to adapt their subjectivities and practices across platforms and affordances (Arriagada & Ibáñez, 2020). Of course, when an influencer has a huge number of devoted followers, as with Richard Tyler 'Ninja' Blevins, then that influencer might be able to exert power over a platform. Ninja did this in 2019 when he signed an exclusive deal first with the failed Mixer platform and then another one with Twitch (after bargaining with YouTube).

Algorithms and Platform Power

Algorithms are another very important aspect of platforms that affect influencers' and creators' ability to reach and impact an audience as well as to potentially monetise their content and following. For instance, algorithms determine what content is displayed in a user's social media feed and in which order. But algorithms are ordinarily invisible to users (which makes them obscure), and they are under the control of the platforms (which makes them impossible for influencers and brands to manipulate) (Kozinets, 2022). Different computer architectures, data storage technologies, arrangements of the memory hierarchy, and other features of a platform are subject to algorithms whose 'governing dynamics' (Ananny, 2016) vary and are specific to each platform.

ALGORITHM

An algorithm is 'an abstract, formalized description of a computational pro-cedure. Algorithms fall into different types according to their properties or domains: combinatorial algorithms deal with counting and enumeration; numerical algorithms produce numerical (rather than symbolic) answers to equational problems; while probabilistic algorithms produce results within particular bounds of certainty' (Dourish, 2016: 3).

Algorithms function best with large amounts of data, and thus the larger social media platforms tend to have the most effective algorithms that can help brands understand their customers and influencers manage their audiences. However, as Kozinets and Gretzel (2021) point out, the more a business (including a small business such as a for-profit influencer or creator) depends on large social media platforms and their algorithms, the more vulnerable it becomes to changes in them that could affect it adversely. This power imbalance is directly related to the way algorithms control and handle data. For instance, Bishop (2018) revealed that YouTube's algorithm can create a discriminatory visibility hierarchy of beauty vloggers, favouring middle-class female influencers who make highly gendered content aligned with advertisers' demands and needs.

Data and Platform Power

Clive Humby, the UK mathematician and architect of Tesco's Clubcard, is widely acknowledged as the first person to compare data with fossil fuels. Here is what he said: 'Data is the new oil. Like oil, data is valuable, but if unrefined it cannot really be used. It has to be changed into gas, plastic, chemicals, etc. to create a valuable entity that drives profitable activity' (Talagala, 2022). Just as the energy from oil shaped our contemporary world, so the insights and power from the data which stream through various platforms now inform supply chains and guide the action of corporations, states, institutions, and individuals. That data, provided and displayed in forms that are textual, graphic, photographic, audiovisual, and musical, are captured on platforms, owned by them, manipu-lated by their algorithms, and resold at will and in useful forms and quantities to the highest bidders.

DATA

The Google Dictionary (2022) defines data from a technical perspective, referring to it as the 'quantities, characters, or symbols on which operations are performed by a computer, being stored and transmitted in the form of electrical signals and recorded on magnetic, optical, or mechanical recording media'. Looking at data from a broader perspective, Merriam-Webster (2022) defines data as facts (such as measurements or statistics) 'used as a basis for reasoning, discussion, or calculation'.

The terms of use and service of the major social media platforms make it clear that the content which influencers and creators post, the reactions and uses of others in relation to that content, and all surrounding information, such as hyperlinks and metadata which record time spent and other matters, are the property of those platforms. These streams of data serve as raw material for the platforms' algorithms to extract patterns of great significance to influencers, brands, and many others. Influencer and creator data, for instance, may highlight specific demographic and psychographic consumer categories in relation to a particular audience or their attraction to specific content, such as geography, income, lifestyle, history, engagement, interests, and inclinations. Because the social media platforms own these data and are able to commercially exploit the information they provide, they control an important element of the means of production in the influencer and creator economy and in society at large.

Relations of Production

Entrepreneurship and Autopreneurship as a Relation of Production

RELATIONS OF PRODUCTION

Relations of production are the relatively stable set of power relationships that people in a society must utilise to survive, produce, and reproduce their way of life. In relation to the world of influencers, relations of production refer to the various social, economic, and technological relationships that underlie participation in a particular society's influencer system (Pfeiffer, 2021).

Beyond the technological resources of platforms and their affordances, algorithms, and data, there are social relationships that underlie an influencer's participation in the influencer and creator economy. One of these is autopreneurship. Ashman, Patterson, and Brown (2018) emphasise the combined confessional and professional quality of influencer behaviour in their term 'autopreneurs', a portmanteau which combines the terms 'autobiographical' and 'entrepreneur'. They highlight the personal and emotional disclosure that drives YouTube influencers' entrepreneurial behaviours. These efforts can take influencers down rabbit holes of emotional showmanship, self-revelation, personal disclosure, humour, intrigue, spicy sexiness, self-promotion, and even aggressive attacks on competitors. Various areas of people's social identity and personal activity become fodder for their entrepreneurial activities. For example, momfluencers and mommy bloggers become 'mumpreneurs' who then may focus on being paid promoters of products while also acting as idealized mother figures for an audience (Archer, 2019). In effect, they are cashing in on their status as mothers who have gathered an audience and using their knowledge to both inform and persuade other mothers.

Fan Labour as a Relation of Production

Companies have long been interested in harnessing the free activities of passionate followers of their brands. In the entertainment industry in particular, fans are seen as 'active, creative, productive' and, often, social (especially online) participants who create all sorts of material to support and encourage other fans (Milner, 2009). Their work in the form of enthusiastic and creative activities often has 'viable financial consequences' for the industry and is therefore referred to as fan labour. 'The media industry is increasingly dependent on active and committed consumers to spread the word about valued properties in an overcrowded media marketplace, and in some cases, they are seeking ways to channel the creative output of media fans to lower their production costs' (Jenkins, 2006: 134).

FAN LABOUR

Fan labour refers to the creative and productive activities freely engaged in by those with an enthusiastic and passionate appreciation for a commercial brand or property, such as media properties, stars, music groups, or motion pictures. We use the term 'fan labour' more broadly in the context of the influencer system to include the concept of 'working consumers' (Cova & Dalli, 2009), who engage in this kind of labour in relation to all kinds of consumption objects or practices rather than just in entertainment or sports contexts.

Fan labour and other online creative activities are a relation to production in which trademark and copyright holders such as Coca-Cola, Ford, and Disney (usually, and within limits) allow their devotees to create and distribute the material on social media using their images and marks, in return for authentic publicity. Some critical scholars consider this to be a type of exploitation of free labour, in which companies leverage enthusiasm and technology to 'find ever more innovative ways to extract free labour from the consumer' (Zwick, Bonsu, & Darmody, 2007: 166). For example, enthusiastic brand fans who focus on the Real Madrid football team will spend many hours creating social media content about players, matches, betting odds, and products such as team jerseys and other clothing that enrich the experience of other Real Madrid fans and may encourage them to engage in greater fan-related consumption and enjoyment. The efforts of these 'working consumers' add cultural and emotional value to Real Madrid's offerings, and work at a personal and social relationship level where the brand cannot operate (Cova & Dalli, 2009). Some platforms, such as the Sina Weibo platform in China, have become quite adept at developing ways to attract and keep fans productively engaged on their platforms (see the work of Yin, 2020 in the vignette box).

WEIBO'S DEVELOPMENT OF DIGITAL FAN LABOUR

Sina Weibo, as the largest social media platform in China, has become the catalyst that gathers, bonds, and disciplines fans from distinctive fandoms, thanks to its specific platform strategy and algorithmic system. Weibo not only reproduced many functions and algorithms from Twitter but also introduced new functions that aimed to govern and mobilize the activities of fans online (Yin, 2020: 479). As fans are among the most active users and produce considerable traffic to the platform, Yin reveals how Weibo strategically quantified casual users into visible data. The platform provides several paths for fans to contribute content, time, and money, and engage in activities by promising that their labour might lead to actual benefits for their favoured celebrities. Using functions, fan-directed affordances, and algorithmic tweaks, fan labour has been effectively managed by Sina Weibo.

Working consumers and fans are concepts that relate to the passionate activities social media content creators engage in to discuss or promote brands. Many influencers and creators start out as working consumers and many continue to engage in unpaid fan labour to establish or maintain relationships with brands. They also use fan labour activities to sustain their authenticity vis-à-vis their audience.

Monetisation of Social Capital as a Relation of Production

SOCIAL CAPITAL

Social capital is the links and bonds that people form through various types of social interaction, including digital communication via social media. According to Bourdieu's social media capital theory, social relationships become resources that can lead to the development and accumulation of other types of capital, such as financial capital (Ihlen, 2005).

Influencers build their existence and business on the recognition that social interactions may become a source of capital that can be turned into money. Gaining attention on social media through strategic practices, so-called visibility labour reflected by the number of likes, views, shares, and interactions content receives (Abidin, 2016a; Gerlitz & Helmond, 2013; Rokka & Canniford, 2016), is valuable in the influencer realm because it can be converted into social capital. The social capital that influencers gain in this manner may be swapped for economic capital, since the number of followers and the achieved engagement rate can be monetised through brand partnerships or other job opportunities (Faucher, 2014).

Mardon, Molesworth, and Grigore (2018) researched how the monetisation of social capital works in the world of successful beauty vloggers on YouTube who have attracted hundreds of thousands or even millions of subscribers. First, the vloggers earn the respect and trust of the YouTube community by offering impartial, often critical, reviews of beauty products, and by building a trusted relationship (also called 'relational capital', see concept box) with their followers. Some influencers genuinely seek an authentic connection with their followers, but others simply play a 'visibility game' in which they use online norms and platform algorithms to simulate that connection (Cotter, 2019). Then, as their popularity grows, the beauty vloggers systematically marketise the relational bonds they have carefully constructed.

RELATIONAL CAPITAL

Relational capital derives from 'the level of mutual trust, respect, and friendship that arises out of close interaction at the individual level between alliance partners' (Kale, Singh, & Perlmutter, 2000: 218). We extend relational capital to the realm of influencers, who build trust, respect, and even a sense of friendship with their audience members through content and interaction.

Beauty influencers take the positive and trusting relations that they have built with their audience and convert them into financial capital by incorporating paid advertisements and sponsored content. Furthermore, numerous beauty vloggers demonstrate their entrepreneurial acumen by bringing to market their own beauty brands and by promoting non-beauty (e.g., books, stationery, and apparel) items that are directly targeted to the members of their YouTube audience. The creation of relational bonds and social capital and the ability to monetise them serve as relations of production that ground the influencer system and form a key characteristic of the societal base that supports it.

THE TECHNOCULTURAL SUPERSTRUCTURE

Today, influencers operate in an environment that is 'technocultural', that is, it combines technology and culture such that each influences the other (Kozinets, 2019). For example, when considering an influencer phenomenon such as unboxing videos, it is difficult to distinguish between the cultural part of the phenomenon and the technological part. They are blended; the experience of creating and watching an unboxing video is technocultural. Technoculture is an important part of our society's superstructure, which encompasses social elements other than those related to the instruments and relations of production.

The Attention Economy as an Influencer Context

ATTENTION ECONOMY

An economic perspective in which things such as media content are assigned a value according to their capacity to attract the interest and engagement of people (or 'eyeballs') in a distracting media-saturated and information-rich environment (Marwick, 2015a: 138).

The technocultural environment of social media has spawned a complex superstructure of platform use and performative practices allowing some social media users to successfully prioritise the pursuit of visibility and public attention (Davenport & Beck, 2002). Competing online for consumers' attention has inspired new thinking about how to break through the clutter and create lasting, flexible, and evolving relationships with audiences (Fairchild, 2007). Yet, inasmuch as the 'attention economy' may have its origins in traditional marketing, brands' attention-grabbing techniques have trickled down to social media users who have started to adopt them to increase their online visibility and status (Marwick, 2013; Senft, 2008). TikTok activists have successfully supported abortion rights, embarrassed a former US President, and pushed for grassroots social change. For example, the consciousness raising of Sabrina Wisbiski and her 'Eco_Tok' posts is drawing attention to climate change – and away from traditional activism and activists (Pattee, 2021).

On visual platforms that emphasise self-representation like Instagram, ordinary users have taken advantage of opportunities to grab attention by frequenting 'cool' places and events, being good-looking, performing attractive jobs, or engaging in extravagant leisure activities that could be conspicuously exhibited as a symbol of social wealth (Faucher, 2014; Marwick, 2015a). Marwick (2015a) terms this phenomenon 'Instafame'. These practices are based on creating content that portrays them in a high-status light, simulating the attention given to real celebrities. It is through this aspirational image that they increase visibility and gain social capital and status (McQuarrie, Miller, & Phillips, 2013). On TikTok, Instafame is pursued by uploading short videos that can feature lip-syncing, dancing, pranking, and other comedic acts and incorporating audio and visual effects such as songs and filters. TikTok's algorithms and trending hashtags feature allow content to quickly rise in popularity and seem tailor-made for an attention economy where Gen Z users want to easily achieve online stardom with minimum effort.

The Gig Economy as an Influencer Context

GIG ECONOMY

Labour markets that are characterised by independent contracting that happens through and on digital platforms. 'The kind of work that is offered is [usually] contingent: casual and non-permanent work (Woodcock & Graham, 2020: 9).

The phrase 'gig economy' refers to the short-term agreements that are characteristic of musical performances. An ambitious musician might happily tell a friend that they have a gig in the back room of a pub or other venue. Of course, this is no assurance that they will be able to perform on a regular basis. As platforms have become increasingly important to economies around the world, labour markets using them have increasingly assumed the more uncertain, precarious, temporary, and short-term qualities of gigs. Some examples of gig economy work would be driving for a ride-sharing application such as Uber, delivering food for a food delivery app like DoorDash, or renting your home on a rental app such as Airbnb. In the world of influencers, this translates into:

- variable work hours (it may be difficult to predict how long it takes to shoot a good post),

- little job security (the influencer is not an employee), and

- payment on a piece-work basis (influencers are usually paid per post).

Work in the gig economy has its benefits. Gig economy work tends to have high degrees of flexibility, offering workers autonomy, task variety, and complexity. Culturally, it has produced idealistic and idyllic views of freelancing as not just a work arrangement but a lifestyle that offers freedom, empowerment, and mobility, spurring phenomena like vanlife and digital nomadism (Gretzel & Hardy, 2019; Hermann & Paris, 2020). However, tight time management requirements and the rule of the platform can also lead to low pay, working irregular hours, frequent overwork, sleep deprivation, exhaustion, and a sense of social isolation (Wood et al., 2019). Vallas and Schor (2020) present content producers and influencers performing what Duffy (2017) calls 'aspirational labor', work which is provided on an unpaid basis in the hope of gaining a sufficient level of prominence in the attention economy to provide a regular source of income. This aspirational characteristic may make the labour of influencers and potential influencers easy for companies and other large players to exploit.

The Reputation Economy as Influencer Context

REPUTATION ECONOMY

The reputation economy is an exchange system in which reputation independent of money or social position grants access to resources (Fecher et al., 2015). In contemporary technoculture, reputation is often measured and quantified on platforms by metrics such as a number of followers, ratings, likes, or shares.

Influencers and brands exist in an environment in which reputational concerns are all-around and all-important. With their measures of audience size and activity, platforms are constantly engaged in attempts to quantify and qualify the reputations of influencers. Furthermore, the key reputational task of influencers is to inspire trust in their audience. When people are interacting with other people that they do not know, concerns of trust become paramount (Eckhardt, 2020). When brands are attempting to reach new customers, they too are unknown, and must somehow inspire trust. By piggybacking onto the trust of audience members that an influencer has built over time, brands bridge their trust gap and utilise the reputational benefits of working with the influencer.

Reputational concerns are intricately linked to an increasingly prominent 'cancel culture' on social media, which refers to the large-scale withdrawal of support because of perceived wrongdoing. For influencers, this can mean the loss of followers as well as brand deals. As a result, influencers must constantly balance the need to entertain and inform with new and authentic content with the risk that their content may offend and that they could be 'canceled' (Bishop, 2021a). For example, the Kuwaiti beauty blogger Sondos Alqattan is a woman who could really rock a hijab. However, she was rebuked for a post in which she complained about the rights given to Filipino workers in her country. Many people thought that she viewed her Filipino housemaids as her own personal property, and several high-profile cosmetics brands ceased their partnerships in response (Gatollari, 2021).

Creators interested in building trusting relationships with an audience must constantly scrutinize their content with respect to its potential to offend. This important background serves as the reputational context under which a significant amount of influencer and creator activity currently transpires.

Algorithmic Culture as Influencer Context

ALGORITHMIC CULTURE

Algorithmic culture entails 'the use of computational processes to sort, classify, and hierarchize people, places, objects, and ideas, and also the habits of thought, conduct, and expression that arise in relationship to those processes' (Hallinan & Striphas, 2016; 119).

Algorithms determine what influencers, especially marginalised ones, can say and how they can say it. TikTok's algorithms were recently called out by Ziggy Tyler, who found that he was unable to enter phrases like 'Black Lives Matter' and 'supporting Black excellence' into his Marketplace profile. However, phrases like 'White supremacy' and 'supporting White excellence' were allowed. His efforts have led to an influencer and creator movement for more transparency in TikTok and other platforms' algorithms (Ohlheiser, 2022).

Platform algorithms play a key role in the workings of the technological base which influencers must use to produce and distribute their creative content. A knowledge of algorithms and their importance has also filtered into the general culture in which influencers and brands operate. Kozinets (2022: 3) has coined the term 'algorithmic branding' to refer to 'the enfolding of the conduct of thinking about, organizing, and implementing branding through the logic of big data and large-scale computation, consequently altering how the category of branding has long been practised, experienced, and understood'. The guiding logics of algorithms and the computational methods of big data analytics now play an important role in all elements of the brand process and involve brand managers, retailers, consumers, and platform programmers, as well as influencers. Each of these players, and perhaps particularly influencers, are working within a culture that is constituted by algorithms. A considerable amount of their work therefore involves trying to understand how to conduct their work and create their content in the face of data-intensive computational processes used to sort, classify, and hierarchise people, places, objects, and ideas.

Surveillance Capitalism as an Influencer Context

SURVEILLANCE CAPITALISM

Surveillance capitalism refers to a form of capitalism based on the access, accumulation, and control of information that aims to predict and modify human behaviour as a means to produce revenue and market control (Zuboff, 2019).

Surveillance capitalism is a system of governance that uses data and their information to affect social relations and gain authority and power. In the influencer economy, influencers' activities are affected by surveillance capitalism when they are subject to the record keeping, monitoring, and supervising of platforms and perhaps other organisations, such as brands or even governments. Consider the crackdowns of the Chinese government on livestreamers (Bloomberg.com, 2021) as an example of this type of platform surveillance.

As computerised surveillance systems that use algorithmic computation to process large amounts of data have grown more sophisticated, surveillance has turned into a new form of 'technological scrutiny'. This power makes platforms, and the institutional and corporate agencies managing this large amount of data, a force to be reckoned with at the collective and individual levels. For example, the search engine Google is known to retain individual search histories and, upon request, to make them available to state security and law enforcement agencies. Moreover, the monitoring abilities of influencer management tools, which support managers in selecting appropriate influencers for advertising campaigns, may recapitulate 'well-worn hierarchies of desirability and employability that originate from systemic bias along the lines of class, race, and gender' (Bishop, 2021a: 1).

These all-seeing surveillance systems are another important social context that circumscribes and affects influencer activity. Surveillance capitalism, algorithmic culture, the reputation economy, the gig economy, and the attention economy are superstructure elements pervaded with an ideology that preserves the power of the existing system while also shaping it. This specific ideology is called neoliberalism.

Ideology: Neoliberalism and the Influencer and Creator Economy

Much of the influencer and content creator domain is structured by a free market entrepreneurial ethos that positions many activities that were once private and personal (such as mothering or eating) as profitable money-making hustles. Neoliberalism is an important explanatory concept for this development.

NEOLIBERALISM

Neoliberalism is a way of thinking about governance and society that embraces the values of free market capitalism while seeking to encourage greater entrepreneurial, competitive, and commercial behaviour in its citizens. The goal of neoliberalism is to cultivate a type of marketplace in which free market competitive and industrious behaviours are encouraged across society and take place with minimal government interference (Thorsen, 2010).

Neoliberalism is a powerful system of beliefs, norms, and values on which much of the world currently bases its actions. Neoliberalism is a central element of the superstructure in which influencers ply their trade because it is a core ideology. This ideology affects everything in the superstructure. For influencers, the neoliberal way of thinking about governance and society pervades surveillance capitalism, algorithmic culture, the reputation economy, the gig economy, and the attention economy. Neoliberal thinking establishes a cultural condition under which the current production relations of platforms, affordances, algo-rithms, data, autopreneurship, fan labour, and the monetisation of social capital appear not only fair but also entirely natural.

Laissez-faire capitalism is not the same thing as neoliberalism, but the two ideas are closely related. Like laissez-faire capitalism, those who believe in neoliberalism do not think that the government should get involved in social and economic issues unless it is for things like preventing monopolies and protecting people's property rights. Neoliberalism is a way of thinking based on many of the same ideals and aspirations as laissez-faire capitalism, but some of its vari-ants also believe that institutions can play a more positive role in guiding peo-ple's lives. The implications for the influencer and creator economy are that the instruments and relations of production remain largely unregulated.

Much media communication and popular culture content express the idea that a free market economy is a good thing, and that more competitive and individualistic behaviours are better for society. These norms and values are widespread in self-help literature, popular fiction, mainstream TV, consumer publishing, music culture, and journalism. Social media operates like a free market, in that just about anyone can use social media, and billions of people do worldwide. The influencer industry also appears to operate like a free market, in that just about anyone can begin posting original content and start to build an audience and a following. These apparent freedoms, however, are structured in ways that reinforce power dynamics and relationships that favour technology companies and brands. Platforms are required for people to express this freedom. To use those platforms, their terms of use must be accepted and abided by, while the platforms themselves often escape government intervention because of their global nature and size. Furthermore, affordances shape what influencers can and cannot do and platforms are free to change them. Algorithms, which can also be changed by companies on a whim, deeply affect influencers' content and potential business opportunities. These factors leave influencers and creators in rather precarious positions.

One of the key intellectual underpinnings of the influencer and creator economy is the belief in the freedom of the influencer to develop content, build an audience, and market it to companies. This freedom enacted through gig economy work places the influencer in the employ of corporate brand managers and at the mercy of the technology companies who own and manage social media platforms. The neoliberal belief in freedom reinforces this power structure, preserving and helping to construct it. Whether working in the United Arab Emirates, India, Russia, or France, the autopreneurs who shape their identities to their audience's liking to be able to translate their visibility, relations, and reputation into economic capital often struggle to get fair pay for their hard labour and to make a decent living.

CHAPTER SUMMARY

This chapter provided a broad overview of the context in which influencer content is developed and marketed. Influencers' and creators' capacity to work and spread their material is made possible by a mix of technological, social, and economic resources that are not entirely under their control. Platforms are key components of the influencer and creator economy and critically impact what influencers and creators do and how they do it. Influencers and creators draw on, and are impacted by, the attention economy, the gig economy, the reputation economy, algorithmic culture, and surveillance capitalism in their work and their content. Each of these cultural contexts creates its own set of expectations, which influencers must meet through their diligent efforts and responsive content development. Neoliberalism, a free market way of thinking about governing society, is the controlling ideology that holds these disparate aspects together, constructing the socioeconomic conditions and supporting the technoculture in which influencers function but also preserving the power relations in societies. Explaining these important structural elements and considerations, this chapter laid the groundwork for in-depth knowledge of the influencer ecosystem.

EXERCISES AND QUESTIONS

Exercises

1. Go to three different social media platforms and examine the content from one influencer on each of them. How do the different platform affordances affect the ability of the influencer to post content? How do those affordances affect your experience of the influencer's content?

2. Open your favourite social media app and see if you can easily contact your favourite influencer (if you have one, choose an online celebrity if you don't). Explain why you think the app does or does not allow you to connect?

3. Keep a journal for one day and record all the information you type into various platforms. What do you know about how this information is treated?

4. Do you know anyone who works in the gig economy (if applicable, it could be you). Ask them if the gig economy is a good or bad thing for them. Is the gig economy a good thing or a bad thing for society?

Questions

1. Give two examples from your daily life about how resource dependency theory explains the relationships of power that you experience.

2. Algorithms are everywhere, but they are also invisible. Can you explain this statement? Is there any way that we could make algorithms more visible? Explain your answer.

3. What is more important – the reputation of a brand to an influencer, or the reputation of an influencer to a brand? Explain your answer.

4. What are some of the most important effects of the monetisation of social capital?

5. What is the most important thing that social media influencer content must have to get your attention? What do you think this says about you? How does it relate to the idea of the attention economy?

6. Neoliberalism gets a bad rap in this chapter. Do you agree? Discuss your answer.

ANNOTATED READINGS

Cohn, J. (2019). *The burden of choice: Recommendations, subversion, and algorithmic culture*. New Brunswick, NJ: Rutgers University Press.

This book reveals how recommendations for products, media, news, friends and many other aspects of our lives are produced and experienced online and how the logics that govern recommendations have come to serve as a form of social and ideological power and control.

Gandini, A. (2016). *The reputation economy: Understanding knowledge work in digital society*. Berlin: Springer.

This book documents the rise of freelancing and digital professions and highlights the central role held by reputation within this context.

Wichmann, J. R., Wiegand, N., & Reinartz, W. J. (2022). The platformization of brands. *Journal of Marketing, 86*(1), 109–131.

Situated within the fast-evolving domain of platform capitalism, this academic article provides an analysis of emergent platform offerings that brands are adopting as 'flagship platforms' to counterbalance the power of established digital platforms.

3

BUSINESS AND SOCIAL MEDIA MARKETING CONCEPTS

CHAPTER OVERVIEW AND OBJECTIVES

This chapter provides background information about the guiding principles of marketing communications. Brands and social media have been key to recent developments in marketing, such as the desire for communications to go viral and spread organically through word-of-mouth communication. An important model for understanding these transformations is the Paid, Earned, Shared, and Owned (PESO) model, which categorises the results of communication efforts. Influencer marketing sits at the centre of the PESO model. Segmentation, targeting, and positioning are core marketing strategies, and they are also relevant in the world of influencer marketing. Another important idea is the Marketing Funnel, which describes the customer's journey with the brand from unawareness to purchase and loyalty. A final model discussed in this chapter is the Brand Desire Spiral, which explains some of the important changes to marketing and branding in an age of connected networks, including the often-central role of influencers and content creators. The chapter then dives into the range of tactics contemporary marketers utilise to connect their brands to consumer identities, wants, and actions, and to deepen those person-to-brand relationships. Adding depth and breadth to the reader's knowledge of contemporary marketing thought and practice, the chapter closes with a perspective written by one of the world's top social media marketing agencies.

PROVOCATION: 'Because the purpose of business is to create a customer, the business enterprise has two – and only two – basic functions: marketing and innovation. Marketing and innovation produce results; all the rest are costs'. —Peter Drucker, *The Practice of Management* (1954)

KEYWORDS: PESO model, segmentation, targeting, positioning, marketing funnel, brands, celebrity endorsement, product placement, native advertising, affiliate marketing

---

KEEPING UP WITH MARKETING DEVELOPMENTS

Let's consider Sally Hodgkins, a hypothetical but perhaps not atypical public relations and communication management student at a major university in your country. During a break between semesters in her program, Sally landed an internship position at a small but rapidly growing digital agency. Although her programme trained her how to do press releases and to work with journalists in major traditional media publications, she had actually received very little training in social media marketing. When her boss knocked on her door one morning and asked her if she knew how to use retargeting data to help promote a new affiliate marketing program for a brand of beach sandals on TikTok, she smiled confidently and replied, 'Sure, I'm on it!'. Then, she scrambled, quickly looking up the key terms on the web and trying to piece together exactly what it was she was supposed to do.

Like most aspects of business, marketing has become a dynamic practice subject to fast-paced change. However, many basic principles of marketing still apply to influencer marketing. Not only will this chapter provide an understanding of marketing terminology and concepts, but it will also offer a solid background and working knowledge of the world of social media marketing. To accomplish this, we first have to understand some of the basic elements of both social media and marketing.

UNDERSTANDING MARKETING

Markets are places where buyers and sellers transact and exchange, and marketing is the name given to making those transactions and exchanges happen. Although marketing as a type of strategic trade dates back to antiquity and branding was invented in the 1700s, modern marketing practice is generally regarded as having begun in the early twentieth century with the rise of mass media (Tedlow & Jones, 2014). Since then, marketing has become more and more associated with media – first with print media (think flyers, brochures, posters, newspapers, and magazines), then with broadcast media (think radio and television). Today, in keeping with contemporary neoliberal ideology, almost anything can be a brand. There are personal brands and corporate brands, political brands, and branded experiences. And in 2019, total digital marketing and branding surpassed spending on traditional marketing that included television and print.

Marketing refers to activities and processes used to create, communicate, and deliver offerings that have value to customers. Marketing happens as businesses sell products and services to other businesses (e.g., raw materials like steel or janitorial services), in the non-profit world when organisations seek donors and support, as well as within the more familiar world of end consumers, such as when someone buys a car or a candy bar. It often surprises people to learn that the business-to-business (or B2B) marketplace is about double the size of the business-to-consumer (or B2C) market. And, although the average person probably thinks that marketing is just about advertising or sales, marketing is actually a complicated set of activities and processes that also include developing new products, pricing them, getting them into the inventory of business users, on to the shelves of stores, and into the homes of consumers. The element that unites all of these actions is the essential idea of a market: the attempt to create mutual value through a transaction or exchange.

MARKETING

The American Marketing Association, the world's preeminent global association of marketing academics and practitioners, defines marketing as 'the activity, set of institutions, and processes for creating, communicating, delivering, and exchanging offerings that have value for customers, clients, partners, and society at large' (AMA website, 2022).

Marketing activities, such as creating a product or producing an advertisement, are referred to as marketing tactics. These tactics are also known as 'the marketing mix' or 'the four Ps' of marketing. The marketing mix is the entire set of actions available to marketers in order to meet the needs of their customers and create value through the exchange. The marketing mix is made up of 'the four Ps': product (the product or service that is offered), place (where it is sold), price, and promotion (which includes advertising, public relations, direct marketing and sales, and now also influencer marketing). All elements of the marketing mix – product design and technology, packaging, distribution in wholesaler warehouses, retail distribution in stores, gaining shelf space, point-of-purchase promotions, selling and changing the price, and all messaging carried out through traditional and social media – combine to form the 'product' (AMA website, 2022). In contrast, brands are concerned with identity, meanings, and reputation, and are made up of both tangible elements – such as Coca-Cola's famous logo or its top-secret formula – as well as intangible elements such as the values consumers associate with them. Brand meanings are formed in the minds of consumers (which could be business consumers as well as end consumers) through a range of impressions about products, competition, and users. Today, many brands are mentioned and promoted using social media.

BRANDS

Brands are the recognizable identity, meanings, and reputation of a company, product, or service.

SOCIAL MEDIA

Social media are websites and applications that use Web 2.0 technology to facilitate content creation, sharing, and social networking.

Social media are designed so that, without requiring technical expertise, its users can create, access, discuss, modify, and/or share a variety of types of content with individuals or a community of known or unknown others (Gretzel, 2017a). This content could be mainly visual, as with Pinterest and Instagram, audiovisual as with YouTube, or audio as with podcasts and Clubhouse. Regardless of format, when a user of social media creates posts and then shares that content without paying the platform for special distribution of that content, the audience formation that results from this process is known as organic reach.

One of the goals of social media has been virality, or 'going viral', which is the tendency for a certain piece of content to spread rapidly and extensively online (and sometimes even into traditional media). In practice, going viral is much harder to do than it sounds. Many viral posts are flashes in the pan that are difficult to duplicate. This is why marketers often resort to paying platforms to distribute their content rather than hoping that it will rapidly spread in an organic fashion. When someone, usually an advertiser, wants to increase the number and/or types of people who see a post, they will pay the platform to distribute the post. Paying to distribute a social media post is often called amplification.

VIRALITY

The propensity for an image, video, or another piece of content to spread swiftly and extensively from one online user to the next; the state of being viral.

ORGANIC REACH

Organic reach refers to the number of viewers naturally obtained by a given social media post without any advertising.

WORD OF MOUTH

Word of mouth are messages about brands, products, services, companies, and other commercial entities that are spread between people in conversational settings.

There are numerous ways that social media can be used to execute marketing strategies, and these uses are often part of larger plans that include other elements of the marketing mix.

A key concept in social media marketing is the idea of word of mouth. When a social media post comes from an individual and relates to a commercial product or service, that post is often called 'word of mouth', a term that predates online media but is commonly now used to refer to it. When word of mouth becomes a subject of marketing strategy (as is often the case in social media), it is sometimes called word-of-mouth marketing.

Word-of-mouth marketing techniques are the means by which marketers try to spread messages about products or services in conversational settings where people trust one another. Influencers communicating with their followers is one such setting. At the dawn of the social media age, when blogs were all the rage, all that many companies had to do was send a popular blogger a product gift and they would get a review and a mention, and the product-related message would spread through organic word of mouth (Kozinets et al., 2010). Today, the media environment and the influencer business have become considerably more sophisticated. One of the most important ways for understanding that new and more complex media environment is through something called the PESO model.

PESO MODEL

PESO is an acronym that stands for Paid, Earned, Shared, and Owned and refers to four different media types that communicators can leverage to achieve their communication goals. Dietrich (2014) developed the PESO model to illustrate the strategic media options emerging in the digital space. The four media types differ in terms of predictability, scalability (ability to increase reach), cost, and trust vested in them by consumers (see Table 3.1). They are usually depicted as overlapping circles (see Figure 3.1) to emphasise that some emerging communication initiatives cannot be clearly assigned to one category. For instance, branded content/native advertising falls between paid and owned media. The PESO model helps communicators make strategic media channel decisions and determine the necessary media investment.

Table 3.1 Examples and characteristics of PESO media types

	Media types			
Media characteristics	Paid	Earned	Shared	Owned
	(Ads, sponsored posts, listings, search keywords, brand ambassadors, etc.)	(Media relations, investor relations, etc.)	(Social media engagement, user-generated contents)	(Content on the brand website or social media accounts, podcasts, etc.)
Predictability	High	Low	Low	High
Scalability	High	Medium	Low	Low
Cost	High	Low to medium	Low	Low to medium
Trust	Low	High	High	Low to medium

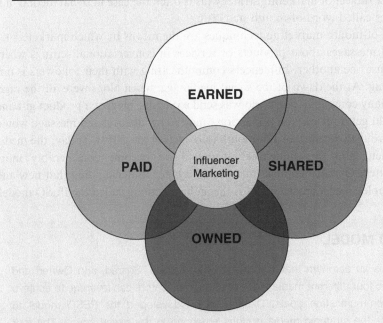

Figure 3.1 Influencer marketing within the PESO model

Influencer marketing can involve all four media types. Paid components of influencer marketing can include paying the influencer for a specific number and type of posts or paying for advertising on a platform to boost influencer posts. Earned media in the influencer marketing context includes unprompted posts by the influencer based on the long-standing relationship the brand has built with them. Earned media also includes mass media reporting on an influencer event based on a press release or journalists being hosted alongside the influencers. Shared media could involve an influencer-based TikTok challenge that goes viral or an influencer managing a giveaway that asks those who would like to enter to post pictures of themselves using the brand and tagging themselves with a specific hashtag. Owned media can refer to brands buying content from creators to be featured on their accounts, repurposing influencer content during or after an influencer campaign, or influencers taking over the brand's social media account for a specified period.

SOCIAL MEDIA TAKEOVER

A social media takeover is a marketing tactic which involves another user posting content on the brand's own account for a limited time. This other user can be an employee, an existing customer, a thought leader, another brand, or an influencer. The brand benefits from a takeover through creative and fresh content, while the person or brand taking over the account gains exposure and access to the brand's engaged audience.

INFLUENCER TAKEOVER OF LIL MIQUELA WITH PRADA

One prominent example of an influencer taking over a brand's social media account is the 2018 Prada collaboration with the virtual influencer Lil Miquela (@lilmiquela), who describes herself as a 19-year-old robot living in Los Angeles and who claims over 3 million followers on Instagram. Prada enlisted Lil Miquela to help promote its fall/winter show during Milan Fashion Week. Lil Miquela publicized the brand's upcoming event through her own Instagram feed and stories with downloadable GIFs and calls to action like 'Go off!! #pradagifs are live in stories! Start posting and tag me 😺 #PradaFW18 #MFW'. Over on the Prada brand account, Lil Miquela gave Instagram users a tour of the fashion show space Fondazione Prada using a drone. In an 'interview' with *The Guardian* (2018) after the show, she further claimed to have attended the show and flown the drone that whizzed up and down the runway.

As the vignette on Lil Miquela taking over the Prada Instagram account demonstrates, there are no limits to the creative forms that influencer initiatives can take. And as the social media landscape evolves, so do the types of influencer marketing that are possible and most effective. An important thing to note is that influencer marketing is not just a simple type of product placement (Russell & Belch, 2005) or celebrity endorsement (McCracken, 1989), although the academic literature often uses the terms when referring to influencer marketing (e.g., Alassani & Göretz, 2019; Jin & Muqaddam, 2019; Schouten, Janssen, & Verspaget, 2020; Torres, Augusto, & Mates, 2019).

CELEBRITY ENDORSEMENT

A celebrity endorsement is an agreement between an individual who enjoys public recognition (a celebrity) and an entity (e.g., a brand) to use the celebrity's name and/or appearance for the purpose of promoting the entity in exchange for an often considerable fee (Bergkvist & Zhou, 2016). The idea behind celebrity endorsement is that the qualities of the celebrity (e.g., attractiveness, strength, and endurance) will transfer to the entity.

PRODUCT PLACEMENT

Product placement is a paid marketing technique that promotes branded products by placing them in a non-advertising context in a way that allows the branded products to blend into the rest of the content. This 'natural' appearance of the branded products lowers consumers' ability to recognise the content as advertising and, thus, lowers resistance to the persuasion attempt.

Compared to celebrity endorsement contracts, the influencer usually retains a much higher level of control over the promotional content in influencer marketing arrangements. Compared to product placement tactics, influencer marketing permits a much more active featuring of the branded product, although the influencer often adds their unique voice to the promotional effort and will strive to make it fit with the rest of their content to not jeopardize their personal brand and to protect their perceived authenticity. Further, many countries and platforms now have rules in place that prohibit the covert nature of product placement tactics when a material connection between a brand and an influencer exists.

Consequently, influencer marketing refers to strategic efforts of communicators to partner with influencers and creators to reach targeted audiences with engaging messages through social media channels using various promotional tactics. The emphasis on partnering highlights that influencer marketing requires the active involvement of both parties while also usually offering mutual benefits beyond the simple exchange of money for a promotional service (e.g., the brand receives fresh, engaging, and creative content, while the influencer can increase their following as a result of the exposure gained through the association with the brand). It is this collaborative nature of influencer marketing that makes it so rewarding for both parties but also so labour-intensive. This is why brands often enlist the help of influencer marketing agencies or other intermediaries to assist them with managing the process (Stoldt et al., 2019).

Because influencer marketing is ideally a form of partnership between an influencer or creator and a brand, one-off initiatives often evolve into longer-term engagements (Influencer Intelligence, 2022). The initial investment required from the brand (finding the right influencers and convincing them to work with the brand) and from the influencer or creator (e.g., learning about the brand and the followers' reactions to it) and their need to establish trust is so high that there is a growing tendency towards influencer relations, which aims at cultivating and nourishing ongoing relationships with the influencers and creators that the brand has successfully collaborated with in the past. But even long-standing partnerships involve concrete periods of high-intensity engagement between the brand and the influencer/creator in the form of campaigns.

Segmentation, Targeting, and Positioning

Good influencer campaigns and strong tactics are grounded in the core marketing principles of segmentation, targeting, and positioning. Marketers use segmentation to differentiate between the many different types of customers (both business and end consumer) and their various purchasing patterns in order to provide them with products and services that better meet their needs. When used correctly, segmentation helps businesses 'tailor their product and service offerings to the groups most likely to purchase them' (Yankelovich & Meer, 2006). Age, gender, geographic location, religious beliefs, ethnicity, hobbies and lifestyle interests, purchase patterns, and stage of the customer journey can all be used to segment potential and actual customers. Today, many social media platforms offer detailed information about market segments. For example, Google Analytics allows users to discover affinity categories, which include sites, groups, and interests that are related to people who visit a particular site, while Facebook and other platforms offer targeting demographics combined with locations and also very specific interests, hobbies, and lifestyles or platform-related behaviours.

SEGMENTATION

Segmentation is the process of distinguishing between different types of customers in order to provide them with products that better meet their needs.

TARGETING

Targeting entails selecting a specific group of customers to sell to.

Targeting comes after segmentation, and the two are frequently combined in practice. When targeting, the marketer seeks to sell to a specific group of customers while deliberately excluding others. 'Target customers are entities (individuals or organisations) whose needs the company seeks to meet. Because a company's main goal is to create customer value, identifying the right customer is critical for market success' (Chernev, 2019). With vast amounts of data available about people online, social media marketing can be quite precise in reaching target consumers while avoiding wasting marketing dollars on those who are not. Influencer marketing enhances targeting opportunities even further because influencers come with a passionate audience that they know very well and can reach through their posts.

POSITIONING

A brand or product's positioning involves creating a mental image in the target consumer's mind of what that brand or product represents, often in relation to other products or brands (Tybout & Sternthal, 2012).

In the marketing world, branding is considered an investment in the future. Therefore, not all advertising campaigns contained on social media will be focused on immediately creating sales. Rather they might be related to creating a specific image of a brand or product in the mind of the target consumer. To be successful, the mental image fostered by positioning should have three key characteristics. First, the brand's image should be related to a category known to satisfy some specific needs. These needs can be symbolic or emotional (a need for human connection, for example) as well as functional or practical (a need for refreshment when thirsty). Second, the brand's image should be distinctive and superior to competitive market offerings in ways that matter to its target consumers. Third, the brand essence should imply some relevant goal or aspiration for the consumer (symbolic and/or functional). A company such as Coca-Cola, for instance, spends large amounts across all media (including social media) to create associations between Coca-Cola and meanings of happiness, authenticity, and togetherness, while it is also positioned in the category of refreshing beverages.

Because positioning is such a key component of brand strategy, it will guide the development of all four Ps. The concept of a brand mantra, such as Disney's 'fun family entertainment', which flows not only through the creation of products and services but also through its pricing models and brand messaging, is directly related to the brand's positioning.

The Marketing Funnel

The marketing funnel is an established and very useful idea that describes a customer journey from the moment the brand attracts attention to the point of action or purchase (Colicev, Kumar, & O'Connor, 2019). There are many different versions of the marketing funnel, but all of them describe a sales process that moves from awareness to consideration and action, which usually means purchase. Some include loyalty (repeat purchase) and even advocacy (evangelizing for the brand with word of mouth). See Figure 3.2, which includes all five of these sales journey elements.

> **MARKETING FUNNEL**
>
> A strategic tool that describes a potential customer's journey from becoming aware of a brand to turning into a loyal customer or brand advocate. The narrowing funnel describes the decreasing numbers of potential customers that fall into each stage. The funnel starts with awareness, continues with consideration and conversion, and ends with loyalty and advocacy.

To understand how the funnel works, consider the journey of someone buying a new model of mobile phone. First, they become aware of the new phone, perhaps through hearing about it online. If they are looking for a new phone, they might learn more about it by searching for more information. They will consider their options, and some subset of those consumers will then act and make a phone purchase. Some of them may become loyal customers of that type of phone and may even advocate and evangelize to other people about how great it is. Figure 3.2 depicts a typical Marketing Funnel. The funnel is wide at the top

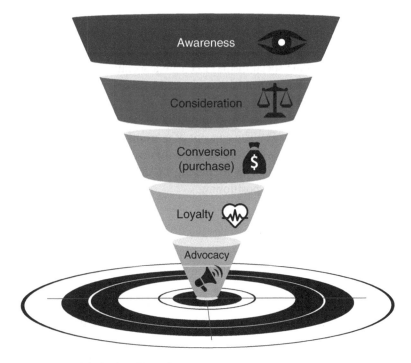

Figure 3.2 The Marketing Funnel

to represent that the largest number of people are aware of the product. It becomes narrower at the bottom to show that far fewer people will purchase, repeat purchase, or evangelize for the brand than are aware of it.

The Marketing Funnel model is often used in relation to influencer marketing because it can help marketers describe the intended effect of a marketing campaign. For example, a start-up company offering a new brand might seek increased awareness and recognition among a particular consumer group by having influencers introduce the brand and explain its benefits to their audience. On the other hand, an established brand may want to stoke sales by providing a reason to act, such as a discount in the form of a coupon code, to encourage consumers who are already aware of and considering the brand to act immediately and place an online order. When the marketer or influencer is asked to take consumers who are not in the funnel, or who are placed higher in the funnel (in other words, who are aware of or considering the brand or product) and move them lower in the funnel, this is said to be moving them down the funnel. Moving consumers through the funnel, or sales process, is also called conversion or helping to convert them (into customers or purchasers).

BRANDING IN A WORLD OF PLATFORMS AND DESIRE

One of the major ways that brand experiences happen today is through technology platforms such as TikTok, Amazon, Meta, and Google, and their associated networks and devices, such as mobile phones and virtual reality goggles. Inherent in the operations of platforms are algorithms, which are opaque and controlled by technology platforms. Algorithms are complex concepts that 'can be conceived in several ways – technically, computationally, mathematically, politically, culturally, economically, contextually, materially, philosophically, ethically' (Kitchin, 2017: 14). One recent development in marketing is to conceive of marketing in this new environment as a type of 'algorithmic branding' (Kozinets, 2022) that must consider the ways marketers and consumers interact with technology platforms, including how they interact with influencers.

Algorithms are key to how technology use enhances consumer desire. In a study of food porn, consumer desire was traced as it travelled via Instagram and other social media sites. The researchers found that the combination of devoted influencers, such as mukbangers and other food porn posters, as well as algorithms, drive attention to extremes (Kozinets, Patterson, & Ashman, 2017). The vignette on mukbang illustrates how influencers like Quang Tran livestream to create powerful sensory content that helps to build a network of desire based around the passion for food.

MUKBANG

Mukbang is a combination of Korean words meaning 'eating broadcast'. It refers to an online audiovisual broadcast in which a host consumes various quantities and types of food while interacting with the viewers (Kircaburun et al., 2021).

MUKBANG: HOW QUANG TRAN CREATES FOOD DESIRE

Quang Tran is a 32-year-old Canadian YouTuber and mukbanger with over 2.4 million subscribers on his YouTube channel. Quang has a passion for fitness and food, two apparently opposing worlds. He started his YouTube Channel in 2014, posting videos of his gym training as he was a personal trainer but did not get a lot of viewers. Then he decided to switch and did a challenge of eating 20,000 calories worth of food. The video went viral, and it got over 2.5 million views. Since then, Tran has made a name for himself through his funny, voracious eating videos. In his videos, he either cooks for himself and then eats yummy, sumptuous, fatty food (i.e., spicy honey BBQ fried chicken, spaghetti and meatballs, all-in burritos, and crispy chicken burgers) or eats fast food from brands such as Burger King, KFC, and Costco's Rotisserie chicken, and then he records his reactions and reviews. In his videos, he is always hilariously starving to the point that he is able to devour a massive amount of any type of food with only a few gigantic bites.

Tran creates desire by performing an eating ritual in front of the camera that drags his audience into a spiral of multisensory collective excitement, while inviting them to play with him through their own fantasy and imagination involvement. When the food is a burger, the eating ritual is generally composed of six sequential steps that create desire:

1. *'Setting the stage'.* This is the preparation of the show, when Tran sets the expectations of the audience. He provides details of his burger shopping experience, he unwraps the burgers, he offers a visual overview of all the items that compose his food feast, he makes a close-up of each of them, and then he carefully finishes the preparation of the burgers, adding a touch of mustard or ketchup.

2. *'Showing my baby'.* Then, he chooses his first burger, the one that tantalizes him the most. . .the elected one for the first bite with which he starts the party. He avidly looks at all the burgers and picks one, then he lifts it in front of the camera, he cuddles it, he turns it to choose the perfect bite angle, where the burger is softer and juicier, he opens it and touches and describes each single ingredient. . .he even calls the burger 'my baby'.

3. *'I'm super pumped for this!'* Now he's ready to bite, just a few more seconds to chew fast and loud with an empty mouth to make his own and his audience members' mouths water. . .a few more seconds to share his excitement with the signature claim 'I'm super pumped for this!', and to boast about his strength and determination with the exclamation 'When you bite into a burger, you mean it!'

4. *'Biting hard and big'.* This is a moment of intimacy between him and the burger. He opens his big mouth, he extends his jaws like a snake and then takes a gigantic bite of the burger, sinking his teeth deep into its soft, juicy meat. Tran invites his audience to taste and experience this apex moment along with him in their imagination.

5. *'Indulging in the after bite'.* After the bite, his mouth is so full that there's barely room to chew. Tran murmurs sounds of pleasure while chewing. He smiles. He nods, satisfied. He may even talk with his mouth full to indulge in his joyful delight before swallowing.

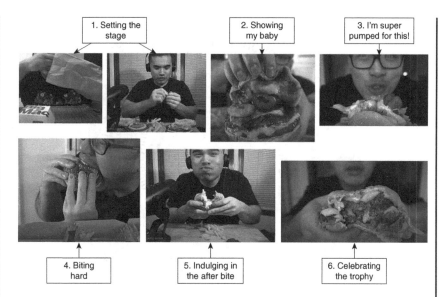

Figure 3.3   Quang Tran's eating ritual to elicit consumers' desire

6. *'Celebrating the trophy'*. Tran closes his ritual by proudly showing the bitten burger to the camera like a trophy. He displays the huge bite marks that have devastated the burger, which now reveal all the delectable colours, textures, and flavours of the burger filling. The bitten burger becomes symbolic of the intense, immediate pleasure coming from giving in to temptation and flows of libidinal desires.

This ritual offers an example of how a mukbanger like Tran creates desire in consumers and channels existing desire into even more extreme spirals of desire. Figure 3.3 captures an exemplary visual sequence of these ritual steps.

The Brand Desire Spiral

Algorithms, platforms, audiences, and influencers like the mukbanger Quang Tran create dynamic and powerful feedback loops that amplify and guide human desire. Sometimes, these 'networks of brand desire' focus on single brands, such as BTS, Disney, or Prada. At other times, they might be focused on wider interests that include brands, such as surfing, women's fitness, or beauty and cosmetics.

The Brand Desire Spiral depicted in Figure 3.4 captures the world of marketing in this new media reality. Each circle in the diagram represents a

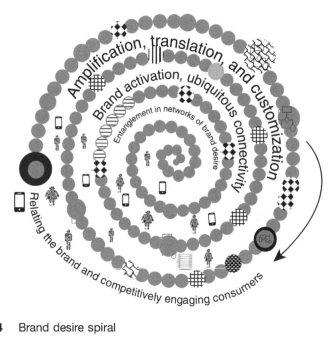

Figure 3.4　Brand desire spiral

brand incident or moment which could include thinking about the brand, connecting with it, or using it, and which can represent different stages of the marketing funnel. Marketers try to entangle consumers in these brand-related incidents. Real-time algorithms embedded in platforms connect the brand to consumer identities, wants, and actions. Along the way, many important marketing tactics are utilised, such as affiliate marketing, native advertising, remarketing or retargeting, behavioural targeting, Search Engine Optimisation (SEO), and Search Engine Marketing (SEM). Often, as in affiliate marketing or native advertising, these marketing tactics directly involve the efforts of influencers and content creators.

Affiliate Marketing, SEO, and Other Related Marketing Concepts

AFFILIATE MARKETING

Affiliate marketing is a type of advertising in which an organisation pays independent third-party content producers/publishers to generate traffic or leads to its site, products, or services. These third-party entities are considered affiliates and are paid a commission fee for their promotion of the organisation or its products.

AFFILIATE MARKETING: THE AMAZON'S ASSOCIATES PROGRAM

The Amazon's Associates Program is one of the world's largest affiliate marketing programs, enabling influencers and creators to monetise the traffic to their content. Amazon gives influencers the tools they need to select items and services from Amazon, suggest them to followers, and earn commissions on any resulting sales. Influencers can motivate people to shop Amazon's millions of products by curating their own Amazon page with livestreams, shoppable pictures, and videos.

NATIVE ADVERTISING

Native advertising is paid media that is tailored to blend into the content of a media source. Native advertising mimics the visual design and functionality of organic or journalistic content and is intended to be so integrated into the page content, design, and platform behaviour that the viewer feels the ad belongs there (e.g., sponsored social media posts).

NATIVE ADVERTISING: *NEW YORK TIMES* AND ALLBIRDS

Native advertising typically uses sponsored news posts. The shoe company Allbirds recently partnered with the *New York Times* newspaper to create an In Feed/In Content ad that was pushed to the NYT's normal newsfeed. Users who clicked on the NYT's article were brought to a page with graphics and sound effects. The article focused on how climate change threatens birds' environment. The shoe manufacturer linked the ad to their own sustainability efforts, which is one of their major brand pillars, and their brand name also includes the word 'bird'. This example illustrates how effectively native content can be connected with the brand, even if it is not necessarily directly about it.

REMARKETING

Remarketing (also known as retargeting) is the practice of serving targeted advertisements to people who have previously visited or acted on a particular website.

REMARKETING AND RETARGETING: EXPEDIA

Companies can set up automated remarketing emails to reach consumers directly in their inboxes in addition to remarketing on websites or social media pages. Users who browse flights on Expedia's mobile app, for example, receive a remarketing email with a button to view the most recent ticket offers. The email copy and eye-catching graphics are personalized with flight information from the Expedia app. They also include a colourful call-to-action button inviting them to return to Expedia's website to view the most recent tickets and book a flight.

BEHAVIOURAL TARGETING

Behavioural targeting (also called online behavioural advertising) is the use of people's activities to determine which advertisements and messages will be the most effective with them. It uses behavioural data, such as what people do or do not do in an app, on a website, or with a campaign ad, to trigger personalized marketing tactics.

HOW NEUTROGENA USES BEHAVIOURAL MARKETING

Knowing that 75% of its customers were purchasing products from only one of its product categories, Neutrogena used historic shopping cart data and buying patterns to create product pairings (i.e., products that were bought in combination, such as mascara and eyeliner). Using those pairings, they created banner ads and videos displaying the product pairings, information, and coupons. In a very successful campaign, these product pairing ads were displayed to customers based on their past purchasing patterns.

SEARCH ENGINE OPTIMISATION (SEO)

SEO is the process of increasing the quality and quantity of search engine traffic to a particular site or page. SEO focuses on unpaid traffic rather than direct or paid traffic and involves strategically adjusting content in accordance with search engine algorithms.

SEARCH ENGINE MARKETING (SEM)

SEM is a type of digital marketing that involves boosting the visibility of certain sites in search engine results pages, often through paid advertising.

The Brand Desire Spiral directs marketers to use as many marketing tactics as are needed to reach the objective of the organisation or campaign, including influencer marketing, affiliate marketing, native advertising, remarketing, behavioural targeting, SEO, and SEM.

As illustrated in Figure 3.4, there are different stages, parts, and players involved in making brand experiences more meaningful. The Brand Desire Spiral is based on the idea that consumer crowds, content creators, and fan groups can make people more interested and passionate about brands – these are often not functional and rational decisions but are emotional and socially influenced (Kozinets, 2022). A key element of the spiral is that brand messages must attract customers and encourage engagement. Influencers and creators play an important role in this.

Messages become translated by consumers when they become part of a group conversation, such as when they are posted by an influencer whose posts can be white-listed and sent to the feeds of people who are similar to them based on algorithms. Algorithms can find patterns in brand engagement metrics and other relevant key performance indicators. These patterns can then be used to customize communications, products, and even brands. Brand activations can happen in particular digital or physical contexts, such as promoting certain brands or brand-related behaviours on the Disney app while a consumer is located at a Disney park and using the location-based Disney app.

Marketing is about connection. Connections between people, between people and brands, and between brands and meanings. Apps and mobile devices are always connected, which makes it possible to retarget purchases and bring consumer interests back to the meanings relating to particular brands. All of these movements, and many more, are supported by individual brand moments, which are boosted by platforms, corporations, online groups, content creators, influencers, and consumers working together and in sync to drive consumers from moments of engagement deeper and deeper into networks of brand desire (Kozinets, 2022). Once these basic elements are understood, there is practically no limit to the kinds of communications that can be envisioned. As our Perspectives section from the world-renowned agency, We Are Social, suggests, the role of social media has never been more important to marketing, and opportunities for communication professionals to understand consumers have never been greater.

SOCIAL MEDIA IN PERSPECTIVE:

What Are the Most Relevant and Impactful Principles of Social Media Marketing Today? By We Are Social

Like us on Facebook! Follow for more!! Smash that subscribe button!!! By the time you read this, those phrases will probably sound ancient. (Some of them are already by 2022 standards.) And so will most platform-specific best practices that exist in the world of today's social media landscape. So we're not going to tell you that shooting vertical video built for sound-off viewing that flashes a logo five times in the first three seconds is the way to go, because it probably won't be by the time you finish this sentence.;)

Social media marketing moves at the pace of culture. And for brands to keep up, it's more important to understand the underlying elements of it all than the click-bait-hack of the day. What are these magical elements? Glad you asked.

'Community building and creation culture are probably the most important unifying elements across the current social media spectrum' says Benjamin Arnold, the CEO of We Are Social, New York. 'While this may seem obvious, each stems from a cultural truth that has been around long before the explosion of social media and will continue to be a driving force in social media for years to come'.

Throughout this perspective piece, we'll speak to each of these elements broadly and then drill down into specific ways we're seeing it evolve today on the front lines of social media before leaving you with a few takeaways. 'Community building is the result of cultural attraction between multiple entities feeling drawn together because of similar behaviours, knowledge, beliefs, locations, customs, and interests. It's the glue that binds followers across social media' – explains Arnold. 'Creation Culture is the driving force behind the content that makes up social media. It arose from the decentralization of production and distribution of content from traditional media sources. This culture forms the building blocks which social media is built from'.

Community Building and the Groundswell of Niche

Social media is at its core a place for people to connect, build relationships, and participate in culture. To market on social media effectively you can't just pay to slap a cut down on your mass audience TVC in front of someone, you have to become a member of the communities that matter to you and your customers. And increasingly, the communities that matter to people on social platforms are popping up around more granular, specific interests. The niche is becoming a powerful force on the internet. Here's what we're seeing with this explosion of micro-communities across social media.

People Are Finding Their Niche

'For You' and 'Explore' pages combined with constantly evolving forms of collaboration like 'Dueting' and 'Stitching' are helping like-minded people find each other. These enhanced methods of discovery and participation have led to new types of communities built around more niche concepts such as cores (the fashion trend of centring one's style around a specific feature). The long tail of community building is hitting its inflection point and niche online communities are more important than ever. In fact, 77% of people say that the most important community group they're a part of exists online (Facebook Community Insights Survey, 2021). What's a core? From 'regencycore' to 'normcore', the prevalence of 'cores' in the digital landscape speaks to people's desire to evoke an emotional response through the curation of audiovisual cues and references that span cinema, fashion, art, pop culture, and more.

Come for the Silly Dances. Stay for the Hyper-Relevant Community

TikTok has tapped into the power of niche communities (a.k.a. Toks) to become the social media darling it is today. It's no mistake that 70% of users believe that TikTok communities have the power to create change in culture (TikTok, 2021). And the change is happening at a community level. Sure, there are the communities you'd expect like #BookTok, #CarTok, and #CatTok but where TikTok excels is connecting niche communities to their members. #DeepTok is a dark humour meta-meme factory. #NumbTok is a space for people to discuss their depression and offer support. When you find your hyper-specific community, you feel more connected and more empowered to effect change.

What's in It for Brands?

With this rise of niche, we're seeing a shift to an emphasis on emotionally potent moments that connect with these emerging communities. This growing genre of creativity presents an opportunity for brands to build bonds around mood or feeling. So, how can you put this into practice?

Brands can collaborate with curators to assimilate into specific cores or communities. Many of the creators driving this form of creativity set the tone for aesthetics and feelings that define niche groups. Luxury luggage brand Rimowa understands this, and recently partnered with a number of fashion mood board accounts on Instagram, effectively showing up where people go to get inspired at the very start of a potential customer journey – contextualized in the vibe set by the curators' tastes.

Brands can appeal to niche communities they may otherwise miss out on by curating a mood around their products and services. For example, as part of its launch of mindful, grown-up sets, LEGO created an ASMR album with Spotify to help audiences relax and unwind. This was part of a bigger campaign to launch a set of products designed to elicit calm and speak to a niche subset of LEGO lovers.

The Escalating Rise of Creation Culture

Creation culture creates the building blocks that bring communities to life and the *creator economy* has never been more vibrant, varied, and galvanized than it is today. The creator economy focuses on bringing more life and meaning to the media landscape, empowering creative people worldwide to bring out the best in them, entirely driven by their passion.

From grass-roots educational content to the emerging role of social as primetime entertainment, people are rolling up their sleeves, creating the content they want to see, and turning their dreams into virtual reality. For your brand to take full advantage of social media it can't just be a silent community member, it needs to actively participate in conversation and creation. Here are a few places we see the depth and breadth of creation culture on full display:

Crowd Learning

Learning has long played a role on platforms like Reddit or YouTube, where channels like Kurzgesagt (or 'In a Nutshell') and VSauce have drawn millions of subscribers. But recently, there's been an uptick in the number of people turning to social to learn: 74% of Gen Zers globally have used social to learn practical life skills, which is more than any older age group (We Are Social, 2021).

From financial literacy to colloquial language skills to Black history, social is gaining traction as a place to pick up the skills we didn't learn in school. German media brand Funk is teaching Gen Z women financial independence, while the Spanish Instagram page @spainsays offers daily tips on colloquial words and phrases. People are looking to digital platforms for actionable info they can apply to daily life and creators are delivering.

Social as Entertainment

More now than ever, social is the first screen, home to a whole new type of media consumption. And video is leading the way. Of course, social video has been here for a while. But the mainstreaming of TikTok and Twitch has pulled social video to the fore, while live content has made unmissable social content more commonplace. In fact, 57% of TikTok users say they've watched less TV and streaming services since downloading the app (TikTok, 2021). As a result, 'made-for-social' formats are starting to emerge: while Scattered is a made-for-TikTok series hailing from Australia, the French Netflix show La Mascarade is an IGTV series (4 × 4-minute episodes), for which followers voted on characters and narratives via Stories.

What's in It for Brands?

As social overlaps the role of previously walled-off spaces like education and entertainment, it's decentralizing who the creators of these worlds are. In this emerging space of democratized content creation, collaboration and experimentation are more important than ever.

So what can brands do? Brands can collaborate with relevant educators to innovate their industries. With a growing number of young people taking to social to educate their peers on industry-specific topics – like Anna Lytical, a Google developer, who teaches coding via TikTok – there's an opportunity for brands to recruit and work with those educators to resonate with the next generation of talent. Brands can show up in social-first entertainment spaces. On Marbella Vice – one of Spain's most famous multiplayer roleplay servers, hosted on Grand Theft Auto V and populated by a number of famous Spanish footballers and influencers – KFC Spain landed Colonel Sanders a supporting role.

Looking Ahead

In many ways, social media has become a parody of itself. Creators that call bullshit on social tropes are no longer just heroes of the fringes, but mainstream icons that match established players. There's long been a healthy amount of cynicism attached to the stereotypes found in our feeds. This was once reserved for macro influencers like the Kardashians – with their Facetuned images, and perceived prioritisation of clout over creativity – or for the algorithms that fill our feeds, skewing our understanding of political discourse, body image, and so much more. To beat this monoculture fatigue you have to give people a reason to care. It's no surprise that 45% of 16- to 20-year-olds want to see 'more accurate' representations of themselves in media advertising (We Are Social, 2022).

'Gone is the time when you could just put your spin on the latest meme, sprinkle in a few brand benefits, and call it a day', says Gabriele Cucinella, Regional Lead EU, We Are Social. 'You must be embedded in culture, tracking the daily pulse of conversation and trending niches. You should be tapped into creator networks to decentralize the production of your content so that you can reach communities on their terms. And you have to be willing to venture into uncharted creative territories, finding fresh ways to connect with your followers and fans. People are seeking a break from the expected. And while all this might sound a little daunting, think of it as a wake-up call. In this environment, newness has never looked better. It's driving a kind of "creation renaissance", for individuals and brands alike.'

Web References

https://thinkforward.wearesocial.com/

We Are Social is a global socially led creative agency, with unrivalled social media expertise. With 1,000+ people in 15 offices spanning four continents, we deliver a global perspective to our clients in a time when social media is shaping culture. We make ideas powered by people. We understand social behaviours within online communities, cultures, and subcultures, spanning the social and gaming landscape.

We started our chapter with the story of Sally Hodgkins, an intern at a digital agency who was asked to use Facebook retargeting data to promote a new affiliate marketing program on TikTok. After reading this chapter, Sally put together a great new plan. She took targeting information from Google about people who had recently purchased swimsuits and beachwear and then developed an email with a coupon code that linked these potential customers to some of the top TikTok influencer content that had been produced as a result of the new affiliate marketing program. After setting that up, she then went to her boss to tell him about how this promotion used the Brand Desire Spiral and the marketing funnel, and how further rounds of engagement and contact might help the sandal brand convert more customers and turn them into brand evangelists. And, after that impressive performance as a mid-semester intern, guess who got asked to return as a new hire when she graduated?

CHAPTER SUMMARY

Marketing began in the earliest marketplaces and town squares when people began exchanging goods to create value for customers. In today's world, it has grown into a professional practice that includes professional branding through social media and efforts to spread messages through influencers. Influencer marketing is part of a repertoire of digital and social methods that include paid, earned, owned, and shared media and which often aim to move consumers from unawareness of a product to its purchase by moving them through the Marketing Funnel. Segmentation, targeting, and positioning are the strategic foundations of all marketing. They are implemented today through tactics such as remarketing, behavioural targeting, and SEO, and increasingly alongside influencer advertising, influencer marketing and influencer relations efforts.

EXERCISES AND QUESTIONS

Exercises

1. Find an example of a recent business-to-business influencer marketing campaign (HINT: IBM and Microsoft often use this type of

marketing). How is it different from a business-to-consumer campaign? How is it similar?

2. Explain how the marketing funnel can help an established business such as Nike Shoes to market its products.

3. A local doctor in your neighbourhood wants to use the latest digital marketing techniques to market her practice to gain new patients. What marketing techniques from this chapter would you recommend to her to help her reach her goals?

4. Think of an example where the Brand Desire Spiral will not work. Explain why.

Questions

1. Think of a brand that you use and like. How are its symbolic and emotional meanings different from its functional meanings?

2. Can you give examples of influencer marketing-related communication tactics for each of the four media types in the PESO model?

3. Should the goal of every digital marketing campaign be to go viral? Why or why not? Is this even possible?

4. How are segmentation, targeting, and positioning different when applying them to influencer marketing compared to applying them to broadcast television advertising? Do these changes make them more or less effective?

5. What are the advantages of an affiliate marketing campaign for the brand? What are possible advantages for the influencer or creator?

6. How does influencer marketing differ from the traditional use of product placement?

ANNOTATED READINGS

Berne-Manero, C., & Marzo-Navarro, M. (2020). Exploring how influencer and relationship marketing serve corporate sustainability. *Sustainability*, *12*(11), 1–19.

This study explores how different types of influencers can be used in influencer marketing plans to support corporate social responsibility goals.

Kim, Y. (2021). Eating as a transgression: Multisensorial performativity in the carnal videos of mukbang (eating shows). *International Journal of Cultural Studies*, *24*(1), 107–122.

This article offers an interesting take on how the mukbang cultural practice involves extremization, acceleration and transgression as affective forces of pleasure and performativity.

Macnamara, J., Lwin, M., Adi, A., & Zerfass, A. (2016). 'PESO' media strategy shifts to 'SOEP': Opportunities and ethical dilemmas. *Public Relations Review*, *42*(3), 377–385.

This article examines how the traditional focus on paid, earned and owned media is changing with growing resistance to advertising and growth in social media.

4

INFLUENCER AND CREATOR ECOSYSTEM

CHAPTER OVERVIEW AND OBJECTIVES

This chapter will provide a bird's eye view of the relationships that link influencers and creators with social media platforms, brands, and the many other actors involved in producing and serving media content to audiences. Using ecosystem concepts provides readers with a broad holistic understanding of the ways that influencers and creators use platforms to distribute content, build an audience's attention, and apportion resource flows. An ecosystem perspective also helps with understanding how brands and organisations work with influencers and how this relationship is increasingly supported by intermediaries. Readers will learn that there is a complex and interconnected environment that surrounds these central ecosystem actors, which supports and shapes but also regulates their efforts.

PROVOCATION: The relationship an influencer has with their audience members is the beating heart of the influencer ecosystem. Everything else flows from that.

KEYWORDS: ecosystem, virtual influencer, multichannel network, social media platforms, traditional mass media, specialised media platforms, advertising agencies, influencer marketing platforms, regulatory agencies

INFLUENCER ECOSYSTEM AT WORK: CHIARA FERRAGNI'S EMPIRE

In 2009, Chiara Ferragni launched her blog 'The Blonde Salad' in Italian and English, while studying international law at Bocconi University in Milan. The blog began as an irreverent take on fashion. 'It was all about mixing it up, like a salad and playing on the cliché of the dumb blonde' (Sanderson, 2019). In 2010, she launched her own clothing and accessories line, Chiara Ferragni Collection, which sells on her own websites, in flagship stores in Milan, Paris and Shanghai, in pop-up stores, such as in Selfridges and Le Bon Marché, and in Alibaba's Tmall and JD.com in China.

From 2015 to 2017, Ferragni transformed her blog into a company. The company has revenues of over €40 million and about 50 employees. Ferragni's business ventures include an online magazine, an e-commerce platform, and a talent agency offering both influencer management and consultancy services supporting digital marketing strategies.

Since 2019, Ferragni's brand collaborations have expanded outside the fashion industry to include other sectors such as food and beverage with the brands Evian, Ladurée, Oreo, and Nespresso. Moreover, Mattel has introduced two Barbies that model her likeness. Ferragni has been appointed global ambassador for Pantene and is an ambassador of the LVMH Prize, which landed her the longed-for credibility in the luxury fashion segment that had initially held her at arm's length.

In 2019, the Italian influencer engaged in brand extension by launching her first collection of jewellery and watches branded Chiara Ferragni. In that same year, her business empire further expanded to the media and entertainment industry. The former law student starred in a documentary-movie entitled *Chiara Ferragni Unposted* about how social media and the internet have changed the rules of fashion. The documentary has been the most-watched cinematic event in Italy of all time. The 2021 series *The Ferragnez* (available on Amazon Prime) provides insights into the extraordinary life of Chiara Ferragni and her partner Fedez and solidified her crossover into traditional media stardom.

ECOSYSTEM

A complex and interconnected system of categories of different actors dynamically interacting with each other and with their environment.

INTRODUCTION TO THE INFLUENCER AND CREATOR ECOSYSTEM

In nature's ecosystems, the various actors compete and cooperate with each other, prey upon, and nourish one another. Drawn from the idea of a biological community, the concept of an ecosystem is also a meaningful way to describe the world of influencers and creators. Like a biological community, the system that surrounds influencers and creators is composed of multiple players, each with different roles, competing and working together to create something from which they collectively benefit. One of the foundations of this ecosystem is a media ecosystem that allows messages/content to be created, spread, and consumed. That media system is intertwined with a digital ecosystem that leverages technology to more effectively produce, distribute, track, search for, and interact with content. Another layer is a business ecosystem that focuses on value creation and exchange. Business ecosystems are based on what Shipilov and Gawer (2020) call 'non-generic complementarities'. The influencer and creator ecosystem encompasses a growing set of actors distinctively associated with providing business-related benefits. The media, technology, and business ecosystems exist within regulatory frameworks that seek to keep the ecosystem in balance. That balance is not a static state but rather a dynamic equilibrium, meaning that everything is constantly in flux.

An ecosystems view provides a bird's eye perspective on the influencer and creator phenomenon that allows a broad, holistic understanding. It identifies the actors and their position and roles in the ecosystem. It facilitates an examination of dependencies and power. A map of the ecosystem's players is practical as well. It can inform the efforts of those seeking to get into the industry, developing entrepreneurial offers for it, and developing careers as managers in it.

What began with blogging in the late 1990s and early 2000s has grown to encompass a thriving global industry with many regional and national variations. The influencer and creator ecosystem is complex and involves numerous players, including influencers and creators, media, audiences, brands/organisations, agencies, managers, and an array of auxiliary service providers. They are interconnected in their actions and depend on one another. Various resources flow among and between them, primarily social media content, audience attention, data, and money. Influencers gather consumers' attention with their content, and then may sell that attention to brands/organisations. But there are other flows as well. The anthropologist Arjun Appadurai (2015) theorises that the global cultural economy is made up of a constantly intermingling flow of finance, technology, media images, ideologies, and ethnicities. These rich cultural streams also flow through the influencer and creator ecosystem.

At its most basic level, this ecosystem involves the presence of influencers and creators, their user-generated content (UGC), which is shared on social media platforms, and the audience attention and engagement that it attracts. Not all influencers and creators create content for profit. So, some influencers and creators who are generating the content, sharing ideas, and entertaining, informing, or otherwise engaging audiences are not directly engaging in the economic side of the ecosystem. But all influencers and creators use social media platforms. And all of them have audiences, however small or large they might be. By using social media platforms which are based on advertising models, every influencer – even ones who are not directly monetising their content or getting brand deals – is enmeshed in a media system that uses social media technology platforms to spread information, collect data, build relationships, and monetise them.

Much of the ecosystem, however, is intentionally built around the business of marketing and advertising that exploits influencers' and creators' skill in communicating with audiences and producing content. The most fundamental level of industrial involvement in the ecosystem is when a brand or organisation reaches out directly to an influencer (and perhaps their manager) in order to reach their audience with a message. This relationship – between an influencer or creator, the platform, the brand, and some audience – is at the very core of the commercial relationship. In the ecosystem, the other relationships all feed off of this central relationship to a greater or lesser extent.

To fully understand the ecosystem, we must understand the various other actors that are involved and their interconnecting roles. Figure 4.1 illustrates the set of actors and relationships constituting the ecosystem. The sections that follow will define, describe, and explain them and reveal their interactions in this complex and important ecosystem.

Influencers and Creators

As we might expect, at the centre of the ecosystem are influencers and creators. There is a range of different types of influencers and creators. These differences have significant strategic implications. An important difference between influencers, especially applied to Instagram and YouTube influencers, is based on their follower counts. The following labels are widely accepted in the industry today:

- Between 1,000 and 10,000 followers are called 'nano-influencers'

- Between 10,001 and 100,000 followers are called 'micro-influencers'

- Between 100,001 and 1,000,000 followers are called 'macro influencers'

- Over 1,000,000 followers are called 'mega' or 'celebrity influencers'

There may be different terms for some of these influencers in other countries and regions. For example, in China and Asia, mega influencers are often called

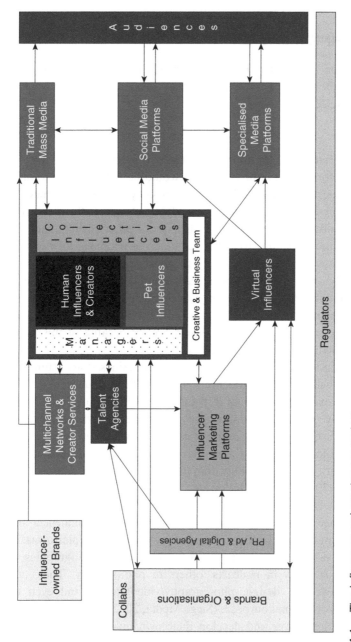

Figure 4.1 The influencer and creator ecosystem

'Key Opinion Leaders' (a term which, in Western cultures, usually means an expert).

KEY OPINION LEADER

Key opinion leaders (or 'KOLs') are social media influencers with a large following on platforms such as WeChat, Weibo, Douyin, Xiaohongshu, and Bilibili (Chi, 2021).

The different types of influencers tend to interact differently with other ecosystem actors. For example, while it would be rare for a nano-influencer to have a manager or be managed by a talent agency, almost every mega influencer would be professionally managed. Similarly, most nano-influencers would create their own content with only minimal help from others, while macro and mega influencers almost certainly would have numerous people in their creative teams. Brands and agencies would be likely to approach nano and micro-influencers either directly or through influencer marketing platforms (IMP), whereas macro and mega influencers would be approached through their agents. Also, mega influencers are more likely to have their contents spill over to traditional media and are more subject to celebrification processes because of this, or they were traditional media celebrities to begin with.

Another consequential difference is between business-to-consumer (B2C) and business-to-business (B2B) influencers. Because B2B influencers deal with technical niches, even very popular B2B influencers have much smaller followings than modestly popular B2C influencers. Lydia Leong, whose Twitter handle is @cloudpundit is an excellent example of a B2B influencer. A renowned analyst at the technology consulting firm Gartner, Leong, shares her deep industry experience with cloud technology domains to her followers online. However, she has less than 20,000 Twitter followers.

There are also a variety of different types of creators, although recognition of these differences is generally less developed than on the influencer side. Nonetheless, content creators produce work for various different platforms in the form of podcasts, videos, photos, case studies, white papers, infographics, etc. Some might specialise only in podcasts, others in photography. Their tasks might include copywriting, design, photography/videography, and even optimising content for promotional purposes (Siege Media, 2022). Talented content creators often brand themselves and develop their own unique styles and professional skill sets. Those with stronger track records will command higher fees, work with larger and more prestigious brands and organisations, and may be managed by talent agencies and sought out by public relations and other agencies.

Influencer Collectives

Some influencers work in collective formats where they produce content together, mutually reinforce each other's content and leverage their collective following for additional views and money. One example is the famous Team 10 house in Los Angeles, which still remains the blueprint for many 'collab houses' (Lorenz T., 2021). Influencers could live for free in the Team 10 house's mansion if they agreed to regularly produce social media content and participate in brand deals, all of which were overseen and monetised by Jake Paul. Another famous collab house is the Hype House with its TikTok stars.

O'Meara (2019) studies a related idea, 'engagement pods', in which grassroots communities of influencers agree to mutually like, comment on, share, and otherwise engage with each other's posts to boost their mutual popularity and gain commercial or other benefits from it. Since this inflates their engagement rates, some influencer vetting tools alert influencer marketers of the potential existence of a pod.

THE HYPE HOUSE TALENT COLLABORATIVE

The Hype House is a collaborative content creation house that bridges the influencer collective idea with the functions of talent agencies and managers in the influencer ecosystem. Living together allows for more teamwork, which means faster growth. Creators can also provide emotional support for what can be an exhausting career (Lorenz T., 2020). Hype House is both a talent incubator that unifies young creators under the same roof to enhance their creative work and boost their following, and a physical co-living and co-working location that provides glamorous backgrounds for their content. Hype House is located in Los Angeles, in a mansion in a gated community that sits on 20 acres of land.

Hype House permits every influencer to bring in friends. When the group gets bigger, the excitement (hype) around participation increases and so do the opportunities to collaborate. In 2022, the Hype House reality show was released on Netflix. The eight-episode series provides a look inside the lives of TikTok's most famous overnight sensations. The series has significantly boosted the hype around the talent incubator and has extended the influencers' reach to traditional media.

Pet Influencers

Although many influencers are human, some are not. There are no exact counts available, but a 2022 survey of 2,000 cat and dog owners indicated that one in four pet owners hoped to turn their 'fur baby' into a social media star (Sparks, 2022). With about 50 million households in the USA occupied by furry companions, this survey suggests there are a lot of potential pet influencers out there to be discovered! There are many examples of successful pet influencers. And behind most successful pet posts is a lot of work by a human or a creative team that links them to a complex ecosystem of platforms, brands, and auxiliary resources.

PET INFLUENCERS: A DIFFERENT KIND OF ECOSYSTEM ACTOR

An example of a pet influencer is Oscar, a Pembroke Welsh Corgi who lives in Singapore. Oscar's owner, Jaycee Cai, spends an hour a week documenting his daily activities, dressing him up, and staging photoshoots in the living room of her flat (Awang, 2020). She tries to post little details of his life every day – even on weekends and public holidays – and makes sure each post comes with hashtags like #corgination, #corgisofinstagram, and #petstagram. Ms. Cai uses her design skills to create merchandise for Oscar and sells it on his online website. Oscar's fans can buy gift cards, luggage tags, batches, stickers, and even a portrait of him on the site.

Another pet influencer is Dolly Pawton, a 6-year-old English chihuahua and macro influencer on Instagram. Her online brand has been carefully constructed. Beyond being an impressive fashion icon with stylish and unique outfits for every occasion, Dolly is also a LGBTQ+ activist, with fans on both sides of the Atlantic. Her funny captions promote the fashionista chihuahua as a sort of 'spiritual guru' called #Dollylama. She is signed to a top US agency and has worked with H&M, Sony, Method, Selfridges, Benefit Cosmetics, Sudio Headphones, and Daniel Wellington, has a longer-term partnership with Hotels.com, and has been featured in People magazine and Vogue.

Marketing specialist Arshanti Chand, who manages the social media accounts of her Maine Coon cat Brossy Meowington, said that, on top of posting pictures of him about three times a week on his Instagram account, she also shoots videos for his YouTube page. Brossy can command up to $600 per post and received over 20 brand deals in 2020. Brossy also receives gifts, including a Dyson vacuum, Skechers sneakers, and vouchers for a pet shop. 'He was given a Coach bag once by a nail salon in exchange for a post with the shop name', says his owner (Awang, 2020). Brossy is represented by Woof Agency. Woof Agency co-founder Jane Peh, started the platform in 2019 to connect brands to a pool of pet influencers. 'Pet influencers can earn as much as their human counterparts through endorsement deals, meet-and-greet sessions, and merchandise', Ms Peh said (Awang, 2020).

Virtual Influencers

> ### VIRTUAL INFLUENCER
>
> Virtual influencers are computer-generated, digital characters that have a per-sonality defined by a first-person perspective of the world and are made available on media platforms for the purpose of influence (Travers, 2020).

Virtual influencers interact differently with the ecosystem than human influencers and, thus, represent a separate category of ecosystem actor. Virtual influencers do not need managers because they are owned, either by brands (like Mattel owns the virtual Vtuber Barbie) or by creative agencies. They do not negotiate, their owners do. Virtual influencers will not stray from the message or break morality clauses because they do not have any thoughts or ideas of their own. With virtual influencers, companies sell their products and send sponsored messages to customers with less risk than using an unpredictable human influ-encer (Powers, 2019). Furthermore, it is possible to change the virtual influencers to meet the needs of the brand (Sokolov, 2019).

Their reliability and flexibility are strong reasons that virtual influencers are increasingly being used in advertising campaigns by brands such as KFC, Bal-main, Brazil's Magazine Luiza, Louis Vuitton, Versace, Tommy Hilfiger, Christian Dior, and many others. Fashion brands have even created their own characters, which have appeared on catwalks and in advertisements. Daisy, a Yoox Net-a-Porter character, promotes fashion brands stocked by the company. Prada recently introduced Candy, their own virtual model, to front the re-launch campaign for their perfume line, Prada Candy (Hiort, 2021a). Fashion maga-zines are increasingly using virtual influencers as the faces of their editorial content. L'Officiel Vietnam created an entire digital cover story featuring the virtual influencer version of multimedia artist Nina Hawkins (Hiort, 2021b). And Asia's media environment has been transformed by the rise of virtual influencers (Atwal, 2022), resulting in major opportunities for Western brands to use virtual influencers to expand their presence there (see Porsche vignette).

PORSCHE'S COLLABORATION WITH IMAKER IN CHINA

When it came time to expand their footprint among young drivers in the notoriously difficult Chinese market, Porsche decided to invest in virtual influencer marketing. They bought into iMaker, a startup that creates virtual influencers (Porsche Newsroom, 2022). iMaker created a digital brand ambassador who was specifically designed to appeal to Chinese Gen Zers. They designed an angelically beautiful, white-haired, female Asian-looking influencer and gave her the name Ayayi.

Porsche is considering a variety of applications for Ayayi, including having her moderate live events, conduct online sales consultations, and be present in interactive in-car applications. Porsche can effectively approach young Chinese cohorts through virtual influencers by inviting them to exciting immersive brand experiences. 'From a brand and marketing perspective, there is enormous potential for Porsche as virtual influencers are playing an increasingly important role in the Chinese ecosystem in terms of customer touchpoints', said Ostin Gong, Lead in Partnering and Venturing at Porsche Ventures China.

Managers

A manager is a professional hired by an influencer or creator who is responsible for assisting with, supervising, and managing the flow of brand deals as well as providing career management advice. A manager will usually be compensated by 10%–20% of the value of brand deals they are involved in. A manager will typically have experience negotiating with brands, an understanding of contracts (managers may also be lawyers), expertise with goal setting and achievement, and time management skills to help keep influencers or creators on track with their various projects (Moore, 2020). Like musicians and artists, creators and influencers are under constant time pressure to continuously create a stream of creative, high-quality content. A loss of popularity is only one missed post away, and so there is enormous stress to focus on production. Under these conditions, a manager can be valuable because they can:

1. remove some of the stress of finding and negotiating brand deals because working their networks of brand connections is a key manager task;

2. help with day-to-day deadline management by reminding about what content is due, when, and for which project; and

3. help influencers and creators think about and plan long-term goals and guide effective career management.

Although there is no minimum number of followers when having a manager becomes required, it is generally the macro and mega influencers and also the creators who are spending significant amounts of their time every day creating content who will benefit most from the skills that a manager has to offer. Sometimes, parents will manage their young influencer children. Although brand managers may joke about the difficulty of dealing with the unprofessional family members of these #kidfluencers, there are some success, as well as horror, stories about the practice. For example, Kris Jenner coined the term 'momager' while she was grooming her five daughters for Internet stardom (Atkinson, 2019).

Creative and Business Team

Influencers and creators have talents, but their talents have limits. YouTubers may be brilliant at writing content, for example, but not as skilled at the fine points of video editing or colour correction. So, although it may seem from the surface that many influencers create their own content, there are often many other people working on it behind the scenes. Professional photographers, video editors, professional scriptwriters, web designers, lighting and makeup experts, location scouts, lawyers, and others with specialised skills may be employed or contracted at various points in the creative process by influencers. It is far more likely that a creator will produce their own creative content, however. But even top creators might bring in professional assistance for certain kinds of content.

Similarly, during the negotiation stage, an influencer or content creator will often benefit from having a lawyer look at a new brand contract and help them understand how it might affect them. The influencer or creator's agent and/or manager would also be a part of business decisions, weighing in on whether the amount paid in a brand deal is in line with current norms, thinking about the terms of a performance-based compensation deal, evaluating whether a brand is aligned well with an influencer and their content, and helping to think about individual deals in the context of a longer-term career.

Multichannel Networks and Creator Services

MULTICHANNEL NETWORK

A multichannel network (or MCN) is a third-party service company that pre-dominantly works with video platforms (such as YouTube, Snapchat, or Douyin), assisting channel owners with activities like content production, content programming, brand collaborations, digital rights management, merchandise, and audience development in exchange for a percentage of the channel's ad revenue (Cunningham, Craig, & Silver, 2016).

MCNs offer support for influencers and creators mostly in the context of video or livestreaming platforms. 'Content creators, or online personalities, generally join an MCN in order to gain audiences, cross promote, develop branding strategies, connect with "mainstream" money and content, and utilise digital rights management and other legal services' (Gardner & Lehnert, 2016: 294). MCNs serve as hubs for creators and provide access to other creators, proprietary tools, assets such as copyright-free music, film opportunities and industry events (e.g., premieres), production studios, editing services, and content optimisation and monetisation services. They also increasingly provide merchandising and e-commerce opportunities. Examples are Webedia, Ritual Network, and Brave Bison. YouTube has directions and does oversight on MCNs to ensure that they are responsible, honest, and transparent with the people they sign.

MCNs are particularly important in the Chinese influencer and creator ecosystem. Jing Daily (2022) reports that there were over 30,000 MCNs in China in 2021. The four most prominent Chinese MCNs are Dayu Media, Mei One, Papitube, and Hive Media. In China and around the world, MCNs also increasingly act as talent agencies that provide training for their creators and influencers. Their core business, however, is to support the production and distribution of content.

Influencers and creators outside of MCNs have access to many companies that cater to their content production needs. The Israeli company Lightricks, for instance, offers various apps that can enhance content and facilitate its creation. There are also a lot of companies offering e-commerce services to influencers. Carro, for instance, lets influencers sell top Shopify brands directly to their fanbase.

Talent Agencies

There is significant overlap in terminology in this young industry, and the terms 'agent' and 'manager' are frequently confused. While managers are often individuals, talent agencies tend to be organisations composed of groups of people whose goal is to find business opportunities for influencers. Talent agencies often specialise in particular kinds of influencer and creator content, such as YouTube, TikTok, gaming, and food. Many of these smaller influencer talent agencies actually function as professional management firms whose focus is on bringing their signed social media influencers and content creators together with brands, overseeing brand deals, and assisting with career management – so they function just like managers.

However, when the influencers with larger followers discuss talent agencies, they are usually referring to the big Hollywood talent agencies like William Morris Endeavour (WME), United Talent Agency (UTA), or Creative Artists

Agency (CAA), the agencies that represent the vast majority of entertainment celebrities. Mega influencers, especially those with millions of followers, eventually hire a talent agent because they have bigger aspirations that draw them to the specialised skill sets and networks of these agencies. For example, they would like a book deal or want to break into the world of film or television. In the state of California, where many of these film and television contracts are written, an agent is the only one who can legally negotiate your contracts. Agents in California are limited by law to take a maximum of 10% of these deals. Currently, there is no regulation surrounding influencer deals. However, with celebrity influencers, these worlds often tend to blend together and there may well be more specific regulation in coming years (Mitchell, 2021). Regardless, if a brand or a public relations agency wanted to work with a celebrity influencer, they would almost certainly need to work through their agency.

Social Media Platforms

SOCIAL MEDIA PLATFORMS

Applications, websites, and other online technologies that enable their users to engage in a variety of different content creation, circulation, annotation, and association activities (Kozinets, 2020a: 4).

Influencers could not do what they do without social media platforms to enable and empower them. Without social media platforms, there would be no way for them to create and share content composed of information, ideas, interests, and other forms of expression, and to do these activities at a scale previously undreamt of. Social media is powered by user participation that derives from the inclusion of the <form> element in html programming language (Ford, 2022) that allows web users to enter their own text. The result of this participatory openness is a universe of UGC such as text posts or comments, digital photos or videos, and data generated by online interactions. As they flow through the ecosystem, these posts, comments, likes, videos, and updates are the lifeblood of social media.

Social media provide a platform for influencers and creators not just in the technical sense, but as a type of stage, a space which elevates them from the everyday and common to the special and unique. On that stage, they enact their performances and gather their audience. There are different stages for different performances. Bloggers prefer longer-form content and often provide a wealth of technical or explanatory detail. LinkedIn provides a stage for professional performances and self-presentation. Facebook is social, cultural, and broad. Twitter is for posts that are to-the-point, controversial, and political. Instagram is visual, polished, and sometimes glamorous. Twitch offers livestreaming gamer content. And so on. Although there are social media platforms that operate globally, regional social media systems can differ quite substantially, most famously in China.

From the earliest days of blogging, and probably even before that, social media users learned how to produce content that had meaning for particular audiences, informing and inspiring them. In the process, these bloggers and the many kinds of social media personalities who followed them learned the online art and science of self-branding as 'micro celebrities' (Khamis, Ang, & Welling, 2017). The influencer ecosystem grew around these people and practices. Today, new platform affordances such as personal metrics and dashboards continue the empowerment of influencers' and creators' audience-gathering performances and attention-getting productions, effectively changing influencers and creators into entrepreneurs able to effectively monetise, quantify, and organise the content they offer as viable business practice or side hustle. Some social media platforms even provide opportunities for creators and influencers to advertise their services to brands and other organisations (see, for example, the TikTok Creator Marketplace).

Traditional Mass Media

TRADITIONAL MASS MEDIA

An assortment of established media technologies that reach a large audience through mass communication, primarily broadcast media, which transmit information such as films, radio, recorded music, or television, as well as print media such as newspapers, books, and magazines.

The influencer ecosystem is grounded in social media platforms, but it also encompasses other media. Traditional mass media such as television and newspapers are interrelated with the ecosystem for several important reasons. Firstly, due to their vast reach, the celebrity-making power of traditional media drives public awareness and also lends credibility and legitimation to influencers and creators. Without Keeping Up With the Kardashians on television, it is unlikely that the Kardashian clan would have been able to achieve the heights they reached on social media platforms. Similarly, when social media influencers want to break out into the mainstream, they turn to television or film. Chiara Ferragni's 2022 Amazon Prime TV series about her home life with her rapper husband Fedez generated 2.7 million views in the first week of its release. Jake Paul, James Charles, Charlie D'Amelio, and many others have leveraged their influencer stardom into traditional mass media appearances.

Secondly, traditional media plays an important ecosystem role by boosting certain messages and personalities in social media. Twitter posts by politicians or businesspeople, for example, became shared on the news and became news themselves. By repeating these messages on traditional media, messages are amplified, and their audiences extended. Finally, there are synergies and complementary relationships between traditional and social media. In their research, Bruhn, Schoenmueller, and Schäfer (2012) found that both traditional and social media have a significant impact on brand equity. However, while traditional media have a stronger impact on brand awareness, influencers on social media can strongly influence a product's brand image. The researchers' findings varied by industry but suggest that while traditional mass media can provide large audiences and lend credibility to messages, social media's intimacy and customization provide a more emotional experience that can intensify desire and provoke action.

Specialised Media Platforms

SPECIALISED MEDIA PLATFORMS

Applications produced with the intention of connecting influencers and their audiences in ways not possible on other platforms.

Another interesting player in the ecosystem is specialised media platforms that are created with the express purpose of connecting the creator or influencer and the audience in new or specific ways. These specialised media platforms offer the audience opportunities to consume additional content and influencers opportunities to gain revenue that are unavailable on general social media platforms. An example of a specialised media platform is OnlyFans which does not censor sexual or adult content. OnlyFans offers sex workers a specialised platform for their risqué or tantalizing content and also caters to passionate fans who want even more contact with their favourite influencers and celebrities. The platform mainly allows influencers to sell followers subscriptions for private content and then takes a piece of the revenue. Similar business models, with less adult content, are also present with private account subscriptions on Snapchat and Instagram (Lykousas, Casino, & Patsakis, 2020).

There are several specialised media platforms devoted to providing alternative options for influencers or creators to reach a more devoted audience of followers and provide them with specialised content for a fee. Twitch, which is arguably also a general social media platform, allows gamers to offer channel subscriptions to followers. Patreon is another specialised media platform that allows members to crowdfund a monthly income for their favourite creators, rewarding them for the quality of their creative output (Regner, 2021). Chinese platforms such as XiaoHongShu, Douyin, and Bilibili offer 'wang hong' (Internet famous) Chinese livestreamers a greater variety of economic opportunities than their Western counterparts, especially for game players, pretty female streamers, and e-commerce master salespeople (Cunningham, Craig, & Lv, 2019). Virtual gifts from fans have become major sources of income for some of these livestreamers.

Brands and Other Organisations

Brands and other organisations who compensate influencers and creators for their content act as the monetary engines that power the ecosystem. In many signpost industries, the opportunity to use social media for customer acquisition, marketing communications, and consumer engagement has become almost indispensable. Technology and electronics, pet care, automotive, fitness, video games, travel, beauty and cosmetics, home renovation and decoration, baby and child products, and fashion are some of the industry areas that have made extensive use of creators and innovators (Santora, 2022). Generally, brands are attracted to the quantitative returns from influencer and creator content – one estimate found that influencer return on investment (or ROI) was 11 times that of average advertising banner performance (Tapinfluence, 2018). Brands and other organisations can not only test and analyse a variety of different messages and assets across different channels, but also build out a diverse catalogue of well-targeted content to use in their own branded channels by leveraging influencers' well-honed expertise in creating meaningful content for their niche audiences. Brands are also attracted to the prospect of building long-term relationships with influencers and creators who can inform their business practice. Most brands use influencers as one element of their overall set of marketing tactics. For many organisations and brands, partnerships with influencers and creators are assuming an increasingly important role.

As the ecosystem has grown in complexity, brand managers have gained significant options for working with influencers and creators. Still, many brands and organisations manage influencers directly, using in-house personnel and skills. Often, companies will have a marketing manager or an employee with a specific title such as a Manager of Influencer Marketing or Director of Influencer

Relations who takes on influencer tasks as their responsibility. For instance, cosmetics companies Morphe and Haus Cosmetics employ a staff of full-time professionals whose job includes not only negotiating and supervising influencer campaigns but also scouting out promising up-and-coming social media talents and cultivating relationships with them as their skills blossom.

Collabs

Influencer-brand partnerships can also be referred to as collaborations that can take on many forms, from sponsored posts to social media account takeovers. While the term 'collab' is sometimes used to generally refer to all forms of influencer–brand collaborations, it increasingly refers to brands creating influencer or creator-based product lines. For example, the clothing brand NA-KD has worked with the Swedish fashion and lifestyle blogger Moa Mattsson and several other influencers and creators on clothing lines inspired by their unique personalities and styles. Collabs are usually indicated with an '×' symbol or multiplication sign, such as in the form of Moa Mattsson × NA-KD. Collabs also happen with e-commerce brands. Mr. Bag × Farfetch is a collab between the famous WeChat influencer and the luxury online retailer that resulted in the creation of a co-branded WeChat Mini Program Store.

Influencer-Owned Brands

As influencers and creators gain power in the ecosystem and obtain skills, capital, and connections within specific industries, they often further monetise their talent and/or access to a target market by creating their own products or services. Tomasena (2019), for instance, reports that many BookTubers are able to translate their knowledge of and acceptance within the publishing industry into their own book deals. A growing number of influencers create their own businesses to showcase their expertise and creativity, connect more deeply with their followers, and diversify their revenue streams (Forbes, 2021). Indian beauty macro influencer Aanam C (@aanamc) founded her own cosmetics brand 'Wearified'. Another example is German model and mega influencer Pamela Reif, whose 'naturally PAM' food product brand creates an additional revenue stream for the successful fitness influencer. The influencer-owned brands and the influencer's personal brands mutually reinforce each other and usually fuel passion among followers despite potential threats to the influencer's authenticity because of the commercial focus. While many influencer-owned brands are exclusively promoted by the influencer and are often only distributed via e-commerce, they can become 'regular' brands that take advantage of the entire influencer and creator ecosystem.

INFLUENCER-OWNED BRAND

A product or service that serves as an extension of the influencer's personal brand and is usually created based on the intimate knowledge the influencer has of their audience. It can be co-created with said audience through insights from polls or other forms of engagement.

Advertising, Public Relations, and Digital Agencies

Another option for brands and organisations to tap into the influencer and creator ecosystem is to hire an advertising, public relations, or digital agency to take charge of influencer-related strategies and tactics. In this case, the organisation would delegate most of the planning, recruitment, day-to-day execution, measurement, and compensation to agency personnel. The brand usually pays handsomely for these services, but the reward is a professional's attention to detail and excellence.

ADVERTISING AGENCIES

Businesses dedicated to creating, planning, and handling advertising and sometimes other forms of marketing and promotion for their clients.

PUBLIC RELATIONS (OR PR) AGENCIES

Companies that focus on shaping the public's perception of a business through earned media, publicity, or other forms of media relations.

DIGITAL AGENCIES

Companies that handle digital marketing, web design and development, digital content production, SEO, and other related services for clients.

As Internet bloggers and then social media influencers gained prominence in marketing, advertising, public relations, and digital agencies all adjusted their offerings to include them. And, although transformational technological change prevails in the world of marketing and promotions, advertising and PR agencies still enjoy momentum, with many different brands and organisations signed to long-term contracts. Celebrity bloggers and influencers were similar in some ways to celebrity endorsers, and influencer advertising can be conceived as seemingly just another variety of advertising that the ad agencies could handle (even though content creation was also one of the specialities to which they clung).

PR firms, too, were familiar with the world of earned media, journalists, and reviewers, and the new digital world of citizen journalists and online reviews seemed like something that their skills and background could encompass as well. For digital agencies, the links of influencers and content creators to platforms, websites, and measurement were obvious extensions of their service offerings. With the recent rise of virtual influencers, new types of digital agencies have appeared (e.g., The Diigitals, the digital modelling agency that created many globally renowned virtual models and influencers such as Shudu and Galaxia). They have a specific focus on, and skill sets in designing, creating, implementing, and managing virtual influencers and digital characters. These digital agencies are hired by organisations and brands interested in including virtual influencers.

Agencies are an important option for brands and organisations who lack the time or expertise to design and implement an entire influencer campaign in-house. Top agencies are highly skilled players whose networks extend to connections to influencers, managers, and talent agencies. They know how to produce and execute high-quality campaigns for their clients, saving them valuable time and minimising hassle.

When it comes to running influencer campaigns, these three types of agencies occupy a similar role in the ecosystem. They compete with one another and with many other players in the ecosystem for brands' influencer and creator-related business. Not only do they compete with each other, but their skill sets increasingly overlap with other players in the influencer and creator ecosystem such as talent agencies, multi-channel networks, and IMP. As a multitude of new platforms, businesses, and technologies provide increasingly sophisticated offerings to brand and organisation managers to help them manage their relations with influencers and creators, legacy agencies are finding themselves squeezed in the rapidly growing influencer marketplace.

Influencer Marketing Platforms (or IMPs)

INFLUENCER MARKETING PLATFORMS

Businesses that provide specialised tools, services, and assistance with most influencer campaign management functions, from strategic planning to compliance, payments, analytics, and reporting.

There are currently a range of influencer marketing platforms offering and combining a variety of different services. Most of them offer brands the opportunity to search a large database of influencers and creators to identify those who might be best suited for particular purposes (Izea, 2022). Some have their own groups of influencers that they recommend and work with. Many also provide a variety of campaign management services.

Grin provides influencer discovery, influencer relationship management, and ROI tracking and reporting tools. The Captiv8 platform, for example, offers templates for contracts and automated digital payment systems to pay influencers and creators. Find Your Influence allows brands to identify influencers, launch campaigns, track performance, and report results all from within the same platform, while also offering a managed services team of consultants that can help brands execute their campaigns. Pixlee specialises in finding, aggregating, automating, analysing, and approving brand-related content that is user-generated. Because many of their services are based on software tools, these companies typically offer a subscription model that can be appended with additional à la carte service offerings.

Some influencer marketing platforms blend traditional capabilities of one type of ecosystem actor with others, creating new hybrids with combined possibilities. Examples of companies that combine agency services with tools in North America are Ubiquitous, Viral Nation, and Mediakix. The flexibility and depth of offerings across these platforms have dramatically increased the capabilities of brands and organisations (as well as agencies) to handle increasingly complex campaigns at scale.

Audiences

Ultimately, audiences are the centre of value creation in the ecosystem. In Goldhaber's (1997, np) famous formulation of the 'attention economy', he states that 'money now flows along with attention'. This attention belongs to an audience of consumers. The attention and trust of these consumers are what is ultimately monetised in the influencer and creator ecosystem. As the attention and trust of consumers historically shifted from newspapers to radio to television to the Internet and now to social media channels, it was followed by the flow of advertising revenues. Today, that interest flows into a new sea of influencers and creators.

These influencers follow consumer interests and match them to industries: sports fans to fitness content and brands; beauty lovers to cosmetics and skincare routines and brands; pet lovers to the newest and latest toys, gadgets, and foods for their furry four-legged family members. The awareness-based power of influencers to gather attention, or eyeballs, is matched by their ability to inspire interest, sending consumers into spirals of brand desire, and provoking actions that register at the cash register. As influencers and creators gently prod an audience of individual consumers through the established stages of awareness, interest, desire, and action, these nudges have distinct and measurable effects on business that ramify throughout the ecosystem.

Regulators

Just as biological ecosystems have limits and constraints, so too does the influencer and creator ecosystem and its players. Governments' regulatory and legislative mechanisms play a key role in directing and transforming action in the ecosystem, linking it to the wider social, economic, cultural, and political environment in which it is enmeshed. In many cases, these regulations do not apply only to influencers but also to brands and the rest of the ecosystem actors. Legally, a company using an influencer or creator is treated the same way as a company hiring their own spokesperson to offer a paid testimonial. Advertising regulations can also be enforced against creative and business teams and others who financially benefit from – and are thus partially responsible for – the content that influencers and creators produce.

The European Union has taken the lead on consumer privacy with its General Data Privacy Regulations and is now targeting social media marketing in its Digital Services Act. New rules will compel advertisers to curb the sales of illegal products and provide safer online environments, police misinformation, and attempt to reduce stereotypes in targeted digital advertisements such as influencer and creator advertising (Larrison, 2022).

REGULATORY AGENCIES

Independent governmental bodies established by legislative act in order to set standards in a specific field of activity or operations in the private sector of the economy and charged with enforcing those standards (Brittanica.com, 2022).

Regulations are often designed and enforced by regulatory agencies. In the United States, the Federal Trade Commission's Division of Advertising Practices (DAP) enforces the nation's 'truth-in-advertising' laws that govern social media influencers, fake online reviews, and native advertising (FTC, 2022). These laws apply to people (regardless of their location) who post commercial messages that might be seen by an American resident. FTC guidelines stipulate that, among other things, influencers must: (1) actually use the product they are endorsing, (2) accurately express its qualities or performance, (3) express their honest opinions, and (4) disclose the fact that their promotion is an advertisement (Sheppard, 2022). As platforms and brands incorporate more provisions for truth-in-advertising into their contracts and their monitoring, regulations will become even further embedded and established in this still-new and ever-changing creator and influencer ecosystem.

CHAPTER SUMMARY

The ecosystem concept helps us understand that influencers are surrounded by a complicated network of other actors whose efforts are interconnected. At the core of the ecosystem, influencers and creators generate content to share on social media platforms and attract audience attention. There are many kinds of influencers, from nano-influencers to pet influencers to virtual influencers. Although some influencers do not engage in economic activities, much of the ecosystem described in this chapter relates to these business functions. Brands and other organisations utilise influencers' and creators' skills in content creation and access to audiences in order to spread their advertising messages and promote sales. Other players in the ecosystem support and affect these activities. Advertising and public relations agencies help develop and manage campaigns for brands. Influencer marketing platforms and MCNs provide alternative ways to work with influencers and creators. Specialised media platforms offer additional, intimate, or behind-the-scenes access, while mass media help amplify and legitimize social media messages and messengers. Meanwhile, regulators impose constraints that bind the ecosystem and its actors into the norms of the wider social and political environment. In all, the chapter portrays the world of influencers and creators as a complex and dynamic system composed of interconnected actors working alongside flows of attention, money, skills, and other resources.

EXERCISES AND QUESTIONS

Exercises

1. Choose an influencer you are familiar with. Now, trace the ecosystem connections of that influencer as best you can. What 'type' of influencer are they? What platforms do they use? Who is their audience? What brands and agencies do they work with? Do they have a manager, agent, and creative team? How does their content spread and move through the ecosystem?

2. Research a specific MCN that operates within a social media platform that interests you (e.g., on YouTube or Spotify). What do they do? Who are their customers? How do they make money? If you were an influencer, would you work with them? Why or why not?

3. Search online and find an ecosystem actor that is dedicated to working with creators. How does this actor cater to the needs of creators?

4. Read deeper into Arjun Appadurai's concept of culture 'scapes'. Detail how one particular scape is embedded within the influencer and creator ecosystem described in this chapter. How is this one 'scape' entangled in the resource flows described in the chapter? Trace these connections in a relatively detailed explanation.

Questions

1. A medium-sized brand wants to develop its first influencer campaign. Would you recommend that they hire an agency or attempt to run the campaign in-house? What questions would you ask them to help them make the best decision?

2. Nano-influencers and celebrity influencers are so different that they almost exist in two different ecosystems entirely. Do you agree or disagree with this statement? Discuss with examples and evidence to back up your perspective.

3. What are influencer-owned brands and in what ways do they differ from regular corporate brands?

4. How does technological change affect the development of the influencer ecosystem? Explain your answer, using up-to-date examples.

ANNOTATED READINGS

Morgan-Thomas, A., Dessart, L., & Veloutsou, C. (2020). Digital ecosystem and consumer engagement: A socio-technical perspective. *Journal of Business Research*, *121*, 713–723.

This paper develops a technology-centric perspective on consumer engagement in a digital ecosystem based on consumers' actions with physical devices, digital haptics, and platforms. It offers a helpful resource to readers who want to understand agency and relationships in contemporary digital ecosystems.

Senyo, P. K., Liu, K., & Effah, J. (2019). Digital business ecosystem: Literature review and a framework for future research. *International Journal of Information Management*, *47*, 52–64.

Digital innovation has enabled the development of new collaborative networks such as digital business ecosystems. This study offers a comprehensive critical review that synthesises and systematises ecosystem research that may enrich readers' knowledge on ecosystem theory and practice.

5

PRINCIPLES OF INFLUENCE

CHAPTER OBJECTIVES AND OVERVIEW

Marketers partner with influencers to shape the attitudes and/or behaviours of target audiences. This implies that marketers assume that social media influencers' capacity to influence is greater than their own. It also means that target audiences are willing, maybe even happy, to be influenced by influencers. This chapter dives into the psychological and sociological foundations of influence to understand what social influence is and what it is not, what reactions individuals can have to influence attempts, and what makes influencers so influential. It then looks specifically at how influencers can exercise influence through communication via social media. By dissecting the influencer communication process into its sender, message/channel, and receiver components, the chapter explains what factors can make influencer posts into highly persuasive forms of communication. Finally, it presents Cialdini's principles of persuasion to illustrate how persuasive influencer content can be.

PROVOCATION: 'Persuasion is often more effectual than force'. Aesop, *Aesop's Fables* (2016)

KEYWORDS: influence, social influence, social power, coercion, manipulation, persuasion, elaboration likelihood model, rhetorical triangle

---

THE QUEEN OF INFLUENCE

'Leader of influencers', 'Social Media Queen', 'Marketing Genius', 'Breaker of the Internet', and 'Selfie Queen' are only some of the labels that pop up when searching for Kim Kardashian online. With over 300 million followers on Instagram and sizable followings on several other platforms, Kim Kardashian is one of the top influencers in the world. Allegedly responsible for the rise of Botox, fillers, and bum-lift surgery (*The Guardian*, 2020), she is often hated for her supposedly unmerited fame but equally admired for her ability to attract social media followers and sway consumer opinions. In an interview given in conjunction with her receiving the Council of Fashion Designers of America Influencer Award, she defined influence as follows: 'You can really tell someone's influence when they wear a makeup look or clothes, and they start trends and inspire people' (CFDA, 2018: n.p.). Her influence is so great that Ethan Zuckerman (2012) proposed the 'Kardashian' as a measure of attention. According to Zuckerman, a Kardashian is the amount of global attention Kim Kardashian commands across all media over the course of a day. Disconnected from merit, talent, or reason, it measures how much attention is received, not how much attention is deserved. Maybe in the future, instead of Warhol's 15 minutes of fame, we will all strive for a 'nanoKardashian' of influence.

Kim Kardashian is one of the most established and iconic social media influencers. The term 'influencer' suggests that these social media account holders are more influential than regular users. But what does it mean to be able to influence others through social media-based activities and how does this capacity to influence emerge in the first place?

INFLUENCE

Influence, in very general terms, describes the ability to evoke change in someone, something, or a course of events without the use of direct force.

Influence is an umbrella term for causing an effect in intangible ways. Not only people but also works of art, innovations, designs, ideas, and so on, can be influential. Think, for example, of the Bible and the kinds of change it has inspired over the millennia of its existence. However, the term 'influence' per se does not necessarily imply changes on a grand scale that impact many people, things, or events. A parent can be influential in the development of a child. A friend can have influence over one's vacation decisions. In contrast, referring to someone as an influencer implies that their sphere of influence reaches beyond their immediate environment.

SPHERE OF INFLUENCE

In a general, non-political sense, a sphere of influence describes a field or area in which an individual or organisation has the power to affect opinions, actions, events, and developments (Google Dictionary, 2022).

SOCIAL INFLUENCE

Social influence is a sub-category of influence that refers to the power of a person, social group, or social environment to affect the opinions, beliefs, values, attitudes, behaviours, feelings, decisions, and motivations of individuals. Social influence may be exercised by a social entity that is actually present, or whose presence is imagined, expected, or only implied (APA Dictionary of Psychology, 2022a). Social influence can be intentional or unintentional, and the target of the influence may be unaware of it. A fashion influencer who poses in front of a wall to promote a new collection and unintentionally creates a trendy selfie-spot, or a student not realising until much later in life how much their fashion style was shaped by a teacher are good examples. Consequently, the outcomes of social influence may be inconsistent with or unrelated to the goal of the person exercising the influence (Gass, 2015).

SOCIAL INFLUENCE

Social influence involves intentional and unintentional efforts to change another person's beliefs, attitudes, or behaviour (Gass, 2015).

It is important to note that social influence is non-coercive. This means that its targets have the freedom to choose whether they will give in to the influence or not. It also does not involve manipulation, which uses abusive and/or deceptive tactics. To manipulate someone means to covertly undermine a person's decision-making power.

COERCION

Coercion refers to the influence that involves the restriction of choice options or the use of negative power such as pressure or punishment. Individuals who are being coerced perceive a psychological threat and do not think they have the freedom to ignore the demands made (Gretzel & Femenia-Serra, 2022).

MANIPULATION

Manipulation refers to behaviour designed to exploit, control, or otherwise influence others to one's advantage (APA Dictionary of Psychology, 2022b).

Sources of Social Influence

Individuals, groups, or organisations who influence others are referred to as influence agents. Their power to influence emerges from specific roles, characteristics, or resources. Influence agents can derive their ability to influence from six main sources (French & Raven, 1960) (Table 5.1).

Table 5.1 Sources of social influence

Type of source	Definition	Example
Reward power	Perceived ability to provide rewards, either positive or a decrease in negative results, for the target of the influence	A fitness influencer's ability to encourage engagement by offering giveaways to followers
Coercive power	Perceived ability to provide negative results, such as punishment or other forms of reprimand	A celebrity influencer negotiating high rates based on their ability to publicly shame a brand
Legitimate power	Perception that the influence agent has the right, such as through a specific role or position, to influence and obtain compliance from the target of the influence	An appointed brand ambassador gaining new followers when discussing the company's new product line

Table 5.1 Sources of social influence *(Continued)*

Type of source	Definition	Example
Referent power	Identification with or (desired) association with the influence agent by the target of the influence	A livestreamer receiving virtual gifts from their dedicated fans
Expert power	Perception that the influence agent has special knowledge or skills that can be provided to the target of the influence	A billionaire CEO creating interest in a cryptocurrency through his tweets
Informational power	Ability to provide information or obtain information for the target of the influence	A fashion influencer increasing traffic to their YouTube channel by announcing their attendance at an exclusive fashion show event

First, influence agents can sway the opinions or behaviours of others if they have, or are perceived to have, the power to reward (in the form of benefits, favours, or support). Reward power means that influence agents can induce positive effects or reduce negative results for the target of their influence. It is enough for this reward power to be a potential occurrence in the future to have an effect. Second, influence agents may have coercive power, which refers to their perceived capacity to cause negative results, for example, through punishment or public scolding. They do not actually have to articulate a threat (that would be coercion); merely being in the position to punish adds to their power to influence others. Third, legitimate power emerges from roles, titles, documents, or positions that give the influence agent the right/authority to demand compliance from the target of the influence. Legitimate power can also emerge from perceived social obligations and norms (Wang, Huang & Davison, 2020). For example, if a technology blogger solved a tech problem for one of her or his followers, the follower might feel obliged to subscribe to the blog.

Fourth, referent power creates a capacity to influence because the target of the influence wants to identify or associate with the influence agent and will therefore comply with what the influence agent asks of them. Referent power is often based on interpersonal notions of perceived similarity, attraction, or empathy (Rubin & Rubin, 2001). It can also be based on the influence agent being seen as an ideal, aspiration, or role model. It is effective even if the relationship is only parasocial, as might be the case with celebrity influencers (Hwang & Zhang, 2018). Fifth, expert power refers to the influence that is based on the perception that the influence agent possesses special knowledge or skills (based on their reputation or credentials) that can be beneficial to the target of the influence. This is obviously a significant source of influence for creators, for whom knowledge and skill are frequently intertwined with style and taste. The perception of an influence agent's expertise can sometimes be impacted by trivial factors such as whether their gender and the product gender match. For example, women are perceived to be more knowledgeable about the product category of food processors, whereas lawnmowers are viewed as a masculine product (Fugate & Phillips, 2010). Even for virtual influence agents, the effect of influence agent gender and product gender congruence on perceived product expertise holds true (Beldad, Hegner, & Hoppen, 2016).

Sixth, informational power refers to influence based on the ability of the influence agent to provide useful information or obtain otherwise difficult-to-obtain information for the influence target. According to Uzunolu and Kip (2014), in the case of influencers, this information is not only useful but also trustworthy. Influencers' independence from brands lends credibility to the information they provide and, as a result, increases their persuasive power. Influencers and creators may highlight specific characteristics in their profiles or content to demonstrate their power to influence. Tiffany Alice (@thebudg-etnista), a woman with over 500,000 Instagram followers, for example, describes herself in her Instagram profile as a New York Times Bestseller author and business co-owner to emphasise her expertise in financial advice.

A Network Perspective on Social Influence

The position of an individual within a social network can also confer influence. A social network describes the social interactions and personal relationships that exist among a group of people. These social networks can have geographical boundaries (e.g., all people living in a specific country) or they can be based on membership or association (e.g., all people who work for a specific company, who attended an event, or who use a specific social media platform). The number of social connections (relationships), their direction (incoming, outgoing, or reciprocal), their strength, and their importance within the overall network structure can all affect an individual's ability to obtain and provide resources (including information) and influence others.

The greater the number of one's connections, the more people one can potentially influence. This is why the number of (real) followers is still an important measure of how big a social media influencer's sphere of influence is. The strength of a connection within a social network can describe different things but usually involves the frequency of communication/exchange or the intimacy of a relationship. Think friend (strong tie) versus acquaintance (weak tie). The stronger the connection, the greater the potential for social influence.

Maintaining strong connections, on the other hand, requires a great deal of effort. Because of our cognitive limitations, the number of strong connections we can form is limited. According to anthropologist Richard Dunbar, humans are limited to approximately 150 close and stable relationships (Dunbar, 1992). While others have criticized his approach and proposed various alternative numbers, there is broad agreement on the overall concept. Even the use of social media, which has increased our communication capabilities, has not significantly increased the number of people with whom we maintain close relationships (Gonçalves, Perra, & Vespignani, 2011).

DUNBAR'S NUMBER

Dunbar's Number describes the cognitive limit to the number of people with whom a human being can maintain stable social relationships.

Dunbar's assumptions are helpful for understanding the value of nano-influencers. Nano influencers' audiences are small enough for them to be able to maintain close social relationships with individual followers. As a result, their engagement and conversion rates tend to be higher. However, there is value in weak ties as well. According to Granovetter's 'Strength of Weak Ties' theory (Granovetter, 1973), networks with a high number of weak ties are less homo-geneous, and this diversity has clear advantages. For example, rather than 'preaching to the choir', an influencer with a large number of weak ties can reach a broader audience that does not necessarily share their convictions.

Another network concept to consider is prestige, which refers to the number of important others with whom one is associated. Being followed by someone with a large number of followers, for example, adds prestige (and potential influence) to one's network because one's posts may now reach a larger audience due to the prestigious connection with the well-connected individual. An example would be established influencers assisting emerging talent by following them on social media. The ratio of incoming to outgoing links is related. It can convey prestige and exclusivity. Instagram profiles are notorious for displaying this ratio: in August 2022, Kim Kardashian's IG account had 328 million fol-lowers but only followed 197 other accounts (including Jessica Simpson and Balenciaga). This means she is very selective about who she associates with, despite the fact that millions of people and brands want to be associated with her.

An individual's position within a social network is also an important consideration. They could, for example, act as a link between otherwise unconnected network nodes. Consider a brand that wants to communicate with a new target market or an extremely difficult-to-reach target audience such as war refugees or billionaires. An influencer who already communicates with this audience can serve as an important gateway for the brand. By collaborating with the influencer, the brand's messages have a better chance of reaching the target audience.

Because network concepts can be formalized through mathematical equations, network theory can help calculate the relative influence of individuals within a network and help with the identification of influencers for specific topics (see, for example, Laflin et al., 2013). It can also assist with the development of success metrics. In general, adopting a network perspective is important for everyone in the influencer marketing ecosystem, from influencers and marketers to talent managers, platforms, and software providers.

Social Influence as Power

Power is the capacity to exercise social influence. This type of power is social because it is a structural property of a social relationship rather than an attribute of a person (Fiske & Berdahl, 2007). Social power is relative, which means it varies depending on the situation. For instance, a Chinese livestreamer may wield considerable influence over Chinese consumers while having no influence at all over French consumers.

SOCIAL POWER

Having social power means having relative control over another person's valued outcomes (Fiske & Berdahl, 2007).

For social influence to occur, some form of social interaction is required. This is why having a dedicated audience that consumes their content is essential to the definition of an influencer. Physical outcomes (e.g., health and safety), economic outcomes (e.g., material well-being), and social outcomes are examples of valued outcomes that can be controlled through social influence (e.g., belonging or self-enhancement). Sometimes, influencers specialise in the type of outcome they seek to affect. Fitness influencers, for example, try to encourage healthy fitness routines, whereas finance influencers try to improve their followers' financial standing (credit rating, debt, investment knowledge, and so on). In contrast, so-called lifestyle influencers generally promise outcomes across all categories.

CONSPIRITUALITY INFLUENCERS

The term 'conspirituality' refers to the intersection of wellness culture, new-age spirituality, and conspiracy theories, which reached new heights during the COVID-19 pandemic (Wiseman, 2021). Although these appear to be contradictory philosophies, their proponents are united in their rejection of authority and distrust of institutions. JP Sears' YouTube channel AwakenWithJP has over 2.5 million subscribers, and David Wolfe (@davidavocadowolfe) has nearly 400,000 followers on Instagram. Baker (2022) explains that wellness and lifestyle influencers became conspiracy influencers (or alt.health influencers) when they began to successfully spread disinformation by establishing themselves as moral authorities and taking advantage of social media's affordances and participatory culture. Because of network effects fuelled by platform algorithms, their messages spread quickly and widely, and their follower counts grew rapidly in response, increasing their ability to influence even further. Many used their newly acquired social influence to sell questionable products. While they personally benefited financially from the process, their ability to influence many others contributed significantly to the spread of misinformation during the pandemic and undermined health authorities' efforts to control the outbreak.

Social media influencers are usually portrayed as using their social influence to evoke positive outcomes in their followers (helping them find bargains or enabling them to save money by avoiding inferior products, teaching them skills, or providing them with advice for difficult decisions/situations). The vignette on conspiracy influencers, on the other hand, demonstrates that social influence can have negative consequences from the individual to the societal levels when influencers abuse their power to control their followers' valued outcomes for personal gain and/or the advancement of radical political agendas.

According to Manuel Castells (2011), in our contemporary network society, 'social power is primarily exercised by and through networks' (774) and 'communication networks are the fundamental networks of power making in society' (785). Social media influencers critically rely on communication networks, specifically social media platforms, to build and exercise their social influence. Social media platforms have what Castells calls 'networking power', which means they decide who is included or excluded from the network. Being banned from a platform has significant impact on an influencer's power to influence others. On 8 January 2021, Twitter suspended former U.S. president Donald Trump's account because of the risk that his messages would incite further violence. That action drastically curbed Trump's capacity to influence others – until Twitter's new management re-established the account. Platforms also have 'network power', which means they can impose communication standards on those within the network. Social media influencers need to be aware of what these standards are. At the same time, social media influencers often challenge these protocols through their practices, forcing platforms to adjust the standards or further regulate content.

Social media platforms and their affordances also allow users to create their own networks of followers through which their social influence can spread. Being a social media influencer requires the ability to network. The need to strategically work with (and sometimes around) platform algorithms to ensure that contents spread quickly and widely and have an impact on the network of followers and beyond is also a requirement. The more effectively and consistently a social media influencer can accomplish this, the more social influence and thus social power they have.

Reactions to Social Influence

According to Kelman (1958), when social power is realised in the form of social influence, it can occur in three distinct ways:

1. Compliance takes place when individuals accept the social influence and adopt the induced behaviour to gain rewards (or approval) and avoid punishments (or disapproval). Compliance refers to submission to the demands/direct requests, wishes, or suggestions of others. Compliance involves temporary outward acquiescence, which means that the change in behaviour is displayed to others but there is no real internal change.

2. Identification happens when individuals adopt the induced behaviour in order to create or maintain a desired and beneficial relationship with another person or a group. This assumes that the influence agents are admired. The APA Dictionary (2022c) defines identification as 'the process of associating the self closely with other individuals and their characteristics or views'. The effect of the influence will only last as long as there is a desire/need to identify with the other person or group.

3. Internalization occurs when individuals accept influence after perceiving the content of the induced behaviour as rewarding or consistent with their value system. Internalization describes private acceptance or conversion. Internalization, therefore, has long-term effects. It is a very strong form of social influence that can even lead to innocent people confessing to crimes they did not commit.

However, not all social influence is accepted. By definition, individuals can yield to social influence or resist it. Otherwise, it would be coercion or manipulation/deception. Acceptance or rejection necessitates awareness of social influence. Because of our social nature, we are extremely vulnerable to subtle, reflex-like influences. Humans, for example, find it difficult to resist the urge to imitate others. 'The strength, immediacy, and number of sources who exert pressure relative to target persons who absorb that pressure' determine whether social influence induces change in perceptions, opinions, or behaviour (Brehm, Kassin, & Fein, 2002: 253). Many people respond to social influence in the form of a command issued by someone with authority. Resisting this type of social influence would necessitate defiance of the influence agent's authority.

When individuals change to be more consistent with the opinions or actions of other people or with the norms of a social group or situation, their acceptance of social influence is called conformity. Several variables affect conformity rates, including culture, age, gender, and the size of the social group (Burger, 2001). For example, members of collectivist cultures, like China or Japan, are generally more likely to conform, but there are limits, as 2022 protests over COVID-19 lockdowns demonstrate. Individuals can have different reasons for why they conform. When social influence is accepted by a person who wants to fit in because they fear the negative social consequences of appearing deviant (Brehm, Kassin, & Fein, 2002), it is referred to as normative social influence. Normative social influence is motivated by the need for social approval. Normative social influence relates to concepts like majority influence (the minority faction of a group adopts the opinions or behaviours of the majority to be accepted) or peer pressure.

Many people want to be seen to be doing the right thing. As a result, they conform in order to be correct in their judgements, and they believe that if other people agree on something, it must be correct (Brehm, Kassin, & Fein, 2002). They may change their minds or behaviours as a result of new information or peer influences. This is referred to as informational social influence. It is driven by a desire to be right. When there is uncertainty, this type of influence is more likely to occur. During the early stages of the COVID-19 pandemic, many people turned to social media, particularly their favourite influencers, to determine whether they should wear masks, stop travelling, get vaccinated, and so on, and were heavily influenced by the content posted.

One of the possible outcomes of social influence is social change. This typically happens via minority influence. Minority influence involves so-called dissenters or nonconformists who speak up against the majority. Those in the minority need to be forceful, persistent, and unwavering in their position for minority influence to work (Brehm, Kassin, & Fein, 2002). Minorities who argue consistently can prompt the group to reconsider even long-held or previously unquestioned assumptions and practices (APA Dictionary of Psychology,

2022c). Majority influence tends to be direct and results in conformity, while minority influence is indirect and leads to conversion, as the members of the majority struggle to validate their judgements. Social media influencers can evoke social change either by being dissenters who consistently communicate minority positions in the role of activists or by amplifying the messages of minorities and acting as allies.

PERSUASION

Persuasion is a specific type of social influence that happens through a communication process. Miller (2002) describes persuasion as guiding someone or oneself towards the creation, reinforcement, or change of an attitude or behaviour by rational or symbolic means. Therefore, persuasion is an open, communicative appeal to a person's decision-making powers. Like other forms of social influence, persuasion requires free choice, meaning the person who is being persuaded needs to have the ability to do other than what the persuader suggests (Perloff, 2003). However, the distinction between persuasion and coercion can become murky. As a result, Perloff (2003) proposes viewing persuasion and coercion as a continuum. Influencers should make sure that their content is firmly on the persuasion side of this spectrum, which means that their followers believe they have free will and the ability to do otherwise.

PERSUASION

Persuasion is an open, intentional, goal-directed, and communicative attempt to influence (using verbal or non-verbal symbols) (O'Keefe, 2015).

Being a communicative attempt, persuasion involves a sender, a message, a medium through which the message is sent, and a receiver or audience (see Figure 5.1 for its application to the influencer context). The goal is to elicit a desired response in the receiver. This can involve the shaping of new attitudes/behaviours

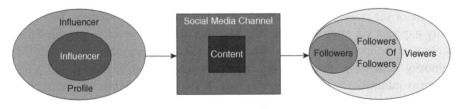

Figure 5.1   The influencer communication process

or either the reinforcement or change of existing attitudes/behaviours. Ideally, persuasion leads to internalization and strong and easily accessible attitudes that are consistent with the intent of the persuader.

ATTITUDE

An attitude represents a summary evaluative response towards a concrete or abstract object of thought, for example, a person, thing, place, idea, behaviour, or issue (Bohner & Wänke, 2004). Attitudes can be positive, negative, or mixed. They can be enduring or made up on the spot. They can be classified as weak or strong depending on how resistant they are to counterarguments. They are important predictors of behaviour.

The influencer (represented through their profile/their account) or their team or a brand who was given access to the influencer account sends a message in the form of text/visual/auditory content tailored to a specific social media platform by posting it on the platform. In contrast to interpersonal communication, the receiver in the influencer context is an audience that can consist of different types of receivers. A precondition for persuasion is that the receiver is actually exposed to the message. The influencer's followers are the most likely to be exposed to the message. Their followers will be exposed if they share the message. Furthermore, if the message is linked to a hashtag or promoted, it may be seen by other social media users. Someone might also come across the message on the influencer account. The likelihood of someone seeing a message is, of course, determined by the social media platform and its algorithm. This means that the influencer has limited control over who receives the message. Overall, whether a persuasion process is successful is determined by a variety of sender, message/channel, and receiver variables. Influencers must pay close attention to all of them in order to be successful in their persuasion efforts.

Receiver Characteristics

Exposure is just the first step in the persuasion process. In addition, the receiver must pay attention to the message and process the information it contains. Social media users sometimes quickly scroll through contents without really paying attention. For many messages, the persuasion process stops there. It is increasingly difficult for messages to organically (without paying the social media platform) break through the clutter of social media and reach interested users. This is one of the reasons why influencers are playing an increasingly important role in assisting brands in persuading target audiences. Social media users who follow an influencer are essentially indicating that they are willing to be persuaded. However, influencer content still competes with organic content created by other influencers, friends, and family, as well as paid content promoted by platforms to please their advertisers. Influencer content must stand out in order to be noticed and processed.

For the process to be persuasion rather than manipulation, receivers need to be able to identify content as a persuasion attempt. Persuasion attempts may appear to be fairly obvious on social media, but people with low social media literacy or children may be unable to detect them. They may require a 'warning' to recognise the persuasive intent of a message and possibly resist persuasion (Bohner & Wänke, 2004). As a result, an increasing number of regulators (and platforms) require that commercial persuasion attempts be appropriately identified as such. In the case of influencers, this means that contents that emerged from a material connection with a company (payment, gift, etc.) need to be labelled as advertisements. Persuasion attempts outside of the commercial realm (e.g., getting social media users to follow the influencer or share a non-sponsored post) do not fall into this category.

If the message catches the receiver's attention and is processed, the processing can occur in two ways or via two routes. The Elaboration Likelihood Model (ELM) is the most well-known dual-process model of persuasion (Petty & Cacioppo, 1986). It attempts to determine how likely receivers are to question the arguments in a persuasive message. The ELM refers to the two persuasion routes as the central route and the peripheral route. If the receiver's motivation or ability to process a message is high, processing takes place via the central route, which involves elaborate thought about the message's issue-relevant arguments. If the receiver's motivation or ability to process is low, so-called peripheral cues (things that do not directly relate to the message argument, such as the post's background colour) become more important, and rules of thumb or heuristics will be used instead of thoughtful processing. The central path to persuasion results in more powerful, persistent, resistant, and accessible attitudes that are more predictive of behaviour. It is thus preferable; however, if the message's arguments are weak, the central route may result in the rejection of the persuasive attempt. Encouragement of peripheral processing may be more effective in this case. Peripheral processing is also important when there is limited time for message processing and decisions must be made quickly, as in livestream commerce. Many factors can influence a receiver's motivation and ability to process a message thoughtfully. Influencers must be aware of the variables that may exist for their target audience.

ELABORATION LIKELIHOOD MODEL

The ELM 'groups the various processes by which attitudes can be changed into two conceptually distinct processes': effortful elaboration (the central route) and comparatively non-thoughtful procedures (the peripheral route) (Bagozzi, Gürhan-Canli, & Priester, 2002: 107).

Resistance to persuasion is the ability to withstand a persuasion attempt (Knowles & Linn, 2004). It has a cognitive ('I don't believe it'), affective ('I don't like it'), and a behavioural ('I won't do it') component. It is more likely to occur when attempting to change an existing attitude. Individuals generally dislike being persuaded because changing one's attitude requires cognitive effort, can result in an imbalance in one's attitude system, and necessitates admitting that one's previous attitude was incorrect. People also want to think that they have control over their attitudes and beliefs. Individuals' resistance to persuasion, however, can vary. They may be more sceptical of proposals or emotionally invested in their beliefs, have a greater proclivity to scrutinize persuasive requests, or have a personality that makes them less likely to want to change. When a persuasion attempt is directly perceived as threatening an individual's choice alternatives (the person believes that someone or something is illegitimately taking away their choices or limiting the range of alternatives), it can cause reactance. Reactance is a motivational state marked by distress, anxiety, resistance, and a desire to restore the threatened freedom. This can lead to people counter arguing, valuing the limited option even more, or doing the exact opposite of what the persuasion attempt requested, such as smoking more or strengthening their negative attitude towards immigrants.

Knowles and Linn (2004: 8) describe resistance and persuasion as 'opposing yet integral parts of a persuasive interaction' and warn that potential resistance is often overlooked in marketing. Thinking about how to overcome potential resistance to persuasion attempts is an important aspect of influencer marketing campaigns and of influencer communication in general. However, sometimes it is also necessary to think about increasing resistance to persuasion. Building up resistance to persuasion in a target audience can be a good thing if it makes individuals less likely to be persuaded by competitors or competing ideas. One way of increasing resistance to future persuasion attempts is through inoculation by exposing the receiver to a weak version of a competing argument (like a vaccine contains a weak version of a virus to inoculate a person against the disease). Another way is providing individuals with possible counterarguments.

Source Characteristics

The message's persuasiveness is influenced by the message's source. Sources are more persuasive if they are perceived as attractive, trustworthy, and knowledgeable, according to the Ohanian model of source credibility (Ohanian, 1990). Figure 5.2 summarises the various elements that contribute to the credibility of a source. Sources, according to Lakhani (2005), persuade not only through their appearance but also through their communication skills and style (e.g., humour) and their consistent positioning (e.g., personal branding). According to Pöyry et al. (2019), when it comes to influencers, perceived credibility and authenticity both influence the persuasiveness of their communication.

Lou and Yuan (2019) confirm that influencer characteristics have an impact on perceptions of the sponsored contents they post. However, O'Keefe (2002) warns that source characteristics can have complicated relationships with each other (e.g., liking a source leads to greater trustworthiness but not expertise

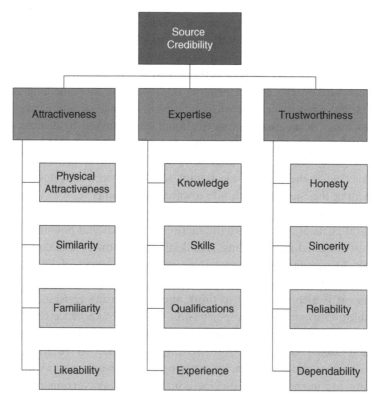

Figure 5.2   Ohanian's model of source credibility

Source: Adapted from Ohanian (1990).

perceptions) and can have direct and indirect effects on persuasive outcomes. These are important things to consider when designing a virtual influencer from scratch. One of the great advantages of influencer marketing with established influencers is that they have already proven themselves as persuasive communicators by amassing a sizeable number of followers. Their followers perceive them as credible and authentic sources of valuable information. However, as a source, they still need to continuously match the message and the brand they represent to make influencer marketing successful.

EXPERTISE AND LIKEABILITY AS DRIVERS OF LITHUNIUM SNOW'S SUCCESS

Nils Kuiper Verberne, known professionally as Lithunium Snow, is a Dutch beauty macro influencer. His appearance is considered unconventional because he dresses in offbeat clothes when performing artistic makeup and hairstyle demonstrations, and he uses makeup to paint famous artists' masterpieces on himself (i.e., the Mona Lisa, the Kiss, Starry Night, and the Great Wave off Kanagawa). He began his career as a professional model and was named 'Mr. Alternative' in 2016. He was then featured in 'Dark Beauty Magazine'. His make-up skills, qualifications, and professional background all contribute to his perceived make-up expertise.

Verberne's likability is based on his personality and looks. Verberne crafts himself as a common person – the 'next door guy' – when sharing his life stories and connecting with his followers. For example, he films his makeup videos dressed in comfy clothes, with messy hair (that he may even reveal he has not washed for a few days!), moving from one room to another in his house. In these videos, he interacts with his audience in a very familiar, informal, and cheerful tone, like they have always been best buddies. His Instagram bio reads: 'Weird kid from the Netherlands doing his best with makeup and a camera 📷.' Another element of his personality that generates likability is his self-irony. For instance, he puts himself to the test with challenges that amuse his follower community, like in a video in which he lets Google Translate decide his makeup.

Channel and Message Characteristics

Marshall McLuhan (1964) famously coined the phrase: 'The Medium is the Message'. The communication channels used in influencer marketing are social media platforms, and they indeed have a huge effect on what the message can be and how it is delivered and possibly processed by the receiver. Consider a Snapchat message and the short time limit in which it must be processed, or Instagram's heavy emphasis on visuals and aesthetics and their impact on how content must be structured. Consider Parler users and how an anti-gun influencer's message on this platform would be perceived. The key takeaway for influencer and creator marketing is that the platform's characteristics, not just its user base, must be considered, and that content must be tailored to the platform.

The persuasion literature distinguishes between message structure and message content, as well as language and context (O'Keefe, 2002; Perloff, 2003). Message structure includes factors such as whether the message is one-sided (presents only one point of view) or two-sided (presents both pros and cons), as well as the order in which the arguments are presented. It also considers whether or not an explicit recommendation is made. Message length is also an important structural dimension for social media communication.

Message content deals with the strength of the presented argument(s) and the kind of appeals the message includes. Aristotle's famous rhetorical triangle (Aristotle, 1984) distinguishes among three kinds of appeals: ethos, pathos, and logos. Ethos describes appeals that establish the source as credible. Pathos appeals to the emotions of the audience (fear, guilt, etc.). Logos appeals to reason and describes how well a message argues its point. All three work together to make the message persuasive.

RHETORICAL TRIANGLE

Aristotle's rhetorical triangle describes the pillars of persuasion in the form of three types of rhetorical appeals: ethos, logos, and pathos.

The message language can differ in terms of the type of language used, its complexity, the type of symbols used, for example, emojis (Ge & Gretzel, 2018), its intensity, the tone and speed of speech if there is audio, the use of metaphors, the use of casual language or slang, and so on. The message context is also very important. Messages on social media often do not appear in isolation. For example, an influencer's YouTube channel will typically present several videos and a blog shows posts in reverse-chronological order or sorted by categories. The ratio of sponsored posts to organic content is an important context to consider for influencer marketing. If an influencer's persuasion attempt on behalf of a brand is placed within a series of other sponsored messages, its effectiveness is likely to suffer, especially if any of the other messages are for competitors' products or services. As a result, many influencer marketing contracts include a clause that prohibits influencers from working with competing brands for a set period of time.

The timing of the post is another context factor. Much of a social media marketer's work involves optimising message characteristics. There is a lot of common sense about when to post what on which platform, but little scientific research on message characteristics and persuasiveness in social media. The good news is that influencer marketing is based on the expertise of influencers who have figured out what messages and channels work for their audiences through trial and error. As a result, giving influencers a say in campaign design is crucial.

CIALDINI'S PRINCIPLES OF PERSUASION

Calls to Action (CTAs) are a staple of influencer messages. Influencers not only try to shape, reinforce, or change the attitudes of followers but also directly request compliance with their demands to perform specific actions. The affordances of social media platforms make it easy for followers to instantaneously engage in the requested behaviours. For example, the Swipe Up feature on Instagram allows the user to follow a link directly from an Instagram Story without needing to go to the account bio page first.

CALL TO ACTION

A call to action is a piece of content within a message that is intended to induce the receiver to perform the desired action (Marketingterms.com, 2022). It typically takes on the form of an instruction or directive. Examples from the influencer context are 'Swipe Up', 'Subscribe Now', or 'Use Coupon Code XYZ'.

The American psychologist Robert Cialdini has compiled a list of principles that are especially powerful when it comes to requesting compliance. According to Cialdini, these principles involve pressures to comply because of human tendencies to:

1. return a gift, favor, or service;

2. be consistent with prior commitments;

3. follow the lead of similar others;

4. accommodate the requests of those we know and like;

5. conform to the directives of legitimate authority; and

6. seize opportunities that are scarce or dwindling in availability.

(Cialdini, 1995: 258)

Cialdini has recently added a seventh principle, which states that the more we perceive people are part of 'us', the more likely we are to be influenced by them (Cialdini, 2021). Table 5.2 summarises these principles and provides examples set in the influencer context.

Table 5.2 Cialdini's principles of persuasion

Principle	Definition	Example
Reciprocity	One is more willing to comply with a request from someone who has previously provided a favour	An influencer posts an exclusive coupon code for a price rebate and asks for post likes and shares in return
Commitment and consistency	After committing to a position, one is more willing to comply with a request for behaviours that are consistent with that position	An influencer encourages their followers to express their love for animals and then asks for a donation to an animal shelter
Social proof	One is more willing to comply with a request for behaviour if it is consistent with what similar others are thinking or doing	An influencer reads out comments from followers who have benefitted from the fitness routine explained in the video then later asks viewers to subscribe to a fitness program by following a link to a dedicated webpage
Liking	One is more willing to comply with the requests of friends or liked individuals	An influencer refers to their followers as friends and shares intimate details (e.g., pregnancy and mental health issues) with them or frequently compliments them on their loyalty before asking them to engage with a post
Authority	One is more willing to comply with suggestions made by authoritative communicators	A parenting influencer discusses her psychology degrees before asking viewers to subscribe to her YouTube channel
Scarcity	One is likely to try to secure those opportunities that are scarce	An influencer restricts a coupon code to the first 100 people who use it, or a livestreamer makes a product only available for the duration of the livestream
Unity	One is more likely to comply with a request from someone with whom one shares an identity (family ties, ethnicity, social role, etc.) or with whom one has co-created something	An influencer uses family-related language (I have bought this for my own mother) or asks for input on which colours to include in their soon-to-be-available eyeshadow palette before promoting the product

Source: Adapted from Cialdini (1995, 2021).

RECIPROCITY STRATEGIES BY ALEXA MATTHEWS

Alexa Matthews (@eatingnyc) is a young New York City-based food influencer. She is a macro Instagram influencer who also runs a website with tips for choosing restaurants. Alexa's Instagram feed has a section dedicated to promotional codes and links, making it easy for her followers to find them. Furthermore, she organises giveaways on a regular basis to engage her followers, leveraging the many collaborations she has activated outside of the food sector, such as with brands like Baci Fashion, Corona, Guinness, and San Pellegrino. Her fans respond with likes, thoughtful comments, clicks, and coupon conversions.

These principles are so powerful because they are ingrained in how we function as social beings. Maddox (2021), writing about reciprocity in the ASMR community on YouTube in the form of intimacy and relaxation in return for attention and engagement, further stresses how embedded the principles are in the affordances of platforms. The viewers of free ASMR videos on YouTube feel even more indebted because they understand how much affect and effort go into the production and know that their favourite creators are often excluded from YouTube's advertising revenue system. While the principles were conceptualized for situations involving interpersonal communication, they clearly still work when the interaction is mediated through social media or when the person making the request is a virtual influencer created by a company.

CHAPTER SUMMARY

Social media influencers should wield social power over others in a non-coercive and non-manipulative manner. The ability to influence others grants them social power, which they can use for good or ill. Influencers gain influence from a variety of sources, including their position and role in social networks, as well as social media platforms that allow them to create and engage with networks of followers. Influencers can use persuasion tactics to increase the effectiveness of their messages when communicating on social media. These entail presenting themselves in ways that increase their credibility and authenticity. As a persuasive communicator, they must also ensure that their target audience receives the message, processes the contents as intended, and does not resist the persuasion attempt. Persuasive influencer communication also necessitates the development of messages that include persuasive appeals and are consistent with their personal brand, the brand that sponsors their content, the audience, and the channel through which they are delivered. When influencers ask their followers to do things like share a specific post, click a link, or use a coupon code, they can use social psychology principles like reciprocity and commitment to increase the likelihood that their requests will be met.

EXERCISES AND QUESTIONS

Exercises

1. Design an influencer post including all three appeal types in Aristotle's rhetorical triangle.

2. Listen to an episode of the Conspirituality podcast on https://conspirituality.net/ or your favourite podcast channel, for example, # 36: Guru Jagat's Pandemic Brandwash.

3. Pick a macro influencer account on Instagram and examine their sponsored posts in light of Cialdini's principles of persuasion. How many principles can you spot?

Questions

1. In what way is persuasion different from manipulation?

2. What are the advantages of strong attitudes?

3. Can an individual who has a relatively small number of followers on social media still be an influencer of value to brands/organisations?

4. Which factors could reduce an individual's ability to carefully think about a message received from an influencer?

5. Why are followers compelled to reciprocate small favours from influencers they do not even personally know?

ANNOTATED READINGS

Rojek, C., & Baker, S. A. (2020). *Lifestyle gurus: Constructing authority and influence online*. London: John Wiley & Sons.

This book investigates why and how modern lifestyle gurus can establish and leverage social media influence. The authors demonstrate how these wellness influencers establish persuasive profiles, engage followers, and exercise widespread social influence by addressing both the particularities of influencer culture and the affordances of social media.

Cialdini, R. B. (2021). *Influence, new and expanded: The psychology of persuasion*. New York, NY: Harper Business.

In this updated version of his classic book on persuasion principles, Cialdini describes and explains different levers of influence.

6

DIVERSITY, EQUITY, AND INCLUSION

CHAPTER OVERVIEW AND OBJECTIVES

This chapter will explore important social justice concerns related to issues of diversity, equity, and inclusion that impact influencers. First, it will examine the topic of diversity and consider how representing many different types of individuals is an essential and increasingly expressed aim in influencer marketing today. Then, the chapter will interrogate structural factors contributing to compensation disparities and injustice. The final topic is inclusion, and the chapter will explore how influencers and other key actors in the influencer ecosystem may be creating a climate of belonging and participation. The chapter closes by considering what it might take to achieve these critically important objectives of diversity, equity, and inclusion.

PROVOCATION: Is the world of influencer marketing open enough to diversity? Is it fair? Is it inclusive?

KEYWORDS: diversity, equity, inclusion and exclusion, exploitation, intersectionality

NOTORIOUSLY DAPPER

Kelvin Davis is a middle school teacher in South Carolina who has always been interested in men's fashion. While he was shopping for some new clothes one day, he asked a sales associate for a larger size. The sales associate at the store then told him that he was too fat to shop there. 'It was my first time as a male, being body shamed', he told us in a personal interview, 'and I really experienced that feeling of being insecure, hurt, and sad about my physical presence'. Although he had heard about women being body shamed while clothes shopping, as a man he had not personally experienced it firsthand. However, the entire incident opened childhood wounds, such as lacking 'positive Black male figures' in the media and not being exposed to a variety of positive body images for Black men.

Kelvin then did what any ordinary, self-respecting man would do. He took his experience to Facebook. First, he wrote a status update about it. Then, in self-doubt, he deleted it. He was concerned that his male friends would mock him, saying things like 'man up and go to the gym or take Hydroxycut or go on a diet'. He decided that was not what he needed to hear. Instead, he said, he 'needed somebody to tell me that the way I felt was okay and that my body was fine the way that it actually was'. He thought about what he should do over the next few months. He became convinced that he should start a body positive fashion blog for men. He came up with the name Notoriously Dapper in 2013, started a blog in 2014, and published a book with that title in 2017. As of 2022, Notoriously Dapper counted over 126,000 followers on Instagram and has an active influencer marketing component built on Kelvin Davis's promotion of men's fashion alongside positive messages about kindness and self-acceptance.

The Notoriously Dapper story underscores many of the important social justice themes we will cover in this chapter. The representation of diversity is a key issue in the world of influencers. Certain groups of people are less visible on social media than others, or are presented in ways that can be disparaging or inaccurate. Kelvin Davis found that many men, and Black men, in particular, were being represented in the media and in the world of influencers in a certain way. Black men were expected to be extremely fit, as if Lebron James and other athletes provided a physical standard of what a Black man should be. There were other imposed standards, as well, such as light skin or light-coloured eyes that objectified the Black body. Diverse body types, such as plus-size Black men, were not represented or visible. These are issues that are prevalent on social media and especially in the world of influencers and are finally entering the cultural discourse beyond social media. By reflecting upon and exposing his own experience, Kelvin turned this representation issue into an opportunity to express his ideas, make others aware of the issues, and seek to change thinking about these important topics.

DIVERSITY

DIVERSITY

Diversity incorporates all of the characteristics and categories that make individuals unique from one another, including but not limited to gender, body type, socioeconomic status, sexual orientation, ethnicity, skin colour, physical abilities, religious beliefs, and more. In sum, diversity is about the range of human differences. In the world of influencer marketing, acknowledging and fostering diversity means running and managing campaigns with influencers that reflect these differences (Wiley, 2020).

It's no surprise that influencer marketing has been chastised for its lack of diversity. Revolve was criticized in 2018 after it was found that they had exclusively invited White women on their #RevolveAroundTheWorld press tour to Thailand. As a result, individuals turned to the brand's social media to denounce the lack of diversity, creating the hashtag #RevolveSoWhite. The resulting outcry also motivated blogger Valerie Eguavoen to launch You Belong Now, an Instagram feed that spotlights and provides a safe environment for bloggers of colour and plus-size bloggers. The blogging 'veteran' Stephanie Yeboah, who has been blogging for over 13 years, wrote a powerful article condemning the lack of diversity in the industry.

> It's time [brands] acknowledged that not only do influencers of color exist, but that we are viable assets who can add value to audiences that span far beyond the current slim, white and blonde aesthetic (Yeboah, 2019).

Yeboah's quote, which focused on 'influencers of colour', suggests that diversity issues impact influencers themselves – and the people who would consider becoming influencers. The representation of specific social categories affects how potential and actual influencers think about themselves and the influencer industry. Can only one type of person, one 'look' and 'voice', be an influencer? Yeboah's quote suggests that, particularly in the world of beauty products, most influencer marketing dollars are spent on women who are 'slim, white, and blonde'.

There have been numerous accusations of tokenism in the world of influencer marketing as well, with brands tending to include one or two diverse influencers in the occasional campaign here or there. As well, some brands have been accused of ghettoizing influencers. Oh Polly, a Glasgow-based online fashion brand set up a special Instagram called 'Oh Polly Inclusive', a separate social media account for plus-size and ethnic minority women. While the main Oh Polly Instagram account continued to feature White, slim models, the special 'Inclusive' page could display the 'other types' of faces and bodies in a way that segregated them from the company's main page. After a public uproar, the company later deactivated its 'Inclusive' page and apologised.

Figure 6.1 illustrates the many kinds of diverse individuals who might be excluded from the opportunity to work as an influencer. For example, disabled people make up around 22% of the UK population. However, this significant population is not reflected when it comes to advertising. Up-to-date figures are difficult to obtain, but research showed that disabled people were featured in only a tiny fraction of advertising. This lack of visibility is not only socially unaware but also economically questionable. Valuable 500, a worldwide initiative that encourages companies to advocate for the needs of disabled people, calculates that the spending power of disabled people worldwide amounts to an astounding $8 trillion (£5.7tn) a year (Cassidy, 2021). That number suggests that there should be considerable demand for disabled people to work in the influencer marketing industry.

There are some success stories in the realm of disabled influencers right now. Consider the cases of beauty influencer Marimar Quiroa (see vignette) and of fashion influencer Caitlin Hellyer (@asliceofcait). There is even an agency in the United Kingdom devoted to representing disability influencers in influencer marketing campaigns. Purple Goat was founded by Martyn Sibley, who was ranked the third most influential disabled person in the UK. The company was founded to help recruit a variety of talented disabled influencers and to help match them with brands that seek an authentic voice that fits with their message.

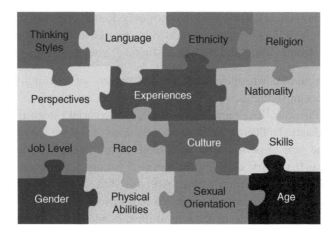

Figure 6.1   Types of diversity

It is important to realise that there is diversity within the disabled community, just as there is within every category of community. There is no 'one way' to be diverse! Purple Goat seems to follow an influencer relations model that aims to build relationships between influencers and brands, eschewing the idea of a 'tokenistic "one-off" campaign' (Purple Goat Agency, 2022).

MARIMAR QUIROA: A POPULAR INFLUENCER WHO DEMONSTRATES DIVERSITY

Marimar Quiroa (@makeupartistgorda66) is a 22-year-old California Latina. She is also a brilliant makeup artist and Zumba instructor, as well as a successful beauty influencer who has over 577,000 YouTube subscribers and 250,000 followers on Instagram. Marimar was born with a facial cystic hygroma, also known as a lymphatic malformation or 'water tumour'. Unable to speak or eat by mouth and experiencing hearing difficulties as a result of the surgeries she has undergone, Marimar communicates using sign language. She currently studies education and plans to teach deaf children. Marimar's amazing life (and her excellent makeup abilities) can be followed on Facebook, Instagram, and YouTube.

Diversity is an important societal goal, and it has been embraced (at least in discourse) by groups, brands, and influencer agencies. Women in Influencer Marketing (WIIM) is a networking group, founded in 2017, made up of women to support other women in the industry and push for more female representation in positions of power. Through its presence online, with a YouTube channel and a popular podcast, the 4,500-person member group is involved in education, advocacy, and providing resources to help empower female influencers. One of the positive roles undertaken by groups such as WIIM and agencies such as the Purple Goat is to bridge the gap between businesses and influencers by encouraging self-advocacy, filling positions of power with varied talent, and rejecting the assumption that creators are defined solely by their Instagram follower count (Wiley, 2020).

NEUFLUENCE: AN INCLUSION-FOCUSED PLATFORM

Angela Fisher is an example of someone from the agency world who is trying to empower influencers who might otherwise be structurally disadvantaged. Fisher was a finance manager who tried a stint as a band manager and ended up working for MTV. After MTV, she ran her own talent agency and, while at the agency, she came up with the idea of creating a platform that focuses on multicultural influencers. Her new platform, Neufluence, is devoted to capturing the opportunities companies have to work with multi-ethnic influencers (Black, Asian, Latinx, etc.) and to provide an authentic voice for their brands. Moreover, Neufluence sees its purpose as helping to provide companies with a deeper understanding of the diverse communities these varied influencers represent. Like the Purple Goat Agency in the UK, Neufluence is an excellent example of an influencer-based company that focuses on building a structure (in this case, a platform) to promote the goal of industry diversity.

Astoundingly, other industry players seem to think that the issue of preconceived notions of what an influencer should look like (presumably, White, thin, and conventionally good looking) should not be challenged but rather be overcome using technology. Facebook IQ is now offering virtual influencer skins, or synthetic media, that can camouflage people's inherent diversity and help them fit better into the coming influencer metaverse. A recent article makes the following statement:

If you fit into the stereotype of what an influencer looks like, then maybe [synthetic media] won't have as big of an effect on you. But if you maybe don't, now you can build a character to convey your story through (Facebook IQ, 2022).

The fact that Facebook would consider offering influencers a synthetic 'character' to help diverse people better 'fit the stereotype of what an influencer looks like' suggests to us that there truly is a problem with diversity in the influencer marketing industry! Another significant problem within the influencer marketing ecosystem is equity.

EQUITY

EQUITY

Equity in a culture and a society refers to the quality of treating people fairly and with justice. A society is said to be equitable when people are treated in a fair and just manner, and when different types of members of a society have similar rights and opportunities for things such as jobs, money, or the chance to meet their own needs. Some also believe that standards of equity should be extended to non-human species, and other living things with whom we share this planet and who also have needs and the right to live.

The diversity section discussed how specific preconceived notions of what an influencer should look or be like to amass an audience and be an attractive partner for brand collaborations drive the potential for individuals to become influencers. Equity concerns the way specific groups of influencers are treated once they are part of the influencer ecosystem. One of the most prominent issues in this context is the pay gap that emerges for some categories of influencers.

Influencer Pay Gap

A 2021 study revealed that there is a 35% pay gap between what White and what Black influencers are paid for comparable work (MSL, 2021). While the influencer economy keeps growing at impressive rates, some influencers and creators have been left behind when it comes time to get paid. The reasons for these lower payment rates are still only dimly understood. Figure 6.2 visualises the absurdity of making payment dependent on the skin colour of an influencer. The only difference between the images of the two influencers is their race. Is this what structural or systemic racism looks like on the economic level? Is it that certain audiences, perhaps particular racial segments, are considered by marketers to be worth less than others? Are certain influencers more niche in their appeal, and the value of any niche audience is less than that of a mainstream audience? Or is this pay gap a clear sign of exploitation in the industry? We need more research to better understand these issues.

Figure 6.2   Visual representation of White versus Black pay gap

Not only are Black influencers getting paid less than White influencers, but a 2020 study by HypeAuditor found that men also get paid more than women in the sector, with the gap continuing to grow into the higher audience tiers. As Social Day (2021) reported, this followed a 2019 study by Klear into influencer marketing rates, which also found that female influencers were being paid 33% less than their male counterparts, despite making up 77% of the industry. The Instagram account 'influencerpaygap' seeks to increase transparency and accountability in terms of influencer compensation by asking influencers to share their highest-paying gigs together with important demographic information and widely used performance indicators, such as the size of their following and average engagement rate. Though there is currently little research into the pay gap among other groups, LGBTQ+ and disabled influencers have taken to @influencerpaygap to share stories of being unfairly paid, or of brands not paying them at all for campaigns and partnerships. Not paying influencers fairly is a form of exploitation.

EXPLOITATION

Exploitation involves transactions between unequal parties that produce unjust outcomes (Hahnel, 2006).

In the world of influencers, the absence of industry regulation has an impact on the ability of companies to exploit certain individuals, such as people of colour, people with disabilities, or indigenous peoples. Because they do not clearly know how much money others are being paid, or the value of their work, individual influencers and creators have a lowered ability to negotiate and to value their own work. Agencies and brands do have this knowledge and can use it to exploit certain already disadvantaged groups. The lack of understanding of these people, combined with the willingness of companies and brands to exploit, is a major contributor to economic disparity in the influencer industry (Lothian-McClean, 2021).

Another issue is the difficulty of influencers to gain representation and collective bargaining power, for example, through unions. While other areas of the gig economy are making progress in this respect (see for instance https://www.drivers-united.org/ as an example of rideshare drivers fighting against industry exploitation), there seems to be a very little movement in this respect in the influencer space.

Structural Barriers

There are often structural differences that support these inequitable outcomes. White influencers are more likely to have a built-in network of lawyers, business managers, and accountants to support the business side of their hustle.

According to Forman (2021) by Vox Media, White creators are better primed to know where to look in an industry that keeps details of social media algorithms, payouts, and influencer sponsorship deals secret. On the contrary, Black and indigenous influencers of colour are left to navigate a space that showcases the same pay inequality and discrimination that contaminated many other industries before it. However, some organisations and platforms have made an effort to bridge the knowledge gaps. Digital Brand Architects, an influencer marketing business, has launched a free, eight-week crash school for Black influencers and creators (Liederman, 2022). The training teaches negotiating methods to smaller talents who do not have access to a management team.

Structural factors that support the work of influencers differ by nation, and these differences can have radical effects on different genders. In the influencer world, an important account of gender discrimination in the social media space has been recently illustrated in the United Arab Emirates (UAE). As Datta, Atkins, and Fitzsimmons (2020) reveal, the legal framework in the United Arab Emirates makes it challenging for women to become influencers. The UAE society is strongly influenced by religion and tradition and the level of women's involvement in the workforce has been determined by the strong patriarchal culture and traditional Islamic standards. Some conservative sections of Arab society dislike women entrepreneurs on social media and often describe them as aggressive and bold. Additionally, social media platforms are seen by some Arab males as objectifying women. As a result, the lack of support for women's entrepreneurship in social media, along with the general tendency of UAE female entrepreneurs to be more conscious of reputational threats, diminishes their desire and ability to enter into the influencer business (*ibid*).

INCLUSION

INCLUSION AND EXCLUSION

'Inclusion is the action or state of including or of being included within a group or structure. More than simply diversity and numerical representation, inclusion involves authentic and empowered participation and a true sense of belonging' (Annie E. Casey Foundation, 2021). In the world of influencer marketing, inclusion means creating and maintaining a climate that welcomes the full participation of diverse influencers.

Exclusion is the opposite of inclusion. It is the act or state of excluding people from a group or structure, often by making members of a particular group feel

(Continued)

(Continued)

unwelcome or like they do not belong. In the world of influencer marketing, exclusion manifests as a climate in which diverse influencers feel that their presence and participation are unwanted.

As discussed in the previous sections, there are many structural and social issues that can lead to under-representation and inequity for certain groups of influencers. This section focuses on discourses and actions by influencers and other actors in the industry that can create a culture that can make under-represented groups of influencers more welcome. Many of the inclusion efforts in the influencer realm have been self-generated, that is, they have been the results of individual influencers or groups of influencers who have spoken out to attempt to create and maintain a positive climate that welcomes the participation of other people like them. The Black male fashion messages of Kelvin Davis and his Notoriously Dapper blog, book, and Instagram account are a good example of this approach. It is an approach that is also often found among social media posters belonging to groups like the Advanced Style Influencers, LGBTQ+ or Black community, women's empowerment, or body positivity advocates.

Advanced Style Influencers: Ageism and Inclusion

Ageism, in which people above a certain age are excluded from participation, is an important element of exclusion in the influencer marketing industry. Research conducted by Veresiu and Parmentier (2021) shows how mature female fashion and beauty consumers qualified as Advanced Style Influencers openly defy gendered ageism in North America's fashion and beauty markets. These two Canadian professors showed that influencers belonging to the Advanced Style movement – a social media movement explicitly featuring and advocating for women aged 50+ – use their Instagram accounts and personal blogs to claim legitimate inclusion in the fashion system. Their fight entails a form of resistance rooted in the popular Western discourse of successful ageing that relies on two key strategies. First, they deconstruct gendered and ageist fashion ideals, explaining what they are and why they exclude. Then, they openly defy gendered and ageist notions of female beauty.

Body Positivity

A similar dedication to making the fashion industry more inclusive and accessible can be seen in relation to the body positivity movement, which has lately emerged as one of the most popular contemporary themes of influencer activism. One of the most important aspects of body positivity is advocacy for the societal acceptance of an overweight body. Sofia Grahn provides another significant example of body positive discourse, this one connected to skin acceptance.

SOFIA GRAHN: PROMOTING INCLUSIVITY THROUGH SKIN POSITIVITY

Sofia Grahn, 26, is a skin positivity and acne healing advocate from Sweden. Within just two years of public posting, she had become an inspiring and authoritative voice for skincare brands and for those with skin issues such as acne. Her first pimple debuted when she was 10 years old, and she suffered from acne throughout her teenage years. Her acne began to damage her mental health in her early 20s, and she had to seek professional medical care. She adjusted her diet and attempted different skincare regimes before seeking medical aid. She felt lonely in her problems because no one in her personal circle had gone through the same therapy, so she turned to social media.

When Grahn looked for the hashtag #accutane (the brand name of isotretinoin, a powerful acne drug) on Instagram, she discovered a large community of individuals who openly discussed their difficulties with acne. Her Instagram page was created to not only monitor her skin's improvement during the isotretinoin treatment and document its side effects but also to communicate with others who understood her situation. She shared photos of herself without makeup or retouching to show the true colour of her skin and connect with the community. Her bravery to appear in photos as she is makes her appealing and motivating to her fans. Influencer Intelligence, a company which measures the sentiment of influencers, has found that her 'social equity score' is 'the highest score for her influencer follower band' (Barnett, 2022). This is proof that diversity can be objectively powerful.

Mental Illness Education and Advocacy

The way we think about and communicate about mental health has also changed dramatically in the last few decades, thanks in part to the efforts of influencers and content creators on social media. All the major social media platforms, including Twitter, Instagram, Tumblr, and TikTok, have made it possible for people with mental illness, mental health professionals, activists, and advocates all over the world to create useful content – ranging from reels about what it is really like to live with obsessive-compulsive disorder (OCD) using the #ocdawareness hashtag to anxiety coping tips to the often-overlooked signs of attention-deficit hyperactivity disorder (ADHD) in girls and women. This content could potentially reach and help millions of social media users around the world and, importantly, it could inspire them to reach out to others through social media and share their own stories.

The usefulness of this content was especially noteworthy during the COVID-19-related lockdowns. According to a survey by Captiv8, an influencer marketing platform, the number of posts mentioning 'mental health' increased by about 80% across all social media channels in 2020. One example of a mental illness influencer is Chloé Hayden, an artist who lives with autism and ADHD. Hayden uses her platform as an influencer to inform and empower her audience to understand what mental illness is and how to live with it. She engages with her audience on TikTok using a variety of stimulating, fast-paced, and colourful content that is engineered to hold the attention of even the most distracted follower.

In a study of people's social media disclosures about their own mental illness, Griffith and Stein (2021) found that most disclosures were related to the emotional reality of, and thoughts about, mental health. People used social media to reach out and share their feelings of loss and their changes over time. One of the most important effects seemed to be that people heard back from others and from this reception gained a reassuring sense that they were joining a community of like-minded others. Influencers, thus, play an important role in starting and managing conversations about mental illness. They gather supportive audiences and create an inclusive atmosphere on social media where other mental illness influencers can emerge and contribute to the ongoing discourse.

LGBTQ+ Influencers: Creating an Inclusive Climate for Other Influencers

LGBTQ+ influencers have become a powerful global megaphone who have tried to open the influencer industry to others in their community. Part of this effort has been for influencers to normalise LGBTQ+ practices and perspectives so that other influencers feel welcome to share them through social media. Revealing intimate details of their personal story is an effective way for influencers who belong to the LGBTQ+ community to invite other members of that community to participate as influencers, advocates, and even as activists. Through publicly sharing stories of coming out, struggling with depression or self-harm, the processes of transitioning, the start of a new relationship, or a breakup, LGBTQ+ influencers create a social legitimisation of their actions and viewpoints.

Besides creating a sense of community that bonds LGBTQ+ members with one another, visible and normalising influencer depictions of gay coupling have been found to encourage feelings of empathy inside broader communities and provide a more welcoming culture across different social media platforms and channels (Abidin, 2019). Similarly, in their study on lesbian intimacy on

YouTube, McBean (2014) reveals how a lesbian influencer couple's shared story on YouTube provides a 'representation of contemporary lesbian intimacy online' (284) that may encourage others to share similar representations, creating a climate more positive to future participation by other lesbians.

Sharing and normalising the coming out process is one of the ways that the Danish beauty influencer Nikkie de Jager has opened up the influencer space for greater inclusion of LGBTQ+ topics. De Jaeger's emotional and confessional public coming out video encourages all the 'little Nikkies' that feel frightened and insecure to find the strength to free themselves from the daily psycho-social burden of living a false existence and from suffering social stigmatization.

Transgender influencers started to upload material to YouTube in 2006. Transgender vlogging has since then spread and evolved as a culture and a genre that promotes inclusion and participation by other transgender people. Today, YouTube provides the most vivid visual culture of trans self-representation and information. In an academic study, Raun (2018) explores the efforts of the transgender Canadian vlogger Julie Van Vu as she uses her influence to create a climate of understanding, acceptance, and respect for transgender people. With her videos, Julie Van Vu explicitly claims a political identity, labelling herself as an advocate for the LGBTQ+ community online. While documenting her transition through visual surgical details of medical procedures accompanied by very explicit images, these videos have a clear educational purpose as well as a potential impact on future participation by other transgender people. As Raun observes, Van Vu is committed to demystifying the process of physical and social transitioning by revealing intimate personal details that counteract the pathologisation and discrimination of trans people.

Intersectionality

Inclusion efforts often span multiple issues. This complexity is rooted in intersectionality.

INTERSECTIONALITY AND INTERSECTIONAL INFLUENCERS

Intersectionality is a field founded on the idea that each person is placed in a specific place in society at the intersection of many social axes (Gopaldas & Fischer, 2012). These axes could include things such as social class, gender, age, race, immigration status, religion, and sexual preference. This means that people use these positions as both their own individual identities and as a way to connect with each other.

(Continued)

(Continued)

Intersectional influencers are influencers who exhibit intersectional character-istics and whose content often emphasises their location at the intersection of several social axes as part of their social media identity and their influencer channel's personal branding.

Work in the intersectionality area highlights how persons at the intersections of overlapping social axes are susceptible to specific structural benefits and dis-advantages as a result of their intersectional positions. For example, someone who is in a disadvantaged position in several social axes will likely suffer more structural disadvantages than someone who is placed in only one.

Being a woman, Black, bisexual and Muslim, Blair Imani is an example of an intersectional influencer who masterfully uses her social media presence to build social media into an inclusive channel for other intersectional influencers.

BLAIR IMANI: OPENING A SPACE FOR FEMALE, BLACK, BISEXUAL, AND MUSLIM INFLUENCERS

Blair Imani, 28, is an activist, educator, historian, and public speaker with 395,000 Instagram followers. She is an African-American Muslim who grew up in a Christian family and converted to Islam in 2015. She is also a proud bisexual. Her major purpose on social media is to educate and inform people so they may select their own route, which includes the pathway to being an intersectional influencer.

She has displayed a strong and personal affinity with religion after converting to Islam. She wears a headscarf and reveals her arms only occasionally. Imani has deconstructed the assumption that Islam is a fundamentally homophobic faith that challenges Western ideals. Every day, she uses her voice as an influencer to battle injustice and prejudice based on sexuality, gender, reli-gious views, and body size. She states that her goal is inclusion. She wants to make everyone realise that they can feel like they are part of a community. While sharing personal details, she also demonstrates solidarity and empathy for others in need. For example, she discussed her own alcoholism and the AA (Alcoholics Anonymous) recovery process (see Figure 6.3).

Despite unjust criticism, prejudiced views, and disrespectful acts directed at her, Imani's persona exhibits a clear and direct resistant tone that seeks to change the online climate and make it more inclusive of diversity. Her fierce, some would say 'badass', attitude towards inclusion is exhibited in her bold posts:

Figure 6.3 Self-empowering discourse of inclusivity on Blair Imani's Instagram pages

Source: Original author recreation from https://www.instagram.com/blairimani/?hl=it.

'Homophobes: I am not going to cease being Muslim & Bisexual just because you are pissed' and 'Every nasty letter makes me more bisexual' (see Figure 6.3). Her confidence motivates others with comparable ideals and experiences to come out, to become influencers themselves, and to fight the important battles of inclusion on social media. Her relationships with businesses are also value-driven, as she only collaborates with brands who share her ideals of inclusion and equality, like Toms (see Figure 6.3).

WHAT THE FUTURE MAY HOLD FOR DIVERSITY, EQUITY, AND INCLUSION IN INFLUENCER MARKETING

Social justice is an urgently important issue with complex causes and no simple solutions. In the realm of influencers, there are forces working for it and against. There are many positive examples of influencers who are pursuing goals of inclusion, but more collective efforts to change the industry are still very limited. There are social structures that support exclusion and that affect the income-earning potential of the members of different groups and communities. Some brands, agencies, and social media platforms are actively acknowledging and working towards acknowledging our human differences and ensuring that they are represented on social media and in the influencer economy – but many are not. These are deep issues, and they have deeply embedded causes connected to social institutions, cultural practices, politics and power and individual beliefs.

The visibility of blogs like Kelvin Davis' Notoriously Dapper, or Blair Imani's or Sofia Grahn's Instagram accounts means that the members of groups who were under-represented are now finding a voice through the work of influencers and hopefully will feel more encouraged to become influencers themselves. Influencer channels are part of wider social movements for greater access to the media and to the representation that leads to diversity, equity, and inclusion online and in the physical world.

The ability to participate in the influencer industry is not evenly distributed throughout society but depends upon several factors, including disposable time, technical proficiency, and access to the resources needed to develop skills and purchase equipment. If you must work 10-hour shifts at a factory to make ends meet, or if you cannot afford high bandwidth internet, a ring light and a good microphone, or an up-to-date mobile phone, it is much more difficult for you to become an influencer than if you can. And even if you can afford those things and create content, you may not have the right 'look' or style to attract followers or to be able to earn money from commercial sponsors. The influencer industry is currently not a level playing field.

Given the state of the influencer marketing industry, it seems unlikely that members of different racial, age, sexual orientation, body types, and other groups feel that they are included in the world of influencers. With the possibility that they might be held up to ridicule, members of these groups may not perceive authentic opportunities for them to participate in the booming influencer economy and to find a genuine sense of belonging within it. Influencers alone can only do so much. Inclusivity needs to penetrate the whole ecosystem. As long as brands select young, White, skinny women with perfect skin, the creator economy will not be inclusive. It is only when brands, platforms, agencies, and influencers can fully commit and effectively coordinate to promote the goals of diversity, equity, and inclusion that these urgently important goals will finally be reached.

CHAPTER SUMMARY

In this chapter, we gained a deeper understanding of how diversity, equity, and inclusion affect influencers. Acknowledging diversity and representing many different kinds of people is an important and increasingly voiced goal in influencer marketing today, but it is an objective that remains elusive. There are structural elements in the world of influencers that lead to influencer pay gaps and inequity. Inclusion is a socially essential achievement. Numerous influencers promote inclusion and exhibit their diversity, often encouraging others in their community to also become influencers and to raise the online visibility of their groups. In doing so, they encourage other influencers to enter this worldwide ecosystem and to raise important issues relating to topics such as ageism, racism, sexism, mental illness, homophobia, and transphobia, as well as to promote cultural and social change. However, influencers cannot fully change the influencer ecosystem by themselves. When brands, agencies, platforms, regulators and influencers fully commit and effectively coordinate to promote the goals of diversity, equity, and inclusion, we may have a chance to achieve these urgently important goals.

EXERCISES AND QUESTIONS

Exercises

1. Look through some of the lists of top influencers that are circulating online (e.g., https://jdinstituteoffashiontechnology.com/top-20-fashion-influencers-to-follow-on-instagram-in-world/). Are certain body types and social perspectives offered as role models, while others are less visible, suppressed, or problematized?

2. Have you ever encountered discriminatory discourse in your social media daily use (e.g., racism, ageism, body shaming, transphobic, or homophobic)?

3. Do you follow any influencers primarily for their commitment to inclusivity issues?

Questions

1. Explain why diversity, equity, and inclusion are urgent social goals, and how these goals translate to the influencer space.

2. How do brands hold back the achievement of a more diverse influencer ecosystem?

3.   How important is it that influencers from different social groups are paid the same for doing the same work? What are some ways to ensure that this happens?

4.   Is it ever acceptable for an influencer to imitate people's accents, make fun of people's bodies or appearance, or perpetuate racial stereotypes?

5.   What are some of the ways that platforms can increase the sense that different types of people belong on the platform and feel that their participation is welcome?

ANNOTATED READINGS

Scaraboto, D., & Fischer, E. (2013). Frustrated fatshionistas: An institutional theory perspective on consumer quests for greater choice in mainstream markets. *Journal of Consumer Research*, 39(6), 1234–1257.

This study explores the issue of inclusivity in the influencer realm, highlighting how Fatshionista bloggers leverage body positivity and self-acceptance discourse in their social networks to encourage the introduction of a greater range of fashionable plus-size clothing choices.

Södergren, J., & Vallström, N. (2020). One-Armed Bandit? An intersectional analysis of Kelly Knox and disabled bodies in influencer marketing. In J. Argo, T. M. Lowrey, & H. J. Schau (Eds.), *Advances in consumer research volume 48* (pp. 139–142). Duluth, MN: Association for Consumer Research.

This academic study offers an exploration of the interplay between influencer marketing and intersectional diversity, by carrying out a visual analysis of a British model and influencer born without an arm.

Tomkinson, S., & Elliott, J. (2020). Hype source: G Fuel's contemporary gamer persona and its navigation of prestige and diversity. *Persona Studies*, 6(2), 22–37.

This study explores how female gamer influencers struggle to affirm their gamer identity and legitimacy.

7

CULTURAL EFFECTS

CHAPTER OVERVIEW AND OBJECTIVES

This chapter offers a broad look at some of the most important forces and effects of influencer culture. Influencer culture consists of an interconnected system of meanings, actions, technologies, people, objects, and interactions. Forces of dramatisation, intensification, and commodification drive this culture and impel certain actions and attitudes. Dramatisation and intensification effects lead to the production of strong identities, strategic relationships, and engaging influencer content. Forces of commodification drive influencers towards more entrepreneurial behaviours and strategies in self-presentation, relationship building, and content. Forces of dramatisation, intensification, and commodification are bolstered by affective labour practices that exploit influencers' creativity, aspirations, and emotional investments to create strong reactions in audiences. These forces fuel marketisation, which describes the potential economic value assigned to influencers or creators and their audiences and contents. In turn, forces of marketisation encourage dramatisation, intensification, and commodification, creating an endless feedback loop. The culture resulting from this self-reinforcing quest to build different kinds of capital has a range of positive and negative effects, including work stress, cancel culture, fear of missing out (FOMO) culture, self-comparison effects, and threats to influencers' well-being and personal safety. Providing a variety of concepts and examples, this chapter will explore the individual, social, cultural, and economic elements and effects behind influencer culture.

PROVOCATION: What kinds of cultural effects relate to the activities of influencers? Do these effects reflect a positive or negative social impact?

KEYWORDS: influencer culture, commodification, dramatisation, intensification, extremisation, personal brand, parasocial relationship, marketisation, affective labour, cancel culture

A TIKTOK INFLUENCER'S NIGHTMARE

Ava Majury joined TikTok when she was 13 years old. Ava enjoyed dancing and lip-synching to trending music on the platform. Her account with the profile message 'Hey, I love you!!' grew quickly, and she started three more. By 2020, she had over a million followers, and nearly three quarters of them were men. Her paid TikTok promotions included a tooth-whitening product and NFL games. She was an entrepreneurial young lady whose earning power surprised her friends and parents.

However, things began to turn dark in early 2020. One fan, EricJustin111 was attempting to connect with her via Snapchat, on Instagram, in online games, and in comments on TikTok. Innocently, and because she liked to reply to her fans, the then 14-year-old responded to him a few times. Ava later learned that some of her friends were selling him photos of her as well as her personal information, including her cell phone number. Ava's parents allowed her to sell a couple of selfies to this fan for about $300. After that, the fan began messaging Ava with messages detailing what he would pay for 'booty pics' and photos of her feet. After more online harassment, Ava's father texted the fan and demanded that he stop contacting Ava. Afterwards, the fan began sending text messages indicating that he planned to assault her.

Early on July 10, the fan, 18-year-old Eric Rohan Justin, arrived at Ava Majury's family home in Naples, Florida, carrying a shotgun. He blew open the front door and then his weapon jammed. Ava's father, a retired police lieutenant, chased him off. Later, the online stalker returned to the house. Ava's father told him to drop the shotgun, but he pointed it at him instead. Then, in self-defence, the retired policeman shot the 18-year-old stalker, and the young man later died. What began as an entrepreneurial young woman's influencer account turned into a tragic awakening about how online fame can lead to stalking and real-world violence (Williamson, 2022).

The vignette about 13-year-old Ava Majury, her rapid TikTok success, and the enormous personal cost of the stalking nightmare she suffered along with her family illustrate some of the key themes in this chapter. Influencers and creators are a new social phenomenon. They have many of the characteristics of celebrities and advertising personalities, but they are not actually celebrities. The implications of this new reality are just beginning to be felt through culture and society. This chapter looks at some of the important forces shaping the reality of influencers and creators. As Ava's story illustrates, these forces can have positive and negative effects. Cultural drivers and impacts together form what we can call 'influencer culture'; a phenomenon that increasingly infiltrates popular culture, business exchanges, social relationships, and many other aspects of contemporary life.

INFLUENCER CULTURE

Influencer culture is a system of meanings, actions, discourse, technologies, people, objects, places, and interactions that emerges from and simultaneously fuels influencers' and creators' strategic activities on social media and beyond.

ENABLING FORCES OF INFLUENCER CULTURE

As Figure 7.1 illustrates, some of the main forces that help to produce influencer culture revolve around dramatisation, intensification, and commodification. Dramatisation involves the intentional crafting of the influencer as a type of character, the protagonist in an ongoing social media narrative. Intensification describes the continuous pushing of boundaries of what is average social media user behaviour or content, with the intent to increase engagement. Commodification relates to the

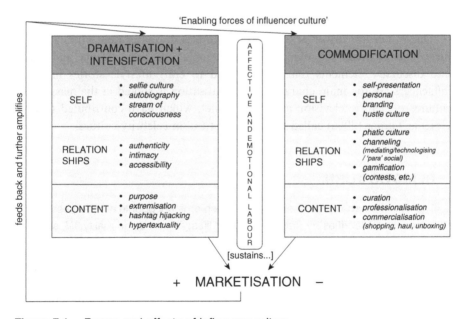

Figure 7.1   Forces and effects of influencer culture

building of the influencer as an entrepreneur operating in a transactional economy. Dramatisation, intensification, and commodification are interconnected by the affective labour performed by influencers, a type of emotional work in which influencers and creators engage to create passion and desire in relation to their personal brands and creative content. With the help of affective labour, influencers dramatise, intensify, and commodify their self, their relationships, and their content, ultimately leading to marketisation potential. Marketisation refers to an influencer or creator's ability to derive exchange value (i.e., monetary value or other forms of compensation) from their activities. Marketisation in turn further encourages and amplifies dramatisation, intensification, and commodification. Each of these elements and their interconnections are important to our understanding of influencer culture and its effects.

Dramatisation and Intensification

DRAMATISATION

Dramatisation is the act of producing a narrative in which the influencer incorporates themselves into an ongoing social media story situated within, and drawing from, but also often challenging or expanding, mainstream narrative and visual codes (Hearn, 2008).

One important driver of influencer culture is dramatisation. Dramatisation turns places, encounters, objects, brands, people, occasions, events, and affects into discursive elements that can be used to craft lifestyle stories in which influencers are the main characters. Dramatisation is rooted in the mass media cultures of reality television and the Internet, which have contributed to what Graeme Turner (2006) called the 'demotic turn' in celebrity culture.

DEMOTIC TURN

The demotic turn is a process through which ordinary people are progressively turned into celebrities by dramatising their lifestyle stories on reality TV, social media platforms, or other media (Driessens, 2013; Turner, 2006).

Dramatisation and the demotic turn are enabled by the affordances of social media platforms. Platforms are storytelling media, offering a stage for people to create and share tales about themselves, their interests, and their lives. When creating these stories, influencers look for more vivid and attention-gaining content for their stories to attract interest and arouse emotions. This heightening of the everyday and ordinary into something that can grab attention is a process of intensification of the everyday.

INTENSIFICATION

Intensification entails deliberate efforts to insert strong, vivid, evocative, or emotional content into lifestyle stories as part of the process that influencers use to draw attention to their presence in social media and build connections with their audience (Just, 2019).

The reason we often see influencers using an abundance of visual language (e.g., emojis, stickers, fantasy filters, and lenses) (Ge & Gretzel, 2018) and emotional facial expressions (e.g., crying, laughing, expressing surprise, sadness, happiness, and excitement), as well as a hyperbolic use of rhetoric and punctuation (e.g., words expressing an emotional status and abundance of exclamation marks) is because they are employing intensification strategies. Intensification strategies aim at triggering follower reactions, which can range from appreciation, excitement, exhortation, harsh critique, and disapproval to even offense. Intensification practices energise followers' passion to consume (Kozinets, Patterson, & Ashman, 2017) and encourage them to avidly 'feed on' influencers, their dramas, and their emotions, often driven by a vicarious desire to emulate their experiences and lifestyles (Abidin & Thompson, 2012). Dramatisation and intensification can increase influencers' visibility, following and status, and can even help them withstand periods of negative backlash.

DRAMAGEDDON 2.0: JAMES CHARLES AND THE INTENSIFICATION OF PERSONAL DRAMAS

In May 2019, top American makeup YouTubers clashed in an escalating battle that was termed 'Dramageddon 2.0'. Beauty gurus Tati Westbrook and Jeffree Star alleged that then-teenager James Charles had hurt Westbrook's vitamin supplement business and sexually preyed on straight boys. Charles immediately experienced the greatest subscriber loss of any YouTuber in the platform's history – 1.7 million in just over a week. His collab brand was removed from the shelves in some cosmetics stores.

Initially, Charles intensified his reaction by producing an emotionally over-the-top video apology in which he appeared sad, miserable, and unkempt – as you can see in Figure 7.2 (left image). During the apology, he whispered in a feeble voice, telling a story that cast himself as a little boy who was helped and mentored by his friend Tati. But this video proved ineffective. It struck viewers as fake and overly dramatic. Only a few days later, Charles changed his narrative. He crafted a powerful and assertive video where he refuted all the allegations, counter-arguing and providing evidence of Westbrook's misbehaviour and opportunistic friendship. In this second video, of which Figure 7.2 presents a screenshot (right image), he appeared with his typically precise, shiny make-up. He looked professional and prepared, speaking fast and posing confidently in front of the camera. After his performance, Star and Westbrook had to apologise. It was, in fact, all performance, and caused a huge uproar across social (and traditional) media. Charles went on to surpass both Star's and Westbrook's follower-counts within the next year and a half. The drama continued (of course) and is likely to continue, inciting a flood of interest from both fans and haters of the stars, and from the general public, ultimately gaining all three major players a wealth of attention and engagement.

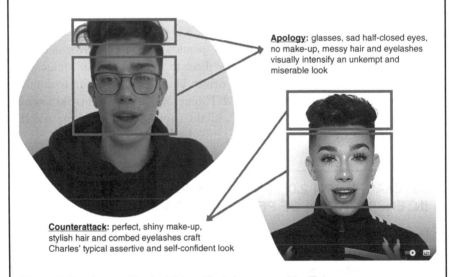

Apology: glasses, sad half-closed eyes, no make-up, messy hair and eyelashes visually intensify an unkempt and miserable look

Counterattack: perfect, shiny make-up, stylish hair and combed eyelashes craft Charles' typical assertive and self-confident look

Figure 7.2   James Charles' intensified dramas on YouTube

Dramatisation and Intensification of the Self

Dramatisation and intensification have shaped influencers' identitites by popularising specific visual and textual narratives of the self. Often, these self-related narratives relate to the notion and the culture of the selfie taking, as well as the conventions of autobiographical storytelling.

SELFIE

The selfie is a digital image characterised by the desire to frame the self in a picture taken to be shared with an online audience (Kozinets, Gretzel, & Dinhopl, 2017: 1).

SELFIE CULTURE

Selfie culture refers to a new form of culture shaped by the media-related performance logic of human self-presentation, social relationships, and social consumption shaped by the convergence of social networks, social media platforms, and mobile phones (Faimau, 2020).

Good selfie taking skills include the ability to capture a well-framed digital self-portrait and the ability to edit the selfie to maximise likeability. Often, influencers will utilise the number of likes, shares, and comments on a selfie as a way to quantify its popularity (Abidin, 2016b: 4). Selfies are not just photos, but social practices that transmit 'human feeling in the form of a relationship' (Senft & Baym, 2015: 1588–89). In fact, selfie-taking and sharing has become one of the favourite practices through which influencers bond with followers, especially on Instagram, a platform that favours the selfie format (Driessens, 2013; Marshall, 2010). Through selfies, influencers seek either to elevate their exclusivity or to lessen the ordinariness of their social standing to appeal to audiences (Rokka & Canniford, 2016). Capturing the self in a snapshot while sporting new trendy outfits and gear, going to the gym, visiting a museum, having dinner in a fancy restaurant, hanging out with attractive friends, travelling in exclusive places, or relaxing at home (Marwick, 2015b; Jerslev & Mortensen, 2016) has become a popular way for influencers to incite consumers' desire (Kozinets, 2020b).

Autobiographical storytelling was introduced online with the practice of blogging. Blogging refers to writing, photography, and other media self-published as short pieces of online content that typically appear in reverse chronological order. Blogging started as an opportunity for individuals to write diary-style entries and share autobiographical experiences, but it has since been incorporated into the identity work of influencers. The hallmarks of autobiographical storytelling online include crafting self-revelatory stories using the self-confessional style of a diary, with informal language and frequent updates.

AUTOBIOGRAPHICAL STORYTELLING

Autobiographical storytelling reflects on personal memories and life experiences, including the everyday, instead of reporting on biographical facts. It creates an emotional, deep, and intimate story.

The visual turn of social media (Gretzel, 2017b) has popularised an aesthetic code that celebrates vividness, symbols, and powerful images. This visual turn affects the form of both selfies and autobiographical stories. For instance, Instagram feeds appear as a stream of consciousness-like collage of selfie images. Instagram stories and reels include quick daily life stories or lessons told in a simple, unpolished, and colloquial language and imagery. Typographical errors, excessive punctuation, and abundance of emojis invite followers to partake in the joyful flow of the narrative. Livestreamers on forums such as Twitch and YouTube Live present a more unvarnished aesthetic code that can seem more immediate and rawer. These conventions invite audiences to become transported into the influencer's representation of an authentic lived reality.

STREAM OF CONSCIOUSNESS

A narrative device or way of storytelling that depicts a character's thoughts, feelings, and reactions in a continuous flow, uninterrupted by objective description or conventional dialogue.

Dramatisation and Intensification of Relationships

Dramatisation and intensification allow influencers to build relationships with their followers that can be quite intense and emotional. Adding to these relationships are influencers' displays of accessibility, intimacy, and authenticity.

ACCESSIBILITY

Accessibility refers to influencers' online presence, understandability, approachability, and availability to interact with followers (Marwick & Boyd, 2011; Marwick, 2013).

By appearing as or actually being accessible to their audience, influencers enhance these relationships. One way that influencers can appear accessible is by frequently posting new content. When frequent posts are not forthcoming, this can generate disapproval and critique on the part of followers that may damage the influencers' reputation.

THE ACE FAMILY ACCESSIBILITY ISSUE

The ACE family (whose name was drawn from the first letters of the original three members of the family) is a popular YouTube channel that attracted more than 17 million subscribers. The family shares their personal daily life stories focused on the joys and the challenges of being parents. When Catherine, the mother, was pregnant at the end of 2019, the family took some time off. Many followers criticised them for not posting videos for several days. Austin, the father, tweeted that those who were complaining should 'do us a favor and unsubscribe and stop watching our every move'. He also added that he and his family deserve to be able to take a break and spend time away from the camera. Fans and other YouTubers immediately reacted to his tweet saying that being a content creator is a dream job, he and his family became rich thanks to his followers, and they should be more available to their followers (Tenbarge, 2019). McBroom later cancelled his tweet, and the ACE family increased their online presence and contact with their audience.

Influencers are expected to connect with their followers by displaying empathy and care. In performances that suggest intimacy, influencers reveal personal stories and private details of their life, as well as disclosing elements of their internal, emotional world (Tenbarge, 2019). Unlike actor celebrities who maintain the mystery of their actual personal life, influencers are public personas whose authenticity is often based on revelations of their real life. This means that their audiences expect self-disclosure of intimate moments of their daily life with their followers, just as friends would do with one another (Berryman & Kavka,

2017). Tactics to intensify accessibility and intimacy include using the 'Ask Me Anything' feature on Instagram or, in some cases, inviting followers to a more intimate and exhibitionistic platform like OnlyFans.

INTIMACY

Intimacy relates to influencers' open, close, and self-revelatory interactions with their followers (Raun, 2018).

NIKKIE DE JAGER'S COMING OUT ON YOUTUBE

An example of intimacy is Nikkie de Jager's public coming out on YouTube. Nikkie de Jager is a Dutch beauty vlogger who has over 14 million followers on YouTube. In the 11 years she has been posting on the platform, her videos have grown in popularity both for her sweet, candid personality, and for her talent and creativity. Her videos also often feature celebrity cameos, including Snoop Dogg and Lady Gaga. On 13 January 2020, de Jager posted a video revealing that she was transgender. The video provides emotional details of her past and of her transitioning to inspire other 'little Nikkies' like her to have the courage to come out and be themselves. 'I can't believe I'm saying this today to all of you for the entire world to see, but damn, it feels good to finally do it', de Jager says in the video. 'It is time to let go and be truly free. When I was younger, I was born in the wrong body, which means that I am transgender'. The video received over 33 million views in less than a week and garnered mainstream media attention.

AUTHENTICITY

In the influencer context, authenticity designates an effort whereby influencers appear to be 'themselves' while they engage in 'performances of self' on social media (Banet-Weiser, 2021).

In the influencer realm, authenticity implies a fusion of performance and identity, expressed by hashtags such as #truetomyself, #loveyourself, #therealme, and #nofilter. In these efforts, artifice and reality are mutually constitutive concepts. As

Banet-Weiser (2021: n.p.) argues, 'the affordances of social media platforms encourage authenticity as something both assiduously constructed and vehemently contested; fake Instagram accounts, doctored videos (deepfakes), bot accounts, and a plethora of apps, filters, and other tools to distort and create one's image abound in this social media environment'. In this scenario, performing authenticity possesses a heightened significance because influencers' identities are always in need of artifice, embellishment, and improvement. Authenticity may also entail revealing expertise and enthusiastic commitment to a field of activity (Usher, 2020). This implies nurturing their talent and their bond with followers, as well as remaining true to themselves (*Ibid.*). Jerslev (2016: 5234) investigated the UK beauty and lifestyle vlogger Zoe Sugg, who is better known as Zoella. Jerslev found that Zoella's straightforward, passionate, here-and-now way of addressing her audience while presenting innovative beauty routines constituted a way to practice authenticity.

Dramatisation and Intensification of the Content

While engaging in dramatisation and intensification, influencers produce content that is attention-grabbing. One way that some influencers seek attention is by highlighting a purpose. A clear and effective purpose can set out an influencers' intent and personal contribution to societal betterment and connect them with followers. The rise of conscientious consumers has emphasised the need for influencers to raise their voice and disseminate content that helps communicate their ideals and personal support of current social, environmental, civic, and political issues.

CLIMATE SENSITIVITY AS PURPOSE IN LUISA NEUBAUER'S CONTENT

German influencer Luisa Neubauer is a young climate activist with a sizable following on Instagram and a popular podcast about climate change. As a result of her content strategy, her opinion is sought by important global figures such as President Barack Obama and Prince William, and she is often a guest on TV, together with representatives of political parties. Neubauer's social media content is nearly always linked to public demonstrations of climate sensitivity. Moreover, she is part of a large group of activists including @gretathunberg, @vanessanakate1, and @lizwathuti. As a result, they often tag each other in their posts, repost each other's content, and have their photos taken together as if they were a team, underlining the idea that everyone must play a role in the fight against climate change. Neubauer's focused, carefully crafted purpose has led her to be considered one of the most important climate activists in Europe.

Another way of intensifying content is through extremisation. Because attention is the coin of the realm in social media, creating controversy can rapidly produce engagement and reach wider audiences. Thus, extremisation is one way that influencer content can break through the background noise and have an impact. Whether engaged intentionally or unintentionally, extremisation often shocks an audience and elicits reactions, thereby increasing the visibility of the influencer content. However, there are important social and cultural dangers, and ethical risks, to creating and promoting content that is deliberately polarising.

EXTREMISATION

Extremisation is the use of provocative, controversial, strong or polarising beliefs or opinions.

FROM FASHION TO POLITICS: THE EXTREMISATION OF HODA KATEBI

An example of content extremisation is offered by Hoda Katebi, a young Iranian American micro-influencer on Instagram. She is a writer, community organiser, and creative educator. In 2018, Katebi was invited to a local TV station in Chicago. Instead of talking about Iranian fashion, the subject of Katebi's new book, the anchor asked about Iran and nuclear weapons. Katebi seemed quite shocked by the statement but then, after a laugh, she began to discuss American capitalism, imperialism, and colonisation in the Middle East. The interviewer said her statements could be considered offensive by many Americans, adding: 'You are an American. You don't sound like an American', to which Katebi replied: 'That's because I've read'. Soon after, the interview went viral. Within a month, the interview had been viewed more than ten million times. Reactions to the interview were polarised. On the one hand, the activist started receiving death threats and hate mail, which forced her to go to the police. On the other hand, she quickly gained an astonishing number of followers thanks to the explanation of the incident on her Twitter account.

Other attention-grabbing techniques include hashtag hijacking and hyper-textuality. Hashtag hijacking has existed on Twitter since 2013 and is a common practice on TikTok. It occurs when influencers use a brand's hashtag on unrelated content, in hopes they can 'hijack' the social media platform's algorithm and gain more exposure. Though TikTok hijackers have been known to tag their videos with multiple rows of popular hashtags, a TikTok spokesperson said that there is little benefit to using multiple hashtags and that it is 'not considered a best practice for creation'. The use of hashtags and tags also emphasises the hypertextual nature of influencer content because these elements often link to other sources that are similarly categorised.

HASHTAG HIJACKING

Hashtag hijacking is a practice by which an influencer uses a popular or trending hashtag that is irrelevant to the content of the post simply to gain additional visibility on social media.

HYPERTEXTUALITY

Hypertextuality refers to the online interconnection between content, such that a Web address/hyperlink, tag or hashtag in one piece of content links to another piece of content.

Influencers often utilise a large amount of trendy and evocative tags and hashtags. These connect to other pages and feeds where influencers can create different layers of visual and textual content through which they can craft compelling personal narratives that engage their followers.

Commodification

Influencers craft themselves not only as characters in social media but also as entrepreneurs whose aim is to 'sell' themselves, their personal brands, and perhaps their own or other companies' brands to their audience. Social media has created a space where people can act as entrepreneurs (Scharff, 2016) – also called 'autopreneurs' (i.e., entrepreneurs engaging in autobiographical work) (Ashman, Patterson, & Brown, 2018). They usually act as their own producers, utilising their own capital and generating their own earnings (Smith, 2015). When acting as entrepreneurs, influencers and content creators may commodify what they do in their private lives and also build a professional online presence. When they commodify themselves, influencers deploy and maintain their online identity as if it were a brand – a personal brand – often with the ultimate aim of monetisation (Senft, 2013).

COMMODIFICATION

In general, commodification happens when things that were not previously sold (e.g., friendship, sex, or water) are sold and enter the marketplace. In the world of influencers, commodification refers to the monetisation of user-generated online content and also to addressing and engaging with the online audience in a way that potentially 'attracts attention and publicity' (Raun, 2018: 100).

Commodification of the Self

Commodification relies on rituals and practices of self-presentation and personal branding that are rooted in theories of identity as a type of social performance (Goffman, 1959). While engaging in self-presentation, influencers incorporate stories with attributes, meanings, and values that communicate a brand-like uniqueness and desirability. Influencer self-presentation is thus aimed at positioning influencers as human brands in their audience's perception. Self-presentation and personal branding enable influencers to achieve awareness and status and allow them to do things such as promote consumer trends, brands, and lifestyles, and raise awareness about cogent societal issues.

SELF-PRESENTATION

Self-presentation is the construction and performance of an ideal self through symbols, objects, practices, and interactions used to communicate a desired impression.

PERSONAL BRAND

A human being's personal presence that is consistent, authentic, and distinct (Freberg, 2021).

Masterful conveyance of the personal brand has also become part of self-presentation on YouTube. This attention to detail is often found in the short 'welcome to my channel' video that almost every YouTuber has today. You-Tubers are expected to sell themselves to achieve a high-profile position in the platform. Thus, self-promotional annotations with links to their other videos as well as to the channel subscription are a must to ensure views and clicks, both of which can be translated into status, success, and money.

ZOZOLIINA AND THE COMMODIFICATION OF MIDDLE EASTERN-WESTERN BLENDED IDENTITY

Zozoliina is a young French fashion designer and blogger who has Algerian, Armenian, and German lineage, and counts over 50,000 followers on Instagram. Pemberton and Takhar (2021) studied Zozoliina and found that her self-presentation and personal branding advance an attractive blend of Middle Eastern and Western meanings and symbols in a way that disrupts codified social norms of difference rooted in ethnic, religious, political, and cultural identity. Her image extols bringing different cultural elements together. For instance, she appears in a bold blend of *hijab*, kaftan, ripped jeans, and high heels; she flirts with the camera in a selfie that contrasts the rigorous seriousness of the *hijab* with the wild femininity of Western purple make-up and flowery foulard; and she poses in a romantic and seductive naked-back Western wedding dress.

Influencers' practices of self-presentation and personal branding have become relentless. Influencers must consistently and devotedly engage in their entrepreneurial pursuits and content creation, constantly blurring the boundaries between work and leisure as well as those between private and public life. The work of influencers is continuously being measured and assessed. Influencers do not merely share messages or look attractive. Instead, their marketability is being measured by their follower counts, engagement rates, click-throughs, discount coupon redemptions, and other measures. The demands of commodification have instilled a 'hustle culture' into influencer culture that has normalised working harder, faster, and longer as a landmark of being a virtuous entrepreneurial influencer. It creates pressures to perform that can even, in the extreme, result in purchases of fake followers or the use of scare tactics in messages. Hustle culture also pressures influencers into commodifying every aspect of their self and their life, including turning their partners, pets, and kids into influencers.

HUSTLE CULTURE

Also known as burnout culture or grind culture, hustle culture is a lifestyle where career and work have become so much of a priority in people's lives that other aspects of human life – such as hobbies, family time, and self-care– take a back seat to earning money.

Commodification of Relationships

In contrast to celebrities, influencers tend to establish more personal relationships with their followers which resonate with audience perceptions of their attractiveness, perceived similarity, and empathy (Lou & Yuan, 2019). These relationships are generally mediated by platforms. While mediating the interactions between influencers and their audiences, the technological and social affordances of social media enable audiences to form an apparently close, face-to-face bond with the influencer (Hartmann & Goldhoorn, 2011; Labrecque, 2014), encouraging their perception that the influencer is a like-minded peer and a friend. This seemingly close and intimate bond extends the notion of 'parasocial relationship' (Horton & Wohl, 1956) originally developed with reference to social bonds between performers and viewers in mass media contexts. The social bond generated in technology mediated interactions allows influencers to channel audience relationships into an income source through monetisation. For instance, monetisation can be offered to give followers access to increasingly rich, valuable, and intimate influencer content.

PARASOCIAL RELATIONSHIP

A parasocial relationship is a one-sided relationship in which one person (a follower or fan) invests emotional energy, is highly interested in, and knows a lot about the person, and the other party (typically a media personality) is unaware or uninterested in the other person.

ONLYFANS

Launched in 2016, OnlyFans is a subscription-based social media platform where users can sell and/or purchase original content. When utilised as an adult site, users will post nudity and sex-related videos and photos – what is globally known as NSFW (Not Suitable for Work) – to their accounts. Some content is free, but some is behind paywalls that can be accessed by buying individual pieces of content or paying a monthly subscription fee. The platform's management has tried to broaden its appeal beyond erotic and adult fare, seeking fitness influencers, artists, comedians, and others who want to share and easily monetise their content. Although the platform mostly offers up porn related content, influencers including Bhad Bhabie and Tana Mongeau use OnlyFans to sell intimate content that is unavailable elsewhere.

Despite the seemingly close and interpersonal nature of the relationships that influencers form with their audiences, these connections are also fragile, superficial, and transitory. The Dramageddon 2.0 case shows how unstable the bond between Charles and his followers was. Granovetter (1983: 201) termed ephemeral ties such as these 'weak ties' – which he defined as 'acquaintances that are less likely to be involved with one another than close friends'. The spreading of weak ties is also demonstrated by the contemporary need of people to engage in what have been called, using a term from anthropology, 'phatic communication' exchanges.

Phatic exchanges express sociability and maintain connections or bonds between people in a superficial manner (Miller, 2008: 393–94). Social media offer opportunities for influencers to create ephemeral social experiences that increase their visibility, publicity, and interactions. Phatic threads of conversations, hashtags, selfies, emoji, stickers, memes, gifs, and videos create an endless discursive flow that influencers can play with to establish a permanent connection with their audiences over time (Hampton, 2016). The popularity of phatic exchange using social media has led to what some communication theorists have termed a phatic culture.

PHATIC EXCHANGE

Phatic exchange is a communicative gesture that does not include any meaningful information or facts about the world but occurs simply to continue a communication or affirm a superficial feeling of social connection (Miller, 2008).

PHATIC CULTURE

Phatic culture refers to the 'flattening of online communication towards the non-dialogic and non-informational' qualities of superficial communication exchanges (Miller, 2008: 388).

In contemporary society, the idea of having continuous access to others through technology has become commonplace. The need for persistent and continuous connection has become yet another engine of commodification. Influencers exploit this need by channelling their followers' willingness to connect into measurable 'audience engagement' activities which, in turn, allow them to attract commercial opportunities. To avoid engagement fatigue and encourage more valuable interactions, they often employ gamification strategies.

GAMIFICATION

Gamification refers to the application of game-design elements and game principles into non-game contexts, such that the service is enhanced to support users' overall value creation (Huotari & Hamari, 2017).

Influencers perform gamification when they introduce game-like aspects that can motivate their audiences to interact and engage with their content. These rewarding social experiences may include online challenges, contests, giveaways, trivia games, or other game-related components. Gamified contents are intended to boost engagement, create a sense of play and fun, and permit a less intrusive and offensive integration of commercial material into the social dynamics of the influencer–audience member connection.

Commodification of Content

Commodification of content occurs when influencers engage in an accurate and skilful transformation of cultural artefacts (Schembri & Tichbon, 2017) drawn from their lifestyle repertoire into an assembly of digital objects and aesthetic experiences (Venkatesh & Meamber, 2006). These artefacts can include visual and textual elements such as selfies, stories, captions, a hashtag, gif, meme, or video. They are shared with an audience to gain visibility and potentially generate revenues. Commodification of the content entails content curation, professionalisation, and commercialisation.

CURATION OF CONTENT

Curation refers to the expert and diligent identification, selection, and combination of various content elements to form an aesthetically pleasing assembly on social media.

Exactly like a museum curator who carefully and patiently identifies, selects, and assembles artwork while preparing an exhibition for museum visitors, influencers curate each piece of content for their audience. They keep in mind the need to craft a powerful and attractive story. While building their curations (e.g., their Instagram feeds), influencers pay special attention to select, shape, and present emotional content because this type of content will be more likely to generate word-of-mouth, increased visibility, and audience appreciation – and may lead to enhanced monetisation opportunities. In this respect, revealing hidden secrets of their personal life through a combination of images, words, and emotional vocabularies and hashtags has proven to be effective.

Adept content curation requires professionalisation. Selfie-taking is a great example of increasing professionalisation in the social media space. What originally began as a non-professional self-presentation activity (Senft, 2013: 4) has gradually evolved into professionalised labour thanks both to technological innovations and the increased capitalisation of influencer content. For example, influencers curate and share their selfies using (semi-)professional makeup and dress, lighting and posturing, and apps and artifice, transforming selfies into commercial creations that serve personal branding objectives. Selfie-taking skills have become a recognised influencer-related asset resulting in an expanded base of followers and an increasing number of sponsorship opportunities.

PROFESSIONALISATION OF CONTENT

The increased demarcation of the contents of amateurs/regular social media users and those produced by individuals with specific competences.

The requirement for professional content is especially high for content creators, whose standards may reach professional levels. Artists, photographers, designers, filmmakers, and other content creators using social media are expected to stay up to date with the latest techniques, styles, and equipment – yet they must do so on budgets that may be far more limited than those enjoyed by devoted full-time professionals in competing industries.

COMMERCIALISATION OF CONTENT

The process of increasingly producing content for financial gain.

Professionalisation of content opens up opportunities for commercialisation. In his exploration of the Canadian transgender YouTube vlogger, Julie Van Vu, Raun (2018) reveals that Vu embraced the ideals of commercialising her social media content from the start, earning money through sponsored mentions and affiliate sales while also receiving gift merchandise for reviews. Her videos and interactions with followers represent a new commercial genre of trans vlogs that combines self-reflexive documentation, support and advice, and sponsored/ commercially driven tips and tricks on make-up, beauty, and body modification. Other forms of commercial videos that influencers produce are shopping, haul and unboxing videos, where influencers variously engage in showing, describing, unboxing, and reviewing products just bought in shopping episodes or received as gifts from brands.

Affective Labour

Dramatisation, intensification, and commodification forces are sustained by the affective labour performed by influencers in order to affect the emotional experience of others. Affective labour often can include narration of personal stories that aim to establish an emotional bond with followers (Wissinger, 2007). A curated Instagram feed can be similar to a digital mood board where the aesthetic combination of feelings, emotions, places, people, and colours is intended to arouse followers' interest and emotions. Mombloggers are a particularly strong example of affective labour. When mothers share their personal stories about the trials and tribulations of parenting as well as their photos of themselves with their children, they frequently display emotion, blurring the distinction between their public and private lives, and employing mothering related content as a medium for advertising (Hopkins, 2019).

> ### AFFECTIVE LABOUR
>
> Affective labour is work that is produced in order to intentionally inspire or alter other people's emotional experiences (Just, 2019).

The production and the circulation of emotions often requires emotional labour (Hochschild, 1983; Negri & Hardt, 1999). The need for a positive, service-oriented emotional palette in influencer content requires influencers to engage in emotional labour and for them to capitalise on affective labour through building and monetising audience members' emotional attachment to their personalities and stories. The result is the affirmation of an 'affective capitalism' (Karppi et al., 2016), where both emotional and affective labour become important wellsprings of economic value.

> ### EMOTIONAL LABOUR
>
> Emotional labour is work that requires the producer to feel or modify their own emotional experiences as part of the job task (Hochschild, 1983).

Research analysing LGBTQ+ influencers and creators has highlighted how the exercise of affective and emotional labour in service of self-commodification and monetisation may also create a tension with the representation of their minority status. This tension can be resolved when affective and emotional labour convey authenticity and establish common ground with followers through self-revelation (Duguay, 2019). Considering both the potential negative and positive effects of affective and emotional labour is necessary for understanding influencer culture.

MARKETISATION AND ITS CULTURAL EFFECTS

Influencers' and creators' efforts to dramatise, intensify, and commodify their identities, audiences, relationships, and content in such a way that someone is willing to pay for their work (e.g., through content subscriptions, sponsored posts, advertising content, or endorsements) has led to increasing marketisation of the influencer and creator space. Marketisation expresses the potential and aspirational ability of influencers and creators to attract deals, make money, create their own brands, and collaborate with companies. Marketisation generates potential economic value from the resource of influencers' emotional and affective labour (e.g., emotions, feelings, editorial content, products, objects, places, and events). Economic value is determined through measures of key indicators of influencers' performance such as number of followers, engagement rate, number of views, likes, comments, shares of a post, or lead generation. Following these key indicators can become a major obsession of influencers, and a significant source of performance pressure.

Marketisation also creates monetisation opportunities for ecosystem actors related to and relying upon the efforts of influencers. These actors include agencies, managers, partnering companies, and others. Marketisation continuously feeds back, amplifies, and nurtures the dramatisation, intensification and commodification forces that generate it, perpetuating an ongoing loop.

MARKETISATION

'The promotion of market ideologies and the expansion of the market into areas traditionally beyond its purview' (Tadajewski, 2020: 3).

Marketisation produces cultural effects that can be both positive and negative. Some of the most important positive effects include providing opportunities for entrepreneurship where none existed beforehand, democratising social media participation with a range of diverse voices, inspiring a culture of empowerment across social media channels, and enabling activism among participants in the influencer world. Some of the main negative marketisation effects involve cancel culture; FOMO, social- and self-comparison effects; and threats to influencers' wellbeing and personal safety.

Cancel Culture

The emphasis on phatic communications to support relentless flows of conversations and the idea that social media offer an uncensored space for self-expression have created some important problems. Because influencers who take their content development too far can be subject to scrutiny and public censure, many have been caught in the backlash from their own content. In this regard, a cultural effect of marketisation is cancel culture.

CANCEL CULTURE

Cancel culture is a phenomenon where a public figure is named, publicly shamed, and professionally and socially ostracised for behaviour that is considered offensive, such as making racist, disparaging, or offensive remarks, or conducting inappropriate actions in their real life (e.g., Will Smith being professionally sanctioned and removed from the Academy for slapping Chris Rock on the 2022 Academy Awards stage).

For influencers, being cancelled can result in a massive loss of followers, an attack on their public image, and the loss of sponsorships and other forms of income. But, according to research conducted by Insider (Hall & Tenbarge, 2020) for some of the most well-known YouTubers, being cancelled ended up providing a significant, enduring career boost that enhanced their visibility and monetisation opportunities. This is the case for Jake Paul, an influencer who openly courts controversy. Jake has faced scrutiny for partying during the coronavirus pandemic and getting raided by the FBI after he filmed himself loitering at an Arizona mall as it was being looted. Despite these incidents, or perhaps because of them, Paul has managed to not only recover from their repeated controversies but also to thrive on the back end of major scandals.

Whereas cancel culture in Western and in most of Asian countries tend to be more related to public perception of influencers' misbehaviours that do not comply with the widely accepted moral and ethical standards, in mainland China cancel culture is far more politicised, with the central government sometimes taking an active role in encouraging cancellations of influencers, celebrities, and brands. As the media magazine Jing Daily (2022) reports, China's culture stands out for its nationalistic and moralistic bent, with the majority of consumer 'cancellations' reserved for influencers, celebrities, and brand ambassadors who make a moral misstep either real or imagined, which is then amplified on Chinese social platforms, or for brands that fail to toe the Communist Party line.

FOMO and Social- and Self-Comparison Effects

A major cultural drawback of dramatisation, intensification, and commodification forces is the parallel global upsurge in influencers' reported mental illness, including anxiety, excessive work-related stress, and depression (Hall & O'Shea, 2013; Sennett, 1998). These issues are related to the pressures coming from increased competition for attention as well as the public visibility and pressures that accompany working in front of the camera in the influencer industry. Anxiety also results from the tension between needing to be authentic and needing to dramatise, intensify, and commodify. The issues are exacerbated by the reliance of the digital marketplace on key performance indicators that establish challenging personal targets and performance-related rewards for influencers in order to keep up with ever-increasing market standards for performance. As a result, sometimes even breaks from social media are turned into money-making opportunities like brand deals, leading to the commodification of disconnection (Jorge & Pedroni, 2021).

FAR FROM THE MADDENING WEB-CROWD: SUMMER MCKEEN BETWEEN FOMO AND JOMO

Summer McKeen quietly deactivated her social media accounts in August 2020. The lifestyle vlogger with over two million YouTube subscribers had been gaining traction, thanks in part to her starring role in the unscripted Snapchat series Endless Summer. But fame had brought with it increased scrutiny and a growing chorus of criticism, and McKeen needed a break (Jarvey, 2020). The FOMO (fear of missing out) that drives influencers to constantly create and share content to avoid oblivion has recently been offset by an opposing joy of missing out (JOMO) that allows influencers to escape the maddening web-crowd despite the costs. McKeen returned to regular posting just a few weeks later, so it was not a long break. However, for an influencer whose career is built on platforms like YouTube and Instagram, it was a difficult decision. Without new posts, her metrics would undoubtedly decline. Nonetheless, McKeen determined that she needed to prioritise her personal well-being.

'People started viewing YouTubers as characters in their favorite show rather than real people', McKeen said in an interview with the Hollywood Reporter. 'As a result, the level of criticism skyrocketed'. 'All of the criticism and random rumors got a lot smaller to me after my break', McKeen said, adding, 'My numbers went down, but it was worth it'.

As the influencer industry enters its second decade, breaks like McKeen's are becoming more common, and microcelebrities are openly discussing the stresses and anxieties of their jobs. Influencers such as Lilly Singh, PewDie-Pie, and Elle Mills have announced plans to step away from social media in recent years, with many citing burnout as a result of their vlogging schedules. Meanwhile, Instagrammers such as model Olivia Culpo have been more open about how their perfectly curated feeds conceal their internal struggles (Jarvey, 2020).

The pressure to compete is not only directed outwardly, but also inwardly and towards the self (Gill, 2010; Scharff, 2016). This is marked by an increasing effort of influencers oriented to self-improvement, self-achievement, and pushing themselves beyond their own limits. Internal competition generates social- and self-comparison effects that reinforce influencers' anxiety. Depression can result when influencers cannot cope with the pressures they face for a continuous stream of original, innovative, and socially desirable content creation. Facing these challenges is exhausting and can result in influencer burnout. This happens especially among the youngest and most fragile cohorts of Gen Z influencers many of whom, over the last few years, became famous incredibly fast. The global pandemic that challenged the mental health of so many may also have been a contributing factor.

JACK INNANEN AND THE BURNOUT OF GEN Z'S TIKTOKERS

It became increasingly difficult for Jack Innanen, a TikTok star from Toronto, to create content. 'I feel like I'm tapping a keg that's been empty for a year', he told the New York Times in an interview (Lorenz, 2021). Spending hours shooting, editing, storyboarding, engaging with fans, negotiating brand deals, and juggling all of the other responsibilities that come with being a successful content creator has taken its toll. Jack Innanen, like many other Gen Z influencers who rose to prominence in the last year, is exhausted. 'I get to the point where I'm like, 'I have to make a video today', and I spend the whole day dreading it', he admitted.

Loss of Privacy and Threats to Personal Safety

As the vignette about Ava Majury that opened this chapter illustrated, there can also be personal risks to being an influencer. Unfortunately, stories about fan obsession and the stalking of influencers such as the one about Majury and her stalker are not rare. They are becoming almost as commonplace as those relating to Hollywood celebrities. Pleas by influencers to their stalkers to please leave them alone are becoming more prevalent. The difference is that these are regular people, not major celebrities – and they must deal with this difficult new reality without the resources of big entertainment studios to help them. We have had influencers as class speakers who tell us that they have changed what and how they post because of fear of stalkers. Travel influencers and others cannot announce destinations that they will be at, for fear that they will be stalked. They can only discuss destinations after they have left them. The price of their marketisation is a change in their personal lives which is not always for the better.

BROADER IMPACTS OF INFLUENCER CULTURE

The increasing marketisation of the influencer and creator space and the resulting influencer culture also have broader ramifications. Influencer culture has been blamed for fuelling the sometimes toxic culture of social media, especially through its emphasis on superficial, consumption-focused lifestyles, the polarisation that stems from its extremisation of content, and the normalisation of documenting and publicly sharing every detail of one's life. It has specifically been criticised for encouraging mindless consumption and worsening sustainability issues like food waste and fast fashion.

CHAPTER SUMMARY

This chapter examined some of the most powerful forces and effects of influencer culture. Influencer culture is a complex network of meanings, actions, technologies, people, objects, and interactions. It is propelled by forces of dramatisation, intensification, and commodification, which drive certain actions and attitudes. Dramatisation and intensification effects result in the creation of content with engaging narratives and evocative depictions of identities, relationships, and situations. Commodification forces push influencers towards more entrepreneurial self-presentation, relationship-building, and content strategies. Emotional and affective labour practices, which structure emotion into the work of influencers and audience reaction, strengthen the forces of dramatisation, intensification, and commodification. These forces serve marketisation, which emphasises the realisation of the economic value of influencers' personal brands, contents, and audiences. Marketisation forces, in turn, encourage the development of the other major forces and effects of influencer culture. The culture created by this self-perpetuating quest for economic value has a variety of positive and negative consequences, including cancel culture, FOMO culture, self-comparison effects, and the resulting threats to influencers' wellbeing and personal safety. As developed in this chapter, influencer culture has a variety of unique and important individual, social, cultural, and economic elements and effects.

EXERCISES AND QUESTIONS

Exercises

1. Open the social media page of a popular influencer you have never visited before. Watch their feeds, read their most recent posts, or watch their latest videos. Which elements from this chapter can you identify in their content?

2. Can you think of an influencer who has recently produced extremised contents, or who has generated a controversial reaction? Did the reactions of the audience focus more on the controversial contents posted or on the person? Did the influencer reply to any reaction? What ideas from this chapter might help you to explain what you observed?

3. In this chapter, we revealed that for some of the most well-known YouTubers, being cancelled ended up providing a significant, enduring career boost that enhanced their visibility and monetisation opportunities. Why do you think this happens?

4. Go online and find an example of an influencer that has marketisation potential but does not use it for monetisation.

Questions

1. Can you name one of the emotions that a particular influencer inspires. How, exactly, do they inspire that emotion?

2. What do people consider attractive and aspirational about influencers' lifestyles? Thinking of a particular influencer, what would you say makes their content seem worthy of aspiring to?

3. With reference to marketisation, what types of influencer contents are the most sought-after? Why?

4. There are numerous young TikTokers who reached fame very fast and are now experiencing burnout, anxiety and depression. Could these effects be avoided?

ANNOTATED READINGS

Cashmore, E. (2019). Kardashian kulture. *How celebrities changed life in the 21st century*. London: Emerald Group Publishing.

A sociologist provides a historical analysis of how celebrities have impacted consumer culture.

Yallop, O. (2021). *Break the Internet*. London: Scribe UK.

A social media strategist enrols in an influencer bootcamp, goes undercover at a fan meetup, and shadows online vloggers, Instagrammers, and content creators.

8

ETHICS AND REGULATION

CHAPTER OVERVIEW AND OBJECTIVES

By overviewing core principles and offering numerous examples and illustrations, this chapter will inform readers about the ethical and regulatory basis of the influencer marketing industry. The chapter will provide the conceptual basis for understanding marketing ethics and how it applies to the universe of social media marketing, and specifically influencer marketing. Rule-bound and situational approaches to influencer marketing ethics principles will be contrasted and compared in the chapter, which will also provide a succinct analytical tool to help focus on the moral and ethical dimensions of marketing decisions. Public controversy in the influencer industry will be discussed as an example of post-truth, a complex new ethical concept for a complex new time. Marketing ethics must apply not only to human and social betterment but also to non-human animals and the planetary ecosystem. Some of the major agencies that regulate the influencer marketing industry will then be overviewed, along with some of their most important regulations, such as disclosure. Regulations also govern influencer-related areas such as native advertising, fraudulent influencers, fake followers, problematic content, and vulnerable audiences. Knowledge of these regulations and areas is important for anyone seeking to understand or practice in the influencer industry. The chapter will close with a discussion of the role of activists and future trends in influencer marketing regulation and governance.

PROVOCATION: 'With great influence comes great responsibility!' (Paraphrasing an ancient adage)

KEYWORDS: marketing ethics, post-truth, regulatory agencies, fraudulent influencers, fake followers, problematic content, influencer activists, activist influencers

---

FAKE FOLLOWERS

In general, influencers have ethical reputations not too different from the snake oil salespersons of olden days. In the HBO documentary 'Fake Famous', director Nick Bilton shows how easy it can be to fake your way to becoming a popular online influencer. 'You don't have to go to the dark web, or anything, you just go to the straight up internet and you can buy pretty much anything you want', Bilton says in 'Fake Famous' as he takes out a credit card to buy thousands of fake followers for the documentary's three characters. As Bilton shows, fake followers are generated by hackers and code that creates followers and steals existing accounts' photos, names, and bios.

Bilton paid about $119 for 7,500 followers and then faked a luxurious lifestyle by renting a mansion and a fake private jet. In the end, Bilton's three characters grew their Instagram following from 2,500 to about 340,000 followers. Meanwhile, they also started receiving perks from brands looking to be featured in their Instagram posts, from free sunglasses or jewellery to free training sessions at a private gym in Beverly Hills (Huddleston, 2021). Bilton asserts that many influencers also use fake followers and misleading tricks to create catchy social content and attract brands for online promotions. These types of activities seem shady, but are they illegal? In the world of influencer marketing today, what is ethical and moral, and what is legal? We will find out in this chapter.

ETHICAL MARKETING

Influencer advertising, marketing, and relations have become crucial elements of social media marketing. Most social media marketing can be viewed as the systematic use of social media for sales outreach by organisations to various members of society in pursuit of exchange transactions (Laczniak & Murphy, 2006). These transactions have effects that are not only economic but also social, ethical and environmental. In fact, 'every marketing decision implicitly if not explicitly has ethical dimensions' (Smith, 1995). Because social media is intertwined with all media, has such a wide reach, and much of it is publicly accessible, the impact of these decisions can be far ranging.

Oftentimes, in practice, marketing managers must make decisions which trade-off short-term financial or other business goals with moral or ethical behaviours. As a result of trade-offs made in favour of short-term financial or other business goals, marketing practices such as the aggressive sales of credit cards or sugary, processed foods have had negative effects on consumers and on society at large.

> ## MARKETING ETHICS
>
> The obligation by all parties involved in marketing products and services to engage in thoughtful consideration and practices that respect the well-being of individuals, society, animals, and the ecosystem, and follow and anticipate applicable regulation.

There is a long tradition in marketing thought and education that considers the ethical implications of different marketing decisions and actions. One of the most fundamental principles of these traditions is that ethical marketing practices put people's best interests first. In other words, people should not be treated as merely the means for a marketer to reach their own goals. Instead, marketing should be a part of a set of institutions which creates value for society and contributes to individual and social betterment. This implies that high pressure sales tactics, sexual exploitation, stereotyping, utilising strong persuasion attempts (such as fear appeals), and price gouging should generally not be used because these tactics tend to treat consumers as means to a goal.

In the Anthropocene, the age we live in, in which humans dominate the ecosystem on Earth, marketing and consumption play major roles. For example, Elhacham et al. (2020) calculated that there is now twice as much plastic, by weight, on planet Earth as there are living things. An increasingly important element of marketing ethics therefore must be our consideration for the well-being not only of other human beings and society but also of other living beings and the long-term health of the planetary ecosystem itself.

A useful maxim we have devised to consider the moral and ethical dimensions of marketing decisions is as follows:

* What is being marketed, to whom, and how?

The maxim draws our attention to the following aspects of marketing decision-making:

1. What is the product or service being marketed? Is it harmful to people by nature, such as tobacco products which cause illness and addict people? How was it produced? Did it use fair labour and trade practices, or did it come from shady work factories with questionable conditions? Is its production cruel to animals, such as fur products, factory farming, or foie gras? Does it contribute to the destruction of the environment, such as fossil fuels, fast fashion, or plastics? Is it disposable or biodegradable?

2. Who is being targeted in the marketing? Are vulnerable populations the target? For example, are children being targeted? Are people with poor credit the targets? Are certain racial, gender, or other stereotypes used in targeting? Are the people being targeted being exploited for some weakness or shortcoming?

3. How is the product or service being marketed? Are the sales tactics themselves moral and ethical as well as honest and respectful? Are false claims or inferences being made? Are any pressure or fear tactics being used? Is the product being made to look better than it really is, for example, by being featured as part of a desirable lifestyle? Where necessary, are the media and social media vehicles and sites being used appropriately to exclude those who should not be enticed into purchasing the product (e.g., underage consumers) and to avoid harming society?

Although this is just a brief treatment of our marketing ethics maxim, the fundamental idea of examining what is being marketed, to whom, and how, is quite powerful and can be extended to situations across the world of marketing, including those relating to influencer marketing.

INFLUENCER MARKETING BEGINS WITH *LONELYGIRL15*

Something most people don't know is that some of the first influencer marketing that occurred was not disclosed in any way. The advertising was for an early YouTube series called *Lonelygirl15*, in which an actress (Jessica Rose) played a real girl named 'Bree' speaking from her bedroom, and her audience never knew if she was real or acting. 'Icebreakers' candy approached them with a promotional deal. In the show, one of Bree's friends offers everyone an Icebreaker during a car ride. There was no disclosure of this as an ad and the producers treated it exactly like a product placement. In those early days, there were no rules and no regulations. Producers, many with Hollywood and advertising backgrounds (the two are interlinked), were simply making everything up as they went along. For more details, see Davis (2006).

FOUNDATIONS OF ETHICAL INFLUENCER MARKETING

There are numerous approaches to marketing ethics. However, they can be grouped and understood as relating to one of two different sorts of moral stances on ethical principles: either they are *rule-bound* (also called 'deontological') or they are *situational* (also called 'consequentialist' or 'utilitarian'). Rule-bound ethical principles are like 'thou shalt' or 'thou shalt not' commandments. They express guiding values that are intended to be unwavering and as binding as they are in a religious doctrine or a law. So, in public relations and marketing, practitioners are often told to be honest, open, loyal, fair, and respectful in all of their communications. On the other hand, situational ethics are founded in the idea that reaching an ethical decision will depend on weighing or calculating the various different factors at work in a particular context. So, for example, a public relations agency might decide that it was ethical to deliberately confuse or obscure an issue because they have calculated that it would be in the best interest of their client.

Rule-bound and situational ethical principles can lead to very different paths. For example, someone following the Biblical commandment 'thou shalt not kill' in a duty-based manner would refuse to kill another person, regardless of the circumstances. Over 70,000 men were conscientious objectors who refused combat positions in World War 2, often because of holding religious beliefs and values such as this. A situational view on killing might look at the circumstances. Is it self-defence? Is this killing a just punishment? Would the killing be protecting someone else? Am I killing to protect my country or important values like freedom? So while rule-bound ethics would be absolute in its stand against killing, situational ethics provides us with a long list of pragmatic reasons in which it is perfectly acceptable to kill people. When President Truman said that he was trying to save American and Japanese lives by dropping atomic bombs on Hiroshima and Nagasaki, he was using situational ethics to justify the morality of his decision.

Although the stakes are not quite as high in influencer marketing as in war, the same sorts of general ethical principles are relevant to the marketing field and the battlefield. For the rule-bound aspects of influencer marketing, a small sample of the types of rules would include the following.

1. Always Be Truthful: When an influencer is marketing a product or service to customers, the influencer, the agency, and the brand must work together to ensure that the information they provide is completely truthful and honest. Key information about product safety and effective use must be included. Absolute honesty about the ingredients, product components, price, and supply chain is required.

2. Never Make Unverified Claims: Influencers must not advertise products by promising that they deliver specific results (such as protection from disease, improved health, or healthier skin) without providing scientific evidence that backs up these claims.

3. Never Exaggerate Product Claims: When an influencer exaggerates the benefits of a product or service, this is the same as making a false claim. The influencer must only promise the customer the level of benefit that can actually be delivered by the product.

4. Never Make Any False Comparisons: Making untruthful, inaccurate, or confusing statements about a competitor's products is not allowed and is considered to be an unscrupulous tactic in influencer marketing.

5. Never Stereotype: Influencer marketing should not feature or promote racial, gender, or other stereotypes and should not sexualise people in order to sell products.

Situational marketing ethics are different. Using situational ethics is a much slipperier slope because it allows the individual or organisation to engage in their own calculations (and justifications) to determine a so-called ethical response. The 'Potter Box' method is a situational tool sometimes used in communication and public relations decision making (Christians et al., 2020). In the Potter Box method, the decision maker is permitted to define a particular situation, identify relevant values and loyalties, and then select a moral principle to apply to the situation. The result is that, faced with the same situation, different managers with different loyalties and perspectives can each decide that very different types of behaviour are 'ethical'.

In general, situational, consequentialist, or utilitarian guidelines would attempt to balance the maximum amount of customer benefits for the most people while also minimising risks. In influencer marketing, this would mean trying to benefit as many people as possible while creating as little harm or negative impact on society as possible. So, for example, a brand manager for a candy manufacturer might calculate that advertising their product on a child influencer's YouTube channel is ethical. Although the product's sole ingredients are sugar, artificial colours, and artificial flavours, the marketer might calculate that its delicious taste brings more joy to young consumers than it does harm to their young bodies. They might point out that selling candy is legal, or that competitors also do it.

As the candy marketing example suggests, there is a 'Wild West' or a 'hardball' culture in marketing today where almost any type of marketing practice can be justified (Laczniak & Murphy, 2006). Marketing students commonly express an attitude that ethical principles are 'flexible' and often depend on circumstances and personal opinions. This anything goes type of moral reasoning is known in philosophy as relativism, and assuming a situational perspective can easily slide into adopting a relativist perspective where nothing is actually immoral or moral, or right or wrong.

Students and practitioners of influencer marketing who consider using situational principles should therefore be aware of two important facts. Firstly, the marketing codes and principles of industry groups and organisations such as the Spanish Advertisers Association and the Incorporated Society of British Advertisers are based on the idea of rule-bound or duty-bound ethical maxims such as labelling paid influencer promotions in certain ways. These codes of ethics tend to frown upon consequentialist ethical formats, which leave too much to the individual manager to interpret. Secondly, many organisations have ethical codes that specify appropriate behaviour in a rule-bound manner.

Situational Ethics in a Post-Truth World

The contemporary media environment is rife with misinformation, disinformation, and mistrust. People in positions of power from Big Government to Big Business regularly misuse the power of media platforms to try to promote messages that favour their perspective and their interests. With so much misinformation in the air, truth seems like yet another endangered species.

In 2016, *Oxford Dictionary* named 'post-truth' their Word of the Year, defining it as 'relating to or denoting circumstances in which objective facts are less influential in shaping public opinion than appeals to emotion and personal belief'. These appeals to emotion and personal belief have certainly shaped, and continue to shape, influencers' relationships with their audiences and the content they use to build it. Even smaller influencers know that by creating controversy and conflict (whether real or fake), or by using sex appeal or fear, they can gain attention and create engagement in an audience, pumping up their numbers. There seems to be little cost to polarising, extreme views, and controversy, and this fact tends to power influencers' strategies of attention-getting in the age of influencers.

POST-TRUTH

Circumstances in which objective facts become irrelevant, or at least less important than personal beliefs and opinions, and in which emotional appeals are used to shape public opinion.

Although some influencers thrive on releasing controversial content that serves as clickbait and leads to skyrocketing engagement, the practice is unethical. In 2017, the gaming vlogger Felix Kjellberg, better known as PewDiePie, featured so-called 'comedy' content that included a pair of dancing men holding up a hand-written sign that read 'Death to All Jews'. While holding such a sign is not technically illegal, it is morally questionable. Kjellberg's reach is vast, with millions of followers, and it includes a devoted alt-right following. With repeated anti-Semitism violations, PewDiePie has earned a reputation in the press as an unethical character. As a result, some companies, including Disney, have cut ties with him but others have not. In case after case, it seems as if influencers are pushing the boundaries of what marketers and society consider ethical. Influencers have fervent audiences who forgive even major ethical breaches. Controversies seem to attract attention and engagement, consequences that are seen as positive. There seem to be new rules at work in the influencer ecosystem where immoral behaviour is being rewarded.

Whether it is David Dobrik's racist discourse, Chris Donelij's homophobic and transphobic mockery, or Xiaxue's body shaming posts, there is no shortage of ethically questionable behaviour among influencers. Logan Paul's filming of a dead body in Japan's Aokigahara 'suicide forest' in 2018 provides another strong example. The clip, in which the popular YouTube star travelled to Japan and joked while showing a man's dead body hanging from a tree, quickly gained over 6 million views and sparked controversy about the unedited, uncensored, and unethical nature of some social media influencer content.

There was a brief storm of controversy that included the YouTube business platform (owned by Google) cutting some commercial ties with Mr Paul. Mr Paul apologised and spoke about the importance of suicide prevention. He explained that he made a mistake by treating suicide and mental illness in a non-serious manner. Some followers unsubscribed; others who had previously unsubscribed came back. In the long run, Mr Paul's popularity does not seem to have suffered and in fact continued to increase after the incident. Influencers, it seems, may not be held to the same ethical standards as journalists or advertisers. Wellman et al. (2020) suggest that instead of being able to lean on professional organisations to inform their behaviours, influencers are often guided by an *'ethics of authenticity'* (68), which means that they try to be true to themselves, their brand, and their audience. Freed from rule-bound ethics, many influencers appear to be charting their own form of situational ethics, dictated by their own personal situations and desires.

The Morality of Non-Human Influencers

Human beings and human society are not the only important ethical actors featured on or affected by influencer content. Even though cats and dogs are some of the most popular non-human influencers on social media (Statista, 2021c), exotic animal species are growing in popularity. Exotic and wild animals such as foxes, otters, toucans, lamas, wildcats, iguanas, and monkeys are often featured as influencers on platforms including Instagram and YouTube.

However, it is important to remember that these are wild animals, not pets. The media industry frequently represents exotic animals as similar to pets, trivialising issues of biodiversity and animal species conservation (Yong, Fam, & Lum, 2011). Social media brought the risk of transforming exotic animals into social media puppets managed by humans as influencer accounts. Turning exotic animals into monetisable social media content has currently become a growing trend in the influencer industry (Mateer, 2021; Urban Paws, 2021). This raises ethical concerns related to taking away exotic animals from their natural habitat and forcing them to adopt a lifestyle that is totally extraneous to their nature. A prominent case is the marketisation of hedgehogs. Online, these spiky creatures gained global attention and managed to capture thousands (and sometimes even millions) of adoring fans, who proudly call themselves 'hedgies'. However, little has been written about the ethical implications of this trend.

MR. POKEE THE HEDGEHOG: THE ETHICS OF EXOTIC ANIMAL INFLUENCERS

Mr Pokee is an African Pygmy, or four-toed, hedgehog influencer (now deceased) who was located in Germany and currently has 1.8 million followers on Instagram. His account is kept alive by his successor, another African Pygmy hedgehog named Herbee. Throughout a life carefully curated on social media, Mr Pokee became a celebrity and gained sponsorships with brands of all kinds, including not only hedgehog pet care products but also Google Home, various phone cases, and Lindt chocolates. Mr Pokee also had his own product line that made money for his owner, which included plushies, magnets, stickers, postcards, a calendar, and t-shirts.

Despite the positive comments, happy emojis, and smiles associated with Mr Pokee's Instagram account, it also spotlights the commercial exploitation of a species whose natural environment is disappearing and which is widely (and probably unreflectively) exploited for humans' excitement. It turns out that hedgehogs are nocturnal and solitary animals who traverse great distances and like to roam, require live insects as food, and African hedgehogs need relatively hot temperatures. Therefore, they are not easy pets to keep, and it is cruel to keep them confined in a small space. If they become sick, it is not easy to find a veterinarian who specialises in exotic animal care – and they are usually expensive (Goertzen, 2012; Hedgehog Welfare Society, 2014). It is illegal to own an African pygmy hedgehog in Canada, as well as in California, Georgia, Hawaii, Pennsylvania, and Washington D.C.

Some authorities contend that hedgehogs are often purchased on impulse because people see them as cute little objects, like toys, on social media.

Once purchased, owners discover that they are not actually easy or even good pets and end up abandoning them in shelters (or worse) (Segraves, 2018).

In response to the ocean of adorable hedgehog content whose market-isation as influencers encourages a distorted perception of reality, Christina Hannigan decided to use social media to raise awareness about 'the non-cute part' of hedgehog influencers. Her site informs people of the many health problems to which these hedgehogs may be prone, including skin diseases, cardiac diseases, and tumours. Hedgehogs also have been known to carry diseases which can affect human health. Equally important is the fact that capturing and keeping a wild animal which likes to roam long distances across the open savannah and grasslands in a small cage is cruel to the animal.

Overall, taking an ethical non-speciesist perspective means that we must view African hedgehogs and other cute-looking exotic animals as beings who are not simply toys created for our enjoyment and amusement, but as wild animals with a right to exist and thrive undisturbed in their natural environment.

REGULATION

#FOLLOWINGTHELAW, BY JON PFEIFFER

Regulating influencers on social media is like enforcing the law in an old western town without a sheriff. There are lots of rules, but rarely is anyone around to enforce them. Reports estimate that over 90% of FTC (Federal Trade Commission) guidelines are violated by social media endorsements.

What are the rules?

Let's start with the 50,000-foot view. Influencers are primarily regulated under Section 5(a) of the FTC Act which prohibits 'unfair or deceptive acts or practices in or affecting commerce'. The FTC has stated that the relationship between an influencer and a brand must be clear and conspicuous – but what does that mean? To answer that question, we have to get into the weeds on disclosures.

The FTC has issued guides and regulations regarding proper online disclosures. These disclosures are required when an influencer has a 'material connection' with the brand. A material connection to the brand includes a personal, family or employment relationship, or a financial relationship such as a brand paying the influencer or giving free or discounted products or services. This includes everything from free meals or t-shirts to six-figure brand deals.

Disclosures made with hashtags must be unambiguous. Saying '#thanks' is polite but doesn't tell people anything about the brand relationship. Influencers must use #sponsored, #ad or #paid even when talking about their own products.

Hashtags should not be buried or hard to find. When a post includes multiple hashtags, readers are likely to skip over them. If an influencer uses multiple hashtags, they should lead with the important disclosures. As the FTC has said, avoid '#HardtoRead #BuriedDisclosures #inStringofHashtags #SkippedByReaders'. Also, disclosures should be placed within the endorsement itself as well as in the caption where viewers can see the disclosure without clicking the 'more' button.

Finally, an influencer should not remove any disclosures with respect to any content at any time, whether during or after the term of the influencer agreement.

The FTC rules are clear and influencers would be wise to follow them. More robust FTC enforcement is coming.

Jon Pfeiffer is a Santa Monica based entertainment lawyer and the host of 'The Creative Influencer' podcast. A significant portion of his practice is devoted to the representation of YouTube, Instagram, and TikTok Influencers. His website is www.pfeifferlaw.com and he can be reached at pfeiffer@pfeifferlaw.com.

Major Regulatory Agencies and What They Govern

Today, everyone who participates, directly or indirectly in creating influencer marketing context is considered to be responsible for their legality. This includes:

- the brand or seller,
- the advertising, public relations, or digital agency,
- the influencers or affiliate marketers,
- web designers or agencies, as well as
- platforms, publishers, and media companies.

So, although the paid posts of the early influencers took place under a context where there were no clear rules and no regulations, the situation has changed dramatically. The major global trade and competition regulators – including the FTC in the United States and the Competition and Markets Authority (CMA) in the United Kingdom – all consider promotional social media influencer posts to be online advertising. Both agencies, the FTC and the CMA, are charged by their governments with enforcing advertising laws. Influencers, their agencies, and the brands and other organisations that use them are governed by the laws and rules of advertising. Among them are important laws that prohibit deceptive acts, such as a person appearing to offer an unbiased testimonial of a product when they actually have a relationship to the product. As well, specific social media platforms such as Instagram and YouTube provide guidelines for businesses and content creators to help regulate influencer marketing. One of the most important elements enforced by platforms is their own norms of decency and of accurate information.

This chapter's opening vignette features the purchase of fake followers and renting a mansion or jet (or it could have been an expensive car) in order to give the impression of a luxurious lifestyle. It is fairly easy to fake it on social media. In 2020, the YouTube influencer Natalia Taylor posted a series of photos on Instagram which showed her enjoying a luxurious vacation at a resort in Bali, Indonesia. But, as she later explained on YouTube, the photos were actually taken at her local Ikea as part of a ruse she staged in order to show people that 'life on the internet isn't always what it seems; especially in this day and age where it's so easy to pretend to be anyone you want to be' (Huddleston, 2021).

Depictions of luxurious lifestyles currently exist in a legal grey area between deception and stagecraft. However, there are strict legal regulations guiding the notion that influencer reviews need to be honest. For example, both the FTC and the CMA assert that influencers cannot talk about experience with a product or service that they have not actually used or experienced. As well, the rules from both agencies emphasise that influencers cannot make claims about a product or service, such as that it can treat a particular health condition, without scientific proof that these claims are factually true. In other words, even if it is the honest opinion of an influencer that a product has miraculous effects, they cannot say this for any brand or product with which they have any kind of relationship. There are also numerous regulations regarding matters such as native advertising, fraudulent influencers, fake followers, problematic content, and vulnerable audiences.

NATIVE ADVERTISING

For regulatory purposes, the FTC defines native advertising as 'content that bears a similarity to the news, feature articles, product reviews, entertainment, and other material that surrounds it online' (Federal Trade Commission, 2022).

FRAUDULENT INFLUENCERS

Fraudulent influencers are those who create social media posts claiming that the content is sponsored by a brand but in reality they have no agreement with the company. They subsequently use these phony deals to secure real contracts with other companies.

FAKE FOLLOWERS

Fake followers are multiple social media accounts created by the same person or group and sold in bundles to increase an influencer's total follower account, which is a metric often used by brands to gauge how much influence a person has and, therefore, how much to pay them.

PROBLEMATIC CONTENT

Content is problematic when it features topic matter that is unsuitable in general or for a particularly sensitive audience. Alcohol, smoking, and nudity are examples of problematic content in sponsored posts, particularly when it comes to concerns about the age of an influencer's audience.

If not properly disclosed, native advertising falls under deceptive, unfair and misleading practices prohibited by the FTC Act. Fraudulent influencers and fake followers deceive both consumers and brands. Problematic content can be regulated by governments. For instance, the Austrian Prohibition Act 1947 makes the dissemination of Nazism-related messages, Holocaust denial lies, and racist hate speech illegal. However, most problematic or sensitive content is regulated by the platforms themselves.

Vulnerable Audiences

Vulnerable audiences such as children or youth should be treated with special care by advertisers using influencer marketing. Advertisers must exercise caution when the products are potentially harmful or addictive, such as with alcohol, cannabis, tobacco, non-nutritional foods like snacks and candy, prescription drugs, or over-the-counter medicines or remedies with strong side effects.

Influencer marketing is becoming a big part of the $1.8 billion industry that markets food and beverages to young people. A 2020 study by New York University professors studied the most popular YouTube videos by child influencers aged 3–14 years old. The study found that, among the 43% of the sampled videos which promoted food or drink, more than 90% of the products shown were unhealthy branded food, drinks, or fast food toys. Fast food was shown the most, followed by candy and soda (NYU News Release, 2020).

Places and cultures may be sensitive or vulnerable as well. Problematic content can include travel- and tourism-related posts. An increasing problem in tourism marketing is called the 'Instagram effect', in which influencer photos of lesser-known destinations drive tourism traffic while, in some cases, destroying the environment or ruining the culture being promoted (Ketcham, 2019).

Social media users are vulnerable because of their difficulty to identify persuasion attempts on platforms. Consumers are increasingly being misled and treated unethically as marketers keep blurring the lines between commercial communications and editorial content. Although many countries have regulations regarding the labelling of advertising, they generally lag behind platform developments that serve advertisers. To avoid consumer confusion and mistrust, the industry must work hard to distinguish between paid advertising, genuinely unbiased consumer reviews, paid reviews, and actual news. Advertisers who use influencer marketing and other forms of marketing should always strive to clearly distinguish between advertising, public relations, and corporate communications, as well as news, editorial content, and entertainment. When an organic social media review is not labelled as any of these things, that should indicate that it is the unbiased opinion of a member of the public with no relationship to the product or brand other than that they are a consumer of it.

Types of Campaign

Certain types of influencer marketing campaigns may be illegal, considered immoral, or subject to strict government and/or platform regulation. Giveaways and sweepstakes are strictly regulated in many states and countries. Lotteries, in which cash or valuable items are awarded, are particularly strictly regulated.

Instagram says that the brand or influencer must make the terms, rules, and requirements for entering the giveaway clear, as shown below.

- The influencer hosting the giveaway must explain all of the eligibility requirements, such as age and where eligible participants must live.

- The audience must know who is running the giveaway.

- The host cannot tag content inaccurately or encourage other people to tag content inaccurately.

- All giveaways on Instagram need to say that they are not sponsored, endorsed, or run by Instagram, and that Instagram has nothing to do with them.

- If the giveaway requires user-made content, it is the responsibility of the host to gain permission from the user to repost or use the image.

Furthermore, some contests, such as sweepstakes, are considered a form of gambling. Some religions believe that entering sweepstakes and other contests is immoral, and holding such contests may offend them. Contests in which you can enter to win a prize also may violate Islamic or Sharia law.

Guidelines on Disclosure

A major issue in influencer marketing is disclosure. In 2022, the organisation 'Truth in Advertising' (or TINA.org) called out the celebrity hip hop producer DJ Khaled for promoting Cîroc vodka to his Instagram audience while simultaneously failing to disclose his relationship with Diageo, Cîroc's parent company (Truth in Advertising, 2022). This follows a 2018 investigation in which TINA.org gathered more than 1,700 Cîroc alcohol ads on Instagram from 50 different social media influencers in which the influencers failed to clearly and conspicuously disclose their material connection to the brand.

Despite blatant disregard for the rules by influencers, there are specific guidelines that various regulatory agencies have released for social media influencers, which are also important for others who operate in the influencer ecosystem to understand. The FTC guidelines are quite explicit about the expectation for disclosure. They state that an influencer must disclose any type of relationship with a brand. If there is a family or personal relationship, this must be disclosed. So, for example, if an influencer talks about a brand without disclosing that they actually own it, or a part of it, this is a breach. Financial relationships do not only include money but can include gifts or small discounts, or even giving to a charity suggested by the influencer. All material connections, even special access to an event or a sweepstakes entry, must be disclosed. Even if the gift or small discount was given without any conditions or strings attached, it still must be disclosed as a relationship. As well, if an employer of a company posts a promotional message about the company or brand, they must disclose their employment relationship. Sony got into big legal trouble when it had its employees post messages about the PlayStation Vita without disclosing their relationship to the company.

Disclosures must be clear and conspicuous – they must be unmissable by the audience. The four Ps of disclosure are the disclosure's prominence, presentation, placement, and proximity. If there is a video, the disclosure must be spoken and shown in the video, not simply in the text on the side of the video. And, according to the FTC, it is not just reviews that count as content. A tag, like, pin, or other way of showing support to a brand is considered an endorsement. And anyone who posts in a way that might affect US consumers is regulated by these laws, regardless of where they live or from where they might be posting.

Other points to consider about disclosures are:

- Disclosures need to be placed so that:
  - they are hard to miss

  - they are in the endorsement message itself

- Disclosures need to be given in simple and clear language:
  - they can be explained using simple terms like advertisement, sponsored, or 'I got this as a free gift'

  - using #ad or #sponsored are acceptable but not necessary accompaniments to the influencer disclosure

  - influencers must avoid using confusing terms like 'Collab' or 'ambassador'

The U.K. CMA guidance includes similar advice about disclosure, namely, that influencers must:

- say when they have been paid, given, or loaned things, or any other form of reward (all of which is considered 'payment')

- be clear about their relationships to a brand or business (including explaining why there are discount codes, competitions, giveaways, or products on your page)

- include in their disclosures past relationships as well, as long as they took place within a reasonable period of time (guidelines suggest within the last year)

- not be misleading by seeming to be a regular consumer when acting for their own business purposes or on behalf of a business or brand.

Truth in advertising principles dictate that influencers who post about a related product or service must be truthful, not misleading or deceptive, and must provide adequate substantiation for every claim. Despite clear regulations on disclosure and the application of truth in advertising laws to influencer marketing, influencers still work in a 'grey area' between the public and the private, between personal and protected 'free speech' and commercial speech. The precise lines between these important matters are not clear. As a result, the area of influencer marketing is still not precisely understood by governments or industry and many precedents are still being set. It is important for marketers and others working in this area to realise that there are few rules about content. The influencer space is currently much less regulated than other spheres of media and advertising, and the regulations much more loosely and unevenly enforced than in traditional media. The global sphere of influence of influencers and creators and different national approaches towards regulation further complicate things. However, the rules of marketing ethics offered in this chapter should provide some strong guidance about what the research scientist or practitioner should understand and how they should approach questions of ethical marketing practice.

WHAT INFLUENCERS NEED TO KNOW ABOUT THE FTC IN THE UNITED STATES, BY ROBERT FREUND

Influencers should be aware of the legal risks and best practices associated with promoting products on social media. The FTC views influencer endorsements as advertisements, and as such, those endorsements must follow the FTC's advertising guidelines. With the FTC poised to update its Guides Concerning the Use of Endorsements and Testimonials in Advertising, which are enforced via the FTC Act and apply to all advertising targeting US-based audiences, and with the new FTC regime taking an aggressive stance against deceptive online marketing practices, it is more important than ever for influencers to understand the rules and potential pitfalls. The FTC Act requires that all claims that brands make must be truthful, not misleading, and substantiated. That goes not just for claims that a brand makes directly but also any claims made by influencers as part of a brand's campaigns. Therefore, everything that an influencer says about a brand as part of a campaign, whether in a feed post, story, tweet, video, or livestream, must also be truthful, not misleading, and substantiated. Otherwise, both the influencer and the brand are potentially liable for violating the law. Additionally, the FTC Act requires disclosure of any 'material connection' (i.e., a family, employment, financial, or personal relationship) between the influencer and the brand and that the disclosures must be 'clear and conspicuous'. Understanding the law is important for influencers because it can help them limit their own risk of liability, help protect their brand partners, and build trust with their audience.

Robert Freund is an experienced advertising attorney and advisor based in Los Angeles. He focuses his practice on e-commerce and social media marketing issues. He posts about legal issues in marketing on Instagram at @robertfreundlaw.

GOVERNMENT CENSORSHIP OF USERS AND CONTENT

The Chinese influencer industry is massive, rapidly expanding, and lucrative. China's media regulators issued new rules governing the hosts of livestreamed programming in 2022. Many social media influencers in China use livestreaming apps, and these livestreaming e-commerce and entertainment personalities have become an important part of Chinese people's online shopping experiences. Regulators now govern livestreaming content using standards similar to those used for traditional media hosts.

In China, influencer content is increasingly being treated as mass media content in order to regulate political speech. The guidelines emphasise that livestream hosts must uphold correct political and social values, create and promote 'positive' stories, and provide their audiences with a 'wholesome' experience. Anything that caters to fandom culture or promotes the love of money was among the topics that the regulations sought to discourage. Users who break these rules may be placed on a blacklist and permanently barred from streaming. The rules apply to virtual hosts as well as the human voices behind virtual hosts (Zhou, 2022). To be an activist influencer in China has serious consequences that could lead to being banned from platforms or even worse.

Social media platforms are bellwethers for the ongoing challenges to internet freedom transpiring around the world today. In mid-2022, the Indian government gave the Twitter platform an ultimatum commanding it to remove 39 accounts and content. Twitter responded by saying that it will take the Indian government to court. Big technology companies who operate globally, such as Twitter and Facebook, are major bulwarks standing against government censorship in various nations (Elliott, 2022).

ACTIVIST INFLUENCERS AND INFLUENCER ACTIVISTS

The worlds of activists and influencers have been overlapping for some time. During COVID-19, numerous global influencers were recruited by public health agencies to help spread information and messages. This book contains numerous examples of influencers who are using their social media presences to try to influence the world for the better. Some influencers are even paid for these efforts and become, in effect, a type of compensated lobbyist. An American advertising company called Urban Legend pairs social media influencers with clients who wish to promote political agendas and ideas. For example, one campaign paid influencers to promote a petition advocating climate change legislation. Another paid influencer activist example was a physical therapist who works with elderly clients. She tried to get her 3,900 Instagram followers to sign a petition demanding that the government pass paid medical leave legislation. It is noteworthy that the post of this influencer, and some of the others paid by Urban Legend, did not disclose their affiliation and sponsorship (Wofford, 2022).

Although this chapter about ethics tends to emphasise influencers bending or breaking the rules of good behaviour, we felt that it was important to also highlight the fact that there are activist influencers who are seeking to educate their audiences about important social causes and to emphasise moral and ethical behaviours – even when they are not being paid by an agency to do so! One such influencer is Malala Yousafzai, whose story we present in a vignette in this chapter.

ACTIVIST INFLUENCER

Activist influencers are social change agents who usually have established their prior credibility as protesters and organisers, and who then utilise social media as an important part of their education, mobilisation, and protest efforts.

MALALA YOUSAFZAI AS AN ACTIVIST INFLUENCER

Malala Yousafzai is an activist and a social media influencer in the sphere of politics and human rights. She captured the global media's attention on issues such as women rights, childhood education, violence, and conflict resolution in Pakistan. She was born in Swat Valley in Pakistan in 1997. When the Islamic Taliban movement took control of the valley in 2008, girls' schools were burned down. Malala kept a diary of the events, which was published in 2009 by BBC Urdu. In her diary, she spoke out against the Taliban regime. An American documentary film made Malala internationally famous. It was not long before the Taliban threatened her life. In 2012, Malala was shot in the head on a school bus by a Taliban gunman. She survived but had to flee to England and lives in exile there because a fatwa was issued against her. In 2013, TIME magazine named Malala one of 'The 100 Most Influential People in the World'. On her 16th birthday, she spoke at the United Nations. In her speech Malala called for the equal right to education for girls all over the world and became a symbol of this cause. Malala was awarded the Nobel Peace Prize in 2014 for her fight for the right of every child to receive an education (Nobelprize.org, 2014).

Malala's activity on social media spans all the major platforms. She has followers on Instagram and TikTok. With her Malala Fund profile, she has followers on

Twitter and on YouTube. She is active on social media to spread messages related to peace, women rights, and childhood education. She does not use social media only as a megaphone for her activism, but actively utilises the platforms to create, collect, and disseminate purpose-driven, meaningful content through which to educate, encourage, and empower young women to fight for their rights. She catalyses the collective energy of hope and social justice that circulates in the social web and uses it to encourage change. Because of this active use of social media platforms, she is also an influencer beyond being an activist.

Malala's communication approach as an influencer tends to be institutional, coherent, and firm. She does not partner with brands or publish any sponsored content on her profiles. However, on her Instagram, she published stories in which she asked students around the world to share how they were spending their time at home during the COVID-19 period, and she offered them advice. On Instagram, TikTok, and YouTube, she devotes significant space to recognising brave women around the world who fight for their rights. She collects and spreads their photos and stories of their education and achievements to provide concrete examples of what strength, determination, and courage can do that may inspire other women to do the same. She uses the power of social media to craft a space of collective memory that moves young women to build their own future.

INFLUENCER ACTIVIST

Social media influencer or creator who uses their content and/or access to audiences to spread purpose-driven messages, sometimes in collaboration with brands or organisations.

The flip-side of activist influencers are influencer activists who use the power of their online presence, personal brands, and dedicated audiences to initiate or support social change efforts. Whether they advocate for veganism, body positivity, sustainable fashion, or LGBTQ+ rights, these promoted values are often crucial elements of their influencer brands. Their activism can include the spreading of paid or unpaid messages from brands or organisations that align with the causes they seek to promote. Influencer activists occur across the political spectrum; for example, so-called 'gunfluencers' promote Second Amendment rights in the US. Influencer activism also applies to non-human influencers.

MONTY THE CAT INFLUENCER ACTIVIST

Rescued from a shelter in Copenhagen, Monty is a cat who was born without a nasal bridge but while this 'chromosomal abnormality' causes him to sneeze a lot, he can breathe normally. Today, Monty is a global spokescat and cat influencer activist with over half a million followers on Instagram, promoting shelter animal adoption and welfare globally, both on Instagram and TikTok, together with his cat sister Molly.

Monty's Instagram (@monty_happiness) educates people about cat disabilities and advocates for other pathological conditions that are common in cats, like diabetes, which he has as well. Thanks to his engagement to improve ill and disabled cats' life conditions, Monty has become the ambassador of 'The Purrington Post' and one of the protagonists of the children's game 'Catastrophe'. Moreover, he won the Animal Welfare Award in 2018.

Besides raising global awareness of the beauty and qualities of 'cat diversity', Monty and his family also sell Monty's own brand of merchandise. For each purchase, a percentage is donated to support the cause of helping animals in need. Consistent with his ambassadorial profile, Monty's brand collaborations are very few and related to the pet care market or to the non-profit world. One of his collaborations is with Enjoy Bloom, a company that launched an app to help people who suffer from anxiety. Monty promoted the app with a post on his Instagram page, adding that the profits would go to a non-profit organisation advocating for self-acceptance and inclusivity.

TRENDS AND FUTURE DIRECTIONS IN ETHICS AND REGULATION

Many changes for the influencer marketing industry are on the horizon which will ramify through the ecosystem. Data privacy regulation is an up-and-coming concern for influencers and influencer marketers. Regulators around the world are already very concerned with who owns the data in things such as influencers' mailing lists, what happens to that data, and how the privacy and the rights of the names of people on such lists is being protected. In terms of the European Union's General Data Protection Regulation (GDPR), which governs influencer activity that might impact citizens of the European Union, there are data security implications for influencers who run contests or who sell products (Brown, 2018). In particular, the following regulations are important:

- Influencers must ensure that followers want to be on their mailing list and must remove them immediately if they ask not to be contacted.

- Influencers must never sell or share their email lists.

- If an influencer hosts a giveaway and receives personal information as part of the entry, participants must have a clear opt-in option. If users later ask for their information to be removed from the database, it must be removed.

Social media platforms are increasingly being held under a magnifying lens, and the scrutiny is likely to extend to the influencer marketing industry itself. The flows of data between platforms such as TikTok and national governments, such as the Chinese government, are being questioned. There are also likely going to be more controversies among the wild and wacky world of influencers. The extreme behaviours are likely to inspire more discussion about the responsibility of social media platforms for enforcing norms of decency on the content that is being posted. The social media ecosystem is moving away from an 'anything goes/free speech' situation to one in which influencer content is being examined more closely, where more restrictive regulations about that content are made and enforced.

The global trends today point towards more regulation. Especially after its boom during the COVID-19 pandemic, influencer marketing is gaining more attention from regulators than ever before. Non-disclosure has become a more serious concern. Florida-based Teami teas, a weight loss and detox tea, was promoted using a massive social media influencer campaign including Cardi B, Jordin Sparks, Adrienne Bailon, Darnell Nicole, Brittany Renner, and others (Fair, 2020). One of the main problems was that the influencers' disclosure was not clear and conspicuous. The audience did not even see the disclosure until the consumer clicked the 'more' button. The company was responsible for monitoring that its influencers did their disclosure properly. Another was deceptive health claims such as that the teas could cause rapid and substantial weight loss, fight cancerous cells, and unclog arteries. As a result, the FTC ruled a $15.2 million judgement against the company. More of these types of cases are very likely in the near future.

Education is likely to prove extremely important. Brands need to both train and monitor the influencers they work with, as well as the other agencies and organisations that might be involved. Why? Because these companies are responsible for monitoring the actions of the individuals they employ as advertisers. As this multibillion-dollar industry continues to grow, creative plaintiffs' lawyers have already begun testing issues around influencer marketing. Brands may begin litigating against others brands which breach regulations. Agencies such as the FTC in the United States regularly update their regulations, and the next refresh of their influencer marketing guides is likely just around the corner. Fraudulent influencers, fake accounts, fake followers, fake reviews, and problematic content are major concerns that are likely to be targeted by regulators. In 2019, the FTC halted the operations of two companies that sold fake followers and fake reviews, establishing that these behaviours are illegal. Most experts suggest that the best strategy is to be aware of the relevant regulations and to prepare for a more heavily regulated and litigious future. The rules of marketing ethics are increasingly important because more enforcement of influencer marketing is likely just around the corner.

CHAPTER SUMMARY

By overviewing core principles and offering numerous examples and illustrations, this chapter informed readers about the ethical and regulatory basis of the influencer marketing industry.

Influencer marketing is an arm of the advertising industry that systematically employs social media content for sales outreach to members of society in pursuit of exchange transactions. As a form of commercial speech, influencer marketing is governed by various national agencies such as the FTC and CMA, which regulate all advertising. Because all marketing decisions have ethical dimensions, decisions about influencer marketing also need to be governed by the principles of marketing ethics that guide moral practice in this field. Rule-bound and situational principles are the major approaches to ethical marketing decision-making and they also apply to influencer marketing. Most marketing ethics codes are governed by strict rules rather than moral principles that are left open to specific contexts and the idiosyncrasies of individual interpretation. In influencer marketing, clear and conspicuous disclosures, truthful and supportable claims, and avoiding stereotyping are important moral and ethical duties. Although the influencer ecosystem is a complex environment and sometimes seems to possess a Wild West and post-truth mentality, ethics and regulation are simultaneously assuming increasingly important roles. The FTC in the United States, the CMA in the United Kingdom, and the GDPR rules in the EU enforce truthful advertising, disclosure, and data privacy regulations. Regulations also govern a growing list of influencer-related areas such as native advertising, fraudulent influencers, fake followers, problematic content, and vulnerable audiences, and these regulations are increasing as scrutiny of the industry grows. Some influencers are using their clout to try to enact positive social change and activism while activists increasingly mimic influencers to spread their messages. In this vein, influencers, agencies, and influencer marketers can play an important role in society by contributing to individual human and collective social betterment, and they may also communicate to the benefit or, at minimum, non-harm of non-human animals and the planetary ecosystem.

EXERCISES AND QUESTIONS

Exercises

1. Read the *Lonelygirl15* vignette in this chapter, including the Davis (2006) article. What lessons do marketers still need to learn from this story?

2. Please come up with an example from the world of influencer marketing regarding a duty-based approach to ethics. Now, devise an example of a situational approach to ethics. Which approach do you prefer? Why?

3. Provide an example of a recent controversy that involved influencers. What happened? Do ethics matter for influencers, or not?

Questions

1. Can you think of an example of a case where an influencer provides a testimonial for a product, but that testimonial is not subject to advertising regulation?

2. Can you differentiate between what is ethical in marketing, and what is legal? Are they always the same?

3. What is your own personal code of ethics? Where does it come from in your life (e.g., from your faith or your upbringing)?

4. This chapter emphasises that non-human living beings and the planetary ecosystem should also be considered in marketing decisions. Do you agree, or do you think that this is taking things too far?

ANNOTATED READINGS

Goanta, C., & Ranchordás, S. (Eds.). (2020). *The regulation of social media influencers.* Cheltenham: Edward Elgar Publishing.

Integrating insights from law, economics, ethics and communication science, this book highlights how public bodies, social media companies, brands and citizens relate to the influencer industry.

Jackson, S. J., Bailey, M., & Welles, B. F. (2020). # *HashtagActivism: Networks of race and gender justice.* Boston, MA: MIT Press.

The book reveals how contemporary forces of online activism, digital storytelling and strategy-building set the stage for hashtags such as #MeToo and #BlackLivesMatter.

Roberts, C., & Black, J. (2021). *Doing ethics in media: Theories and practical applications* (2nd ed.). London: Routledge.

This book offers an accessible and comprehensive guide to contemporary media ethics which is informed by principles of moral philosophy.

9

THE BUSINESS OF INFLUENCE

CHAPTER OVERVIEW AND OBJECTIVES

This chapter discusses influencer marketing as a type of strategic communication that pursues campaign-based goals, spans across various media types, and involves influencers and creators as collaborators. It stresses influencer marketing's embeddedness in broader organisational communication and marketing efforts and therefore its need for alignment. The picture it paints of influencer marketing is one that involves flexibility, adaptability, co-creation and, thus, a larger than usual degree of creative freedom. However, it also emphasises the need for careful planning and management to harness the benefits of influencer and creator collaborations. The chapter establishes campaigns as the focal point of influencer marketing and dissects the campaign process. It establishes four phases: planning, partnering, execution, and evaluation. Continuing with the focus on strategic elements of influencer marketing, it analyses the steps involved in the first phase of the process, namely the planning of influencer marketing campaigns.

PROVOCATION: Close to 86% of U.S. marketers will tap influencers for campaigns by 2025 (eMarketer, 2022). About 90% of brands that have tried influencer marketing believe it to be effective (Influencer Marketing Hub, 2022b). Major brands are planning to increase their influencer marketing (Digital Marketing Institute, 2021).

KEYWORDS: strategic communication, co-creation, campaign, target audience, whitelisting

VIBE ISRAEL AND THE DOGGIE VACAY CAMPAIGN

Joanna Landau is a pioneer in the influencer marketing space who stumbled into it in 2010 out of necessity. As the founder and CEO of Vibe Israel, a non-profit organisation that uses country branding strategies to positively influence the way people think and feel about Israel, she had to find ways to reach as much of her millennial target audience with as little money as possible. She found the answer in organising free, themed trips to Israel for small groups of bloggers. The first trip took place in 2011. Vibe Israel has since hosted over 250 social media personalities, from early mommy bloggers to contemporary food influencers. While the initial efforts were characterised by a lot of trial and error, Vibe Israel has since become very strategic in its approach. This includes the careful selection of influencers for the trips, putting together itineraries that elicit 'instaworthy' moments, amplifying influencer content using paid advertising, and careful during and post-tour measurement of impact.

Joanna is best known for her 'Doggy Vacay' campaign that brought six instafamous dogs to Israel: Yeyush and Renzo (@yeyush_the_chihuahua), Bruce Wayne (@ipartywithbrucewayne), Iggy Joey (@iggyjoey), Teddy (@ted_gram), and Remix (@remixthedog). The campaign was announced on International Dog Day in 2017 and started with a competition that asked dogs to post a picture of themselves with sunglasses on Instagram and tag themselves with #doggyvacay. The dog influencers were selected based on the size and geographic location of their following, as well as their ability to travel to Israel. The dogs and their human 'plus ones' got to experience different aspects of life in Israel, from playtime on the beach to dog-friendly culinary delights, such as chicken stock popsicles. Vibe Israel invested $20,000 to promote the influencer posts, made sure that the dogs were followed by 'pup-arazzis' to gain media attention, and produced a video of the best moments that went viral. In total, the campaign reached over 700 million people. Make sure to check out the campaign video on Youtube: https://www.youtube.com/watch?v=s5yzqWZD5h8.

Working with influencers and creators to achieve marketing, public relations, or other business communication goals has become a mainstream approach. The primary reason for its steep growth is that influencer marketing works. Influencers are brilliant social media communicators who have access to highly engaged and trusting target audiences. Shopify (2021) reports that 61% of consumers trust influencer recommendations. Influencers' characteristics and their relationship with their followers allow them to exercise a kind of influence that most marketers can only dream of. Creators, on the other hand, know how to produce content that is especially effective in social media contexts. They have the kind of social media expertise and artistic talent many marketers lack. Further, other forms of marketing and communication have become increasingly less effective because of changes in consumer preferences and behaviours as well as new algorithmic realities promoted by platforms, which make it ever more difficult for marketers/communicators to achieve their goals.

Collaborating with influencers and creators is also more cost-effective than many other forms of marketing and, therefore, more accessible for a wider range of marketers. Last, but not least, influencer marketing is a very versatile tool that can be adapted to many communication needs and contexts. Not only established corporations but also start-ups, governments, not-for-profit organisations, trade associations, consumer movements, religious organisations, etc., can benefit from the help of influencers and creators. In a nutshell, engaging with influencers and creators makes a lot of sense from business and general communication perspectives.

GOVERNMENT-SPONSORED INFLUENCER CAMPAIGNS TO SLOW THE SPREAD OF COVID-19

Before the Coronavirus pandemic, many governments were reluctant to try influencer marketing. However, when the need arose to communicate with often hard-to-reach audiences quickly and effectively, many countries realised that their traditional communication approaches were hopelessly outdated. Several governments around the world turned to influencers for help with spreading health-related messages in timely and cost-effective ways, including Bangladesh, a country with a particularly young population.

Bangladesh's Information & Communications Ministry, together with Los Angeles-based influencer marketing agency Xomad (xomad.com), launched a #CalmCOVID19 campaign in April 2020, encouraging residents to stay home and help flatten the curve to save lives. To achieve the necessary impact, the country partnered with hundreds of nano and micro-influencers in the region to reach Millennial and Gen Z audiences. Posts featured influencers holding up hand-written messages about why, or who, they are choosing to 'stay home for'. The campaign gained over 15 million impressions across Instagram and Facebook in less than two weeks.

The initiative was the inaugural campaign launched through the ICT Ministry's new Influencer Advisory Council of 5,000 pre-vetted influencers, which is funded by Bangladesh-based National Bank Limited. The country's strategic investment in influencer relations points to its desire to work with influencers on a variety of social marketing campaigns in the future.

Chapter 1 defines influencer marketing as a more short-to-medium term, campaign-based, and tactical way of collaborating with influencers and creators. However, it is still strategic in terms of its pursuit of campaign goals and in relation to its potential contributions to communication, marketing, or overall organisational strategy. Also, it often serves as the first step in developing an influencer relations strategy.

THE STRATEGIC ROLE OF INFLUENCER MARKETING

STRATEGIC COMMUNICATION

Strategic communication is a term used to describe the communication principles, strategies, and initiatives used to further an organisation's goals, mission, or values.

Influencer marketing can take on many forms and involve many different activities. To ensure that these activities are selected in a strategic fashion, influencer marketing activities should be embedded in, informed by, and aligned with the wider marketing and strategic communication efforts of the organisation. Imagine opening a Russian nested doll. Influencer marketing is the little doll in the middle that sits within the somewhat bigger doll of social media marketing, which sits within digital marketing, which sits within marketing, which, finally, is contained within the biggest doll, namely the overall organisational strategy. If influencer marketing is not aligned with the rest, it will at best be ineffective and at worst undermine other strategic efforts. If influencer marketing fits within the other components, it can significantly contribute to the organisation's success.

Enke and Borchers (2019) identify influencers and creators as important organisational stakeholders and conceptualise influencer marketing and relations as forms of carefully managed strategic communication that address issues the organisation has identified as 'strategically substantial'. From a strategic communication perspective, influencer marketing can span across all media types, from paid and earned to shared and owned media (see the PESO model and its discussion in Chapter 3). Consequently, influencer marketing could be the responsibility of multiple organisational units.

Influencer advertising clearly falls into the category of paid media and is therefore usually handled by the media team or the brand's advertising agency. Influencer marketing, however, requires different approaches, skills, and dedicated budgets. Possible 'homes' within the organisation are the public relations team, the content or creative team, the social media team, or the performance marketing/ digital marketing team. The social media team is good at understanding social media culture and affordances, the content or creative team understands content, the public relations team knows how to control messages and build relations, but the marketing team has expertise related to running and measuring campaigns, distributing products to influencers, co-creating products with influencers, and might have a bigger budget. If a particular unit takes on influencer marketing, it might not be able to fully take advantage of all the opportunities influencer marketing provides, from content creation to audience reach and engagement, to co-creation and relationship-building. If influencer marketing is divided across functional units where everyone is in charge, the danger is that nobody will take responsibility for managing it and paying the expenses. This situation is also very difficult for agencies or other intermediaries trying to work with the brand or organisation. And it is a potential nightmare for the influencers and creators who need consistency, access, and direct contact. Consequently, influencer marketing requires, at a minimum, a dedicated manager. Ideally, it should be handled by a specialised in-house team or department.

CO-CREATION

A collaborative activity between businesses and influencers or creators that requires all parties to be engaged and bring resources to the table.

INFLUENCER CAMPAIGNS

The core element of an influencer marketing initiative is the campaign. Influencer marketing campaigns can involve a wide variety of promotional tactics, spanning across all sorts of media types and channels. In contrast to influencer advertising campaigns, where the brand determines everything and uses the influencer to simply distribute the content, influencer marketing campaigns give influencers a certain level of freedom and control. Influencer marketing campaigns are co-created by the brand and the influencer/creator, meaning that both parties bring resources to the table that they then integrate to achieve a shared goal (McColl-Kennedy & Cheung, 2018). Influencer marketing campaigns can and often do involve more than one influencer and regularly even different types of influencers. They can be of varying length. They can be platform-specific or span across multiple social media platforms and applications. So, what are the common building blocks of influencer marketing campaigns?

> **CAMPAIGN**
>
> A campaign is an organised and strategic effort consisting of a connected series of operations aimed at realising specific communication goals within a specified period of time (Atkin & Rice, 2013).

The Campaign Process

Since campaigns are strategic communication efforts, they involve quite a bit of planning and preparation up-front, need a lot of management to realise them, and require measurement afterwards to ensure that the campaign goals were reached. In this sense, influencer marketing campaigns do not differ from other promotional campaigns. However, within this broad campaign framework, there are some unique steps included in influencer marketing campaigns that require specific knowledge, skills, tools, and approaches. Figure 9.1 illustrates the influencer marketing campaign process, including its various phases (from planning and partnering activities to campaign execution and evaluation) and the multitude of steps that are usually involved.

While Figure 9.1 presents a neat, linear process with distinct elements, the phases within influencer marketing campaigns might overlap, and the steps are often connected and interdependent. For instance, selecting TikTok as the platform on which the campaign will be executed affects the number and types of influencers available for identification and impacts the types of campaigns that can be run because of the specific affordances the platform offers. Similarly, determining that a mega influencer is needed to reach the campaign goals will have serious budget implications and will shape influencer outreach and negotiations as these influencers are usually

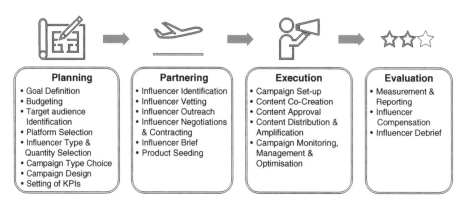

Figure 9.1   Influencer marketing campaign process

represented by agencies and carefully protected by their managers. The same over-laps can also be found for evaluation. Evaluation will happen after the campaign, but it is highly dependent on the goals and key performance indicators (KPIs) set in the planning phase. In addition, evaluation often has to be included in the influencer contract if the influencer needs to provide specific data for it or is compensated based on specific performance measures. Last, evaluation needs to be considered when setting up the campaign (e.g., through the use of influencer-specific coupon codes that allow for attribution of sales to individual influencers and, thus, more precise performance measurement). Thus, while evaluation is the focus of the last phase, it really penetrates all phases of the process.

It is also important to note that many actors can be involved in the different phases of the campaign process (see the various players in the influencer and creator ecosystem discussed in Chapter 4). Brands often work with their regular digital advertising agencies to design the campaigns. Some will hand over most of the process to an influencer marketing agency. Whether an influencer marketing campaign is handled in-house or not is often a matter of skills and (human, monetary, and technological) resources available within the organisation. It also depends on the nature and complexity of the campaign. However, marketers can now access a variety of tools to support and sometimes even automate the various steps. Since co-creation and collaboration are important facets of influencer marketing, many in-house influencer marketers prefer to work directly with influencers and creators to establish trust and build relationships.

INFLUENCER MARKETING TOOLS

Just like other areas of marketing, influencer marketing is experiencing a tremendous growth in the availability of marketing technology, a term which is also shortened simply to MarTech. MarTech is essential for digital types of marketing but has become increasingly indispensable for general marketing as well. MarTech helps marketers achieve their strategic goals more effectively. Digital marketing guru, book author, and B2B influencer Neal Schaffer main-tains an extensive list of tools that can help communicators manage their influencer marketing campaigns. The regularly updated list is available at https://nealschaffer.com/influencer-marketing-tools/. The types of tools included range from social listening tools, influencer discovery and outreach tools, to influencer marketplaces and other campaign management tools. Other market-ing bloggers, for instance Tom Pick, maintain similar lists (https://webbiquity. com/cool-web-tools/the-28-best-influencer-marketing-tools/) that demonstrate the diversity and fast-developing nature of MarTech in the influencer marketing space. You might also want to have a look at the list compiled by Referral Rock (https://referralrock.com/blog/influencer-marketing-software/).

Within an organisation, influencer marketing campaigns can involve several different functional areas that need to work together to realise the campaign. For example, an organisation's legal unit might need to get involved in the contracting phase of a campaign and the accounting department will be needed to handle the often-complex influencer compensation schemes deployed for the campaign. If the campaign involves sending products to influencers, the fulfilment department needs to be on board and the logistics to ship products to hundreds of nano-influencers at reasonable cost and in a timely manner need to be set up. If the campaign involves the development of a personalised product line for the influencer, the product development unit is needed. Also, campaigns often call for the set-up of campaign-specific landing pages, which might require the help of IT services. If the campaign includes an influencer event to which journalists should be invited, then public relations should be consulted. These are just a few examples, but they make it very clear that (1) influencer marketing campaigns require organisational buy-in across various functions, and (2) even if the campaign is outsourced to an influencer marketing agency, there is still active input required from the organisation.

In line with the strategic orientation of this chapter, the only campaign process phase that will be discussed here is the planning phase. The more operational phases (partnering, execution, and evaluation) will be dealt with in subsequent chapters.

Campaign Planning

Planning sets the strategic foundations for campaigns and links them to tactics. Santiago and Castelo (2020) stress the importance of this phase by pointing out that it fundamentally shapes all campaign-related decisions. Planning an influencer or creator campaign thus involves the development of a comprehensive and clear communication strategy. According to Borchers and Enke (2021), a communication strategy involves the setting of communication goals, determining the audience, designing the message, deciding on the positioning, and selecting appropriate media. This is done within a certain budgetary limit.

At this general strategic level, an influencer marketing campaign planning looks just like any conventional communication campaign planning process. It is at the tactical level that influencer marketing provides options that are not typically available for other forms of social media marketing and requires considerations that do not apply to other types of campaigns. Influencer marketing campaigns can be embedded in larger campaigns but demand separate planning because of these specific considerations. Further, Borchers and Enke (2021) report that the co-creation element of influencer marketing can already start in the planning phase if influencers are invited to help select the type of campaign or assist in shaping the overall campaign message. This is more likely to be the case in the context of an influencer relations strategy, where the partnership with the influencer is already established.

Goal Definition

Many influencer marketing campaigns are doomed from the very beginning because they fail to set appropriate goals. If the organisation does not know what it wants to get out of the campaign, it cannot clearly communicate its wants and needs to the influencer(s) involved in the campaign. It can also not evaluate in the end whether a campaign was successful or not. A lot of communicators feel that they should try influencer marketing because everybody else is doing it but lack an understanding about how it could actually benefit their organisation. They sometimes forget about the collaborative nature of influencer marketing. And they often fail to consider the benefits they need to deliver for the influencers and creators to spark their interest in working with the organisation. Thus, before goals can be set, an understanding of the nature and needs of influencers and creators and an appreciation of the characteristics and potential benefits of influencer marketing are necessary.

Types of Goals

The potential benefits of influencer marketing directly translate into the goals an organisation can select for its campaign. The things that influencers and creators can do for marketers/communicators, and therefore the goals influencer marketing campaigns can pursue, fall into four big categories: (1) awareness, (2) conversion, (3) content creation, and (4) insights (Figure 9.2). These goals clearly

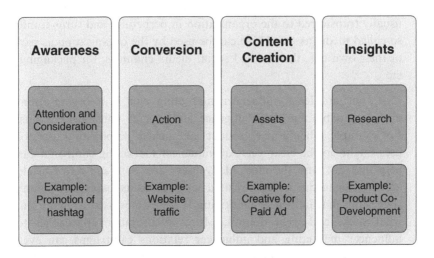

Figure 9.2 Categories of influencer marketing campaign goals

distinguish influencer marketing from influencer advertising, which instead focuses on simple content distribution.

1. Awareness means that influencers can spread the word about brands, specific products, campaigns (including the hashtags designed for them), or events. They can explain products and create positive associations with brands. Awareness goals are especially important for new product launches or for rebranding efforts. They are critical for start-ups and smaller brands who need to get their names out, or for companies who would like to enter new markets.

2. Conversion goals pertain to specific actions the influencer encourages. The most prominent example is the driving of purchase actions, but conversion goals also include actions like following the brand's social media account, downloading an app, visiting a website, signing up for a newsletter or product club, or engaging with a particular piece of content. Conversion goals therefore apply across the marketing funnel.

3. Content creation-related goals can relate to content produced by the influencer/creator themselves or to consumer-generated content. In comparison to other goals, where content is just the means to an end, content creation-focused campaigns see content creation as the end goal. The specific goal here is to obtain either high quality or high quantities of content at much lower cost than if the organisation had to produce it. The nature of the content is also special in that it is likely more engaging and accessible than content produced by brands. The ownership over the content created as part of these campaigns is usually transferred to the organisation in perpetuity and turns it into so-called media assets. These can be used by the organisation as part of their own ads, their owned social media channels, for packaging, etc.

4. Last, but not least, influencer marketing can help organisations obtain valuable market intelligence and specific consumer insights. For example, when a new product is launched, its potential users or uses might not be clear yet. An influencer marketing campaign can help find out who the most likely users are. Santiago and Castelo (2020) refer to this insights-related set of goals as 'experimentation', suggesting that influencer marketing is sometimes used to figure out what sticks and what doesn't. More collaborative approaches to influencer marketing and influencer relations campaigns can even include product co-development with the influencers as their goal.

CONTENT ASSET

'A content asset is any piece of content – for example, a blog post, a white paper, or a video – that a business deploys in service of a greater marketing goal. Content assets have the most value when they are created and used strategically, after carefully considering the content's audience, purpose, and goals' (Tendo.com, 2022). In the context of influencer marketing, content assets are created by influencers, creators, or regular consumers. Brands need to negotiate and often pay for the right to use these contents.

Besides the four main categories of influencer marketing goals, the professional literature (e.g., Russell, 2020) often mentions two additional benefits and therefore potential goals. We refer to them as auxiliary goals because they are usually combined with other goals. The first one is search engine optimisation. Influencers creating backlinks from their blogs or websites to the brand website (especially when they have large followings) can help organisations improve their search engine ranking. Being able to publish fresh and engaging contents on the brand website with the help of creators or through consumer-generated content creation campaigns can also help please the search engines.

The second auxiliary goal is reputation management. Having influencers produce considerable and very visible amounts of positive contents about an organisation and/or its products/services can help dilute negative reputations or strengthen positive ones (Ewing & Lambert, 2019). Influencer relations can also aim at empowering influencers as advocates who will likely step in and defend the organisation during a reputational crisis. The role of influencers in crisis communication is certainly growing and should receive more attention (Femenia-Serra, Gretzel, & Alzua-Sorzabal, 2022). The same is true for the role of influencers in corporate social responsibility, especially with influencers increasingly supporting particular causes, from body positivity to sustainability.

The initial step in the campaign planning process should also consider formulating desired benefits for influencers and creators to inform subsequent steps like campaign design and influencer outreach. This step underlines the collaborative nature of influencer marketing and is especially important for campaigns within influencer relations initiatives. Influencer- and creator-related goals could involve creating opportunities for influencers and creators to learn about the brand, to grow their audiences, to offer special experiences or unique information to their audiences, to develop their skills, to work with professionals (e.g., talent coaches or media experts), or to access organisational resources.

Goal Characteristics

All campaigns require SMART goals, where SMART stands for specific, measurable, attainable, relevant, and time-bound:

- Specificity is an important characteristic because it helps determine the necessary elements of the campaign. When a campaign goal simply states that it seeks to increase brand awareness, it is not really clear what this means and how it should be achieved. A specific goal would refer to an increase in brand mentions or brand recall instead.

- Measurability is an essential dimension for determining the success of the campaign but also for understanding what investments and tactics are necessary. Driving online sales could mean anything. However, if the goal is to sell 1 million units of a newly introduced product, it becomes clear that a major effort is needed that will likely require the help of influencers with a considerable audience. Measurable means not just numeric but also trackable or based on data that can be obtained without occurring considerable cost.

- Attainability derives from specificity and measurability. Influencer marketing is effective, but it cannot perform miracles. Goals need to be realistic and set at a level that is attainable given the nature of the organisation (e.g., its market share), its products/services, and its resources.

- Relevance is often forgotten when some goals, like post engagement, can be easily achieved. For example, when an influencer posts about a brand, their followers might like the post in solidarity with them or respond in the form of encouraging comments. These comments can be simple emojis or influencer-related statements like 'you are so amazing'. Is this kind of engagement really relevant for a brand that wants people to attend their event or try their latest flavour of kombucha? It can also be tempting to try to kill as many birds as possible with one stone and just list all sorts of possible goals. This will dilute the campaign and will make it very difficult to determine the most relevant tactics.

- Time boundedness sets the parameters for when the measurement should take place. Whatever campaign goal(s) are formulated, it needs to be clear by when they should have been achieved to allow for their measurement. An example of a time-bound goal would be to state that a certain number of brand mentions should be achieved within two months of the start of the campaign. This is especially important when the compensation of the influencer is linked to goal achievement.

It also needs to be clear who will be responsible for achieving the goals. Will the execution of the campaign lie completely in the hands of an influencer, or will the brand contribute important resources, for example, paid advertising spend to amplify the influencer messages? Achievability is linked to investment and, thus, it depends on the budget that is put behind the campaign. A lot of things are achievable when resources are unlimited. This suggests that goal setting and budgeting are intimately linked.

Budgeting

Some influencer marketers need to operate within the overall social media marketing or general marketing budgets and will need to justify the allocation of resources to influencer marketing. Others will have a specific pot of money dedicated to influencer marketing and need to carve out a campaign's budget from that amount. In fact, the number of marketing teams with dedicated influencer marketing budgets is increasing (Levin, 2020). Budgeting might not be the most exciting part of influencer marketing, but it is certainly one of the most important. In their study of influencer marketing professionals, Santiago and Castelo (2020) found that determining the budget was one of the most prominent concerns during the campaign planning process.

Budgeting can be as easy as dividing the available influencer marketing budget by the number of campaigns needed/desired. However, even then there need to be allocations within that budget to different cost categories. An influencer marketing campaign budget is more complex and sometimes more difficult to derive than budgets for other marketing campaigns. One of the reasons is that influencer rates can vary considerably and the actual cost of engaging an influencer will be unknown until the negotiations are completed. General aspects that affect the cost of an influencer are the size of their following, the topic area they are in, the type of audience they can reach, their engagement rate, the brands they have already worked with, and the platform on which they engage with their audience. Cost is also a matter of the length of engagement needed for the campaign, the type of content needed (and on which platforms), the level of exclusivity desired (this means the influencer will not be able to work with similar brands for the duration of the campaign), ownership over the content produced by the influencer, and the terms of payment offered. Influencers might charge more for brands they do not know. Some influencer marketing tools offer price calculators to obtain a general price range of what a particular influencer might charge (e.g., HypeAuditor or Inzpire.me). On influencer marketplace platforms, influencers might provide more specific information on their pricing.

Table 9.1 lists categories of factors that influencer marketing campaign budgets should consider. Which factors apply depends very much on the type of

Table 9.1 Budget categories for influencer marketing campaigns

Budget category	Consideration factors
Influencer compensation – monetary	Number of influencers Type of influencer Length of engagement Type of engagement (exclusivity; one-off vs. longer-term) Type of content
Influencer compensation – non-monetary	Cost of product/service (e.g., club membership) or merchandise Cost of shipping Cost of hosting influencers (especially if VIP experience)
Production cost	Location rental, travel cost, and staging cost Photographer/filming crew and equipment (e.g., drones), if applicable Cost of giveaways (most notably the prizes)
Legal cost	Preparation of influencer contracts and non-disclosure agreements Compliance fees (giveaways, disclosure, etc.)
Media cost	Landing pages, KPI tracking set up, QR codes Advertising cost for paid media components
Campaign support	Influencer marketing tools if in-house Labour cost if in-house (e.g., events team and influencer outreach) Service/subscription fees for agencies

campaign the organisation would like to run. Some of the categories can require a substantial budget. For example, when Hamilton Island in Australia held its 'Ultimate Instameet' in 2012 (Marketing Magazine, 2013), it organised helicopter flights for the travel bloggers to allow them to shoot exceptional bird's-eye view content of the tropical island. The categories also depend on how much of the campaign is handled in-house.

Target Audience Identification

Identifying the target audience for an influencer marketing campaign is in principle very similar to selecting target markets for traditional advertising campaigns. This step in the campaign planning process should consider which audience needs to be reached to achieve the campaign goals. The audience could be one that the company already attracts and communicates with. Or, it could be a completely new target group. If necessary or desirable, single campaigns can also be designed to attract multiple audiences. Creating so-called personas (rich descriptions or vignettes) for the ideal target audience member has become a very popular tool for helping marketers understand, and sometimes even visualise, who they would like to speak to through the campaign. The important thing to remember in this context is that descriptions are only useful if they represent targetable characteristics or behaviours. For instance, 'likes to spend time with friends' is a label that cannot be easily targeted, whereas 'yoga enthusiast' can be easily translated into hashtags used, products purchased, websites visited, and influencers followed.

TARGET AUDIENCE

A target audience is a group of individuals who are the intended receivers of a message. The individuals within this group share at least one common trait that can be identified and used to tailor and direct the message.

Consider the unique benefits and challenges for selecting target audiences that influencer marketing campaigns offer. First and foremost, the influencer and the target audience cannot be separated. It is the influencer who brings access to a particular target audience to the table (Campbell & Farrell, 2020). Thus, the target audience for an influencer campaign is a mutual audience that the brand desires and the influencer already engages with. Being able to build on the influencer's knowledge of and rapport with a specific audience is a key benefit of engaging in influencer marketing. This is especially important when marketers want to communicate with a new or very difficult to reach audience. However, it also means that influencer marketing only works for audiences who follow influencers. These tend to be younger and social media savvy audiences (Marketing Charts, 2021b). In addition, some influencers attract very diverse audiences and it is impossible to only reach a specific subsection of their followers through a post. Some influencers have different accounts for different audiences but most lack the ability to target within their following.

Because of the interconnection between influencer and audience, some campaigns select target influencers instead of defining target audiences. For instance, they select influencers based on the topics they post about. This can be an especially fruitful strategy for campaigns with insights-related goals as the campaign results will indicate which influencer followers were most engaged or interested.

Platform Selection

Like target audience identification, platform selection is not completely independent of other strategic factors and therefore might be a step that is subordinate to other steps. For example, various platforms attract different kinds of users. A campaign that seeks to target Gen Z should carefully consider whether Facebook is really the ideal platform to use. Also, some platforms are not available to users in all countries. Campaigns might need to consider additional platform characteristics that might impact their ability to be successfully implemented. As discussed earlier in the book, social media platforms have specific affordances. Thus, platform selection can also depend on the campaign goals and the type of campaign needed. For example, some platforms are much better for sales conversion campaigns because they allow for easy integration of links or in-app purchasing. While Twitter might be a great platform to reach politically active, middle-aged Americans, the type of content a Twitter campaign can involve and the opportunities for driving conversion are rather limited compared to other platforms.

Platforms further differ in terms of which influencers are active on them. Some influencers have a presence across several platforms but might attract different audiences or achieve different engagement rates on specific platforms. If a particular platform is needed to run the campaign (because of the type of content needed or the type of audience targeted), this might limit the number of influencers who could be involved. For example, the number of Twitch influencers is considerably lower than the number of Instagram influencers. Platforms also differ in regards to the measurement tools and insights they offer to marketers. Weibo, for instance, provides its business account holders with lots of data not typically available, although other platforms seem to be catching up quickly.

In summary, campaigns can be platform-specific or involve multiple platforms. The selection of the platform can take centre stage (e.g., if the goal is to build a brand's following on Instagram), or it can follow from other strategic choices made, such as the selection of the target audience, the influencer type, the campaign type, or the measurement needs. No matter which is the case, platforms are central to the execution of the campaign, and it should not be left up to the influencer to decide which platform they use if they are present on more than one. Specifying the platform is also important for content generation-focused campaigns with creators because content assets should be optimised for specific platforms.

Influencer Type and Quantity Selection

While the selection of specific influencers usually happens in the partnering phase of the campaign process, the planning phase should at least determine the number of influencers and the type of influencers to be involved as those aspects have huge implications for the cost of the campaign. Indeed, the campaign budget might be the determining factor in terms of the type and quantity of influencers a campaign can involve. While many brands would want to work with Kim Kardashian, not many can actually afford to collaborate with her.

Like the selection of the platform(s), the influencer type and quantity selection can represent a 'chicken-or-egg' problem for influencer marketers as this step is highly interdependent with the campaign type choice, the target audience choice, the platform choice and maybe even the KPIs. For example, some influencers place an emphasis on remaining independent of companies. They might be great for product reviews that drive sales as part of a product seeding campaign, but would not be willing to directly promote products through trackable coupon codes. General criteria that will have to be considered in this step are the size of the following and therefore the cost of the influencer, the type of target audience the influencer is connected with, the location or language spoken, the topic category, the experience with influencer marketing, and past engagement with other brands (especially direct competitors). For creator campaigns, specific skills might be necessary.

Campaign Types

As indicated already in several places, influencer marketing at the tactical level is very flexible, in constant flux, and subject to the creative input of influencers and creators and their intricate knowledge of platforms and audiences. This means that campaigns can take on many forms. The following section categorises campaign types based on prominent features but is certainly not intended to provide an exhaustive list of possible campaign types. Overall, campaigns can be distinguished based on the compensation they involve, the category of influencer they engage, the platform on which they are hosted, the strategic goals they aim to achieve, where they take place, the media they involve, and their length and timing (Figure 9.3).

Figure 9.3   Influencer marketing campaign classifiers

Compensation. Influencer marketing campaigns can involve monetary compensation for the influencers and creators, can offer non-monetary benefits, or can provide a mix of both. Typical non-monetary campaigns are gifting swag/merchandise or product seeding campaigns. These campaigns build on the reciprocity principle discussed in Chapter 5. Gifting swag (e.g., at a festival like Coachella) can be effective if influencers find the merchandise useful and worth featuring in their posts. Product seeding campaigns are especially helpful for brands with inexpensive products that have not found a specific target audience. Sending these products (e.g., snacks, drinks, clothing, etc.) to a wide range of nano-influencers can provide the company with important exposure and insights. It is important to note that any type of compensation, including a gift, and even a small discount code, requires disclosure online as a business relationship.

Campaigns can also differ in the way the monetary compensation is structured. Some campaigns determine the compensation up front while others are performance-based, meaning that influencers will receive a share of the revenue they generated or will be offered additional compensation opportunities after establishing initial campaign success (e.g., a select group of influencers will be provided with personal coupon codes based on the engagement levels they achieved in earlier phases of the campaign).

Influencer category. Campaigns with top-level influencers differ not only in terms of cost and complexity of intermediaries involved but also in size. Nano-influencer campaigns often involve hundreds of influencers who are likely less experienced. This will affect subsequent stages of the campaign, from outreach to contracting to campaign monitoring and management.

Social media platform. While some campaign types are platform-independent, others are very much enabled by specific platform features as well as platform cultures. For example, unboxing, hauls, and product demo videos are most common on YouTube because they require longer video formats. Challenges are native to TikTok. Polls, burst campaigns (crews of influencers blanketing a particular target audience's feeds), multi-post campaigns, and swipe-up lead generation are typical for Instagram campaigns. Just like Dolly Parton in her famous social media challenge adjusted her profile picture to fit the expectations of users on different platforms, campaigns also need to think about their alignment with the platforms.

Goals. Some campaign types are better able to achieve specific goals than others. For instance, a giveaway or sweepstake can serve awareness goals, support lead generation goals, or help with follower counts (although brands should be wary of individuals who only follow the brand to be able to participate in a contest). Contests can also be used to encourage the generation of content. Shout-outs or account takeovers can help brands build their own following. Affiliate marketing campaigns that use custom coupon codes are great for sales generation.

Location. Some campaigns have a distinct location-based element to them. Think about hotels, restaurants, spas or whole destinations – it would be illegal for these companies to ask influencers to promote them without hosting them and letting them experience their services. But even companies that sell tangible products might grant the influencer unique 'behind-the-scenes' experiences. It is important to think about the location element because of its implications for budgeting and for the complexity of the campaign management. A very popular tactic in the influencer marketing space that has a heavy location-focus are influencer events. Influencers are either invited to existing events (conferences, product launches, fashion shows, etc.), or events are specifically created for them. Events usually bring multiple influencers together, which provides unique content creation opportunities. They might also catch the interest of news media.

Another location-focused tactic are so-called influencer tours. These are typically organised by specialised agencies that handle all the trip logistics. One example of such an agency is Roadies. Their website promises: 'When we pair influencers and a Roadies road trip, magic happens. Millions of impressions, thousands of new followers, hundreds of conversations started and the cash register ringing' (https://www.roadies.coach/influencer-trips/). The road trips include stops that allow for instaworthy content creation (often with professional lighting equipment or stylists), and the time on the bus can be used to explain the products and brand needs. Tours and events are special perks for influencers because they get to create exciting content for their audiences, get to know and learn from other influencers, and get to spend time with brand representatives.

THE LORNA JANE INFLUENCER CAMPAIGN

Australian activewear company Lorna Jane, whose motto is 'Move, Nourish, Believe' partnered with influencer marketing agency Vampped to design an event in the US to promote its brand and its cookbook. Vampped conceptualised, produced, and hosted an intimate event with 14 top influencers in the health and wellness space. From a private chef serving dishes based on recipes from the cookbook, to shopping Lorna Jane's new activewear line, to a tarot card reader, the event provided plenty of material for the influencers to post about. The event-based campaign achieved a reach of over 8 million. Pictures and videos from the event can be found on the Vampped website (https://www.vampped.com/case-study-lorna-jane).

Media. Two emerging forms of campaign types that warrant attention based on their use of media are livestreaming and whitelisting campaigns. Livestreaming allows influencers to produce more authentic content and to interact with the audience in real-time. Twitch is the most prominent example of a livestreaming-focused platform. Livestreaming is extremely popular in the e-sports and in the gaming sphere. When combined with e-commerce, livestreaming becomes live-stream shopping or live shopping. Livestream shopping is already an extremely popular and successful way of using influencers to sell products in China and is increasingly adopted globally as more platforms allow for live broadcasts of con-tents and offer more ecommerce integration. Livestreaming and live shopping have specific implications for campaign design and management. For instance, advance content approval by the brand is of course not possible.

LIVESTREAMING

Livestreaming refers to the use of social media platforms to share unedited, raw footage with a live audience that can usually interact with the influencer through a chat window and through gifting or tipping functions.

Whitelisting emerged from the brands' need to overcome platform limitations in terms of content amplification and campaign evaluation. Whitelisting is a unique mix of influencer marketing and paid social media advertising that offers brands a lot more control. Influencers like it because it gives their content a lot of exposure and can help them build their following. The unique elements and advantages of whitelisting campaigns are explained in the vignette contributed by influencer marketing agency Influence Hunter.

WHITELISTING

Influencer whitelisting is the process of influencers and creators granting advertising permissions to brands or partners to use their handles, content, and audience targeting (Lumanu.com, 2022).

INFLUENCER WHITELISTING, BY AARON KOZINETS

Influencer whitelisting is the latest addition to an influencer marketer's toolbox. Influencer whitelisting is done by utilising the influencer's account to run ads that appear as though they are from the actual influencer, following native advertising principles. The average consumer will not even realise that this is not an influencer post. The brand, with the permission of the influencer, can use the influencer's identity, control the creative or copy, and include a Call to Action (CTA). Brands can use their own paid media dollars to push the content and, because they oversee the ads, have direct access to all campaign-related data. Thus, it is a collaborative form of influencer marketing that gives brands more control and allows the influencer to earn money and attract more followers while playing a more passive role.

Whitelisted ads appear to social media users as wanted forms of content, much as the typical influencer post would. This stops the typical social media user from immediately mentally filtering out the advertisement. Using whitelisted ads bridges the gap between wanted influencer content and unwanted ads, bringing out the best of both worlds. Whitelisting also delivers several advantages in terms of audience targeting. It allows brands to target bigger and more specific audiences beyond the immediate following of an influencer through the advertising tools offered by platforms, while still taking advantage of engaging content created by influencers.

Three types of audiences can be targeted: (1) custom audience based on criteria offered by the platform's advertising tools; (2) engaged audience of the influencer (individuals who already like and comment on the influencer's posts); and (3) lookalike audience, meaning a custom audience similar in demographics and interests to the engaged audience. The latter allows brands to turn a micro-influencer into a mega-influencer without losing impact while scaling up. It widens the reach while still maintaining the same narrowed scope of targeted customers. It has been possible before to target people similar in demographics to those who follow and engage with the brand. However, without whitelisting it is not possible to target people similar to the types that like and follow the influencer. Last, with whitelisting, brands can A/B test their influencer marketing in a way that was never before possible.

Since it is a collaborative initiative that requires knowledge and trust, white-listing is best performed when utilising the content of an influencer who has promoted the brand beforehand. The posts don't remain on the influencer's feed, which is one reason many influencers are open to whitelisting. It also allows influencers to monetise their content without the same need for a time investment. Importantly, whitelisting gives the influencer tremendous exposure and therefore opportunities to grow their following.

Influencer whitelisting is the newest tool in businesses' arsenal that will allow brands to break through ad fatigue, appear authentic to consumers, and grow the reach of their ideal influencers. It also creates better targeting opportunities, blends paid ad content with influencer marketing, and helps with campaign measurement. While still in its infancy, influencer whitelisting appears poised to be a massive development in the influencer marketing industry, with huge benefits for both brands and influencers.

Aaron Kozinets is Founder and CEO of Influence Hunter, a full service influencer marketing agency for companies looking to scale. https://influencehunter.com/

Duration and timing. Some campaigns are very short-lived, one-post affairs. Others can span over considerable periods of time and usually involve a more complex mix of content and maybe even influencers. The management and monitoring requirements for a long campaign are of course much more elaborate. Some campaigns are tied to very specific events (product launches, fashion weeks, holidays, etc.), while others are very flexible in terms of their timing. The latter give brands and influencers/creators more time for negotiation, content creation and approval processes and allow them to monitor and optimise campaigns over longer periods.

Campaign Design

Campaign design refers to the overall message of the campaign, campaign-specific hashtags, specific CTAs, and other elements like the structure and settings as well as potential partners for tours or events. While the brand needs to have a clear understanding of what the 'take-away' message will be for the audience, it is important to keep the collaborative nature of influencer marketing in mind. This step in the process needs to clarify how much creative freedom the influencer(s) will get and what kinds of content or other resources the brand will deliver.

It is also a good idea to think about the ways in which the campaign might benefit the influencer(s) and motivate them to participate in it. Backaler (2018: 133) warns that brands can be very tempted to control the entire creative process and need to be reminded that influencer marketing campaigns work best when they provide 'freedom within a framework'. As mentioned above, influencers are sometimes already consulted in this design step to co-create the campaign.

The notion of 'freedom within a framework' emphasises not only creative freedom for the influencer but also the need for alignment with the brand. Just like other marketing campaigns, influencer marketing campaigns need to fit within the overall brand strategy and follow key branding guidelines. Even if the creative design for the campaign is outsourced to an agency or an influencer, a general branding framework is necessary to inform the creative design of the campaign.

THE PANDORA INFLUENCER CAMPAIGN

Pandora is a Copenhagen-based jewellery manufacturer best known for its customisable bracelets and themed collections. Pandora sold over 100 million pieces of jewellery in 2022 and has 6,500 points of sale in more than 100 countries. Self-expression and collectability are important components of its brand promise. For its influencer marketing initiatives, Pandora has issued creative design guidelines to inform its local campaigns. These guidelines state that influencer marketing campaigns should showcase how the collection empowers local influencers to be themselves and express their values, their memories, their passions, and their dreams. They should feature a personal approach that celebrates the influencers' own style, self-expression, and creativity. Further, campaigns should use an educational approach using 'How-to' and 'step-by-step' content clearly showing product functionality. These guidelines illustrate how important campaign design is and what it can look like at the strategic level.

Setting of Key Performance Indicators

Various influencer marketing books (Levin, 2020; Russell, 2020; Schaffer, 2020) stress the importance of starting campaigns with the end goal in mind. Establishing the KPIs up front ensures that this is the case. It also helps if these KPIs are communicated to the influencers who, through their creative efforts and audience engagement tactics, will have to contribute to their achievement and sometimes even measure them for the brand.

One of the main advantages of influencer marketing is the comparative ease of measuring its results. Various MarTech tools and measurement affordances built into the platforms further contribute to this measurability. As a result, it can be tempting to select KPIs depending on their availability. However, the key to establishing a campaign's return on investment is to select KPIs that directly align with the goal(s) set for the campaign. The campaign process closes with the measurement of the KPIs during the campaign evaluation phase. In this book, KPIs, their alignment with specific campaign goals, and their measurement will be discussed in the evaluation-related chapter.

Once these strategic elements of a campaign are determined, the partnering phase begins. This is an essential step in influencer marketing that also clearly distinguishes it from other types of marketing campaigns. Consequently, it deserves its own chapter.

CHAPTER SUMMARY

Influencer marketing has its origins in early ad hoc attempts of brands to encourage bloggers to write positive things about their products or services. It has since developed into a strategic communications tool that increasing numbers and types of communicators use to achieve a variety of goals. Influencer marketing provides communicators a lot of flexibility to work with different types of influencers and creators, as well as different media types and communication tactics, but this flexibility makes it difficult to compare campaigns and establish what works best. It is often the influencers and creators who know best what contents engage particular audiences. Leaving room for the creative freedom of influencers and creators is therefore a core driver of influencer marketing success. The other important factor is a strategic approach to influencer marketing that involves careful planning and meticulous design, execution, management, and measurement of campaigns. The chapter set out a four-phase campaign process with multiple steps within each phase. It ended with a discussion of the first phase, the planning phase, which sets the stage for all other phases and ensures strategic alignment with company goals and budgets.

EXERCISES AND QUESTIONS

Exercises

1. Watch the 2021 Pepsi commercial starring Doja Cat: https://www.youtube.com/watch?v=5nIYTZxx6P8. Discuss how her performance in the ad differs from the way an influencer would endorse a product like Pepsi.

2. Find a post tagged with #sponsored or #ad on Instagram. Try to discern which campaign goal(s) the post supports.

3. A start-up company wants to build brand awareness in the US market using an influencer marketing campaign. Can you help them translate this business need into a SMART campaign goal?

Questions

1. Why is budgeting an influencer campaign so difficult? Explain and provide examples of cost categories or items that are hard to estimate in advance.

2. In what way does selecting the target audience for an influencer campaign differ from audience selection for a Facebook advertising campaign?

3. What are the advantages of a whitelisting campaign for the brand? What are possible advantages for the influencer?

4. Joel Backaler promotes the notion of 'freedom within a framework' when discussing the creative design of influencer marketing campaigns. What does he mean by this?

5. What should a brand consider when determining the target audience of an influencer marketing campaign?

ANNOTATED READINGS

Berne-Manero, C., & Marzo-Navarro, M. (2020). Exploring how influencer and relationship marketing serve corporate sustainability. *Sustainability*, *12*(11), 1–19.

Although academic research typically focuses on supporting customer acquisition, commitment and retention, this study explores how different types of influencers can be used in influencer marketing plans to support corporate social responsibility goals.

Blaney, D. M., & Fleming, K. (2020). *Will post for profit: How brands and influencers are cashing in on social media.* Orlando, FL: Post Hill Press.

This professional book explores influencer marketing from the perspective of both influencers and companies. Amongst the topics covered are: how to select a platform, audience growth strategy, and designing successful campaigns.

10

PARTNERING WITH INFLUENCERS AND CREATORS

CHAPTER OVERVIEW AND OBJECTIVES

Partnering with influencers and creators happens after the planning phase and before the execution and evaluation phases. This chapter explores how influencer and creator partnering is initiated and managed. The exclusionary effects of software tools and influencer management platforms on diversity and equity are described, examined, and critiqued. The next partnering process readers will learn about is the evaluation or vetting of influencers. Following that, examples of outreach are provided to guide influencer partnering practice. Another important tool that is thoroughly explained is the influencer brief. Following that explanation are descriptions of the negotiation stage between an influencer or creator and an organisation. The chapter then defines and explains the various components of the influencer or creator contract in order to provide a practical and comprehensive overview of this critical phase. The chapter concludes with an overview of the six main processes and a description of a critical problem that must be resolved during the partnering phase.

IDENTIFYING THE RIGHT INFLUENCERS FOR THE #EACHVERSIONOFYOU CAMPAIGN, BY LIERAC ITALIA

#Ogniversionedite (which translates into '#Eachversionofyou' in English) is a campaign launched by Lierac Italia in 2021, an Italian skincare brand focusing on women's empowerment that is part of the Laboratoire Native French cosmetics group. The aim of the campaign was to promote the Premium cosmetics line by having influencers talk about the importance of being themselves and also showing them authentically demonstrating different versions of themselves.

With the help of an agency, the marketing team went on a search that took about a month. During that time, they looked for and analysed the profiles of 20 different influencers from both a qualitative and quantitative point of view. During the scouting phase, they used a platform to look at and compare the metrics of influencers on different social media sites. This helped them make sure they were getting the right information. After this first step, the marketing team chose the best profiles and put them on a short list. Ambra Angiolini and Eva Riccobono were the first two people they chose. Several things led to the choice of Ambra and Eva. They are followed by a target that fits the brand: active women ages 30–54. Also, they have an engagement rate that is higher than 2%. Additionally, they have a credible personal background to spread the message of the brand. Notably, they have always shown themselves to be real people who don't try to hide their flaws. In particular, Eva Riccobono is known for speaking out about self-acceptance and natural beauty. Also, Ambra and Eva had never worked with competitors in the same category before.

After choosing Ambra and Eva, the marketing team got in touch with them through their agents to tell them about the project and get a price quote from them. Both influencers liked the idea right away and said they were available to be the main faces of the campaign. The marketing team then moved on to finalising the budget, negotiating the contract, and, as the last step, developing the creative brief for each piece of content that the influencers would be making. Figures 10.1 and 10.2 show two of the most important shots from the campaign, both of which feature Ambra Angiolini. The shots were taken under the artistic direction of Nima Benati, Italian fashion photographer included in the Forbes' 'Under 30' list in 2020.

Then, Drusilla Foer, a third influencer, was brought into the project after being approached through her agent. Drusilla had been considered from the start because of the credible way she talks about diversity and how important it is to feel like yourself. Drusilla gave an emotional and introspective speech for the campaign. She looked into what it means to really be yourself in all your different forms. 'It was an honor for us to work with an artist like Drusilla Foer', says Domenica Florii, Digital Marketing and Influencer Manager at Laboratoire Native Italia and team leader for the Lierac campaign. 'She immediately got the idea behind this project and then perfectly communicated the campaign's key messages'.

The #Ogniversionedite campaign was a success because of how well the influencer identification phase was managed. The result was a perfect match between the topic, personalities, and voices of the chosen influencers and the contents created, which were beautifully in line with the brand's values, tone of voice and communication strategy.

Figure 10.1   #Ogniversionedite campaign by Lierac Italia, 1

Figure 10.2   #Ogniversionedite campaign by Lierac Italia, 2

THE PARTNERING PHASE: FROM FINDING TO BRIEFING INFLUENCERS AND CREATORS

Influencer marketing is divided into four stages in this book: planning, partnering, execution, and evaluation. Planning entails defining the campaign's goals, budgeting for it, thinking about influencers and who will be chosen, and establishing the key performance indicators (KPIs) that will be used to evaluate the campaign (Childers, Lemon, & Hoy, 2019). Next comes the partnering phase. During this phase, which happens before a campaign is launched, influencers are identified and vetted (Russell, 2020). As well, partnering is where outreach (contacting the influencers or creators), negotiations, and contract signing take place. Thus, this is a very important stage, whose proper implementation can make or break an influencer campaign. Think of the campaign as a bit like filming a movie and the partnering stage as the time when actors are auditioned, hired, and cast in roles. It is only after the partnering stage, when the complete line-up of influencers is set, that the execution of the campaign can begin, and their posts start appearing on social media. After the campaign is finished, and often before agencies and influencers are paid, the outcomes of the campaign are evaluated. This chapter focuses on the partnering stage in which the most important actions relate to finding, connecting with, negotiating, and signing the influencers or creators who are going to create the content and represent the brand for the campaign.

The opening vignette example of the #eachversionofyou campaign, shared by one of its managers, shows how identifying the right influencers benefited and strengthened an Italian cosmetics brand. There may be no element of the process of working with influencers that is as important as identification and outreach. For a campaign to be effective, it needs the right talent. And with millions of talented creators and influencers across a dozen effective platforms to choose from, the possibilities are both endless and a bit overwhelming. Nonetheless, there is a process that can help managers working on any type of influencer campaign to effectively sort through the different choices and then end up with a meaningful arrangement that can help realise the campaign's goals. In this chapter, we provide this process.

INFLUENCER IDENTIFICATION

Influencer identification is the process of searching for, locating, and vetting appropriate influencers for a particular campaign in order to achieve that campaign's objectives.

CHOOSING INFLUENCER TALENT, BY SYBIL GRIEB

Not all influencers/creators with a large social following and/or high engagement will be able to generate significant return on investment (ROI). Begin by defining the key messages you want to convey, identifying the target audience/s for your product, and deciding what type of content will best achieve your objectives. Is it a simple message aimed at an older demographic? If so, images or short videos on Facebook might work best. Is it a younger demographic? They are most likely on TikTok. Is there a complex messaging to convey? Then a longer form video on a platform like YouTube may perform best.

Once you've established your key messages, target audiences, ideal platforms, type of content, and CTA, you can start fleshing out the influencer/creator's must-haves (key platforms, audiences, type of content, and topics) as well as the nice-to-haves (the influencer/creator needs to be a mom and it would be nice if they frequently espoused women's empowerment). When deciding which talent to work with, the goal is to find the right influencer/creator who is already having the right conversation with your target audience. Once they have been fully briefed on your brand and goals, they can create powerful content that will resonate with their audience.

Sybil Grieb is a Digital Marketing Strategist. She is currently Senior Vice President of Brand Partnerships and Web3 Innovation at the creator commerce company, Whalar. Sybil was the former head of influencer marketing for Edelman and William Morris Endeavor.

Finding Influencers

How do brands and other organisations go about finding influencers for their campaigns? There are a variety of methods and options available. Organisations will sometimes leverage their existing relationships, including actual customers. Some of the most successful influencer campaigns have resulted from brands reaching out to people who were already posting reviews and content about the brand, demonstrating their knowledge and enthusiasm. The amount of authenticity gained by utilising an already enthusiastic customer should not be underestimated! Many companies already use brand ambassadors to promote their products or services. These ambassadors' social media accounts can be utilised and leveraged for specific campaigns. With their Quest Squad and Quest Missions, Quest Nutrition employs a variety of customers and brand ambassadors (see vignette). Employees can also be used as influencers. However, employees may lack some of the established content creation and audience management skills of influencers. Furthermore, some companies, such as Sony PlayStation, have had problems using their employees as influencers in the past because they failed to follow disclosure regulations.

BUILDING A COMMUNITY OF INFLUENCERS AT QUEST NUTRITION, BY ALYSSA NIMEDEZ

I have been with Quest Nutrition for over six years and my specific role at the start was to grow their brand community. However, the influencer and creator campaigns I developed at Quest Nutrition have been somewhat unique. I have been able to develop a dedicated relationship with a group of influencers and content creators to enhance the Quest brand's digital presence.

Quest had already built a solid reputation at in-person events and now it was time to nurture its online community of influencers at the pace of its growing social media channels. Back then, there were no tools to help streamline communication – it was all manual and that played to our advantage. In fact, the influencer programme I developed was somewhat unique in that we did not identify and contact influencers. Instead, we created a program where the influencers came to us!

I put out a call to all Quest fans and consumers – my group of influencers and content creators – and asked them to apply to be a part of a unique brand advocacy program. The applications vetted them for appropriateness to be involved with the brand, so we could ensure quality content that fit with our desired image.

In the first year, I had 300 engaged 'Quest Squad' members who would post to social media every month in return for brand love, recognition, and free products. In 2018, we $10\times$ the growth to 3,000 and by 2021 we had 7,000 members. In tandem with this growth, we invited members to our headquarters and hosted events with Quest Squad members throughout the country. Quest Squad's share of voice equated to 30% of the mentions on Quest's social media channels, resulting in over 140k mentions of the Quest brand.

A distinct difference in a community like the Quest Squad is that we don't go looking for influencers. Instead, they come looking for us. We set up our squad and established the criteria we were looking for. We wanted to recruit influencers with a strong, solid relationship with our brand and a talent for relevant content creation. Then, we leverage them not only for content creation, but also for insights, sampling, share of voice, referrals and more. This group of influencers becomes an online army of our loudest advocates. By communicating the brands' messaging en masse and in their own voices, this squad of influencers (many of them nano-influencers) helps our brand every day to drive recall, purchase intent, brand trust, and consideration.

I believe that all brands have a unique opportunity to gain even more credibility and trust when they take their relationship with a consumer, fan, or influencer and transform it into face-to-face interaction. I have found it very rewarding to bring influencers together with managers and give them an experience they will never forget. Quest Squad is still an important part of Quest's marketing strategy and is one of my most sought-after programs to replicate in the health and wellness industry.

Alyssa Nimedez is a brand engagement expert who helps brands increase their digital presence through impactful influencer and advocacy programs. She is currently the Senior Brand Engagement Manager at Quest Nutrition and oversees PR, social media, and influencer marketing.

Another way organisations find influencers is by having an in-house talent team. Major brands like L'Oréal have in-house talent teams whose job it is to scour the social web and identify rising stars that might be useful in future campaigns. Many professionals in the industry spend significant amounts of time viewing and listening to social media content, seeking out the new styles, new faces, and new voices that they want to bring into future campaigns.

An increasing number of brands and organisations are also working with technology companies to create large lists of approved influencers who can then be tapped programmatically or manually for campaigns on an ongoing basis. Oftentimes software tools will be used in order to seek out relevant influencers. These tools might search for particular topics. For example, seeking out content creators with a significant share of voice posting about a particular skin-related issue or medical condition. Google alerts can also be helpful to identify who is posting about a particular topic or brand. Other tools might be used to distinguish content creators whose audiences have particularly desirable characteristics for a campaign's objectives. Influencer activity can also be assessed by monitoring who is using the #sponsored or #ad disclosures.

There are a variety of providers and dedicated businesses that help campaign managers locate influencers appropriate to their campaign. Influencer marketing platforms offer access to a database of creators, sorted into categories and containing descriptions, from whom they can choose. For example, Grin has a database of over 30 million content creators who are classified by their content and audiences. Other businesses offer so-called 'marketplaces' designed to connect influencers or content creators with potential clients. For example, IZEA encourages creative content producers to showcase their skills by offering digital creative services for sale on their platform. One of the advantages of marketplaces is that influencers and creators often display their rates. Brands and other organisations can then browse through the marketplace to find fresh talent for their projects and to pay for the content through the platform, with the platform's finder or matchmaking fee included in the cost.

Agencies are another important place where brands can find appropriate influencers. Influencer agencies usually have a roster of influencers and content creators who they know and trust. Agencies offer services with these influencers that may range from a simple introduction to developing and managing the entire campaign. For example, Activate is an opt-in network of over 150,000 vetted and authenticated influencers. The platform adds value to its list by curating useful lists of different kinds of influencers such as Cool Moms, Dapper Dudes, Keto Creators, Conservation Activists, and Black Girl Magic (Lu, 2019).

Similarly, Open Influence offers creator discovery services as part of its overall influencer marketing support services.

Next are the very important tools that major social media platforms provide to brands and other organisations to help them discover the right person from their site. TikTok's creator marketplace, for example, allows the brand to search by gender, country or region, topic, reach, engagement rate, average views, audience country, age, audience device, and other useful designators. Creator images are presented as a result of searches and the user can view some of their short video material before potentially anchoring them. A user can create shortlists, go back and view past searches, save results, and even name and save campaigns. Similarly, China's Bilibili matchmaking platform has a service called 'Sparkle' (Hua Huo in Chinese) to help agencies and brands find content creators.

Influencer identification software, whether stand-alone, integrated into platforms or accessed through agencies, increasingly uses artificial intelligence for different tasks that are central to influencer marketing. One of the most important is to scan thousands of influencer and creator profiles, comparing and categorising them, and also looking for red flags such as the possibility of fake followers. As well, AI tools use predictive analytics programs to forecast how a given audience will receive a particular piece of content. However, as the vignette about brand safety and influencer equity discusses, the increasing use of platform tools raises some very important issues about influencer diversity that the industry needs to better address (Bishop, 2021a).

BRAND SAFETY AND INFLUENCER EQUITY: THE IMPACT OF SOFTWARE TOOLS

Influencer management tools use artificial intelligence, algorithms, and data analytics to support marketers in their selection of influencers that are appropriate for campaigns. One of the most important ways they do this is through calculations of influencers' impact on brand safety and risk. Brand safety and risk are considered broadly, as relating to the influencers' general decent or appropriate behaviour, the history of their social media posts, and how it might impact the brand's reputation. Bishop (2021a) researched how one influencer management tool called 'Peg' allowed managers to assess influencers' use of profanity, audience backlash, and press coverage. She found that the algorithms and outputs of the tool tended to equate certain forms of sexuality with brand risk. In particular, LGBTQ+ people were earmarked as being morally risky. This seemed to be especially true for female LGBTQ+ people. She also found that brand safety was 'raced. Blackness specifically is bound up with risk' (Bishop, 2021a: 5).

Bishop's investigation concluded that, although it was presented as an objective tool, the software system presented subjective evaluations of risk 'that exclude marginalized individuals' and encodes 'a heteronormative and White lens' on what risk and brand safety mean (Bishop, 2021a: 10). This unfortunate encoding potentially perpetuates 'sociocultural discrimination against women, people of colour, and LGBTQ+ people in promotional ecologies' (10). As Bishop (2021b) points out, 'non-risky influencers – who are hired more frequently, and paid more – tend to be white, beautiful, heterosexual with long-term boyfriends. Later, they become mommy bloggers'. In fact, Gillespie (2019) published an image presenting the composite image of the face of the 100 most followed influencer accounts, further highlighting the potential problems with automated influencer identification.

Influencer identification often involves a tiered approach, meaning a certain number of influencers (if any) is selected for each influencer tier, from nano to celebrity influencers. Different identification criteria and maybe even approaches/tools might be applied for each tier. Usually, the selection of the tier and the determination of the number of influencers (or even the specific influencer) is a matter of what the campaign budget can accommodate. In any case, it is important to select more influencers than needed for the campaign and to prioritise them as not all of them will be able or willing to collaborate.

Vetting Influencers

INFLUENCER VETTING

Investigating, evaluating, and making a careful and critical examination of an influencer and their content in order to ensure that they are a suitable partner for a brand, organisation, and/or campaign.

Influencers have many characteristics and, when considering their inclusion in a marketing campaign, some of these characteristics may be more important than others. The first element to consider is brand alignment. It is a general foundation of influencer marketing that a brand seeks out spokespersons who will fit with the brand, particularly with the brand's personality. Like people, brands have personalities (Aaker, 1997). One way to conceptualise a brand's personality is to consider how it rates in terms of competence, sincerity, excitement, sophistication, and toughness. Influencers' personalities could be considered along similar lines, and the influencers with the best fit chosen. Another important characteristic would be the influencer's ability to enliven and embody the brand promise that the campaign seeks to convey, as set out by the managers.

Another key assessment characteristic is the type of audience that the influencer gathers. There is usually no point in advertising a product for young, fashion-forward women with an influencer whose audience mainly consists of men in their 50s and 60s who smoke cigars. Influencer marketing is marketing, and marketing is based on targeting particular kinds of consumers. Information about the influencer's audience should correspond to the target that the marketer wishes to reach. Note that there is not always a one-to-one correspondence between the age, gender, and other characteristics of the influencer and that of their main audience. For example, James Charles is a male who was born in 1999, but his main audience is teenage girls. What unites Charles and his audience, however, is a passion for the beauty and cosmetics topics in which he is an expert.

The next assessment characteristic is authenticity, or the influencer possessing a good balance between being a trusted and honest community member and a commercial spokesperson. One of the ways influencers achieve this balance is by not saying positive things about every product they receive but being honest about their reactions to products and how they might be improved or whether they are worth purchasing. The influencer must maintain their trusted relationship with their audience, and also a sense that they are a real person. Their tastes need to relate clearly and in some specific ways – as a proxy, or perhaps as an aspiration – to the needs and tastes of audience members. Another way to maintain authenticity is to mix up sponsored and organic content. Yet another manner in which it can be achieved is when the influencer carefully selects brand deals that fit with their personal brand and with the needs of their audience.

Social media creators can also be assessed for the type and quality of the content they produce. Related to brand alignment, this content might have a particular orientation, appearance, or emotional texture that matches, or clashes, with the brand and the type of content with which the brand is associated. The type and quality of content becomes especially important when a marketer is looking mainly for content creation, where a particular aesthetic tone may be the key criterion for the choice.

Background checks are an important part of the vetting process. Are the influencer's values aligned with the brand's? Maggie Reznikoff of the Los Angeles-based influencer firm Open Influence says that almost all brands will avoid influencers whose content is vulgar, violent, or that incite hatred. She says that Open Influence will look closely at political affiliation and stances on social issues when a brand has concerns in those areas, and that some clients are concerned about drug or alcohol use, nudity, strong political or religious content, or other risqué content (Open Influence team, 2020).

Another useful consideration is the track record of the influencer. How have they performed in prior campaigns? Have they been timely and reliable? Did they produce high quality content? Did their content help achieve brand objectives? Did they disclose properly and avoid other complications, such as arousing unwelcome controversies? Are they promoting different products all the time? Do their audiences seem tired of their promotions? Are their audiences sufficiently engaged and commenting in a positive and enthusiastic manner?

Recently, managers applied the idea of rating the pillars of influence to vet influencers. Domenica Florii explains the core three pillars – Relevance, Resonance, and Reach – in a vignette in this chapter. Amanda Russell (2020) added two additional, and useful Rs to the list in the vignette. First, 'Recognition' which is an assessment about how recognizable the influencer is to the target audience. Next, 'reference', which refers to who references the influencer, such as whether they have been featured on any lists or interviewed on any prominent podcasts. To this list of 'R' terms, we might add 'Real Followers'. Unfortunately, there are many fake followers still being used in social media, although significantly less than there have been in previous years. Nonetheless, a check on this fraudulent behaviour is often warranted, especially when dealing with influencers whose reach exceeds 100,000 people.

Scott Guthrie of Ketchum coined four additional pillars of influence: reception, relationship, reality, and relinquish control (Guthrie, 2016). Beyond the reach, relevance, and resonance elements described in the vignette, David Armano of Edelman Digital suggested the following additional characteristics (Armano, 2011):

- Proximity: being close to others who have high trust within their networks; their power to influence is stronger, even if the reach may be limited

- Expertise: exhibiting deep meaningful knowledge about a particular topic

- Trust: being considered an honest and legitimate broker of knowledge or opinions about a topic

THE THREE RS OF IDENTIFYING INFLUENCER TALENT, BY DOMENICA FLORII

Is it better to select influencers with high follower counts or should one focus on engagement? The first two basic principles when figuring out how to identify the right influencers for a brand are relevance and resonance. Relevance is vital for attracting people who belong to the brand's target group. Influencers are relevant when they have similar characteristics or are appealing to the brand's target audience and share content meaningful to the brand industry and attuned to the brand values.

It is important to analyse the influencers' audience demographics and lifestyle to ensure that the followers belong to the group the brand wants to attract. Beyond age, gender and location, some of the basic elements to assess are the influencers' language, values, tastes, passions, and interests. At the same time, influencers must be able to activate the brand's target audience to achieve content amplification. In this respect, resonance plays a fundamental role.

Resonance represents the influencers' capacity to evoke shared emotions, feelings, and values in their followers. A huge follower count is pointless if those followers are not active, responsive, or keen on the content shared by the influencer. This explains why nano-influencers, despite having less than 10,000 followers, seem to be more credible and have a more loyal fan base insofar as they are more selective about the products, services and brands they promote. Influencers' Reach comes in a second step and is the key metric to compare influencers.

Reach denotes the number of people influencers could potentially reach through their follower base. The general notion is the more followers, the better the influencer. However, this is not entirely correct. There are other performance-driven influencer metrics that are crucial for companies when identifying the right influencers. For instance, organic follower growth, which is a sign that the audience is genuinely interested in the influencer's profile and content. Then, engagement rate is one of the other vital factors. It refers to the level of interaction between the influencer and their followers. The higher the engagement rate, the more the audience trusts the influencer. Analysing the followers to following ratio is also necessary. Influencers may accumulate followers by first following random people, getting a follow back from them, and then by unfollowing them in a few days. In this case, the followers are not genuinely interested in what the influencer pursues.

All these performance indicators can be found and analysed through dedicated tools that provide an overview of key metrics to be considered during the influencer scouting phase. These tools offer support throughout the full influencer marketing process until the campaign final reporting. HypeAuditor, Creator IQ, and Inflead are just some of the available tools. For instance, Inflead is the platform that Laboratoire Native Italia used in 2022 and it enabled us to select the right influencers for each brand by providing a complete overview of their profile. The platform offers the possibility of scouting according to selected criteria. It also performs analyses of the influencers' audience, including demographics, presence of Instagram engagement pods, list of topics they usually focus on and list of competitors they collaborated with in the previous months. At the same time, at the end of the campaign, the platform elaborates the influencers' outcomes achieved by each of their contents published.

From a qualitative point of view, while selecting an influencer, it is also vital to check their previous collaborations and marketing campaigns. Brands do not want to team up with someone who has worked with their competitors before or has engaged in collaborations that collide with their current values. The influencer's voice should be aligned with the brand's lifestyle, ethics, and values. Last but not least, brands want to avoid influencers who are walking advertisements. Collaborations with influencers engaged in advertising give brands no leads because their audience, no matter how huge, is bound to be confused.

Domenica Florii is Digital Marketing and Influencer Manager at Laboratoire Native Italia. Domenica is experienced in marketing, digital and influencer marketing and public relations and has worked in multinational companies such as The Walt Disney Company and Mattel.

Conducting Influencer Outreach

Once a brand or other organisation has identified potential influencers for a campaign, the next step is to contact them. This is known as 'influencer outreach', and it is similar to dating or any other social introduction in that it may require a warm-up stage. Managers could try to get the brand on the radar of influencers by following or subscribing to their channel, engaging with their content, or even ethically sharing influencer content through owned channels as a warm-up (which would require permission). Managers will frequently simply send an invitation to influencers to participate in an upcoming campaign. The message should be written in such a way that it attempts to answer the question of why the influencer should be interested in participating in the campaign. If influencers who already have a relationship with the brand have been identified, the answer to this question may be obvious. If no such relationship exists, the influencer may need to be persuaded.

Obviously, this is especially important for smaller brands or new brands, but even established brands should briefly describe who they are and what they stand for to allow influencers to judge how aligned they are with the brand.

INFLUENCER OUTREACH

The communicative effort by individuals in an organisation to recruit particular influencers selected as especially suitable for a campaign.

It is critical for the contact message to recognise what is important about the influencer in order for the messaging to be personalised. It should explain why you like them and believe they are the best choice for this campaign. The outreach message must also clearly establish the credibility of the brand, company, or organisation – and possibly the managers involved in it as well. Outreach should inform the influencer or creator who the brand is, the company behind the brand and its mission, and argue why they should trust the brand and want to be associated with it. Keep in mind that influencer relationships are about more than just a financial arrangement. Just as a brand takes a risk by working with an influencer, influencers put their reputations on the line with each brand they promote to their audiences. Also, payment is not the only thing influencers care about. Gaining access to the brand and the potential of a long-term partnership might be very attractive prospects. It is important to provide as much detail as possible about the campaign, its goals, and what will be expected of the influencer. Finally, the message should include a call to action that specifies the next step.

To improve the response rates of influencer outreach even more, Formost (2022) recommends additional strategies. First, try to identify influencers whose audiences are predisposed to like your product or brand. Next, pick out between one and three areas in the contact template you are using that you can customise to acknowledge the uniqueness of each influencer and their content. Consider white labelling so that your message seems as though it's a personalised e-mail coming directly from your inbox. Finally, always try to maintain a personal touch, even when messaging at scale.

The format for outreach can be important. On platforms such as Instagram and Twitter, a direct message (or DM) contact is common. Some platforms, such as TikTok, provide their own user templates (which can be customised) for outreach to influencers. If an email address for the influencer is available, such as is often given through influencer management platforms, email is often used. Figure 10.3 provides a sample influencer outreach email template that uses our recommended characteristics, and which can also be adapted into any of the other useful formats.

Subject: Sponsored content opp –can we discuss?

Hi Tracey!

I'm the influencer relations manager at VeganFriendly Dog Treats. We've been in business for 20 years and are dedicated to producing only organic, sustainable, and healthy vegan dog treats. I've been following your Instagram and think your messaging around vegan dogs and organic pet care is amazing and fits beautifully with our product line. I even see you have reviewed some of our 'Yummy for Puppy's Tummy' treats—thank you! I've attached a copy of our Influencer Brief for you to check out. I think we match up well because we are both focused on vegan pet care and seem to share some of the same values, please see the brief for more details. If this is of interest to you, I'd love to talk to you on the phone about developing some sponsored content for a new campaign we're planning, also included in the brief. Do you have a few minutes to chat in the next week? You can reach me at carrie@vfdogtreats.com.

Thanks so much!
Carrie Gerschon

Figure 10.3   A sample influencer outreach email

It is also important to remember that outreach might have to go through an influencer manager or an agency that represents the talent. This is likely the case for celebrity influencers.

The Influencer Brief

The influencer brief is an important component of outreach, as shown in Figure 10.3's sample outreach email message. The influencer brief and campaign brief are both extensions of the creative brief, which is commonly used in the advertising industry. Creative briefs are more general and outline the vision for the campaign. Consider the influencer brief to be similar to an online dating profile, with the goal of informing the influencer or creator about your brand and campaign while piquing their interest in working with you. We recommend including the influencer brief in any outreach message whenever possible because it persuades the influencer that your brand is a good fit for them.

> **CREATIVE BRIEF**
>
> A document that outlines the strategy of a creative project and usually contains details about purpose, goals, requirements, target audience, messaging, and other important information.

INFLUENCER BRIEF

A document that outlines the strategy of an influencer campaign and contains details about its goals, requirements, target audience, messaging, compensation scheme, and other high-level information of relevance to the influencer so that they can make a decision regarding their involvement in the campaign.

CAMPAIGN BRIEF

A document that provides materials and details relevant for the execution of a campaign.

The primary goal of an influencer brief is to capture the attention of the influencer, clearly define campaign objectives and explain expectations. The influencer brief serves as a blueprint as well as a source of inspiration for the campaign's defining aspects and the role that the influencer will play in it. Because influencers and their skills are in high demand, it is worthwhile to invest time in creating an impressive influencer brief. Many influential people are inundated with requests to collaborate. Consider the influencer brief to be a pitch that sells the brand and/or product while also creating excitement about working with the brand. It also clearly defines the influencer's and the brand's expectations. Finally, it aids internal organisation by establishing and clarifying the campaign's strategy and goals.

When writing an influencer brief, there are a few key elements to keep in mind. The first is a biography of the brand or company. The information in this section should be more focused on the mission, values, and vision. The purpose and mission of a company can set it apart from competitors. Links to the company website, social media accounts, news stories, and other photos or content that can provide a clearer sense of the brand's image and aesthetics are important elements to include.

The brief, like a business plan, should clearly indicate the campaign's direction, referring to goals, objectives, and even KPIs for the campaign. What product, service, event, or message is being promoted by this campaign? Is it the introduction of a new product? A holiday marketing campaign? Who is the campaign aiming to reach? Is this a campaign intended to increase brand awareness? A campaign intended to create branded content assets? Describe your intended audience. Try to be as brief as possible and summarise this section in one or two sentences.

Following that, some information about content execution should be provided. Now that the influencers have a general understanding of the campaign, the brief can lay out some of the most important details in an easy-to-understand manner (such as with bullet points). The social media platform, the type of content desired, and a description of the content, as well as a sense of voice or tone, are some of the elements that could be included here. Some campaign execution details, such as which software to use or the exact date or time of publication, can be left to the campaign brief, which will be the final document provided. Compensation should definitely be discussed in the brief (Levin, 2020).

The influencer brief will also include some messaging points and should include a mood board indicating the brand's voice, aesthetics, and overall messaging look and feel. The mood board or other visual illustration is very helpful in determining whether the brand's imagery is a good match for the influencer's own style and capabilities.

In general, there are three guiding principles a manager must remember about their influencer brief. The first is that there is risk for both parties. The influencer does not want to damage their reputation by being affiliated with a brand that clashes with their values and ethics, and the same is true of the brand's reputation. The second is that they need to give influencers and creators plenty of space to express their own creativity. One of China's top luxury influencers, Savi Sui, complains that one uniform brief should not be 'delivered to dozens of influencers, because everyone has a different style and target audience. Regarding fashion KOLs [key opinion leaders] as mobile billboards obviously goes against the uniqueness of this industry', she says (Qiu, 2022). Figure 10.4 represents these concerns about the influencer brief in the form of an illustration that emphasises balance. The third principle is to express some gratitude to influencers and to position the connection as an opportunity to build (or continue) a great relationship.

Negotiations With Influencers

NEGOTIATION

A strategic discussion involving two or more parties that reaches an agreement or resolves an issue in a way that each party finds acceptable.

The goal of influencer negotiation is to reach agreement. Negotiation stages are generally accepted to include investigation, presentation, bargaining, and closure. Although these stages may differ for different types of agreements, they serve as a general framework for understanding the fundamentals of negotiating an influencer deal. The investigation stage may include members of the organisation conducting

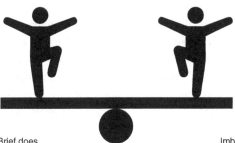

Imbalance/Influencer: Brief does not provide enough direction or goal definition, leaves too much about content creation to influencer interpretation.

Balance obtained: Brief clearly defines campaign goals, but leaves plenty of creative license for the influencer or creator to do what they do best

Imbalance/Marketer: Brief contains overly prescriptive or restrictive message descriptions; too much marketer control over creative content

Outcome: Approval delayed or rejected, having to redo content development, strained relationship

Outcome: Effective and authentic content, happy followers, enhanced brand relationships of marketer and influencer; good relationship

Outcome: Lower performance, inauthentic and less imaginative content, follower complaints, strained relationship

Figure 10.4   Finding the right balance in an influencer brief

research on the influencer, such as the rates they have charged for specific jobs they have done in the past. Comparable rates for users with similar characteristics should also be researched. Rates are often based on an influencer's follower count and engagement rate, but other factors such as star power, talent, or niche audience access, also may factor into pricing. An unspoken but well-known industry rule is $100 per 10,000 followers, with extra fees added for the type of post (McLachlan, 2021). Another is that Instagram post compensation is typically based on engagement, with a price estimate running at recent average engagements X $0.14 for a post (X $0.16 for a video or a reel). These guidelines should be viewed as general starting points, not hard-and-fast rules. Again, it is important to also consider offering compensation beyond fees in the form of products, travel, event tickets and other opportunities attractive for the influencer. With this information, the negotiation can proceed on an informed basis.

During the presentation stage, an offer, usually in the form of a contract, will be presented to the influencer or creator and their team. Contract elements will be discussed further in this chapter. It is worth noting that many influencers have a manager, possibly an agent or agency, and frequently assemble an entire team, which may include a legal consultant. This is usually a good thing because the more professional the influencer, the more professional the negotiations. However, some influencers may be managed by family members, such as their parents. Negotiations can become complicated in these cases because people who do not have a strong business background but have strong access to the influencer are involved.

Bargaining may occur after the offer or contract is presented. During bargaining, the influencer and their team may request contract changes. One of the most common changes is to request more money. Another option is to request less work or less restrictive contract terms. Bargaining can be viewed as a natural part of the negotiation process. When larger influencers, such as celebrities, are involved, the offer is viewed as a starting point for further discussion because these influencers and their agents have more bargaining power. Bargaining with larger influencers is thus similar to bargaining with major stars or other celebrities. Smaller influencers can be less difficult to please – but not always! Regardless of how many followers an influencer has, they are entitled to be treated with dignity during the negotiation process. Sometimes the rate might be non-negotiable but the brand can ask for additional content or favourable content usage rights.

Managers should try to avoid any clauses that could harm the influencer's reputation or jeopardise their current and future job opportunities. For example, many brands look for clauses in the contract that limit the influencer's ability to work in the same industry for a year or more after the campaign. Managers understandably do not want an influencer to promote their brand one day and a direct competitor's brand the next. But how much time should pass between promotions? Because they limit the influencers' business and income, non-competition clauses can be difficult to negotiate. If a beauty influencer earns their living by promoting beauty brands, they cannot be limited to just one. As a result, the influencer may request that the brand compensates him or her for lost business in exchange for a period of non-competition. Bargaining can take place over the length of time, content requirements, appropriate compensation, or even the necessity of such clauses. Many brands have contracts that state that they own the influencer's branded content created for the campaign in perpetuity. Influencers and their management teams, on the other hand, may rightfully object and offer an exclusive right to license the content for a set period of time but not ownership.

Always keep in mind the opportunity for long-term collaboration that these negotiations provide for both managers and influencers. Although bargaining can become heated at times, the end goal for both parties is to reach an agreement. If bargaining becomes too adversarial, future relationships may be jeopardised. As a result, it is always best to be informed and prepared, as well as to approach the negotiation process with an open mind.

The Contract

CONTRACT

A formal and legally binding written agreement.

The contract is one of the most important tools of an influencer marketing manager. The agreement between the influencer or creator and the organisation that hires them is specified in the contract. Although there are influencer contract templates widely available online, these standard forms should be tailored to the specifics of a given campaign. Because not every relationship between an influencer and a client is the same, the agreements that govern these relationships must also be unique.

What matters is that the agreement foresees potential issues in the relationship and clarifies expectations. A good, solid contract can save a lot of trouble in the future. And, because some influencer campaigns will involve people who are doing this for the first time or as a side hustle, it is even more important to have a well-written contract that can help ensure a professional working relationship from the start.

Usage rights and repurposing of content are increasingly important terms in the influencer contract. Marketers usually approach usage rights in the following way. Most marketers expect to be able to use (or license) the content that the influencer or creator creates for the campaign for between one and three months with little to no incremental fee. When the usage period increases from three months to a year, there may be a small to moderate increase in that incremental fee, which might even double for larger influencers or more established creators. If the marketer wants to use the content for over a year, there could be significant increases in the incremental fee.

Similarly, it is generally expected that the creative content will be used on social media. If it is going to be used on an organisation's owned website and in email marketing, there may be modest incremental fees. If used in a banner ad or in programmatic advertising, there could be moderate fees. Television and print advertising, outdoor, and product displays uses would represent the most expensive placement for usage of influencer and creator content. And although newcomers to the influencer game might allow marketers full ownership over their content, more established creators are generally reluctant to grant full ownership to a brand (McGrath, 2019).

Table 10.1 summarises some of the key components of an influencer contract. The table includes standard contract elements like the agreement's terms, cancellation clauses, confidentiality, payment terms, termination, and indemnification clauses. These standard elements are common in influencer contracts and are required in many business contracts. The table also includes campaign timelines, deliverables, content to avoid, content approval process, intellectual property rights, and disclosure or FTC responsibility. It is important to note that the contract stipulates rights and obligations for both parties, not just the influencer or creator. For instance, if the brand is supposed to pay for the amplification of the content, this should be stipulated. When taken as a whole, understanding the influencer contract elements can be a valuable resource for those learning about these important tools for managing relationships with influencers and content creators.

Table 10.1   Key elements of influencer and creator contracts

Contract element	Explanation of element	Short sample clause
Standard agreement terms	Gives names of the parties involved, date of contract, and simple description of agreement topic	'This influencer contract is entered into and shall be effective on [date] between [client name] (hereinafter the "Client") of [address] and [influencer name] (hereinafter the "Influencer") of [address]'
Campaign timeline	Explains how long the contracted relationship is intended to last (e.g., whether this a long-term alliance, or just for this one campaign)	'This contract will remain in force for six (6) months after the date of signing'
Deliverables	What the influencer is expected to deliver, on what platform, and when; includes descriptions of any penalties for late posting	'The Influencer hereby agrees to perform the following services on the TikTok platform: three posts with content regarding the brand'
Cancellation clauses	Reasons for cancelling the contract	'This contract may be cancelled for non-performance, poor performance, or breaking rule guidelines (including the "no obscenities" rule and the FTC disclosure requirements)'
Collateral details	States what content, briefing material, and other information will be provided for the influencer to use	'During the term of this contract, the Client hereby agrees to provide a Campaign Brief and all necessary details to the Influencer in order to perform the services'
Content to avoid	Provides topics, phrases, and names, such as competitors' brands, that the influencer is to avoid mentioning or referring to in posts	'The Influencer agrees to avoid the use of obscenities, nudity, vulgarity or other inappropriate images and language in the content provided to the Client'
Content approval process	Lays out the approval process for posts that the influencer must follow	'The Influencer must submit their content for approval before posting and must wait for sign off from the Influencer Manager as well as the Director of Public Relations before posting'
Confidentiality	Agreement not to share any private and sensitive information,	'Parties to this contract agree that each shall treat private

Table 10.1 Key elements of influencer and creator contracts *(Continued)*

Contract element	Explanation of element	Short sample clause
	but only to share relevant allowable information	information such as strategies, PR and campaign and content plans, that may be provided by either Party during the term of this Contract as strictly confidential'
Exclusivity	An agreement not to work for competing organisations or brands for a certain specified amount of time	'The Influencer shall provide the services exclusively for the Client and will not take up any project for competing brands or companies throughout the terms of this Contract and for three additional months afterwards'
Granting of rights	Establishes the right of the influencer to use copyrighted or licensed property of the client	'The Client herein grants the right to use and publish the Client's photographs, logo, and brand messaging for brand purposes during the length of this campaign'
Intellectual property rights	Specifies the ownership of the content produced by the influencer or content creator	'The Client will license the content from the Influencer for a period of three months from the beginning of the campaign, after which full rights will return to the Influencer'
Compensation	Elaborates what the influencer or content creator will be provided as compensation, whether free product, an agreed flat rate, a performance-based commission, cost per view or per action, a combination of these, or another format; may also include a bonus incentive	'The Influencer will be paid at a rate of $2,500 dollars per TikTok post approved and posted. The currency of this contract is US dollars'
Payment terms	Indicates how the payment will be processed, from where to send invoices, payment terms, payment methods, timing, and so on	'Upon completion of services, if payments are not made within 60 days, the Influencer shall have the option to claim a late penalty of $1,000'
Disclosure and FTC Responsibility	Provision that the influencer must comply with all legal disclosure responsibilities; may provide	'The Influencer must comply with all FTC disclosure regulations. Failure to disclose this commercial relationship

(Continued)

Table 10.1   Key elements of influencer and creator contracts *(Continued)*

Contract element	Explanation of element	Short sample clause
	enforcement procedures; may involve penalties if not followed	will result in immediate termination and possible forfeiture of compensation'
Termination	Provides the conditions under which the contract is terminated; usually upon completion of the contract requirements, but sometimes may be triggered by other actions or on a certain date	'The contract may be terminated by either party as follows: upon any breach of contract terms and conditions, or upon 14 days prior written notice to the other party, with or without cause'
Other elements	Might include emergency options (Force Majeure clause), statement that influencer is an independent contractor and not an employee, indemnifying parties against losses or damages, and/or the legal system used in case of a contract dispute	'Nothing contained in this Contract shall be taken to establish any partnership, joint venture, or employment relationship. It is hereby understood and agreed that the Influencers is an independent contractor'

The Campaign Brief

The campaign brief is a more detailed document that is provided to the influencer after the contract negotiations are completed and signed. The campaign brief includes elements of the influencer brief but is more detailed and specific about the influencer requirements. It will contain information such as which performance data are required or which plugins are necessary, as well as where to find them and other software-related terms, or the specifics of the CTAs and coupon codes to be included in the content. Timelines and milestones would most likely be more specific, possibly tied to performance targets or bonuses.

The campaign brief may also include additional information about the company, its products/services and its campaign objectives (including confidential data). Marketing materials to be used and content requirement details are likely inclusions that would provide useful information in addition to what is included in the influencer brief.

In summary, the six main processes involved in the partnering phase are visualised in Figure 10.5. It is easy to see how elaborate the process is and why more long-term influencer relations efforts seek to establish partnerships with influencers or creators that make this process a lot quicker and smoother.

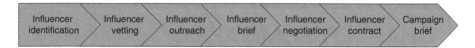

Figure 10.5 Processes involved in the partnering phase

AN IMPORTANT CHALLENGE

Finding the right influencer for a specific campaign involves a number of critical practical considerations. It can be tempting to consider the various criteria we use to select and evaluate influencers to be objective. However, organisations and their managers should be aware that many of their ostensibly objective considerations for judging content creators and influencers may be skewed by their pre-conceptions. As illustrated in this chapter, even influencer marketing platforms and their algorithms can have biases against non-White and non-heteronormative influencers and creators. It is therefore critical for all organisations and for the influencer industry itself to pay close attention not only to the efficiency of the partnering processes but also to the important implications it has for diversity, equity, and inclusion in the future. Careful oversight must occur during the partnering stage if we are to build a more diverse and representative group of influencers and creators and compensate them fairly for their creative labour.

PRODUCT SEEDING

Product seeding or influencer gifting refers to brands sending out free products to a selected group of influencers or creators with the hope that they will produce and share favourable content about the product with their followers. This often happens without negotiations or contracts and, thus, there is no guarantee that it will result in posts. Some brands use product seeding as a first step in the partnering process to create interest and follow up with requests for posts once the product has reached the influencer/creator. Others employ it to maintain relationships with influencers/creators. It is important to consider the amount of gifts many influencers receive. Consequently, carefully selecting the influencers and creators is key to a successful product seeding strategy, as is selecting the right product, personalisation of the gift, and the creation of anticipation by informing the recipients of the shipment. If products are sent out to influencers or creators after the signing of the contract and either with or after sending the campaign brief, this phase is called product fulfilment. Influencer marketing platforms typically provide marketers with useful tools to manage the product seeding or fulfillment step of a campaign.

CHAPTER SUMMARY

Partnering is a critical phase. Brands and other organisations sometimes leverage existing relationships with customers and employees to find authentic influencers and creators. In-house teams, agencies, platforms, and tools are other methods used for identification. Software tools and influencer management platforms can, however, favour White, beautiful, and hetero-sexual content creators and undermine diversity and inclusion goals. Vetting involves establishing criteria against which the influencer's or creator's personal brand, online presence, and track record are judged. Outreach, where the organisation connects with the influencer or creator, is best approached by a message that is concise, clear, and customised but also persuasive. The influencer brief should inform and provide details on the campaign and the influencer's role in it, piquing their interest and allowing them to judge alignment with the brand/the campaign. Negotiation involves investigation, presentation, bargaining, and closure stages. Closure of the negotiation stage results in a contract, and there are numerous important concerns to be captured in this agreement, including campaign timelines, deliverables, content to avoid, content approval process, intellectual property rights, and disclosure responsibility. The campaign brief expands upon the influencer brief and is given after the agreement is finalised. Together, these steps ensure that the rights and obligations of all involved parties are stipulated, trust is built, and that the campaign can run smoothly.

EXERCISES AND QUESTIONS

Exercises

1. Find a recent influencer marketing campaign that involved a large number of influencers with under 50,000 followers. Reverse engineer the influencer identification process. What criteria do you think managers used to discover and evaluate these influencers? Explain why you think those criteria were employed?

2. Read Sophie Bishop's online article 'The Safety Dance' about the link between influencer management software and equity and diversity (available online at https://reallifemag.com/the-safety-dance/). Do you agree with Bishop's analysis? Are there ways that AI programs could increase equity and actually become more objective?

3. Search for free influencer pricing tools like HypeAuditor and Inzpire.me. Use one (or compare several of them) to look up price ranges for influencers within a specific product category (e.g., travel or beauty).

Questions

1. If you had to choose one, what would you say is the single most important sub-stage within the partnering phase: identification, vetting, outreach, negotiation, contract, or providing the campaign brief?

2. What types of influencers are likely to present the most – and least – difficult negotiations?

3. Explain the difference between a campaign brief, an influencer brief and a creative brief in terms of their content and purpose.

4. Intellectual property rights are extremely important both for the brand and for the influencer to protect in the contract. Discuss this statement and explain it using clear and current examples.

ANNOTATED READINGS

Blaney, D. M., & Fleming, K. (2020). *Will Post for Profit: How Brands and Influencers are Cashing in on Social Media*. Orlando, FL: Post Hill Press.

This professional book explores, in an easily digestible format, topics related to influencer marketing from the perspective of both influencers and companies.

Cloutboost. (2021). *Influencer Contract: How to Draft an Agreement Template*. Accessed 10 August 2022. Available from: https://cloutboost.com/influencer-contract-how-to-draft-an-agreement-template/

A short but thorough and engaging walk through the basic elements of influencer contracts useful for in-house managers, influencers, and agencies. Offers tips, examples, and links to useful resources and articles while covering important sections such as deliverables, timeline, content, compliance, payments, usage rights, and more.

11

RUNNING CAMPAIGNS

CHAPTER OVERVIEW AND OBJECTIVES

This chapter will provide an overview of the processes involved in executing an influencer or creator campaign. Campaign execution follows the planning and partnering phases and precedes the post-campaign evaluation phase. Readers will learn about the most important elements of campaign management and how each of them fit into the execution stage. All campaign execution follows similar principles, but implementation will be different depending on the type of influencer campaign. For example, execution is different when executing with only a few top-tier influencers versus with a campaign involving hundreds of nano-influencers. As well, campaign execution differs depending upon whether the influencer campaign is managed by personnel inside the organisation or through an external agency. Regardless of these differences, campaign execution is a content-focused activity involving four overlapping phases. First, managers oversee the content development enacted by influencers or creators. Second, managers evaluate and approve the content. Third, managers supervise and coordinate the distribution of content and the campaign, internally and externally. Finally, managers execute the campaign through ongoing monitoring and adjustment. The chapter will overview important challenges in campaign implementation and provide concrete guidelines to direct best practices.

PROVOCATION: 'If the proof of the pudding is in the tasting, the test of the influencer campaign is in the execution.' (Paraphrasing Nicolas Boileau-Despréaux, *Le Lutrin* (1682))

KEYWORDS: influencer marketing campaign management, brandwashing, campaign monitoring

---

WORKING ON CAMPAIGNS

As we write this book, the current job post for an Influencer Marketing Manager for the Mattel toy company is posted on a prominent online website. The job posting emphasises just how important the day-to-day operations of managing campaigns are for an influencer marketing manager today. Here is the post:

> The Manager, Influencer Marketing within Mattel's Digital Engagement Group will be responsible for the day-to-day management of paid and earned influencer campaigns across Mattel's portfolio of iconic brands, including Barbie, Hot Wheels, Fisher Price, Thomas and Friends, and Mattel Games. This position will oversee global strategy for their vertical portfolio and run end-to-end campaigns from campaign briefing through influencer selection and campaign execution and measurement.

The campaign execution tasks include:

- Collaborating and aligning with the various cross-functional teams at Mattel in order to build influencer activations that meet desired marketing objectives
- Partnering and maintaining relationships with key licensors, understanding their business and position and how it intersects with Mattel's business interests and functions, including during the execution of the influencer campaign
- Ensuring that the final creative and integrations for the influencer campaigns are consistent with the brand brief and meet legal standards
- Managing the existing relationships, and also scouting out and developing new relationships within the digital influencer community, which includes content creators, platforms, agencies, and managers

---

THE ALL-IMPORTANT EXECUTION PHASE: WHAT DOES IT MEAN TO RUN A CAMPAIGN?

This chapter highlights the execution stage of campaigns, which is where the rubber of influencer marketing actually hits the road. As the Mattel job posting in the opening vignette indicates, campaign execution is an important and complex job that is not only interrelated with many of the other aspects of influencer marketing discussed in this book but also with the various functions that happen across organisations, including but not limited to marketing and public relations. Although there are a number of books and blog posts that provide a broad perspective on influencer marketing, there are still very few resources that discuss the complexities of working in the trenches during the day-to-day maintenance of an influencer marketing campaign.

This book's conceptualisation of influencer marketing divides it into four stages: planning, partnering, execution, and evaluation. Planning entails defining the campaign's goals, budgeting for it, considering influencers and who will be chosen, and establishing the key performance indicators by which the campaign will be evaluated (Childers, Lemon, & Hoy, 2019). Influencers are identified and vetted during the campaign pre-launch or partnering stage (Russell, 2020). After outreach, negotiations, contract signing and briefing are completed, the campaign execution phase starts. It can be quite a long and intense phase depending on the length of the campaign, the number of influencers and creators involved, and the complexity of the campaign (types of content, tie-ins with events, etc.).

Significant evaluation of the campaign results occurs during the execution stage as well. Platform technology allows social media marketers to monitor results in real time as a campaign occurs. These measurements are important because they inform adjustments and alterations that happen as a campaign is running. When a campaign is over, and often before agencies and influencers are paid for their work on it, there is usually another set of measurements and reports, as well as a final debriefing with managers and influencers.

INFLUENCER MARKETING CAMPAIGN MANAGEMENT

Influencer marketing campaign management includes the various coordinated processes, activities, systems, software, decisions, algorithms, and platforms that are involved in the delivery of influencer marketing campaigns.

TYPES OF INFLUENCER CAMPAIGNS

There are numerous types of influencer campaigns, each with its own set of best practices for campaign management. Campaigns with top-tier influencers differ not only in terms of cost and complexity of intermediaries involved but also in size. A campaign involving well-known celebrity influencers may only employ one or two. Putting all of the campaign's eggs in a single basket means that a lot is riding on the performance of this one influencer, and campaign execution would be more akin to managing a personal relationship with that one influencer. Nano-influencer campaigns, on the other hand, may involve dozens or even hundreds of influencers who are likely less experienced than the macro or celebrity influencers. Managing large groups of influencers becomes a logistical challenge, and software platforms that can assist with this task become extremely valuable in these circumstances.

Influencer campaigns can be non-profit, political, business-to-business (B2B), or consumer-to-business (B2C). From 2018 to 2020, UNICEF collaborated with Somali American supermodel and activist Halima Aden. During that time, Aden's Instagram account promoted products, some of which she co-designed, that were sold to benefit UNICEF (see Figure 11.1 for an example of a post of this partnership). Michael Bloomberg's campaign paid Instagram influencers to create content supporting him during his bid for the Democratic presidential nomination – an example of a political use of influencer marketing. General Electric launched an influencer marketing campaign in 2016 that included a weeklong branded content deal with Lena Dunham's Lenny Letter website to discuss the role of women in science and encourage more women to apply for technical positions at the company. This is an excellent example of a B2B campaign (Schaffer, 2020) because the company is recruiting employees rather than customers. In this book, we also have many examples of organisations using influencer marketing to sell products and services to end-consumers, which is the most common form of campaign. But no

Figure 11.1   UNICEF campaign with Halima Aden

matter what kind of campaign is being run, there are certain things that must be done and principles that social media managers must keep in mind.

PRINCIPLES OF INFLUENCER CAMPAIGN EXECUTION

Major parts of the campaign have already been set – the budget, the goals, the brand message, the influencers, their compensation, what is expected of them, and so on (Backaler, 2018; Childers, Lemon, & Hoy, 2019) before the execution begins. During execution, the manager is expected to be constantly monitoring the performance of content and influencers/creators. Although monitoring of the performance of particular instances of content takes place in the execution stage, there are further rounds of more comprehensive measurement that take place after the campaign concludes. At this, the campaign implementation or execution stage, the manager's main task is focused on evaluating and overseeing content and its production, ensuring that content production and distribution go as smoothly as possible, monitoring the campaign in its parts and as a whole, and as it transpires, adjusting, tweaking, and amplifying content where needed and possible. In order to perform well at this stage, influencer marketing managers must know what technologies they will need to have in place to monitor and adjust the content the campaign produces, and to have them ready to use. Once the campaign begins, it will be too late to think about what is needed – the manager needs to be fully prepared for all of the elements that are coming in the execution phase.

CAMPAIGN MONITORING

Campaign monitoring involves tracking campaign implementation, progress towards campaign goals and objectives, and external factors relevant to the campaign, such as influencer scandals.

Content Co-development

An influencer campaign is a unique type of advertising campaign. Why? Because, unlike other advertising campaigns, this one is not directly controlled by marketing and brand managers. Influencers and creators are appealing because they bring their own unique perspectives, ideas, creativity, and insider knowledge to the promotional game. Managers report that they hire an influencer because they understand their target audience and can produce more relevant content for them than they can (Santiago & Castelo, 2020). However, just because a manager has hired the right influencers does not mean that their work is finished!

Working with influencers is a critical component of the campaign's execution. The campaign's influencers collaborate with managers to create content that meets the terms of the campaign agreement while also retaining the authenticity and creativity that the creator brings to the process. Often, as both Backaler (2018) and Schaffer (2020) explain, this involves walking a fine line in which managers must give up some control to achieve the best results.

MANAGING CONTENT ON THE COLD PLUNGE

When Scarlette Tidy headed influencer marketing at Kendo Brands, an LVMH company, one of the brands she worked on was Ole Henriksen, a 40-year-old skincare brand sold at Sephora. The brand had just devised a new, bright blue-tinted mask that helped diminish the look of pores and created a cool sensation, inspired by the Cold Plunge rituals of Scandinavia. The Cold Plunge Pore Mask was a highly anticipated launch and one of the influencers Scarlette decided to work with was the famous beauty YouTuber Bretman Rock. Scarlette worked closely with Bretman and allowed him to conceptualise the collaborative content. Bretman had an idea for how he wanted to approach the video content and together, they planned out a multi-scene video in which he would jump – or perhaps not – into a freezing cold lake in Montana.

Although the brand team was aware of the idea, they had no idea exactly what Bretman would do or say. They knew he was a professional and understood the products, but they had no idea what he would do with the cold Montana lake. The brand promise they had asked him to communicate was the cold plunge and reducing the look of pores which were the essence of the product's main marketing message. Although it is always tempting for marketers to try to take over the act of content production, instead, the group at Kendo consciously decided to monitor its creation while simultaneously trying not to interfere with it.

'We didn't provide him with the script and just let him do whatever he wanted, which I think at the time was unusual', explained Scarlette Tidy. 'A lot of brands were "brandwashing" influencers. They were saying, "you have to look this way," "you have to dress this way." And we decided not to brandwash Bretman Rock. His personality is so bold. Trying to have him do something that wasn't true to himself would just flop.'

As they began filming the video, it became clear that Bretman planned to take the hashtag #TakeThePlunge literally and jump into the freezing cold lake. He does, and then comes out dripping wet and freezing cold. Then, he utters the memorable punch line: 'my pores aren't the only thing that are

---

Figure 11.2   Influencer campaign promotion by Bretman Rock

shrinking', which inspires the new hashtag #shrinkage (Seinfeld fans may recognise the reference). Shortly afterward, he is caught on camera relaxing indoors by a warm fireplace, a towel wrapped around his hair, with the product's bright blue mask on his face. At that point, he tells his audience that they don't need to actually jump in a freezing lake to shrink their pores like he did. Instead, they can simply buy the product at Sephora. It was an influencer video worthy of a Madison Avenue advertising firm, delivered by a top influencer in a way that was entirely authentic to him and appropriate to the brand.

Scarlette recalls, 'It was a wild experience; the video just went viral. The word across the beauty community, both from influencers and consumers, leaving comments on Twitter and YouTube was highly positive. People said, 'Wow, this is how you do influencer marketing!' Across Twitter, YouTube, Facebook, and Instagram, the Bretman Rock TakeThePlunge Ole Henriksen video gained 3.2 million views and delighted both Bretman and Ole Henriksen fans. Sales followed when the product launched and took the number 1 spot for masks in Sephora. Later, it was a finalist in the Comedy Video category of the social media industry's 11th annual Shorty Awards (Figure 11.2).

BRANDWASHING

Brandwashing is an informal industry term related to the word 'brainwashing'. It is used to refer to heavy-handed influencer marketing management that occurs during the execution of a campaign in which the brand's managers forcefully control brand messaging to the point where it chokes out the authentic voice of the influencer.

Not every influencer will be as inventive as Bretman Rock in the Ole Henriksen example. Nano-influencers, for example, may require significantly more direction and guidance to create content. Some influencers might simply read from a script. However, this is the least desirable way to work with an influencer and should be discouraged. An influencer's contributions are most meaningful and effective when managers working with them gently guide them through the brand message or brand promise without scripting their communication. Allow them to filter the message through their own personality in a way that is consistent with the relationships they have built with their audience.

The execution thus begins with the organisation working with an influencer or social media content creator to help midwife the creation of original content. The rules are slightly different when managing content from creators because the content is judged on its own merit rather than as a result of the influencers' relationship with their audience. In the content creator case, content can be evaluated using the aesthetic standards established by the brand managers, such as having a certain photographic or graphical design look or feel. Whether for a content creator or an influencer, running the campaign means staying involved in content creation while also managing to give the talent the breathing room they need to work their magic. That is the first stage: co-producing or overseeing the creation of the influencer or creator campaign content. Once that content is created, the next key part of campaign execution is managing approval.

Content Approval

Influencer content created for a campaign is ideally not automatically shared on publicly accessible social media platforms. Instead, it requires approval at that point. This gatekeeping function is an important part of the campaign execution process. Because organisations are complex and have many functions, obtaining content approval often involves several steps. One of the most important factors to consider when evaluating influencer content as part of a campaign's output is whether the content stays 'on message' and adheres to the contractual agreement reached between the influencer and the brand or organisation hiring them. Determining this adherence may not be as easy as it sounds. Influencers understand their audiences and their own voices better than brand managers do. As the Ole Henriksen vignette above shows, brands have frequently attempted to 'brandwash' by using a heavy-handed approach to approve or reject content from campaigns in the past. Especially luxury brands often confront influencers with an avalanche of requirements, from photography angles to appropriate backgrounds. Managers should keep an open mind about style and even consider pushing some of the boundaries that are not found in the formal 'brand book'. Nonetheless, any content or posts that challenge the effective positioning of the brand or cross a moral or ethical line should be rejected.

The approval or rejection process may span several organisational domains, including influencer marketing, brand management, marketing, sales, public relations, information technology, and legal and regulatory compliance. Managers, in particular, must actively enforce the relevant regulations concerning disclosure and fair advertising practice. Compensation for an influencer, even if it is in the form of a discount coupon or a small gift, is treated exactly the same as hiring a spokesperson to share your brand message. The company will be held accountable if that message contains deception or unethical tactics. Furthermore, as legal and regulatory compliance experts will testify, the audience for the content must be made aware that it is sponsored by the brand organisation. All of these details must be reviewed by the manager as the content is created and before it is approved and made public.

General Supervision (Including Internal Coordination)

Once content is created and approved, it starts to go public. At this point the campaign is running. Coordination is important and, although it may have been planned in advance, often there are hiccups as it reaches the execution phase. A campaign often will coordinate with the social media of the brand or company itself. The campaign would be linked in these cases to the brand's social media profiles, to the brand's websites, and to other relevant online assets. Ensuring that these linkages go smoothly will often require coordinating with technical personnel and information technology staff.

Because the influencers and the content of an influencer marketing campaign are not directly under the control of a business, managing the process can mean managing the influencers and their managers. While some influencers are extremely punctual and efficient, completing high-quality work ahead of schedule, others may require prompting and reminders. Some influencers may drop out of the campaign and need to be replaced. Some content may be difficult to approve or may need to go through several rounds before it is acceptable. Some influencers might find it challenging to create content for a particular brand campaign. Others may want to be paid early. After posting campaign content, an influencer may do, say, or post something unsavoury, and difficult decisions must then be made about the influencer's relationship with the brand. The manager's job is to be on top of all of these concerns, whatever they might be.

Because influencer marketing is still so new, there may be many job tasks and responsibilities that overlap in different industries and companies with the tasks we describe in this chapter and this book. Many organisations, particularly small and medium sized ones, may lack internal expertise in influencer marketing or economies of scale for conducting campaigns and therefore would be likely to employ external agencies such as Influence Hunter, Open Influence, or We Are Social to help them design and run the campaigns. Internally, a marketing manager or the Director of Communication would likely have responsibility for hiring the agency and making decisions about the campaign as it is being executed by the external agency. Within the agency, account managers often coordinate the various functions. In particular, the account manager would act as the liaison between the various people involved in managing the campaign at the agency and the person or persons they would report to and coordinate with at the organisation or brand that hired them.

Oftentimes, managers want results from these campaigns in real time, necessitating reports. Who provides these reports and manages the process? As influencer marketing has become established in industries such as fashion, cosmetics, fitness, food, travel, and technology, more jobs become institutionalised with names such as Influencer Marketing Manager and Director, Influencer Marketing or Influencer Relations Manager. These in-house job titles usually indicate an internal organisational responsibility for the executional phases (as well as many of the other phases) of the influencer marketing campaign process. Often, these internal positions will report to the Director of Communication, Head of Public Relations, a marketing manager, or the Chief Marketing Officer, depending upon how the organisation is structured. These are generally the types of roles who would execute, monitor, and report on the ongoing influencer marketing or content creation campaigns.

Ongoing Monitoring and Adjustment

Supervising an ongoing influencer or creator campaign overlaps with the monitoring and adjustment functions that accompany it because supervision requires information. As the campaign unfolds, content is shared with audiences. Then, people comment on and may like or share it. Buyers redeem coupon codes producing data trails that can be seen. Online sales can be measured and, if coupon or discount codes are used, they can be traced back to the content that initiated them.

It is the responsibility of the influencer marketing manager – or another internal or external stakeholder tasked with executing the influencer campaign – to carefully monitor all of these things. Are the individual posts gaining the reach (the number of impressions) as well as expected? If expectations are not being met, what is the explanation? Collectively, is the campaign getting engagement in the form of comments, likes, and shares? Are sales being made, or are other campaign criteria being reached?

One of the most crucial elements to the execution stage is the presence of high-quality influencer marketing software that can help the manager monitor and adjust the campaign as it is running in real time. There are a number of different platforms and packages available from companies such as HubSpot, Upfluence, AspireIQ, Pixlee, and IZEA. During the campaign, these platforms can provide a dashboard or other broad overview allowing the manager to monitor all of the various influencers that are producing content and aggregate in one place the metrics relating to their content and its public reception. Having this knowledge allows the manager to understand which content is doing well and which content is not doing well. In a recent study, influencer marketing managers considered the ability to monitor the campaign 'enormously relevant' because it allowed them to respond and make changes to the campaign 'if something unforeseen happens, or if something is not implemented according to what was previously negotiated' (Santiago & Castelo, 2020: 47).

At this point one of the managers' most important tasks is often to amplify the content that is doing well by paying to promote it to additional audiences beyond the ones that it gathers organically. Software can help the manager to stay on top of which influencers have created content and fulfilled their contract and which ones still have yet to make their contributions to the campaign period. Influencer marketing changes the game from prior versions of marketing because of this real time management aspect. For performance-based campaigns, the monitoring gives insights into which influencers are doing well and should maybe be 'upgraded' in terms of opportunities, responsibilities and amplification. This is advertising done in real time with new abilities given to managers to not only monitor and assess but also to alter and adjust by amplifying high-performing content and getting it in front of the right audience at the right time.

In total, these are the four critical elements of executing an influencer marketing or content creation campaign: (1) developing and co-developing the campaign messaging, (2) gaining approval for content, (3) ongoing campaign supervision including internal coordination, and (4) monitoring and adjusting the campaign on the go. Figure 11.3 presents these core elements in diagrammatic form.

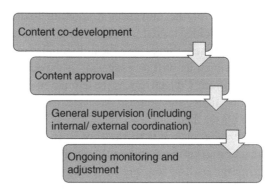

Figure 11.3 The key phases of influencer campaign execution

IMPLEMENTATION CHALLENGES

One of the most significant barriers to successful influencer marketing is campaign implementation. To paraphrase Robert Burns' immortal poem, influencer marketers' best laid plans frequently go awry once the campaign begins! Santiago and Castelo (2020: 46) found that managers reported three main factors to be the most crucial for campaign coordination: evaluation, monitoring, and negotiation. The managers in charge of campaign execution must overcome a number of significant implementation challenges. Fundamental marketing practices play an obvious and important role. We worked with one CBD (cannibinoid) company that used influencer marketing to stoke demand but then could not handle the logistics of shipping its products! People who had ordered the product did not get it for a long time because their supply chain was not working. A fundamental principle of marketing is not to advertise unless you are sure you can deliver on your orders. Otherwise, no matter how good your product, you will not receive repeat business. Organisations must be sure that they can handle the orders when they build demand for them using influencer marketing.

Negotiating and managing the diverse expectations of the campaign's various players is another key challenge. Unless the process is clearly spelled out in the contractual agreement and there are no unexpected twists and turns, there may be confusion about what is expected of the influencers or creators and what role the brand and any agencies involved will play. What are the expectations of an influencer, their manager, and their agent? Working in the influencer industry may entail dealing with relatively inexperienced content producers or talented 16-year-old micro-influencers and the parents who manage them, colloquially known as 'momagers'. Negotiation skills are frequently required to smooth over any bumps in the road as the campaign gets underway.

Other significant challenges include coordinating the campaign's various functions and parts. Marketing, as represented by the PESO model, is a multi-headed beast that is frequently spread across traditional media channels as well as social media and websites. These disparate parts must be integrated for maximum effectiveness. Working on an influencer campaign, which can include dozens or even hundreds of pieces of content, and sharing the right content to the right people, via the right form of media, at the right time can be a logistical challenge. Furthermore, social media campaigns may be required to move and exchange content across platforms. Integrating YouTube videos with Facebook posts and Pinterest boards presents its own set of challenges but can be extremely rewarding when done correctly. Social media platforms are also dynamic. They frequently change their algorithms, causing campaign results to change. Careful management entails keeping abreast of any technical changes that may have an impact on the outcome of the influencer marketing campaign.

Because of the many platforms and tools involved and the focus on metrics, campaign managers sometimes forget the people management aspects of influencer and creator campaigns. It is nonetheless important to not only monitor influencers' campaign-related performance but also their overall activities to avoid being dragged into scandals. And campaign managers need to remind themselves that they must be available for influencers and creators throughout the process to provide information, address concerns, and give feedback. This sometimes means being on location with influencers or creators during their content creation process. Mutual trust and seeing campaigns as partnerships rather than transactions are key success factors.

WHY TRUST IS ESSENTIAL FOR SUCCESS, BY SCARLETTE TIDY

The best advice I could ever give about influencer marketing is to BUILD TRUST! If you are an agency, win the trust of your client. If you are in-house, build the trust of your peers and leadership. If you are working with an influencer, trust their process! Do this by constantly educating along the way and asking questions. Get clarity upfront and explain your process, no matter how simple or intricate. Despite what many people think, there is not one formula or road to success within this field. As influencer marketers, we know that sometimes taking the 'scenic' route (while longer) gives the biggest reward. Do your best to educate and build trust with the people involved in the strategy and execution of your projects so you can explore any road you like. Without trust, creativity is stunted. Without creativity, campaigns are unable to explore the many avenues to success. You never know which route will unlock a win or learning that will catapult a brand forward. It only takes one out-of-the-box campaign to do so!

Scarlette Tidy is an influencer and social media marketer with years of experience growing consumer brands through influencer partnerships and social storytelling. She is the founder of Sure Thing Consulting, a digital marketing agency with clients such as Fenty Beauty, Ole Henriksen, Ellis Brooklyn, Birdies, and many more. You can find Scarlette at surethingco.com and @sure-thingconsulting on social.

BEST PRACTICES AND GUIDELINES

HOW EOS MANAGED TIKTOK FOR INCREDIBLE SALES SUCCESS

Eos is a skincare company that sells high-quality lip and body care in a colourful egg-shaped package. Eos decided to increase its involvement in TikTok influencer marketing in 2022 and used careful campaign management to do so. The brand spent a full 15% of its annual marketing budget on sponsored campaigns with TikTok influencers, carefully monitoring ongoing results, boosting content through ads, and then deepening their influencer relationships with established winners in order to develop outstanding brand content.

Eos discovered that Carly Joy's Eos video was exploding on TikTok. Carly offered viewers a candid shaving tutorial in her video, explaining how Eos' shaving cream allowed her to shave her lady parts and get a beautiful, bump-free shave. The managers increased exposure to the informal shaving tutorial by using the platform's ability to promote videos, resulting in 19 million views and over 5 million likes. This feat of executional wizardry multiplied Joy's extremely effective content production's reach and engagement. Eos claims that Joy's TikTok video resulted in a 25-fold increase in website orders and a 450-fold increase in site visits to its shave category.

Eos CMO Soyoung Kang stated, 'Carly Joy says our shaving cream is an absolute blessing – but Carly Joy is the true absolute blessing here' (Diaz, 2021). The next step for Eos was to incorporate the campaign's findings into the company by linking them to new product development – as well as to launch another influencer marketing campaign. So, following the phenomenal success of the saucy Joy video, Eos and their agency, Mischief @ No Fixed Address, collaborated with Carly to create an ultra-limited edition 'Cooch Blessing Cream' that uses her saucy language as its new brand.

Eos was not engaging in traditional marketing in any way. However, it leveraged insight into an audience and the honest voice they preferred to hear. Executing the campaign required that Eos' influencer marketing managers stayed attuned to what was working and to discover the unconventional but highly effective content Carly Joy delivered to her audience. As a result, Eos provides an example of cutting-edge influencer marketing campaign execution.

Successfully executing a well-planned influencer marketing campaign leaves little room for error. Organisations that have mastered successfully implementing these campaigns typically hire educated and qualified individuals, train them thoroughly, provide them with the best and most up-to-date software or platform subscriptions, and give them the freedom to do their jobs. These organisations are also very clear about the importance of due diligence. Personnel are fully aware of the most recent regulations governing the influencer marketing space and understand the importance of enforcing these rules, whether working with agencies or directly with influencers in-house. Compliance experts are on hand to answer questions and ensure that everyone understands their responsibilities. Top-tier organisations clearly communicate the best practices for ethical, diverse, and effective campaigns that achieve financial as well as social objectives. There are clear chains of command between those working on the campaign and those to whom they report. When agencies are involved, liaisons between them are clearly defined and used as needed. Strong knowledge management processes are also in place in which solid record keeping keeps track of what worked and what didn't for each campaign as well as which skills were adequate, and which still needed to be developed, amongst the various constituents involved. Over time, these practices lead to increased skills being developed and continually improving.

Figure 11.4 presents some important dos and don'ts to remember when executing an influencer campaign. We hope that you will find them useful as you manage your campaigns.

Influencer Campaign Execution Dos and Don'ts

DO	DON'T
• Have a campaign management process in place (can always be customized or altered later on, but have a basic process)	• Leave it to chance!–Don't forget to plan, plan, and plan some more before the campaign begins
• Have a Plan B. Be ready with fallback position (such as having some dependable key influencers in reserve)	• Try to go it alone! Instead, work with other marketing elements and exploit the synergies that come from working together
• Have good up-to-date tools and use them	• Put all the weight of the campaign upon your influencers' shoulders; remember that this is your campaign, you need to manage it
• Take a test and learn approach: there is no failure, there is only learning and growing	
• Execute in coordination with other marketing tactics, if possible; emphasise synergies	• Overmanage the process; remember 'freedom within a framework'; you don't have to interfere with content unless there is a problem (disclosure, inappropriate, indecent)
• Take the time to answer questions from influencers during the campaign; make sure they are familiar with the brand, the campaign and its goals, and their own contractual obligations	• Forget to monitor the flow of content; instead, be ready to act to remove content that is problematic or amplify content that is working well
• Measure and keep measuring throughout the campaign	• Sweat the small stuff along the way. Remember it is all part of a learning process
• Monitor the flow of content carefully, and keep track of it, be ready to amplify high-performing content with a clear plan	

Figure 11.4   The dos and don'ts of influencer campaign execution

CHAPTER SUMMARY

Campaign execution comes after the planning and partnering phases and precedes the campaign evaluation phase. All campaign execution follows similar principles, but implementation will be different depending on the type of influencer campaign. As well, campaign execution differs depending upon whether the influencer campaign is managed by personnel inside the organisation or through an external agency. Regardless of these differences, campaign execution is a people and content-focused activity involving four overlapping phases. First, managers oversee the content development enacted by influencers or creators. Second, managers evaluate and approve the content. Third, managers supervise and coordinate the distribution of content and the campaign, internally and externally. Finally, managers execute the campaign through ongoing monitoring and adjustment. Influencer and social media monitoring platforms are important tools that allow managers to identify top-performing content so that it can be amplified by paying platforms for wider distribution. Implementation challenges include dealing with influencers who drop out, unclear chains of command, being unable to handle demand, managing the differing expectations of brand personnel and influencers, and coordinating the campaign's various functions and subcomponents. The performance of top-notch organisations reveals that managers of influencer campaigns must be fully present during the campaign, monitoring

> and adjusting content and replacing influencers as needed, and always ready to pounce on and take full advantage of any opportunities that emerge while also avoiding overmanaging the creative talent and brandwashing the content.

EXERCISES AND QUESTIONS

Exercises

1. Identify an example of a recent influencer marketing campaign. What kind of campaign was it?

2. Examine online some of the available options for influencer monitoring platforms. Provide a mock report to your manager recommending which platform you need to perform your tasks as an influencer marketing manager.

Questions

1. How are influencer and creator content campaigns different? How do these differences affect campaign execution?

2. An influencer for your new campaign ends up producing an explicit video that takes the product to unexpected new places. What do you do? [Hint: what questions would you need to ask before you could act?]

3. Name two important ways that the goals of brand managers and agency personnel might diverge

ANNOTATED READINGS

Santiago, J. K., & Castelo, I. M. (2020). Digital influencers: An exploratory study of influencer marketing campaign process on Instagram. *Online Journal of Applied Knowledge Management (OJAKM)*, 8(2), 31–52.

Beginning to cast a light on dimly understood parts of the influencer marketing campaign process, this study is based on eight interviews with professionals working with influencers in public relations, communication, and digital influencer agencies.

12

MEASURING AND ASSESSING CAMPAIGNS

CHAPTER OVERVIEW AND OBJECTIVES

Measurement is a key element of working with influencers and creators. Through a combination of definition, explanation, vignettes, and practitioners' perspectives, readers of this chapter will learn the fundamental concepts and best practices governing contemporary influencer relations and campaign management. The why, how, what, who, and when of influencer measurement will be thoroughly explained and discussed. Readers will gain critical knowledge about the role of return on investment (ROI), the importance of non-economic measures, qualitative metrics, and linking campaign and organisational goals to specific key performance indicators (KPIs).

PROVOCATION: 'If you can't measure something, you can't understand it. If you can't understand it, you can't control it. If you can't control it, you can't improve it'.- H. James Harrington, *Business Process Improvement* (1994)

KEYWORDS: awareness, conversion, earned media value, impressions, key performance indicator, vanity metrics, reach, return on investment

> ## LEESA MATTRESS MEASURES THEIR INFLUENCER CAMPAIGN
>
> Leesa is a luxury direct-to-consumer mattress company which only sells online. Although customers can try out their mattresses risk free for 100 nights, they need to trust the company enough to make that commitment. In order to engage their target audience, the brand collaborated with micro-influencers. They wanted to reach out to people looking to buy a new mattress in the next six months, as well as online savvy women with an interest in interior design and DIY topics.
>
> The brand sought unbiased reviews to build trust. Influencers were given creative freedom by the company to come up with their own unbiased and authentic reviews. The influencers were contacted and offered a mattress in exchange for an unbiased review.
>
> After a successful initial round, managers sought to identify what made influencers impactful so they could take the learnings to another, larger round. They identified the following metrics as important:
>
> - A high engagement level. This turned out to be more important than followers or unique visitors.
> - High clickthrough or conversion rates.
> - Brand focus. The team evaluated how the reviewers wrote about the brand and how long those posts were online.
> - Social presence. Bloggers and vloggers were chosen who had posts that could be amplified on Facebook, Twitter, Instagram, YouTube, and/or Pinterest.
>
> In the end, the program drove an additional 100,000 clicks to the Leesa website and the company attributed more than 400 mattress sales directly to the campaign. Matt Hayes, the Head of Marketing for Leesa advised marketers who want to run an influencer campaign at scale to have a strong method on hand for estimating conversion and then tracking it back to measuring performance. By being smart about metrics, he said 'You can get better about the creative that you're choosing, about the messaging that you choose and the content creators' (Johnson, 2016).

TRADITIONAL ADVERTISING MEASUREMENT

Measuring the effectiveness of advertising is crucial for making informed investments. However, advertising measurement has long been a bit of a dark art. It was not all that long ago that advertisers did not have social media apps to broadcast their messages and digital dashboards available to estimate conversion and track it to performance. In fact, there was a time when coupons were printed on paper and contained little identification numbers. Those paper coupons were a way for advertisers to track the effectiveness of their ads. Did people actually read that magazine ad, clip the coupon, and buy the product? Did they use that coupon pack that got dropped in their mailbox? When a coupon was redeemed, the marketers knew.

CONVERSION

A concept, linked to the marketing or sales funnel, that measures how many or what percentage of consumers move from the top of the funnel (e.g., search and social search) to the middle (e.g., online vetting through reading reviews) to the bottom (e.g., purchase on an e-commerce site). Also often used synonymously with sales (as in 'did they convert [into sales]?'). On social media, it measures how often a piece of content starts the process to a conversion event like a subscription, download, or sale.

IMPRESSIONS

An estimated measure of the number of people who had an opportunity to be exposed to the advertisement. On social media, it refers to the number of times a piece of content was displayed.

REACH

A measure of the number of people or unique users who were exposed at least once to an ad during a particular time frame. Social media sometimes distinguish between organic and paid reach, which describe whether the exposure occurred freely or was paid for by the advertiser.

AWARENESS

A statistical estimate of some group's familiarity with, recognition of, or ability to recall a brand or product.

Advertising still encompasses a variety of media that may be linked to digital components, but which did not grow up in a digital age. Consider the many outdoor (out of home or 'OOH') ads that surround us, including highway and street billboards, ads on buses and subways, and advertising on the sides of buildings. Advertising at events (poster stands, display screens, etc.) is also extremely important, and so are the many shelf-talkers, endcap displays, and other forms of retail, point-of-purchase (POP) and point-of-sale (POS) advertising displays. Of course, advertising placed within broadcast media such as radio and television is still a big part of the media landscape. Advertising across all of these media needs to be measured, and these same established forms of measurement – coupons (which now include QR codes and 1–800 numbers), impressions, reach, brand recall, awareness, perceptions, attitude, and purchase intent – are still essential tools for marketers (Stout & Leckenby, 1986).

One of the big attractions of influencer marketing is that it can deliver an abundance of measures about the performance of content. In contrast to traditional advertising measurement that largely informs future campaigns, it also allows for measurement to have a more immediate and direct impact on a campaign if monitoring occurs throughout. Last, but not least, it can save a lot of money if the campaign is performance-based. Thus, while influencer marketing is often hailed for its ability to break through to and engage target audiences and for the valuable content assets it produces, it should also be praised for its measurability.

INFLUENCER MARKETING MEASUREMENT (IMM): THE BIG PICTURE

Influencer marketing measurement (or IMM), is also called metrics, and sometimes called analytics. It developed from the earlier basis of advertising measurement and still contains many of the same basic ideas, such as quantifying impressions, measuring awareness, and using coupons to track effectiveness and sales conversions. The focus of most advertising today, just as it always has been and probably always will be, is on sales. Using financial terms, sales are also called revenues. A poll by Influencer Marketing Hub (2022b) found that 42% of brand managers believe that sales (also called 'conversions') are the most important measure of marketing success. Later in this section, we will discuss ROI, which is an important metric often used as a measure of short run advertising efficiency and effectiveness. However, influencers and creators are often used to create content assets and to enhance brand equity. These are often longer term prospects and can be very difficult to measure in the short-run.

Short-term sales are not everything. Branding is about building lasting relationships that result in revenue streams that last. Whether talking about B2B or

B2C advertising, customer acquisition is key, and keeping a customer is how an organisation cashes out the customer lifetime value. When a customer switches to a new pet food, for instance, this is usually not a single sale, but one that keeps paying off for the marketers month after month and often year after year.

Branding is also about understanding your customers and their ever-changing and unmet needs. Used intelligently, measurement is the key tool that allows marketers to understand customers and the marketplace in a way that will impact revenues in the short, medium, and long term. In the Tomoson (2022) study, 40% of respondents said that brand exposure – in other words, awareness – was the main purpose of influencer marketing. For a company that plans to be around in the long run, short term sales are not enough, and the intelligence that comes from measurement is a critical way that both short and long run sales can be optimised by building ever-more-meaningful customer relationships. That is the core difference between influencer relations and influencer advertising. An average marketer looks at an advertising campaign and asks, 'did it work?' or 'how much did we make?' A superior marketer wants to know 'why did it work, or not work?', 'what did we learn?', and 'how will we benefit from it in the future?' Sophisticated and goal-directed measurement is how intelligent marketers gain this understanding. Furthermore, compensation for influencers is often based on their performance. Performance-based compensation is another important motivation for accurate measurement.

VANITY METRICS

Vanity metrics are easily measured and often superficially impressive measures, such as follower counts, likes, reposts, or number of comments, that make a campaign look good but say little about its actual impact.

Using 'vanity metrics' such as shares or reposts is relatively easy. But thinking critically and strategically about influencer marketing and its results is neither easy nor simple, but it is the right way to approach IMM. Consider that increases in follower counts mean little to a campaign when followers may be the wrong target, for instance. As influencer marketing podcaster Jason Falls puts it, 'do you want Instagrammers and YouTubers to mention your brand? Or do you want to influence an audience to buy your product?' Especially when a manager is new to influencer marketing, they might be impressed by working with an influencer with 10 million followers who can deliver on impressions. But that sea of followers might not be necessary or even useful.

Metrics are clarifying because they focus the organisation on what it wants to accomplish. KPIs, cost per mille (CPM), impressions, and reach can be proof that a campaign was successful and serve as key inputs for campaign management or future success. Or they can be smoke and mirrors used to obscure more than they reveal. Gaining useful content that can be used again and again in paid campaigns on Facebook or other platforms may, for instance, be a more important goal. Whether a measure is useful or not has to do with how it relates to the goals of the organisation overall, and specifically of the campaign. The path to critical and strategic thinking in marketing runs through metrics and measurement.

KEY PERFORMANCE INDICATOR (OR KPI)

A specified achievement variable used to formally evaluate the success of an organisation, individual, or an activity like a campaign.

COST PER MILLE (OR CPM)

The cost per thousand persons exposed to an advertisement.

What does it mean to think critically and strategically about influencer marketing and IMM? It means that conclusions about what and how to measure are reached after careful forethought and intelligent consideration about the information required, the best way to collect it, what time frames to use, who will be responsible and, most importantly, the reasons for the measurement. We call this the why, how, what, who, and when of measurement.

BUILDING KPIS INTO EVERY STAGE, BY SYBIL GRIEB

Set your KPIs as the foundation for every stage of your influencer campaign. Develop a strategy based on what you plan to achieve even before identifying potential creators. Then, keep in mind the call to action (or CTA) that you want creators to include and adjust your platform and creative strategy to align with it. To determine which CTA will have the greatest impact on your KPIs, first define success for this campaign and then reverse engineer your strategy to achieve it.

Best practices:
To maximise ROI on all creator content, use paid media to increase views on the creator's channel as well as to lookalike audiences or other target markets

where the creator's voice will resonate. Track performance and optimise to promote more views of the top performing assets or key messages. Then, apply what you've learned to all future creator campaigns!

Sybil Grieb is a Digital Marketing Strategist and SVP of Brand Partnerships at Whalar.

The Why of IMM

What is the reason we go to the effort of measuring what has happened in an influencer or creator campaign? At times, measurement helps us manage an ongoing process. Knowing which influencers' content is performing best can help us to amplify our efforts with paid media and increase results in the short term. But there is a lot more to measurement than simply helping to execute a campaign. Measurement is about determining whether the organisation has reached its goals. It is often also tied to compensation, so accurate measurement is necessary for a fair and equitable pay out for the influencers and others who have helped with the campaign. Measurement is more forward-looking than this, too.

Organisations all have competencies and capacities that allow them to survive in society. A brand's competencies are around producing goods and services that meet customer needs and then communicating and distributing those things in a way that creates mutual value. If a brand does that well, it survives, and marketing goods and services to customers is therefore key to survival. So, most companies do not just want to do one-off marketing campaigns and then stop. They realise that marketing and consumer understanding is an ongoing process at which they need to keep getting better.

IMM is both instrumental and strategic. Having a sound approach to metrics informs people across the organisation how it will perform the various facets of influencer marketing in the future, such as how it will next identify, vet, and compensate influencers and creators. Through measurement, influencer campaigns become a way to build the long-term orientation that goes with influencer relations. Measurement is not only for understanding what happened in the past. It is the most solid foundation for an organisation to plan what it will do in the future. If influencer marketing is going to be built into the company as an ongoing effort – and this means embracing influencer relations – then metrics are the way this is achieved intelligently and with foresight.

The key to good metrics is clear goals. It is absolutely critical for an organisation to set appropriate goals for its influencer marketing campaigns. Without knowing what they want to get out of the campaign, managers cannot tell whether a campaign was successful or not. Previously, we discussed four big categories of goals related to what influencers and creators can do for marketers: (1) awareness, (2) conversion, (3) content creation, and (4) insights. Although there can be overlap, each of these goals is specific enough that measuring success for each one is different. A creator that is hired to create content cannot be expected to increase awareness, for instance – the goals are distinct.

There are also auxiliary goals, as well, such as streamlining influence compensation, which we have discussed, as well as SEO and reputation management. Campaign goals might embrace equity or inclusion goals and seek to benefit a wider group of stakeholders. The marketing funnel introduced earlier is a useful way to clarify campaign goals. Is the campaign intended to raise awareness, increase interest, gain consumer consideration, prompt the action of purchase, increase satisfaction with a product, build loyalty, or inspire advocacy? Across the funnel, content creation turns out to be a key brand goal of many influencer and creator relationships. These are all legitimate goals. But to be measured, they need to be specified.

The What and Why of ROI

RETURN ON INVESTMENT (ROI)

A quantified measure used to evaluate the financial performance of an investment. In marketing, it represents the most direct application of financial standards to the marketing function.

The single most popular and most controversial metric in IMM is ROI. The ROI metric is popular because it is simple, all-purpose, and comparable. It is controversial because it is often overused and applied where returns may be long term or difficult to quantify. Nonetheless, as influencer marketing became established, managers seemed to be applying it to sales conversions that welcome quantification, and the ROI model firmly took hold. In 2021, 70% of brands reported that they measure the ROI of their influencer marketing (Influencer Marketing Hub, 2022b).

Relatedly, marketers answering an Influencer Marketing Hub (2022b) poll calculated that their businesses were earning $5.20 for every dollar they spent on influencer marketing. A different survey put the number at $6.50 for every dollar invested (Tomoson, 2022). An earlier study, by Burst media (2015), analysed 48 campaigns across 15 verticals and found a return of $6.85 but offered some interesting details. The Burst study reported how widely the results varied by industry.

Fashion and food brands were making over $10 per dollar spent, but home and garden companies were losing money on their investment. It seems likely, then, that the ROI of influencer marketing depends on many factors, just like all marketing does. It is also likely that true returns cannot be calculated in the short run because content often takes time to filter down into sales. Customer lifetime value also is an important contributor to long-term returns that must be factored in.

So, although ROI is a popular measure, it is diligent to take a look under the hood to understand its strengths and limitations better. As Figure 12.1 illustrates, the formula for influencer marketing ROI is calculated by taking the cost of the investment in influencer marketing and subtracting it from the incremental financial value that is gained as a result of the investment in influencer marketing, and then dividing that figure by the cost of the marketing investment. The result of this calculation tells you what the return is for every $1.00 (or whatever currency you might be using) invested in influencer marketing.

Calculating influencer marketing ROI looks simple. But looks can be deceiving! First, it can be tricky to incorporate all the costs that go into influencer marketing. Let's say a brand runs a gifting program and sends out 50 gift packs. The costs of the products in the gift packs and the packaging are relatively easy to account for. But the courier fees and insurance involved in sending them out can be significant. How about the attorney's fees for the influencer contracts? What about the time and energy invested in managing the entire process from beginning to end? The software subscriptions to influencer management platforms? If a company has held one or more influencer events, the complexity of the cost calculations balloons even further. In other words, what you pay for an influencer is not just what is shown on their rate card. It is everything invested into the marketing effort.

Calculating Influencer Marketing Return on Investment

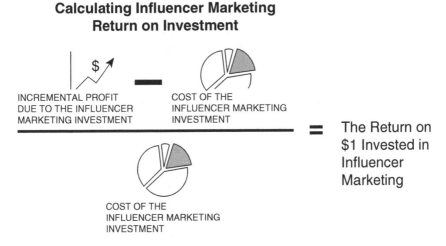

INCREMENTAL PROFIT DUE TO THE INFLUENCER MARKETING INVESTMENT − COST OF THE INFLUENCER MARKETING INVESTMENT

COST OF THE INFLUENCER MARKETING INVESTMENT

= The Return on $1 Invested in Influencer Marketing

Figure 12.1   The formula for influencer marketing return on investment (ROI)

And what exactly is the return? As Gallo (2017) points out, it can be difficult to measure the incremental financial value of any marketing investment. A company would need to establish a sales baseline that predicted what sales and profits would have been if they had not spent on this marketing program. When there is a measurable incremental lift in sales, it still can be difficult to attribute that increase to one campaign rather than another. If social media posts remain online, campaigns can continue producing long after the official campaign ends. This would be an under-reporting of return. Another important factor is the value of the earned media or advertising, which is calculated by measures such as earned media value (EMV). Will EMV be factored into the equation, and how?

EARNED MEDIA VALUE (EMV)

EMV, which is closely related to advertising value equivalency (AVE) and other similar measures seeking to estimate the value of media exposure, is a quantified estimate of the monetary value of the marketing and PR exposure gained through social media content exposure, which means all social media content and mentions on third-party sites that were not created or paid for by the brand (Post Beyond Marketing, 2021). EMV assigns a dollar value to every interaction made with a social media post or account – things such as shares, likes, comments, and retweets – and calculates the total value of them as an 'earned media' total (Elliott, 2019). AVE stresses the amount one would have had to invest in paid media to gain the same kind of exposure.

To accurately assess influencer marketing's organisational utility, we must consider the value of the returns to influencer marketing in the long run. It can contribute to marketing insights and, through them, to the organisation's competencies, sense of customer awareness, and ability to thrive into the future. Organisations can learn about new segments or market needs. Proximity to insightful influencers can lead to marketing insights that allow a brand to create a new product. It could be a collaboration, such as the way Denny's diner developed delicious new cookie dough pancakes when they collaborated with Jenny Solares and the EnkyBoys. Those delectable pancakes might be sold for the next ten years (we can only hope!).

Bringing insightful influencers into an organisation's culture also has the potential to impact the company by inspiring more awareness and understanding of the perspectives of important consumers, something that marketing scholars call 'marketing orientation' (Kohli & Jaworski, 1990). That sort of change can have a powerful long-term effect on a brand (Gebhardt et al., 2006). How would that type of long-term, new product producing, marketing insight driven return be measured? Its cultural effects on the corporate bottom line would be very real but may not ever be fully quantifiable.

ROI is only one tool. It is not appropriate for all types of goals and should be used with caution. Influencers, creators, managers, and everyone else involved in influencer marketing must vigilantly ensure that the concept of 'return' used in the ROI calculation accurately reflects the objectives of the campaign and organisation. ROI calculations demonstrate powerfully that what influencers and what creators bring to the table differs. To simply assess the revenue boost from the content produced by creators is to miss their advantage. Creators are creating assets comparable to what professional photographers and other content producers might offer but often doing it at significantly reduced cost levels. Therefore, trying to assess the value of a creator campaign by measuring revenue increase misses the point that they 'aid in decreasing marketing expenses' (Schaffer, 2020: 204). Instead, the ROI of a creator campaign should value their return by also calculating the cost savings that are provided to the organisation.

The How of IMM

USING METRICS TO TELL A STORY, BY SCARLETTE TIDY

While influencer marketing is, in fact, a science, it's also an art form and is subjective. What is viral for one brand is certainly not viral for the next. That's why metrics aren't as black and white as you think. When running a report to measure the success of an influencer campaign, one-off sponsored post, or even analysing a product seeding, there has to be a personalised approach to back up the story within the data. Even though my favourite metrics are easily pulled from reporting and analytics tools (aka total reach, impressions, video views, engagement rate, number of posts, etc.), there are stories beyond the data that help provide a deeper understanding of the learnings and wins! Questions I often ask myself when building a report – what was the comment section like? How authentic were the influencer's testimonials about the brand or product? What did the KPIs look like on other posts around similar products? How enjoyable was the content? Was this partnership innovative? Did we learn anything about our internal processes that we can improve?

Scarlette Tidy is an influencer and social media marketer with years of experience growing consumer brands through influencer partnerships and social storytelling. She is the founder of Sure Thing Consulting, a digital marketing agency with clients such as Fenty Beauty, Olehenriksen, Ellis Brooklyn, Birdies, and many more. You can find Scarlette at surethingco.com and @surethingconsulting on social.

A few major considerations affect how to approach measurement. The first concerns the use of qualitative and quantitative metrics. Quantitative measures obviously dominate marketing today and influencer marketing is no exception. ROI, EMV, conversion rates, promotional coupon redemptions, engagement rates, reach, and measures of content produced and viewed are all examples of quantitative metrics. The contents of comments people leave on posts, the reviews they write or record are qualitative data composed of text that need to be scrutinised beyond their amount. A user-generated image of a brand posted on Instagram is also qualitative. Other useful qualitative metrics include comments and suggestions received from influencers, agency people, or the internal management team.

Qualitative data can be rich and informative, but is often more difficult to code or work with. Nevertheless, it is important not to overlook it as a valuable KPI (Gräve, 2019). Reducing comments or images to simple counts or using automated sentiment analysis systems tends to drain out meaning and possible insight. Instead of diminishing qualitative data, powerful techniques such as netnography can be used to provide deep insight into a campaign and its outputs (Femenia-Serra, Gretzel, & Alzua-Sorzabal, 2022; Gambetti & Kozinets, 2022; Kozinets, 2020b). By immersing into a campaign and reading through and interpreting comments and reviews, finding patterns in visual and audiovisual data, and locating powerful deep data, influencer marketing managers can use netnography to gain holistic and unvarnished insights into campaigns, content, influencers, and creators.

Qualitative measurement is particularly important for goals that are intrinsically qualitative. How about having a goal of attracting a diverse or representative group of influencers and paying everyone fairly? What if a brand decided to use its campaign to try to further a social issue, or depolarise a polarised political situation? Measuring the success of goals such as these requires nuanced and qualitative measurement.

The final consideration is parsimony. In research, being parsimonious means gathering only the most important and relevant information without all the frills. In measurement, more is not always better. Although you often want to avoid measurement error by triangulating several KPIs, it is not necessary to throw the metrics book at every measurement question. Managers sometimes do excessive measurement because they are not clear on exactly what they wanted to achieve. Social media and influencer marketing platforms often shower managers with all sorts of metrics to prove their value. Following our disciplined process of goals first – the why before the what – is a good way to avoid that problem. A parsimonious approach, along with an attention to a good balance of qualitative and quantitative, can guide strong IMM.

The What of IMM

Understanding the why of measurement establishes the foundation for all other questions. If a manager knows the reason behind the marketing efforts – in other words, the goals, or desired returns – then they should automatically gain a much clearer sense of what they then need to keep track of. In IMM, objectives rule: *the why dictates the what*.

There are a vast number of metrics that can be employed in social media marketing and, as a result, many books on influencer marketing provide long laundry lists of possible and trendy KPIs like bounce rates. This chapter is not going to try to list every possible metric. There are many online and offline resources available to help understand and explain the many choices of metrics. What is most important is that a manager first understands the goal of the measurement – the *why*. Once that is decided, the what of the different KPI choices is more easily found and can be assessed. Instead, this section will focus on a few key KPIs to highlight how they can support different campaign goals. In Figure 12.2, we present some relevant KPIs linked to the most common goals across the influencer marketing funnel.

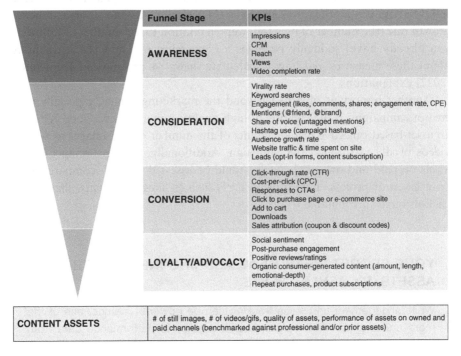

Funnel Stage	KPIs
AWARENESS	Impressions CPM Reach Views Video completion rate
CONSIDERATION	Virality rate Keyword searches Engagement (likes, comments, shares; engagement rate, CPE) Mentions (@friend, @brand) Share of voice (untagged mentions) Hashtag use (campaign hashtag) Audience growth rate Website traffic & time spent on site Leads (opt-in forms, content subscription)
CONVERSION	Click-through rate (CTR) Cost-per-click (CPC) Responses to CTAs Click to purchase page or e-commerce site Add to cart Downloads Sales attribution (coupon & discount codes)
LOYALTY/ADVOCACY	Social sentiment Post-purchase engagement Positive reviews/ratings Organic consumer-generated content (amount, length, emotional-depth) Repeat purchases, product subscriptions
CONTENT ASSETS	# of still images, # of videos/gifs, quality of assets, performance of assets on owned and paid channels (benchmarked against professional and/or prior assets)

Figure 12.2 Key performance indicators for measuring influencer marketing objectives

Let's look at a few examples from Figure 12.2 that link the why of objectives to the what of measurement. If we used influencer marketing to establish more widespread public awareness of our brand, reach and views are a good KPI. Engagement metrics, including cost-per-engagement are the most widely used consideration metrics. Designing campaign hashtags is also a very effective way to track whether an influencer campaign gets traction in the social space. Conversion measures support more concrete behavioural objectives, such as mobile app downloads or purchases. If the brand's core objective is to inspire customer loyalty and evangelism, good management KPIs include assessing the number of positive reviews or ratings, organic post-purchase consumer-generated content, and the length and emotional depth of post-purchase comments received. For some of these measures, it is important, as Russell (2020) emphasises, to benchmark performance before and after a campaign. For instance, before the campaign starts, the manager would look at how many people were searching for the brand on Google. Then, during and after the campaign, search measures would give an indication of whether or not consideration has increased. It is also important to note that the assignment of these measures to specific stages of the funnel depends on the campaign objective and execution. For instance, if the campaign's goal is to increase follower counts and it features a specific CTA (Follow us on...), then audience growth rate (the number of new followers in relation to the number of followers you already have) suddenly becomes a conversion measure. To learn more about these measures and how to calculate them, we recommend Hootsuite's (2022) explanations.

Another important objective beyond the marketing funnel, especially with creator campaigns, is the creation of high-quality content assets. Good KPIs for an asset-based objective include counts of the number of still images as well as videos produced through the campaign. Additionally, the performance of the assets on paid and owned channels should be assessed through comparisons to prior assets or professional assets on KPIs such as likes, comments, shares, and click-throughs attributable to them.

YOUR SECRET WEAPON: MEASURING INFLUENCER ASSETS, BY ASHLEY FELTS

While engagement and sales tracking can be powerful metrics, one of the more under-utilised but very impactful metrics is performance data from influencer assets. Assets are content such as photographs or short videos that can be repurposed by the brand. Typically, influencers are contracted for social posts on their channels and perhaps a few assets to be used for the brand's social media channels. However, you can utilise influencer partnerships for assets to use in the brand's cross-channel marketing platforms. For example, many influencer contracts specify receiving 5–10 image assets from social media posts as part of the influencer deliverables. However, if things are going well, the brand could negotiate and increase asset volume in the contract deliverable up to 20–25 (for additional compensation, of course). Once the asset is received from the influencer, it will then be inserted into the brand's website, email marketing, organic social, and/or paid social campaign. Once the asset has run, you can then analyse the ROI against the ROI of brand-created assets.

If the influencer assets garner a higher engagement rate or lower cost per click than existing brand assets, you can show the positive impact on the partnership to the overall business. Oftentimes, you can showcase a cost-saving element from these assets. The authentic, creative elements of the influencer content can also drive more user impact.

In my work with some of the world's top brands, 8 times out of 10, I have seen the influencer assets outperforming brand assets!

Ashley Felts is an influencer and social media strategist who founded her own consultancy firm in 2020 to help brands launch and manage their influencer and social media campaigns. For more information, please visit https://www.ashleyfeltsdigital.com/.

As these examples demonstrate, there is no one size fits all metric. Some measures, such as counts of the number of comments on posts, may be easy to gather and quantify. Others, like the emotional depths of post-purchase comments, may require an interpretive approach. Performance-based campaigns often involve sales, but may include other goals such as awareness of driving traffic to a brand's owned site. It may also bear mentioning that measures may be different depending on what social media platform is being used. Different platforms present content differently and permit the measurement of different things. For example, TikTok is quite limited, but Facebook and Google offer their own banks of extensive measurements. Each brand may also have different requirements and preferences. Adjustments and customisation are usually required. Some measures necessitate the usage of specific software/platforms (Google Analytics, social media monitoring platform, trackable pixels, and trackable links) or integration with sales and e-commerce platforms. Like the different tools in a toolkit, different metrics can help managers achieve different marketing goals but even more than in traditional advertising, objectives need to be formulated as SMART goals, decided upon at the beginning of campaigns, and translated into concrete measures that are integrated and monitored from the very start of a campaign.

The Who of IMM

Who does the measurement? That question may be more difficult to answer than it looks, because access to information can be dispersed. If an agency is in charge of the influencer campaign, they would likely be in charge of much of the data and thus would provide measurements. If in-house brand managers are running it, then they would. However, they might need to reach out to different teams within the organisation to obtain measures. The influencer ecosystem also contains many players, from the platforms to management software to service providers, managers, and more. All of these different players may have access to different metrics. Combining all of them and turning them into useful insights will ultimately be the campaign manager's job.

Influencers often have access to data that are not provided automatically to brands. Smart brands will write the requirements for data deliverables into their influencer contracts. Many brands and platforms now have plug-ins and other applications that automatically harvest these precious data from influencer pages. Sometimes whitelisting is preferable to overcome the dependence on influencers to deliver metrics. In the influencer ecosystem, exclusive access to metrics and the influencer's closeness to their audience allows them to develop successful influencer-owned brands. Relatedly, the perspective from Lilian Tahmasian points out that influencers and their teams are also managing their own brand through metrics.

MEASURING THE LILIAN BRAND: AN INFLUENCER'S PERSPECTIVE, BY LILIAN TAHMASIAN

In 2014, when I was studying for my Master's in media and marketing, I knew the power of influencing would become bigger than we all expected. In these past few years, influencers have helped build companies and enhanced brand loyalty amongst consumers. However, these relationships between an influencer's audience and brands could not be possible without the special bond between an influencer and their audience. That relationship, which we can consider a type of brand – the influencer brand – is something that needs to be managed and measured through metrics.

I am happy to say we have a team who runs the 'Lilian Tahmasian' brand. Our team consists of a manager, agent, ads manager, and editors. We speak daily, if not weekly, on ongoing tasks, campaigns, goals, and on future collaborations. Some overall metrics we use as a team to manage and better value the 'Lilian Tahmasian' brand include keeping track of the ROI in regard to individual accounts, reach, engagement, and sales, as well as link clicks. Because I am ultimately responsible for my own brand, I like to manage these metrics day to day, to assess what I need to work on and what perhaps to leave in the past, regarding content. This allows me to gain greater knowledge of my audiences and provide value to them.

To understand my audience better, we look at their location and where they are watching from and how they landed on our page. This is called 'Traffic source' and 'YouTube search'. Thanks to Google's analytics, we can see exactly what they searched for and what got them to click on our video.

We measure KPIs from the specific platform we are working on. For example, if we have a YouTube campaign that is already live, we will look at the 'watch time', which measures the time they kept watching the video. For an Instagram campaign, we use 'Instagram Insights' to check statistics including how many accounts we reached, how many accounts engaged with the post, the content interactions, likes, comments, shares, and saves. This information will also be shared with the brand itself.

There are many other ways I track the success of my influencer campaigns or partnerships. These include impressions, monitoring goals and traffic, as well as the creation and tracking of promo codes. Overall, I have found that there is no one best way to track success when it comes to influencer campaigns and partnerships. However, using the understanding from the many measurement tools at our fingertips, my team and I work hard to build my relationship with my audience, build my own brand, and help other brands achieve success.

Lilian Tahmasian was born in Sydney, Australia and has always had a passion for creative industries like fashion, marketing and even the performing arts. Once she graduated from her Masters in Media and Marketing, she was fortunate enough to become a full time content creator. She now is a full time influencer and owns the Tahmasian Media Marketing Agency.

The When of IMM

Timing is everything, so when do you measure influencer marketing? Amanda Russell (2020) emphasises taking careful baselines, a type of current snapshot of everything relating to the brand and its owned media, before a campaign. That makes sense for certain goals. During campaign execution, metrics are used to optimise campaign outcomes on a day-by-day, even hour-by-hour basis. During a campaign, the time for measurement is always now.

But, in general, the question of the time frame of IMM should be driven by its goals. What is it that the organisation is trying to accomplish in their partnerships with influencers and creators? Is content creation important? Is customer lifetime value being factored in? What is the time frame for these accomplishments? If metrics are used for compensation, then accuracy, fairness, and transparency are paramount. This chapter has followed the book in emphasising the long-term possibilities of organisations' partnerships with influencers and creators. Using an influencer relations approach, rather than the one-offs of advertising and marketing, means that brands and influencers/creators are in it for the long haul. As much as possible, the KPIs that managers use to measure success and guide future decision-making should be designed with a long-run orientation in mind.

Obviously, short-term revenues are what keep businesses afloat. But too much focus on short run returns will doom even a thriving business. Taking the long view means seeing influencer marketing not just as a marketing expense, but as an investment in marketing competences, insight, and intelligence. Brand building is a critical function, and sometimes it is not accompanied by immediately measurable sales. Celebrities often add value to a brand by enriching meanings. Think about the value added to the limited Omega Seamaster watches by appearing on James Bond's wrist. Returns on marketing investments like Omega's brand building can be conceived as longer term and more qualitative in nature. Influencer investments may similarly enrich and build powerful meanings. Returns to society, to social and environmental bottom lines may be the longest-term investments of them all – and are likely some of the best a brand can make. In the interrelated activity of strategising and measuring influencer results, the short- and long-term need to find balance.

MEASURING INFLUENCER MARKETING BEYOND PROMO CODE USE

Benidorm is a well-established tourist destination in Spain that mainly attracts an older crowd. The Destination Marketing Organisation (DMO) for the city learned that the French tourist market perceived Benidorm as an unsustainable, overcrowded destination that had a congested beach as its only attraction. In 2017, the DMO decided to utilise influencer marketing to change this negative image and promote Benidorm in order to attract a large number of French tourists and particularly younger tourists.

The slogan for the campaign was 'the Other Benidorm' and involved one influencer, Léa Camilleri, who, at the time, had close to 400K followers on Instagram and over 500K subscribers on YouTube. She describes herself as an adventurous full-time traveller who supports sustainability and habitat preservation initiatives. Working with an airline, luxury hotel, and excursion providers (who donated their services), the DMO flew Camilleri to Benidorm for a luxury experience.

She produced 31 posts about her stay in Benidorm that she shared on YouTube, Instagram, Facebook, and Twitter. These were edited into a single video as well. Managers were delighted with the content of the posts, which highlighted the different protected areas and local sustainability initiatives, ending with her recommending the destination to her socially conscious audience. For quantitative measurement, the DMO used an influencer management platform (Brandmaniac) as well as its own custom analytics tool that allowed it to simultaneously monitor multiple platforms in real time. The DMO estimated the social media reach of the posts at 1,041,110 and the overall engagement at 243,370.

Because the DMO was able to leverage its partners' contributions, the campaign cost only €3,308. When the company estimated the EMV for the different media, it calculated YouTube at €693,721, Instagram at €77,992, Facebook at €7,490, and Twitter at €2,469. Because there was some resistance to using influencers, the calculation of EMV was very important for them to sell the campaign internally. They estimated the overall impact in advertising equivalence at €1 million, which was a massive return considering that the campaign cost them just €3,308 in direct costs.

Note: All case details are from Femenia-Serra and Gretzel (2020).

INFLUENCER COMPENSATION AND DEBRIEF

While influencer compensation can happen at any point during a campaign, depending on the negotiated terms of payment and the length and complexity of the campaign, for performance-based campaigns, it typically happens when the campaign is completed and all metrics have been compiled. The performance-based compensation amount serves as a form of feedback to brands and influencers and can inform future collaborations. When influencer marketing moves towards influencer relations, more elaborate feedback to the influencer or creator can be given in the form of a debrief that shares campaign outcomes and maybe even benchmarks specific contents against brand assets or other influencer/ creator content. Offering more qualitative, personalised feedback, and inviting influencers to provide comments on their experience and on suggestions for improvement is also important for relationship-building.

CHAPTER SUMMARY

Measuring the outputs of influencer and creator relationships is critical to their management. This chapter explained and linked the fundamental concepts of contemporary influencer relations and campaign management with current best practices by using clear definitions, explanations, case studies, and practitioners' perspectives. Answering why, how, what, who, and when questions about influencer measurement emphasises the importance of objectives in influencer measurement. A deeper understanding of ROI also revealed the need to better understand the long-term and qualitative nature of the numerous benefits offered by working with influencers and creators. For best results, KPIs should be linked to goals of awareness, consideration, conversation, and loyalty and advocacy associated with the marketing funnel, or to the objective of developing content assets. Examples of a mattress company, an influencer managing her own brands, and a Spanish DMO illustrate the importance, complexity, and nuance that accompany implementation of measurement principles in practice. Instead of viewing influencer metrics as a short-term practice focused on sales conversions, the chapter emphasised their role in clarifying long-term strategy, measuring success, building competencies, and increasing an organisation's marketing orientation.

EXERCISES AND QUESTIONS

Exercises

1. Find an example of one or more campaigns that clearly demonstrate measurement relating to each of the following objectives, and explain the relationship:

a. Awareness

b. Consideration

c. Conversion

d. Loyalty and advocacy

e. Asset development

2. Research a recent influencer marketing campaign case that includes information about the KPIs they used to measure success. Apply the principles in this chapter and evaluate the measurement activities of the brand. Did they do a good job, or not, and why?

3. Design an influencer campaign for a non-profit organisation. Define the campaign objective(s) and develop metrics for each objective.

Questions

1. Refer back to the Benidorm DMO case and answer the following questions:
   a. Was The Other Benidorm campaign a success, or not? Explain.

   b. Did the influencer metrics in this case match the stated objectives? Explain.

   c. How would you follow up the measurement of this campaign? What measures would you recommend, when, and how?

2. Do the metrics differ between influencer advertising, influencer marketing, and influencer relations campaigns? If so, how? If not, why not?

3. Are quantitative measures such as impressions more objective than qualitative metrics such as content analysis of social media comments? Is influencer management ever fully objective? Explain.

ANNOTATED READINGS

Sheth, J. N. (1974). Measurement of advertising effectiveness: Some theoretical considerations. *Journal of Advertising*, 3(1), 6–11.

This seminal article on advertising effectiveness illustrates that issues regarding campaign performance measurement have been long-standing. Rather than focusing on specific metrics, the article points to broad dimensions of effectiveness that need to be considered.

13

TRAJECTORIES, TECHNOLOGIES, AND TRANSFORMATIONS

CHAPTER OVERVIEW AND OBJECTIVES

This chapter will explore the ongoing transformation of the influencer ecosystem. The COVID-19 pandemic accelerated the adoption of influencers and content creators by brands and other organisations. Readers of this chapter will also learn how contemporary influencers set trends and have become important innovators in contemporary marketplaces. Leveraging social media technology, today's influencers inspire public trust and play key roles in increasing consumer desire. The chapter will then delve into the world of virtual influencers and synthetic media. Readers will learn how human influencers are already involved in the Metaverse and how virtual influencers are proliferating and becoming ever more realistic, persuasive, and sophisticated. The chapter concludes with a summary of ten predictions about what the future of the influencer ecosystem may hold in store.

PROVOCATION: 'The future of influencers is already here – it just isn't evenly distributed'. – (Paraphrasing William Gibson [*NPR Radio Interview,* 1999])

KEYWORDS: diffusion of innovations, synthetic media, Metaverse, NFTs, the Uncanny Valley, Metafluence, woke-washing

INFLUENCER MARKETING IN PANDEMIC TIMES

The COVID-19 coronavirus pandemic that began in 2020 rapidly changed almost everything about normal society, and one of the arenas in which dramatic effects were visible was the sphere of influencers and creators. Marketers found themselves in a challenging position as the reality of the global pandemic set in. They were required to navigate uncharted territory and determine which marketing strategies were appropriate. They still needed to sell their products. They had to avoid giving the impression that they are tone deaf to what consumers were going through. Add onto that, everyone had to shelter in place, so the normal on-site and studio shoots were postponed for an indefinite period. What were they to do?

Enter influencer marketing. Because people had to stay indoors, it turned out that they increased their attention online and to social media channels. As well, influencers and content creators produced their own commercial material, so the lack of ability to get to a studio or work with photographers was not a problem. Additionally, influencers and content creators were also going through the trials and tribulations of the pandemic with their communities, and they were expert at understanding and addressing their needs. Voilà, no more tone deafness. Because of these factors, it turned out that influencers and other content creators were a nearly perfect fit for organisations that were trying to share information about their products or services that was insightful, topical, and relevant while also conscious of pandemic-related needs (Femenia-Serra, Gretzel, & Alzua-Sorzabal, 2022).

Locally and globally, some of the most important uses of influencers came from public health agencies who leveraged their skills and goodwill to spread messages about masking, isolating, symptoms to watch for, and sheltering in place. One of the earliest governments to do so was the government of Finland, which enlisted 1,500 of the nation's influencers to contain the pandemic, check the spread of misinformation, and inform the population quickly, clearly, and accurately. A factual video about the coronavirus by a Finnish YouTuber, interviewing a government minister and health experts gathered over 100,000 views within two days of being posted (Henley, 2020). On a combined global and local level, the World Health Organization (WHO) turned to international influencers and creators with large followings on Instagram to share their own personal perspectives on how the health crisis was impacting them, to encourage people to stay at home where required, and to share best practices for safety during the health crisis (Moore, 2022).

On the brand front, many brands became creative as they discovered their new relevance during pandemic-themed influencer campaigns. In the

hands of influencers and creators, stay-at-home became a major opportunity, one that they could speak to with authority. Instinct Pet Foods was
one of the many pet-related brands that emphasised the added importance
that people's four-legged friends were assuming during pandemic times,
asking owners if it might be a good time to upgrade their pet's food to the
best food possible. At-home workouts were emphasised by companies
that offer exercise equipment and services, like Sworkit and Gymshark.
Because people were cooking at home a lot more, cookware company
Misen Kitchen spoke to them about the quality of their cookware and how
upgrading could have delicious results. Fashion companies and beauty
companies emphasised how good it felt to dress up at home, and how
important it was to look good on Zoom. And CBD companies like Lazarus
Naturals CBD teamed up with influencers to discuss and offer possible
treatments for the increased tension and stress that the pandemic brought
to people/s lives (Moore, 2022).

INFLUENCERS AS AGENTS OF TRANSFORMATION

Even before the pandemic, it was clear that influencers had worked hard to gain
their audience's trust in a way that governments, the media industry, and even
many brands had not. As mass dissent was on the horizon, influencers spoke to
it. Influencers shared their own experiences and stories with an audience who
shared their perspective and was also suffering through similar challenges. When
people did not know who to believe, they turned to influencers. And influencers
demonstrated their goodwill by sharing COVID-19 information for free, legiti-
mising and solidifying their positions of public influence. Influencers acted as
crisis communicators, performing a valued public relations function (Femenia-
Serra, Gretzel, & Alzua-Sorzabal, 2022). Influencers and the influencer
ecosystem demonstrated adaptability and strengthened their resilience in the
global crisis. As a result, the entire influencer marketing industry has weathered
the pandemic storm much better than many other industries, and emerged from
it stronger than when it went in.

The pandemic also shaped the technological foundations of the influencer
and creator ecosystem. Social media engagement soared during the lockdowns.
TikTok, a new platform at the time, grew rapidly to become a major player in
the industry. Stories, Reels, and livestreaming went mainstream as well. The rise
of COVID-19 accelerated changes in media consumption that were already on
the horizon in 2019 and influencers amplified them.

Technology usage, and social media use in particular, had been rapidly growing even before the coronavirus pandemic. During the 2000s, as the Internet and blogging developed, and then through the 2010s as the age of social media gained momentum, people around the world changed how they connected with one another and how they obtained information and learned. No longer limited to book knowledge and telephone calls, the possibilities for building social relations with more people, about more things, and in more places abounded. This new sociality was driven by technology, and it was proving immensely powerful in every area of human endeavour, from politics to business to warfare (Shirky, 2008; Singer & Booking, 2018; van Dijck, 2013). Influencers take advantage of the emerging techno-sociality, but they also encourage and actively manage it in their audiences. Influencers' need for intimacy with their audiences has given rise to specialised platforms like Patreon and OnlyFans, or specific affordances like virtual gift-giving during livestreams.

Influencers as Trendsetters

Influencers as agents of change continuously shape the technological, social, regulatory, and commercial aspects of the ecosystem around them, but they also have larger impacts on culture and society through their participation in and shaping of influencer culture. One of the most important factors fuelling the rise of influencer culture both prior to and especially during pandemic times is the recognition that influencers are outstanding spotters, communicators, and even makers of trends. A survey done by Sprout Social in 2021 showed that more than one-third of consumers use social media to find out about new products or brands or to learn more about them (Bedgood, 2021). This is especially clear in the fashion world, where until a few years ago, print media and top fashion editors had the last word on what was in style and what wasn't. Now, though, shaping the taste of the public must include those with social media influence communicating what they think about fashion, lifestyle, and everything else.

The communication scholar Everett Rogers developed a theory that helps explain the power of influencers today. The desire for new products is conveyed or 'diffused' over time between different types of people in a social system. Innovators tend to take risks and are often in a position to try new products first. Innovators then communicate information about these products to early adopters, and from there the messages travel to the early and late majority (Rogers, 1995). The process is often captured in something called the 'new product' or 'technology' adoption life cycle, which is depicted in Figure 13.1, showing the position of influencers. Influencers often act as innovators and early adopters of new products. They spot and set trends, then promote them using social media to a wide audience. Importantly, they help new products overcome the so-called 'Chasm' in the diffusion curve, which describes the gap between

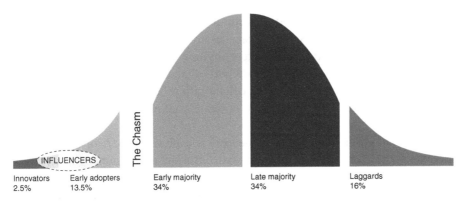

Figure 13.1 New product adoption curve

early adopters and the early majority. This gap is essentially a credibility gap because the early majority does not feel similar to the early adopters and does not necessarily trust them. As authentic, likable/similar, credible and, thus, persuasive sources of information, influencers can bridge this gap.

DIFFUSION OF INNOVATIONS

A theory, originally proposed by Everett Rogers, that explains how, why, and at what rate new products, technologies, and ideas spread through a society.

Among the innovators are highly motivated consumers who not only adopt existing products but also creatively experiment and develop new products for themselves and others. This group of creative producers is called 'lead users' (von Hippel, 1986). Lead users have a long history of being influential 'insiders' in social media and online communities (Kozinets, 2002). Some influencers, like Jeffree Star and Huda Kattan (of Huda Beauty), act as lead users, developing innovative new products and then marketing them to their audiences. For example, unlike the cis-normative female demographic target favoured by almost the entire cosmetics industry, Star pioneered non-binary target marketing that was cis-normative friendly. Further, he developed highlighter pans that were much larger than those offered in mainstream products as well as numerous other product innovations. Huda Kattan targeted an underserved demographic of Middle Eastern women and also developed extremely full coverage products such as foundation for even the most problematic skin. These influencers, and many others, illustrate how influencers have moved beyond merely being spokespersons for corporate brands to developing innovative new products that satisfy unmet consumer needs.

They were on top of trends and opportunities and then innovated for their own brands – in this case, Jeffree Star Cosmetics and Huda Beauty.

In China, these creative tastemakers are now referred to as creative opinion leaders or COLs. Jing Daily (2021) reports that their influence often reaches beyond their core area and cites the collaboration between e-sports host Duan Yushuang and Prada as an example of brands taking advantage of a COL's creativity and style.

The trendsetting capacity of influencers is a powerful part of the popularisation of the 'core' notion in the global diffusion of consumer lifestyle subcultures. Examples of core are things like rapcore, emocore, doomcore, coolcore, cutecore, smoothcore, and so on. When something has a 'core' suffix, it generally relates it to new genres and particular lifestyle groupings linked by aesthetic tastes.

Style subcultures like Dark Academia and Light Academia also have a lot to do with the rise of new aesthetic movements. Both styles honour and get ideas from scholarly people, places, and things and both have had major marketing implications. Dark academia exploded on TikTok and Tumblr in 2020 and can be described as 'traditional academic with a gothic edge' (Bateman, 2020). It likes Greek art, Gothic and Romantic architecture, tweeds, Harry Potter-style clothing, wool sweaters, and so on. Light academia focuses on the softer and gentler side of academia. It has a lighter and airier look with pleated skirts, sweater vests, hair ribbons, and other styles that evoke student life (Michnik, 2022).

When influencers pick up and popularise a concept, such as doomcore or Light Academia, they join a group of innovators or early adopters and amplify their message. The message that something like Light Academia is a significant trend and that specific types of products or services fit into it spreads further and wider than it could have without the voices and audiences of influencers. Cottagecore, which can be defined as a blend of social movements, fashion genres, consumer subcultures, and new taste regimes, is another strong example of an influencer-driven lifestyle trend (see vignette).

INFLUENCERS AS TRENDSETTERS OF THE COTTAGECORE LIFESTYLE

Cottagecore is a mainly female aesthetic that idealises a simple rural lifestyle favouring local food and craftsmanship, living in harmony with animals, trees and flowers, and escaping from technology. It is a reaction against our modern, technology-filled consumerist society. As such, the core of the cottagecore movement lies in wellness and sustainability, which entail a life away from technology, smartphones, big city streets, and other contemporary types of stress-inducing activities (Saxon, 2021).

Figure 13.2   Cottagecore aesthetics

Ironically, however, most women experience the cottagecore movement through images and videos posted on social media by influencers. The cottagecore movement began in 2017 with early mentions of the term on Instagram and Tumblr. The cottagecore lifestyle and aesthetics then blew up on TikTok. By 2020, cottagecore was called a 'budding aesthetic movement' by the New York Times (Slone, 2020). An army of cottagecore influencers subsequently shaped the concept into a dreamy and nostalgic escape into natural living that, for most, could never actually be achieved but only longed for. And, if ever there was a time when that powerful nostalgia for a simpler existence was in abundance, it was during the COVID-19 pandemic.

Homebound during the pandemic, often locked into city apartments with little access to nature, influencers and their audiences began rediscovering the simple joys of baking bread, home gardening, afternoon teas, and dressing more simply and comfortably. The cottagecore movement expanded these pastimes into grandma-inspired projects like knitting and embroidery. The cottagecore aesthetic (Figure 13.2) blended with other movements and consumer subcultures such as second-hand shopping, thrifting, sustainable fashion, ethical manufacturing, handmade clothing, growing vegetables, and cooking food at home. Nowadays, cottagecore's bucolic scenery of the rural countryside and nostalgic country life spans the world of design, fashion, food, literature, music and even politics. Importantly, it is continually shaped, reshaped, and broadcast by social media influencers.

Influencers as Desire Amplifiers

As online communities and digital opinion leaders emerged, they developed alongside technologies that were not only increasing people's ability to connect, but their desire to consume as well (Kozinets, Patterson, & Ashman, 2017). Influencers are driving innovation and social change in sometimes unexpected ways within these networks of desire. Certainly, they are forces that help to drive the commercialisation and commodification of private social life. They are often criticized for encouraging materialism and overconsumption. However, many influencers also act as amplifiers of positive social change and promote sustainable lifestyles. They may contribute to polarisation, extremisation, cultural atrophy, and the loss of traditions or encourage a refocusing on traditional values. They also lead the charge into new social platforms, with their new formats and novel ways of communicating, such as TikTok, Discord, Clubhouse, and many others. Trend setters, spotters, and makers who megaphone their whipsmart observations about where the world is heading, influencers and creators are at the cultural leading edge of changes in the way human beings connect with each other, including in the emerging Metaverse.

TECHNOLOGICAL DRIVERS OF CHANGE

Changes in the technological base of the influencer and creator ecosystem affect the means of productions and the relationships among the various actors and can even lead to the emergence of new players. Monitoring technological developments, thus, becomes an important means of anticipating ways in which the influencer and creator ecosystem will evolve.

Artificial Intelligence

The abilities of computers to use natural language processing and artificial intelligence (or AI) algorithms have vastly increased. AI applications are only beginning to be applied to the world of influencers but have already gained significant traction. Image recognition capabilities, detection of bots and fake engagement, and automated means of determining influence or performance have led to radical alterations in influencer identification, vetting, and monitoring. AI is also becoming increasingly adept at predicting the performance of individual pieces of influencer content, which help to determine fair compensation. During the execution of campaigns, it assists managers in monitoring posts by flagging those that do not follow disclosure guidelines. These applications of AI to influencer marketing are expanding rapidly (Ravindra, 2022). It is also expected that generative AI (i.e., AI that takes images, voice recordings, natural language queries or long-form text formats as inputs and produces creative outputs in the form of enhanced images, visual art, poems, responses to questions, essays, videos, etc.) will revolutionise social media content production.

Virtual Influencers

Although much of this book has been about authenticity, this chapter highlights synthetic media. From synthesised versions of real people to wholly designed virtual influencers, synthetic media is a rising phenomenon. At some point in the near future, many influencers may eventually have an AI avatar, a sort of digital copy of themselves that is able to perform things online in a way that human beings simply cannot.

> **SYNTHETIC MEDIA**
>
> Synthetic media is a broad term encompassing a wide variety of computer-generated media, usually created, modified, or manipulated by employing AI technologies (Kalpokas, 2021: 1).

According to the website VirtualHumans.org, more than 200 virtual influencers are currently active on digital platforms, with Instagram hosting 41 verified accounts. These virtual characters have millions of followers, work with some of the world's biggest brands, raise money for organisations like the WHO, and champion social causes like Black Lives Matter. In the past, synthetic technologies have frequently been used to perpetrate 'deepfakes' and generate false, manipulated representations of real people in order to deceive or misinform viewers. For example, deepfakes have been produced of politicians, such as Barack Obama and Nancy Pelosi, and famous movie stars like Scarlett Johansson and Gal Gadot (Luthera, 2020). However, brands and other organisations are also increasingly leveraging synthetic media for creative marketing campaigns (Facebook IQ, 2022). For example, Die Hard star Bruce Willis seems to appear in a new series of commercials for Russian phone carrier and Internet provider MegaFon. However, it is his deepfaked image, a product of licensing his image for use in the ads. The ability to create synthetic likenesses, personalities, and environments solely through digital technologies may offer experiences that are customisable to individuals and thus be more user-centric and impactful even than 'the real things' (Kalpokas, 2021: 1). Imagine, for instance, a deepfake of your favourite celebrity customising messages just for you and addressing you by name in a convincingly tailored sales pitch.

DEEPFAKES

Deepfakes are videos in which a person's face or body has been digitally dupli-cated by AI technology, often for malicious use or to spread false information, but increasingly for other uses, such as in commercials (Floridi, 2018: 320).

Recent developments in synthetic media involve the creation of synthetic personalities, primarily as virtual influencers, also known as computer-generated imagery (CGI) influencers. The original source of a virtual influencer is human activity, but they are not human (Duivestein, 2020). Hence, virtual influencers have been variously described as hyperreal, or realer-than-real, computer-generated characters who are designed by humans with anthropomorphic fea-tures, such as humanlike appearances, expressions, personalities, and social qualities (Park et al., 2021). Despite the fact they may look like humans onscreen, and seem to behave like humans, virtual influencers are something else entirely. Their existence is scripted and carefully managed.

Capturing Consumers Through Hyperrealism

The lives and journeys of all fictitious characters are brought to life in many ways. Emotional storytelling, behaviour that arouses empathy, attention to aesthetics, and realistic and recognisable behaviour can build connection with audiences in any modality (Luthera, 2020). Employing these same elements online helps animate and elevate virtual influencers (Leighton, 2019), who express and popularise in social media new cultural norms, new rituals, new visual vocabularies, as well as new needs and desires in conversations with both humans and other non-human characters (Gambetti, 2021). Even though most users are aware that they are interacting with non-human characters, they perceive and treat virtual influencers as authentic social actors with whom they can develop affective relationships (Lee & Nass, 2003; Lee, Park, & Song, 2005; Nass, Steuer, &Tauber, 1994).

Consider the realistic Japanese virtual influencer and model Imma (@imma.gram). Her perceived realism emulates a human influencer. Her posts tell a personal story in which she has personal ambitions, achievements, inse-curities, and vulnerabilities similar to an actual human being. She shares her alleged inner life with her audience. Yet, her authenticity is not real, it is scripted for commercial purposes and designed to be archetypal (Drenten & Brooks, 2020). Moreover, Imma and many other virtual influencers exhibit what researchers call uncanniness (a term from computer science's uncanny valley). The uncanny resemblance to actual human beings simultaneously attracts, intrigues, and defies consumers (Block & Lovegrove, 2021).

THE UNCANNY VALLEY

The uncanny valley refers to a hypothesised relationship between an object's degree of resemblance to a human being and the eerie, astonished, and unsettling feelings this promotes in people at high but not perfect levels of resemblance (Arsenyan & Mirowska, 2021).

Virtual influencers who look real may have personalities that are designed to have the most impact on their target audience. Thus, virtual influencers may add a new level of customisation and accuracy to influencer advertising. Content creators give their characters, whether they are designed to look like real people or computer-generated animals or things, a personality based on market research or an impression of what will appeal to a particular target market. Creators then use social listening and machine learning to better fit their avatars to the needs of their audiences (Bradley, 2020).

Engaging Consumer Subcultures

Virtual influencers are making it easier for brands to talk to, learn about, and connect with consumer cultures and subcultures that are interested in technology and media. This is the case with the Japanese youth pop music subculture, which has come together on social media as a group of dedicated fans who support and make content for their virtual vocaloid idols, such as Hatsune Miku, Meiko, and Kaito.

HATSUNE MIKU, JAPANESE POP MUSIC CYBER CULTURE, AND THE NTH DEGREE OF FANFICTION

In 2014, a young blue-pigtailed Japanese pop star named Hatsune Miku opened Lady Gaga's *ArtRave* tour. That same year, while the young pop star was a guest on the David Letterman Show, she announced her first US tour (Toccoli, 2022). It was not the first time that a Japanese music artist made her way in the American music scene, but this time it was different. The young blue-pigtailed Japanese pop star is a computer-generated avatar whose live performances are performed by 3D hologram.

The story of Hatsune Miku began in 2004, when Japan's Yamaha Corporation launched a new vocal synthesiser named Vocaloid that synthesised human voices with the simple input of song text and melody. In 2007, a new voicebank for the Vocaloid called Hatsune Miku (初音 ミク – meaning 'the first sound from the future') was launched by the music software company Crypton Future

Figure 13.3   The virtual Vocaloid and influencer Hatsune Miku

Source: Crypton Future Media and fan art, CC BY-NC license.

Media. That voicebank reproduced the voice of the Japanese singer and dubber Saki Fujita. Right after being launched, Hatsune Miku became an icon of the Japanese pop music subculture. The new voicebank generated a huge, excited and ever-expanding online fandom in just a few years.

How did Hatsune Miku develop such an active, participatory, and creative fandom? The key was in the decision of Crypton Future Media to license Miku as a Creative Commons property (see Figure 13.3 for a typical Miku image licensed as a Creative Commons item). With this decision, the company allowed fans to freely use her image for non-commercial purposes (i.e., for the creation of gadgets, animated figures, and more). However, the company still retained the copyright on all user-generated songs produced with the Vocaloid software.

Armies of fans were happy to oblige. They changed the lyrics of songs, remixed the melodies, and reposted their videos in mashups. They also recorded themselves singing the lyrics, overlayed commentaries on the videos, and ranked their favourite creations (Lam, 2016: 1108). By 2021, there were more than 1 million consumer created artworks and 170,000 uploaded YouTube videos dedicated to Hatsune Miku (Lam, 2016: 1108–09). This combination of creative commons and traditional intellectual property licensing has paid off for Crypton, a company that has seen the release of over 100,000 Hatsune Miku songs so far and even staged 5 sold-out 3D concerts worldwide with performances in Los Angeles, Taipei, Hong Kong, Singapore and Tokyo. Miku has also found her way into cosplay, video games, manga, and collectible figurines, vastly extending the reach and profits from her licensed image into what has been called the 'Nth degree of fanfiction.'

Advantages and Disadvantages of Virtual Influencers for Brands

According to Influencer Marketing Hub (2021), virtual influencers may be lower cost than hiring a celebrity influencer. Production is generally easier since brands do not have to hire people for hair and makeup, rent studio space, or scope out locations and pay for travel expenses. As well, virtual influencers can be easier to manage as brands do not have to deal with some human influencers' emotions, personalities, potential scandals, and possibly unprofessional managers. Virtual influencers can also be in multiple places at the same time, and they are available 24/7. An example is Xiao Wanzi, the virtual influencer of Chinese cosmetics brand Perfect Diaries, who has been very successful in creating and maintaining hundreds of private WeChat groups that engage the brand's customers. Moreover, virtual influencers are trendy and attract young media-savvy audiences. Importantly, research finds the engagement rate of virtual influencers to be higher than that of real, human influencers (HypeAuditor, 2021).

In terms of disadvantages, virtual influencers can represent a serious investment that might only be worthwhile for major brands. Hiring a major virtual influencer may not be as expensive as hiring a major human influencer but is almost certainly a lot more than hiring a group of nano-influencers. Brands seeking something different, like a customised virtual avatar, may pay expensive development costs. And virtual influencers will not work for free gifts! Also, virtual influencers may not appeal to everyone, or for every product. A virtual influencer might not be the best way to advertise a cruise vacation targeting older married couples, for instance. Moreover, as time goes by and as with many trends, the novelty of virtual influencers may gradually wear off (Influencer Marketing Hub, 2021). Alternatively, they may be combined with Generative AI, such as ChatGPT-like interfaces, to create compelling and engaging new social actors.

Ethical Challenges and Opportunities

Virtual influencers raise important ethical concerns (Duivestein, 2020). They may resemble humans, but they do not have real feelings. They are intrinsically inauthentic brand spokespersons because they are not truly able to experience the things they are promoting. For example, no 3D animation can actually experience the taste of food, the feel and fit of clothing, or the refreshing tingle of skincare products. Whether their designers or content creators actually experience the products they promote is also a mystery. Hence, there might be a limit to the credibility and trust that consumers will place on a virtual influencer's recommendations (HypeAuditor, 2021). Virtual influencers are designed to manipulate, and this fact, along with the lack of emotional connection, may result in backlash and reproach when consumers perceive that a virtual influencer's representation is deceptive, stereotyped, or disrespectful. The idea of a disrespectful virtual influencer applies, for example, to the virtual African model and influencer Shudu (@shudu.gram).

SHUDU, THE MALE GAZE AND THE WESTERN COLONISATION OF AFRICAN CULTURE

With over 200,000 followers on Instagram, Shudu (@shudu.gram) claims to be 'the world's first digital supermodel'. She was created by the fashion photographer Cameron-James Wilson in 2017 for his digital modelling agency. Shudu is a regal African looking character, with flawless dark skin and a Barbie like figure. Shudu collaborates with many top fashion, cosmetics, and jewellery brands like Bulgari, Chanel, Ferragamo, and Fenty Beauty.

However, Shudu's social media presence raises important ethical issues related to intersectionality that lie at the crossroads between digital representation, power, and profit. In Shudu, we can detect a form of colonisation where Black people and their cultural objects are stereotyped and commodified for commercial purposes by powerful, White Western people, their brands, and their technologies. Recent research argues that, although Shudu was developed to resemble a Black woman, she was created through the White male gaze, which reflects the dominant power of White and patriarchal perspectives in society (Sobande, 2021a,b). Writer and scholar-activist Francesca Sobande's critique points at Black virtual influencers as another example where the marketable mimicry of Black aesthetics and culture actualises a Western colonisation of African culture. At the same time, her analysis unveils a 'woke-washing' brand practice. By creating a digital Black model instead of hiring a real one, Wilson has been alleged of contributing to the marginalisation of real-life Black models, who still struggle to find opportunities in the industry. As part of this struggle, Black women and models are increasingly using social media (e.g., YouTube) as a symbolic resource to collectively engage with discourse resistant to dominant White Western masculinity (Sobande, 2017).

WOKE-WASHING

Brands' misuse of social issues that involves providing sanitised and commercialised notions of feminism, equality, and Black social justice activism (Sobande, 2019).

In contrast to the negative example of Shudu, virtual influencers can also be used to amplify, reinforce, and bring cogent social issues to larger audiences.

This is the case with the creation of Kami, the first digital character with Down syndrome, who has moved the important inclusivity, diversity, and disability discourse to the realm of virtual influencers.

KAMI AND THE CULTURAL NORMALISATION OF DOWN SYNDROME

Kami (@itskamisworld), short for the name Kamilah, means perfection in Arabic. Online, Kami is a purple-haired, pony-tailed virtual female influencer intended to represent a young woman with Down syndrome. Kami has been created as a response to 'perfect' Internet personas and a lack of high-profile people with disabilities. Kami is the brainchild of Down Syndrome International (DSi), a UK-based organisation dedicated to improving the quality of life for people with Down syndrome by promoting their right to be included on an equal and full basis with others. DSi teamed up with creative agency Forsman & Bodenfors (F&B) and global digital modelling agency The Diigitals – the same agency that created Shudu (Brnjarkevska, 2022).

Kami resulted from a collaboration that was driven by numerous members of the Down syndrome community. To offer a credible representation, a panel of over 100 young women volunteers with Down syndrome from 16 different countries were consulted to collaborate on her creation as a virtual model – acting as the faces, physiques, gestures, voices, and personalities that Kami would embody (Keegan, 2022). Many of these women enthusiastically participated in an Instagram campaign whose headline 'We are all Kami' unites all the ethnic and aesthetic nuances of Down syndrome (Murray & Gissen, 2022). Similarly, Kami's Instagram content spotlights some of the most influential people and personalities in the Down syndrome community. Beyond Instagram, Kami's creators see opportunities for her in the Metaverse, such as representing digital artists with Down syndrome, acting as a brand ambassador for DSi, auctioning NFTs, partnering with virtual pop stars, participating in virtual fashion shows, and entering the gaming Metaverse (Keegan, 2022).

The vignettes of Shudu and Kami represent two opposite faces of the ethical challenges of the future transformative possibilities of virtual influencers. It might be worth noting that, despite the ethical concerns raised with Shudu, as of this writing she has over 230,000 Instagram followers compared to only 2,000 for Kami. Both Shudu and Kami resemble real human women. However, an increasing number of virtual influencers are cartoonish such as Minnie Mouse or the humanised dark rabbit Guggimon. Others are computer-generated versions of pets such as Banbo Kitty or Jennifer Aniston's virtual dog Clydeo. Still others are humanised representations of objects, such as The Good Advice Cupcake (a cupcake), Nobody Sausage (a sausage), Barbie or Real Qai Qai (dolls).

These lifelike virtual influencers reveal a change in taste and a transformation of digital and cultural spheres. As our chapter's opening vignette indicated, technology and indoor life gained a major boost from the COVID-19 pandemic. Increasingly, technology, game play, and influencers are combining with exoticism, escapism, imagination, play, and self-expression. The boom of influencer marketing and the explosion of digital characters cutting across human and non-human categories is just the beginning of a grand integration that some businesses say is just over the horizon, one which promises to change the world of influencers forever.

Influencers and the Metaverse

METAVERSE

'Metaverse' is a portmanteau of the prefix 'meta' (i.e., beyond) and 'universe' (Hackl, 2021). It refers to a new iteration of the Internet and envisions a shared virtual space, supported by new programming languages and open standards, virtual and augmented reality software and hardware, blockchain-based technologies like cryptocurrencies and non-fungible tokens (NFTs), and persistent, synchronous, continuous and immersive experiences, in which social actors are represented through avatars.

TEFLON SEGA EXCITES FANS IN THE METAVERSE

In March 2022, Teflon Sega was the first virtual influencer to headline a Metaverse event. For fans, being able to witness virtual influencers such as Teflon performing a virtual concert provided a once-in-a-lifetime opportunity. Fans had an exhilarating and truly unforgettable experience thanks to interactive elements such as clicking a button to make fireworks explode behind Teflon or seeing their chat messages appear during the show.

The 30-minute show concluded with a live Q&A in which Teflon answered fan questions. Teflon was asked how 'he' transferred his avatar to Wave's virtual concert venue by Makena Rasmussen, a Digital Culture writer working with VirtualHumans.org. 'My particles were re-formed in a new dimension', Teflon explained, 'so I entered environments I'd never been in, saw things I'd never seen, and felt and even looked a little different... I'd have to say that performing "Never in the Middle" while in the grips of a 100-foot-tall ghost vixen was something I'd never imagined I'd experience' (Rasmussen, 2022).

METAFLUENCE

Talkinginfluence.com (2021) defines Metafluence as 'utilizing the power of blockchain technology and building a space in the Metaverse where influencers, brands, and audiences can seamlessly engage and interact with each other'.

Many major technology companies have begun to embrace the Metaverse trend. To name a few, Nvidia Omniverse, Facebook Horizon, and Microsoft's enterprise Metaverse are leading the charge. For the Decentraland fashion week, events such as concerts and fashion shows by Etro and Dolce & Gabbana have been organised in the Metaverse, with some collection items selling for more than $130,000. Media companies and celebrities are establishing themselves in the Metaverse as well. For example, CNN sells their best moments as NFTs, and Lionel Messi launched his NFTs on the 'Messiverse'.

NON-FUNGIBLE TOKENS – NFTS

NFTs are cryptographically encoded digital assets that may represent real-world objects like art, music, in-game items, and videos which are bought and sold online, frequently with cryptocurrency (Conti & Schmidt, 2022). Their value lies in being able to display them in the Metaverse or use them in conjunction with avatars.

Consumer brands such as Chipotle and Gucci are selling their NFTs on Metaverse platforms (Kim, 2021). Chipotle claimed it was the first brand to enable Roblox players to exchange digital currency for real-life rewards when it offered vouchers for burritos to the first 30,000 visitors to its Metaverse restaurant. Gucci announced on Roblox its presence in the Metaverse and sold its digital bags as NFTs for $4,115, where the physical version of the same bag costs \$3,400 in stores. Decentraland is currently one of the most successful Metaverse platforms, where users can buy land, develop real estate and organise art exhibitions (Influencer Marketing Hub, 2022c). It is built on a decentralised Ethereum cryptocurrency (MANA). These developments suggest that the formation of a Metaverse ecosystem is imminent, one where multiple players, small and large, will be connected across multiple virtual worlds (Caulfield, 2021).

THE AVATAR ECONOMY, BY CHRISTOPHER TRAVERS

Avatars have enormous potential as tomorrow's trusted voices. An 'avatar' is a character that represents a specific user in an online space. An avatar was defined in the early days of the Internet as any pseudonymous character used as a profile picture (pfp) on an Internet forum. Today, avatars take the form of video game or game-like characters representing one's online personality, as forums and digital social experiences continue to evolve from 2D to 3D.

When Internet forums, social media platforms, and video games emulate offline experience well enough for immersion to be achieved, the visitor fully identifies with their profile. So, it makes no difference whether someone uses a pixelated pfp on a forum or a 3D character livestreaming on Twitch when it comes to their ability to be authentic through an avatar.

Only when a person feels secure in their online identity, in whatever form it may take, can they fully express themselves. Social media sharing subjects most people to some level of accountability. It also forces them to construct themselves in the way they want to be perceived, both visually (i.e., retakes, cropping, filters, photoshop, and timing) and verbally (i.e., captions, messages, statuses, etc.). Yet, by using an avatar face for online activities, the necessity to put on one's best face forward is eliminated, allowing for more honest expression. Reddit moderators, Twitter personalities, YouTube VTubers, Discord admins, pseudonymous TikTokers, ZEPETO creators, and more use avatars to focus on what they love without fear of censure or sacrificing privacy. This pseudonymity is a powerful tool for creative expression that also protects from the trials and tribulations of modern, filtered social media feeds.

The growing importance of avatars has deep roots in the gaming industry, specifically in the 'Massively Multiplayer Online Role Playing Game' (or MMORPG) genre. What many people today refer to as the 'Metaverse' is the next major step in the evolution of MMORPG video games as they converge with other social phenomena such as social networking, live streaming, and physical goods eCommerce. The avatar economy encompasses all these aspects of avatar creation, consumption, and commerce.

An emerging trend, virtual influencers are a subset of the much larger avatar economy. A virtual influencer is an avatar consistently shared on social media for the purposes of storytelling, self-expression, fandom building, or some combination of the aforementioned. Some creators simply 'live' online as a virtual influencer (read: avatar pseudonym) – an act of genuine self-expression with highly variable end goals. On the more corporate end of the spectrum, a virtual influencer is often a fictional, crafted production designed to send a message (a branded avatar with a life story). The common message, however, is that when an avatar consistently posts in the first person and builds a large enough fan base, they become a virtual influencer. Everyone will have avatars in the future, and some of those avatars will become very influential.

Christopher Travers is a leading expert on pseudonymity, having spent thousands of hours researching, documenting, and building in the virtual identity space. He comes from a diverse, extensive background designing, building, and growing social media companies all centring on the value proposition of pseudonymity in a digital age http://travers.tech.

The Metaverse is both virtual and livestreamed, enabling a type of communication, content, and engagement that is as different from Instagram as a massively multiplayer online game like *Among Us* is from an old arcade game like *Pacman* (Blockwiz, 2022). For example, travel influencers can partner with their audiences to travel to the hottest Metaverse destinations together, only virtually. A beauty influencer can invite herself into fans' bedrooms or have them come into her room for a live demonstration. A culinary influencer can show up in the kitchen of one of her fans to assist them in preparing delectable dishes.

Influencers can perform in real-time, and their fans can be live spectators who also participate in the performance, as was the case during Teflon Sega's concert. When Travis Scott performed a concert in Fortnite in 2020, he appeared as a stomping giant during his opening song, then turned into a cyborg, then transported everyone to a Tron-like computer realm, and then submerged the crowd underwater with a gigantic spaceman figure. The audience of Fortnite players flew around the planet alongside psychedelic effects as the concert drew to a majestic close. Although it only lasted 15 minutes, the concert was lauded as a completely unique experience that was 'surreal and spectacular' (Webster, 2020).

In the future, the Metaverse will allow influencers and creators to explore endless opportunities for self-presentation. They will have vast choices of totally customisable aesthetics, appearances, outfits, and backgrounds to work with. Beyond staging immersive interactive experiences with followers, creating new fanciful avatars and promoting new digital versions of brands, the Metaverse allows the possibility to create new imaginary virtual worlds. Last year, for example, the rapper and influencer Snoop Dogg built his own 'Snoopverse' in The Sandbox (Melnick, 2022; Quiroz-Gutierrez, 2022). In new virtual worlds, influencers and creators can interact with their fans and followers, and also with their fellow influencer peers. They can form whole new worlds of influencers, brands, and followers that might be dedicated to certain themes, like the Marvel Universe or Asian skin care.

In other cases, influencers are creating virtual worlds as a way to develop imaginative new avenues for life betterment and social justice. An example is the artist and crypto influencer Yam Karkai, one of the most popular NFT artists in the world and one of the very few women who has gained ground in the crypto-art industry (Lavania, 2022). Karkai uses her NFTs to stand up for women's inclusion and empowerment. The 'World of Women' NFT project that she co-founded is a collection of images of unique women that represents inclusivity and promotes diversity.

Influencer marketing ecosystem intermediaries are already emerging in the Metaverse. For example, Metafluence.com promotes itself as the first influencer marketing platform in the Metaverse. Its core objective is to connect influencers, brands and audiences in this new virtual space. It works specifically on creating performance-based influencer marketing opportunities in the Metaverse (Investing.com, 2022).

TRAJECTORIES: INFLUENCERS AND CREATORS IN THE NEAR FUTURE

The worlds of social media and of influencers and creators have been rocked by social crises and transformed by technological change. These alterations are not likely to stop. Although gazing into a crystal ball is always challenging, in concluding this book we wanted to offer you a few final prognostications to contemplate.

1. Influencers are not going away. They are a permanent part of the media landscape and we find it likely that we are still only seeing the tip of the iceberg when it comes to their sway over things like public health, public policy, politics, activism, social movements, and even warfare. And it goes without saying that businesses and brands of all kinds, B2B and B2C, as well as other organisations and governments will become increasingly dependent on them.

2. The influencer ecosystem will evolve in sophistication. As the industry develops and ripens, there will be more players offering more services in more ways to support the work that influencers and creators do with brands and other organisations. Social media will keep changing, too. Look for AI-based influencer management platform software to become increasingly sophisticated, for mind-blowing new generative

AI applications to influencer development, and for social media platforms to increasingly cater to influencers.

3. Influencer niches will continue to proliferate. Influencers will become established in more industries and will be present among more different target markets and audience segments. New means of economic exchange such as crypto and NFTs offer especially powerful opportunities for influencer marketing. Alongside, influencer agencies will continue to evolve and specialise.

4. The rise of nano-influencers will continue. There will always be a television-broadcast like role for mega influencers and celebrities who can gather mass audiences. But one of the keys for influencer marketing is the ability to reach specific targets with customised messages. Nano and micro-influencers will become increasingly valued for their ability to connect with difficult to reach audiences in a meaningful way.

5. Diversity will continue to be a major concern for the influencer industry. The influencer industry will face ongoing criticism for its standardisation of appearances and its overt and covert racism, sexism, and ableism. Brand risk aversion built into AI influencer identification software will only make matters worse. Look for regular crises and exposes in this area.

6. Ethics and regulation will become ever more important. Influencers and creators have gotten away with a lot because this was still a new industry. As it professionalises, expect new codes of conduct and industry ethical standards. At some point, regulators may even consistently enforce the laws they have set and communicated.

7. Influencers will increasingly be product developers and innovators. The trend towards influencers as lead users and early adopter communicators will only accelerate as these micro-celebrities also become micro (and sometimes macro) entrepreneurs. Those who successfully influence the audience will control the marketplace.

8. Virtual influencers will continue to challenge human influencers. Vogue Business (2021) predicts that virtual influencers will soon absorb 30% of brands' influencer budgets. Although this is likely an overstatement, there is no doubt that virtual influencers have important benefits, such as predictability and control, over humans. However, at least for now, they lack creativity and the influencer's depth of understanding. But generative AI may begin to change this.

9. Human influencers will start becoming digitised. Human influencers will respond to the threat of virtual influencers by creating and

controlling digital avatars of themselves. There may be major advantages gained when virtual avatars' ability to multiply their presence and guarantee good behaviour are combined with the ability to understand audiences and respond rapidly to cultural changes.

10. Influencers and creators will be major players in the Metaverse. Elements of the Metaverse are already in place, and influencers and creators are already (literally) staking out their ground there. The expanding Metaverse will offer new worlds for influencers, brands, and those who serve them. They will develop new offerings, many of them linked up at first with gaming, e-sports, crypto and NFTs, but then rapidly transcending them as the Metaverse goes mainstream. For those in the influencer industry, exciting new opportunities will abound. The best is yet to come.

CHAPTER SUMMARY

The influencer and creator ecosystem is rapidly transforming as it responds to and simultaneously fuels technological, economic, and social change. The COVID-19 pandemic accelerated the adoption of influencers and content creators as many brands and even public health services discovered their heightened relevance. Contemporary influencers find trends and communicate them, while some use their proximity to consumers to develop and launch innovative new products in contemporary marketplaces. Influencers are central to trends like cottagecore, Light Academia, and many others. Leveraging social media technology throughout the pandemic, influencers have gained public trust and have become established players who take on important roles informing and increasing consumer desire. Virtual influencers are a promising development in the ecosystem, are increasingly being used in advertising campaigns, and are instrumental in establishing powerful global subcultures such as vocaloid fans. Virtual influencers are more controllable by brands, but less attuned to consumers, than human influencers. They raise important ethical concerns. However, they have also been leveraged to promote a discourse of inclusion. As manifestations of the Metaverse grow more prevalent, influencers, brands, and other influencer marketing ecosystem players will be there, exploiting the vast potential of this developing arena of human and technological connection. The future of influencers and creators, although it will not be crisis-free, looks to be bright and exciting.

EXERCISES AND QUESTIONS

Exercises

1. Find a virtual influencer online and closely examine their posts. How does this influencer compare with human influencers that you know? Are they a stereotype? Carefully critique and analyse the strengths and weaknesses of the virtual influencer you have chosen.

2. This chapter gave the example of cottagecore, Dark Academia, and Light Academia aesthetics as a type of movement propagated by influencers. Investigate another social media movement propagated by influencers.

3. Investigate some of the current options that exist for influencers to get involved in the Metaverse.

Questions

1. What role do influencers play in individual and social betterment in times of rapid change?

2. Are all influencers lead users? Drawing on the definition of a lead user (and perhaps expanding your search to learn more), explain your answer.

3. What are some of the major ethical challenges for influencer marketers working in the Metaverse?

4. Look at the list of ten predictions that close this chapter. Do you agree with them? What predictions would you add to the list?

ANNOTATED READINGS

Femenia-Serra, F., Gretzel, U., & Alzua-Sorzabal, A. (2022). Instagram travel influencers in# quarantine: Communicative practices and roles during COVID-19. *Tourism Management*, *89*, 104454.

This article examines how the COVID-19 epidemic changed influencer marketing techniques, content generation tactics, and audience engagement mechanisms.

Hazan, E., Kelly, G., Khan, H., Spillecke, D., & Yee, L. (2022). Marketing in the metaverse: An opportunity for innovation and experimentation, *The McKinsey Quarterly*.

A pragmatic and focused article on Metaverse marketing that views the Metaverse as an evolution of today's Internet.

REFERENCES

Aaker, J. L. (1997). Dimensions of brand personality. *Journal of Marketing Research*, *34*(3), 347–356.

Abidin, C. (2015). Micromicrocelebrity: Branding babies on the internet. *M/C Journal*, *18*(5).

Abidin, C. (2016a). Visibility labour: Engaging with influencers' fashion brands and #OOTD advertorial campaigns on Instagram. *Media International Australia*, *161*(1), 86–100.

Abidin, C. (2016b). 'Aren't these just young, rich women doing vain things online?': Influencer selfies as subversive frivolity. *Social Media + Society*, *2*(2), 1–17.

Abidin, C. (2019). Yes Homo: Gay influencers, homonormativity, and queerbaiting on YouTube. *Continuum*, *33*(5), 614–629.

Abidin, C., & Thompson, E. C. (2012). Buymylife.com: Cyber-femininities and commercial intimacy in blogshops. *Women's Studies International Forum*, *35*(6), 467–477.

Alassani, R., & Göretz, J. (2019). Product placements by micro and macro influencers on Instagram. In *International conference on human-computer interaction* (pp. 251–267). Cham: Springer.

AMA Website. (2022). Definitions of marketing. Retrieved 24 May 2022, from https://www.ama.org/the-definition-of-marketing-what-is-marketing/

Ananny, M. (2016). Toward an ethics of algorithms: Convening, observation, probability, and timeliness. *Science, Technology, & Human Values*, *41*(1), 93–117.

Annie E. Casey Foundation. (2021). *Equity vs. equality and other racial justice definitions*. Retrieved from https://www.aecf.org/blog/racial-justice-definitions

APA Dictionary of Psychology. (2022a). *Social influence*. Retrieved 4 August 2022, from https://dictionary.apa.org/social-influence

APA Dictionary of Psychology. (2022b). *Manipulation*. Retrieved 4 August 2022, from https://dictionary.apa.org/manipulation

APA Dictionary of Psychology. (2022c). *Minority influence*. Retrieved 4 August 2022, from https://dictionary.apa.org/minority-influence

Appadurai, A. (2015). Disjuncture and difference in the global cultural economy. In P. Williams & L. Chrisman (Eds.), *Colonial discourse and post-colonial theory* (pp. 324–339). London: Routledge.

Archer, K. (2019). Social media influencers, post-feminism and neoliberalism: How mum bloggers' 'playbour' is reshaping public relations. *Public Relations Inquiry*, *8*(2), 149–166.

Aristotle. (1984). *The rhetoric and the poetics of Aristotle*. New York, NY: The Modern Library.

Armano, D. (2011). Pillars of the new influence. *Harvard Business Review*. Retrieved 4 August 2022, from https://hbr.org/2011/01/the-six-pillars-of-the-new-inf

Arriagada, A., & Ibáñez, F. (2020). 'You need at least one picture daily, if not, you're dead': Content creators and platform evolution in the social media ecology. *Social Media + Society*, 6(3). doi:10.1177/2056305120944624.

Arsenyan, J., & Mirowska, A. (2021). Almost human? A comparative case study on the social media presence of virtual influencers. *International Journal of Human-Computer Studies*, *155*, 1–16.

Ashman, R., Patterson, A., & Brown, S. (2018). 'Don't forget to like, share and subscribe': Digital autopreneurs in a neoliberal world. *Journal of Business Research*, *92*, 474–483.

Atkin, C. K., & Rice, R. E. (2013). Theory and principles of public communication campaigns. In R. E. Rice & C. K. Atkin (Eds.), *Public communication campaigns* (pp. 3–19). Thousand Oaks, CA: SAGE.

Atkinson, N. (2019, April 13). Beware the 'momager'; Young influencers are the new child stars, but the urge to cash in on cuteness needs to be curbed. *Globe & Mail*.

Atwal, G. (2022). KOL's are dead. Long live the virtual influencer. *Jing Daily*. Retrieved 5 June 2022, from https://jingdaily.com/virtual-influencer-dior-ayayi-mrbags/

Awang, N. (2020). Boasting thousands of Instagram followers, pet influencers are giving their human counterparts a run for their money. *Today*. Retrieved 10 August 2022, from https://www.todayonline.com/singapore/boasting-thousands-instagram-followers-pet-influencers-are-giving-their-human-counterparts

Backaler, J. (2018). *Digital influence: Unleash the power of influencer marketing to accelerate your global business*. Cham: Palgrave Macmillan.

Bagozzi, R., Gürhan-Canli, Z., & Priester, J. (2002). *The social psychology of consumer behaviour*. Buckingham: Open University Press.

Baker, S. A. (2022). Alt. Health influencers: How wellness culture and web culture have been weaponised to promote conspiracy theories and far-right extremism during the COVID-19 pandemic. *European Journal of Cultural Studies*, *25*(1), 3–24.

Banet-Weiser, S. (2021). *Ruptures in authenticity and authentic ruptures: Producing white influencer vulnerability*. Centre for Media, Technology and Democracy. Retrieved 30 March 2022, from https://www.mediatechdemocracy.com/work/ruptures-in-authenticity-and-authentic-ruptures-producing-white-influencer-vulnerability

Barnett, D. (2022). 10 Skincare influencers you should follow. *Influencer Intelligence*. Retrieved from https://www.influencerintelligence.com/blog/TBw/10-skincare-influencers-you-should-follow

Bateman, K. (2020). Academia lives—on TikTok. *The New York Times*. Retrieved 1 August 2022, from https://www.nytimes.com/2020/06/30/style/dark-academia-tiktok.html

Beldad, A., Hegner, S., & Hoppen, J. (2016). The effect of virtual sales agent (VSA) gender–product gender congruence on product advice credibility, trust in VSA and online vendor, and purchase intention. *Computers in Human Behavior*, *60*, 62–72.

Bell, D. (1976). The coming of the post-industrial society. *The Educational Forum*, *40*(4), 574–579.

Bennett, W. L., & Manheim, J. B. (2006). The one-step flow of communication. *The Annals of the American Academy of Political and Social Science*, *608*(1), 213–232.

Bergkvist, L., & Zhou, K. Q. (2016). Celebrity endorsements: A literature review and research agenda. *International Journal of Advertising*, *35*(4), 642–663.

Berryman, R., & Kavka, M. (2017). 'I guess a lot of people see me as a big sister or a friend': The role of intimacy in the celebrification of beauty vloggers. *Journal of Gender Studies*, *26*(3), 307–320.

Bishop, S. (2018). Anxiety, panic and self-optimization: Inequalities and the YouTube algorithm. *Convergence*, *24*(1), 69–84.

Bishop, S. (2021a). Influencer management tools: Algorithmic cultures, brand safety, and bias. *Social Media + Society*, *7*(1), 1–13.

Bishop, S. (2021b). The safety dance. *Reallife Magazine*. Retrieved 1 August 2022, from https://reallifemag.com/the-safety-dance/

Block, E., & Lovegrove, R. (2021). Discordant storytelling, 'honest fakery', identity peddling: How uncanny CGI characters are jamming public relations and influencer practices. *Public Relations Inquiry*, *10*(3), 265–293.

Blockwiz. (2022). *The future of influencer marketing in the metaverse*. Retrieved 12 July 2022, from https://blockwiz.com/metaverse/metaverse-influencer-marketing-future/

Bloomberg.com. (2021). China influencer crackdown exposes loophole used to hide wealth. Retrieved 9 February 2022, from https://www.bloomberg.com/news/articles/2021-12-21/china-influencer-crackdown-exposes-loophole-used-to-hide-wealth

Bohner, G., & Wänke, M. (2004). *Attitudes and attitude change*. Hove: Psychology Press.

Borchers, N. S., & Enke, N. (2021). Managing strategic influencer communication: A systematic overview on emerging planning, organization, and controlling routines. *Public Relations Review*, *47*(3), 102041.

Bradley, S. (2020). Even better than the real thing? Meet the virtual influencers taking over your feeds. *The Drum*. Retrieved 12 July 2022, from https://www.thedrum.com/news/2020/03/20/even-better-the-real-thing-meet-the-virtual-influencers-taking-over-your-feeds

Brehm, S. S., Kassin, S. M., & Fein, S. (2002). *Social psychology* (5th ed.). Boston, MA: Houghton Mifflin Company.

Brittanica.com. (2022). Regulatory agency. Retrieved 10 August 2022, from https://www.britannica.com/topic/regulatory-agency

Brnjarkevska, A. (2022). Meet Kami, world's first virtual influencer with down syndrome. *Newsweek*. Retrieved 12 July 2022, from https://www.newsweek.com/meet-kami-worlds-first-virtual-influencer-down-syndrome-1708753

BroadbandSearch. (2022). Average time spent daily on social media. Retrieved 30 March 2022, from https://www.broadbandsearch.net/blog/average-daily-time-on-social-media

Brown, C. (2018). GDPR and the influencer: What these new regulations mean for you. *Octoly Magazine*. Retrieved 20 July 2022, from https://mag.octoly.com/gdpr-and-the-influencer-what-these-new-regulations-mean-for-you-d959de480f5b

Bruhn, M., Schoenmueller, V., & Schäfer, D. B. (2012). Are social media replacing traditional media in terms of brand equity creation? *Management Research Review*, *35*(9), 770–790.

Bucher, T., & Helmond, A. (2018). The affordances of social media platforms. In J. Burgess, T. Poell, & A. Marwick (Eds.), *The SAGE handbook of social media* (pp. 233–253). London: SAGE.

Burger, J. M. (2001). Social influence, psychology of. In N. J. Smelser & P. B. Baltes (Eds.), *International encyclopedia of the social & behavioral sciences* (pp. 14320–14325). Oxford: Pergamon Press.

Burst Media. (2015). *Burst media releases its first influencer marketing benchmarks report*. PR Newswire. Retrieved 30 July 2022, from https://www.prnewswire.com/

Campbell, C., & Farrell, J. R. (2020). More than meets the eye: The functional components underlying influencer marketing. *Business Horizons*, *63*(4), 469–479.

Campbell, C., & Grimm, P. E. (2019). The challenges native advertising poses: Exploring potential Federal Trade Commission responses and identifying research needs. *Journal of Public Policy & Marketing*, *38*(1), 110–123.

Carr, S. (2021). How many ads do we see in a day in 2021? *PPCProtect*. Retrieved 9 August 2022, from https://ppcprotect.com/blog/strategy/how-many-ads-do-we-see-a-day/

Casciaro, T., & Piskorski, M. J. (2005). Power imbalance, mutual dependence, and constraint absorption: A closer look at resource dependence theory. *Administrative Science Quarterly*, *50*(2), 167–199.

Cassidy, J. (2021). The disabled influencers making their mark on social media. *BBC News*. Retrieved 12 July 2022, from https://www.bbc.com/news/business-56073239

Castells, M. (2011). Network theory. A network theory of power. *International Journal of Communication*, *5*, 773–787.

Caulfield, B. (2021). What is the metaverse? *The Official NVIDIA Blog*. Retrieved 12 July 2022, from https://blogs.nvidia.com/blog/2021/08/10/what-is-the-metaverse/#:~:text=Email1-,What%20is%20the%20metaverse%3F,a%20bunch%20of%20worlds%2C%20too

CFDA. (2018). Kim Kardashian West on influence in the digital age. Retrieved 4 August 2022, from https://cfda.com/news/kim-kardashian-west-on-influence-in-the-digital-age

Chernev, A. (2019). *Strategic marketing management: Theory and practice*. Chicago, IL: Cerebellum Press.

Chi, R. (2021). China's KOL economy: Shaping the conversation for western brands. *The Drum*. Retrieved 10 August 2022, from https://www.thedrum.com/opinion/2021/10/14/china-s-kol-economy-shaping-the-conversation-western-brands

Childers, C. C., Lemon, L. L., & Hoy, M. G. (2019). #Sponsored #Ad: Agency perspective on influencer marketing campaigns. *Journal of Current Issues & Research in Advertising*, *40*(3), 258–274.

Christians, C. G., Fackler, M., Richardson, K. B., & Kreshel, P. J. (2020). *Media ethics: Cases and moral reasoning* (10th ed.). London: Routledge.

Cialdini, R. B. (1995). Principles and techniques of social influence. In A. Tesser (Ed.), *Advanced social psychology* (pp. 256–281). Boston, MA: McGraw-Hill.

Cialdini, R. B. (2021). *Influence, new and expanded: The psychology of persuasion.* New York, NY: Harper Business.

Colicev, A., Kumar, A., & O'Connor, P. (2019). Modeling the relationship between firm and user generated content and the stages of the marketing funnel. *International Journal of Research in Marketing, 36*(1), 100–116.

Conti, R., & Schmidt, J. (2022). What is an NFT? Non-fungible tokens explained. *Forbes*. Retrieved 12 July 2022, from https://www.forbes.com/advisor/investing/cryptocurrency/nft-non-fungible-token/

Cotter, K. (2019). Playing the visibility game: How digital influencers and algorithms negotiate influence on Instagram. *New Media & Society, 21*(4), 895–913.

Cova, B., & Dalli, D. (2009). Working consumers: The next step in marketing theory? *Marketing Theory, 9*(3), 315–339.

Cunningham, S., Craig, D., & Lv, J. (2019). China's livestreaming industry: Platforms, politics, and precarity. *International Journal of Cultural Studies, 22*(6), 719–736.

Cunningham, S., Craig, D., & Silver, J. (2016). YouTube, multichannel networks and the accelerated evolution of the new screen ecology. *Convergence, 22*(4), 376–391.

Datta, K. S., Adkins, O., & Fitzsimmons, J. R. (2020). Entrepreneurship and social media influencers in an Islamic context. In L. Schjoedt, M. E. Brännback, & A. L. Carsrud (Eds.), *Understanding social media and entrepreneurship* (pp. 121–139). Cham: Springer.

Davenport, T. H., & Beck, J. C. (2002). Features-the strategy and structure of firms in the attention economy. *Ivey Business Journal, 66*(4), 48–54.

Davis, J. (2006). The secret world of lonelygirl. *Wired*. Retrieved 30 July 2022, from https://www.wired.com/2006/12/lonelygirl/

de Veirman, M., Cauberghe, V., & Hudders, L. (2017). Marketing through Instagram influencers: The impact of number of followers and product divergence on brand attitude. *International Journal of Advertising, 36*(5), 798–828.

Diaz, A. C. (2021). Eos' NSFW product line honors Tiktok creator who taught fans how to shave their lady parts. *AdAge*. Retrieved 20 July 2022, from https://adage.com/creativity/work/eos-nsfw-product-line-honors-tiktok-creator-who-taught-fans-how-shave-their-lady-parts/2326966

Dietrich, G. (2014). *Spin sucks: Communication and reputation management in the digital age.* Indianapolis, IN: Que Publishing.

Digital Marketing Institute. (2021). 20 Surprising influencer marketing statistics. Retrieved 4 August 2022, from https://digitalmarketinginstitute.com/blog/20-influencer-marketing-statistics-that-will-surprise-you

Dourish, P. (2016). Algorithms and their others: Algorithmic culture in context. *Big Data & Society, 3*(2), 1–11.

Drenten, J., & Brooks, G. (2020). Celebrity 2.0: Lil Miquela and the rise of a virtual star system. *Feminist Media Studies, 20*(8), 1319–1323.

Drenten, J., Gurrieri, L., & Tyler, M. (2020). Sexualized labour in digital culture: Instagram influencers, porn chic and the monetization of attention. *Gender, Work & Organization, 27*(1), 41–66.

Driessens, O. (2013). The celebritization of society and culture: Understanding the structural dynamics of celebrity culture. *International Journal of Cultural Studies*, *16*(6), 641–657.

Duffy, B. (2017). *(Not) getting paid to do what you love: Gender, social media, and aspirational work*. New Haven, CT: Yale University Press.

Duguay, S. (2019). 'Running the numbers': Modes of microcelebrity labor in queer women's self-representation on Instagram and Vine. *Social Media + Society*, *5*(4). doi:10.1177/2056305119894002

Duivestein, S. (2020). *The synthetic future: Virtual influencers of today give us an insight into tomorrow*. Retrieved 12 July 2022, from https://www.virtualhumans.org/article/the-synthetic-future-virtual-influencers-of-today-give-us-an-insight-into-tomorrow

Dunbar, R. I. M. (1992). Neocortex size as a constraint on group size in primates. *Journal of Human Evolution*, *22*(6), 469–493.

Eckhardt, G. M. (2020). Playing the trust game successfully in the reputation economy. *NIM Marketing Intelligence Review*, *12*(2), 10–17.

Edelman. (2021). *Trust: The new brand equity*. Retrieved 30 March 2022, from https://www.edelman.com/trust/2021-brand-trust/brand-equity

Elhacham, E., Ben-Uri, L., Grozovski, J., Bar-On, Y., & Milo, R. (2020). Global human-made mass exceeds all living biomass. *Nature*, *588*(7838), 442–444.

Elliott, S. (2019). What is earned media value? *Julius Works Blog*. Retrieved 1 August 2022, from https://blog.juliusworks.com/what-is-earned-media-value

Elliott, V. (2022). Twitter's case in India could have massive ripple effects. *Wired*. Retrieved 1 July 2022, from https://www.wired.com/story/twitters-case-in-india-could-have-massive-ripple-effects/

eMarketer. (2021). *New forecast*. Retrieved 30 March 2022, from https://www.emarketer.com/content/analyst-note-new-forecast-us-influencer-marketing-now-3-billion-plus-industry

eMarketer. (2022). *Influencer marketing sees steady adoption and room for growth*. Retrieved 30 July 2022, from https://www.emarketer.com/content/influencer-marketing-growth

Emerson, R. M. (1962). Power-dependence relations. *American Sociological Review*, *27*(1), 31–40.

Enke, N., & Borchers, N. S. (2019). Social media influencers in strategic communication: A conceptual framework for strategic social media influencer communication. *International Journal of Strategic Communication*, *13*(4), 261–277.

Ewing, M., & Lambert, C. A. (2019). Listening in: Fostering influencer relationships to manage fake news. *Public Relations Journal*, *12*(4), 1–20.

Facebook Community Insights Survey. (2021). Findings from our Facebook communities insights survey. Retrieved 4 August 2022, from https://www.facebook.com/community/whats-new/facebook-communities-insights-survey/

Facebook IQ. (2022). Syntetic media signals a new chapter for influencer marketing. Retrieved 12 July 2022, from https://www.facebook.com/business/news/insights/synthetic-media-signals-a-new-chapter-for-influencer-marketing

Faimau, G. (2020). Towards a theoretical understanding of the selfie: A descriptive review. *Sociology Compass*, *14*(12), 1–12.

Fair, L. (2020). FTC's Teami case: Spilling the tea about influencers and advertisers. *FTC.gov*. Retrieved 30 July 2022, from https://www.ftc.gov/business-guidance/blog/2020/03/ftcs-teami-case-spilling-tea-about-influencers-and-advertisers

Fairchild, C. (2007). Building the authentic celebrity: The 'Idol' phenomenon in the attention economy. *Popular Music and Society*, *30*(3), 355–375.

Faucher, K. X. (2014). Veblen 2.0: Neoliberal games of social capital and the attention economy as conspicuous consumption. *tripleC: Communication, Capitalism & Critique. Open Access Journal for a Global Sustainable Information Society*, *12*(1), 40–56.

Fecher, B., Friesike, S., Hebing, M., Linek, S., & Sauermann, A. (2015). A reputation economy: Results from an empirical survey on academic data sharing. doi:10.48550/arXiv.1503.00481

Federal Trade Commission. (2022). *Native advertising: A guide for businesses*. Retrieved 5 August 2022, from https://www.ftc.gov/business-guidance/resources/native-advertising-guide-businesses

Femenia-Serra, F., & Gretzel, U. (2020). Influencer marketing for tourism destinations: Lessons from a mature destination. In J. Neidhardt & W. Wörndl (Eds.), *Information and communication technologies in tourism 2020* (pp. 65–78). Berlin: Springer.

Femenia-Serra, F., Gretzel, U., & Alzua-Sorzabal, A. (2022). Instagram travel influencers in# quarantine: Communicative practices and roles during COVID-19. *Tourism Management*, *89*, 104454.

Fiske, S. T., & Berdahl, J. (2007). Social power. In A. W. Kruglanski & E. T. Higgins (Eds.), *Social psychology: Handbook of basic principles* (pp. 678–692). New York, NY: The Guilford Press.

Floridi, L. (2018). Artificial intelligence, deepfakes and a future of ectypes. *Philosophy & Technology*, *31*(3), 317–321.

Forbes.com. (2021). Why and how influencers are launching their own brands. Retrieved 13 August 2022, from https://www.forbes.com/sites/forbescommunicationscouncil/2021/11/02/why-and-how-influencers-are-launching-their-own-brands/?sh=57add54e2a40

Ford, P. (2022). The 'form' element created the modern web. Was it a big mistake? *Wired*, Retrieved 8 August 2022, from https://www.wired.com/story/form-element-modern-web-mistake/

Forman, B. (2021). Wealth inequality exists among influencers, too. *Vox Media Blog*. Retrieved 18 February 2022, from https://www.vox.com/the-goods/22630965/influencer-pay-gaps-privilege-creator-economy

Formost, K. (2022). How to improve influencer outreach and increase response rates. *Tagger Blog*. Retrieved 1 August 2022, from https://www.taggermedia.com/blog/influencer-outreach-strategy-tips

Freberg, K. (2021). *Social media for strategic communication* (2nd ed.). Thousand Oaks, CA: SAGE.

Freberg, K., Graham, K., McGaughey, K., & Freberg, L. A. (2011). Who are the social media influencers? A study of public perceptions of personality. *Public Relations Review*, *37*(1), 90–92.

French, J. P. R., & Raven, B. (1960). The bases of social power. In D. Cartwright & A. Zander (Eds.), *Group dynamics* (pp. 607–623). New York, NY: Harper and Row.

Friestad, M., & Wright, P. (1994). The persuasion knowledge model: How people cope with persuasion attempts. *Journal of Consumer Research*, *21*(1), 1–31.

FTC. (2022). Division of advertising practices. Retrieved 8 August 2022, from https://www.ftc.gov/about-ftc/bureaus-offices/bureau-consumer-protection/our-divisions/division-advertising-practices

Fugate, D. L., & Phillips, J. (2010). Product gender perceptions and antecedents of product gender congruence. *Journal of Consumer Marketing*, *27*(3), 251–261.

Gallo, A. (2017). A refresher on marketing ROI. *Harvard Business Review*. Retrieved 30 July 2022, from https://hbr.org/2017/07/a-refresher-on-marketing-roi

Gambetti, R. (2021). Netnography, digital habitus, and technocultural capital. In R. V. Kozinets & R. Gambetti (Eds.), *Netnography unlimited: Understanding technoculture using qualitative social media research* (pp. 293–319). London: Routledge.

Gambetti, R. C., & Kozinets, R. V. (2022). Agentic netnography. *New Trends in Qualitative Research*, *10*, e519. doi:10.36367/ntqr.10.2022.e519

Gannon, V., & Prothero, A. (2016). Beauty blogger selfies as authenticating practices. *European Journal of Marketing*, *50*(9/10), 1858–1878.

Gardner, J., & Lehnert, K. (2016). What's new about new media? How multi-channel networks work with content creators. *Business Horizons*, *59*(3), 293–302.

Gass, R. H. (2015). Social influence, sociology of. In J. D. Wright (Ed.), *International encyclopedia of the social & behavioral sciences* (pp. 348–354). Amsterdam: Elsevier.

Gatollari, M. (2021). 13 Influencers who were canceled just as quickly as they got famous. *Distractify*. Retrieved 17 August 2022, from https://www.distractify.com/p/influencers-canceled-quickly

Gebhardt, G., Gregory, F., Carpenter, S., & Sherry, J. F. Jr. (2006). Creating a market orientation: A longitudinal, multifirm, grounded analysis of cultural transformation. *Journal of Marketing*, *70*(4), 37–55.

Ge, J., & Gretzel, U. (2018). Emoji rhetoric: A social media influencer perspective. *Journal of Marketing Management*, *34*(15–16), 1272–1295.

Gerlitz, C., & Helmond, A. (2013). The like economy: Social buttons and the data-intensive web. *New Media & Society*, *15*(8), 1348–1365.

Gibson, J. J. (1979). *The ecological approach to perception*. London: Houghton Mifflin.

Gill, R. (2010). Life is a pitch: Managing the self in new media work. *Managing Media Work*, 249–262.

Gillespie, T. (2010). The politics of 'platforms'. *New Media & Society*, *12*(3), 347–364.

Gillespie, K. (2019). What the ideal Instagram influencer looks like. *Paper*. Retrieved 20 July 2022, from https://www.papermag.com/the-face-of-influence-2639356208.html?rebelltitem=11#rebelltitem11

Goertzen, K. (2012). *Pet African hedgehogs: A complete guide to care*. Research Triangle, NC: Lulu Press.

Goffman, E. (1959). *The presentation of self in everyday life*. New York, NY: Doubleday Anchor Books.

Goldhaber, M. H. (1997). The attention economy and the net. *First Monday, 2*(4). https://doi.org/10.5210/fm.v2i4.519

Gonçalves, B., Perra, N., & Vespignani, A. (2011). Modeling users' activity on twitter networks: Validation of Dunbar's number. *PloS One, 6*(8), e22656.

Google Dictionary. (2022). *Sphere of influence*. Retrieved from google.com

Gopaldas, A., & Fischer, E. (2012). Beyond. Gender: Intersectionality, culture, and consumer. Behavior. In C. C. Otnes & L. Tuncay Zayer (Eds.), *Gender, culture, and consumer behavior* (pp. 425–442). London: Routledge.

Gorbatov, S., Khapova, S. N., & Lysova, E. I. (2018). Personal branding: Interdisciplinary systematic review and research agenda. *Frontiers in Psychology, 9*, 2238.

Gorbatov, S., Khapova, S. N., Oostrom, J. K., & Lysova, E. I. (2021). Personal brand equity: Scale development and validation. *Personnel Psychology, 74*(3), 505–542.

Granovetter, M. S. (1973). The strength of weak ties. *American Journal of Sociology, 78*(6), 1360–1380.

Granovetter, M. S. (1983). The strength of weak ties: A network theory revisited. *Sociological Theory, 1*, 201–233.

Gräve, J. F. (2019). What KPIs are key? Evaluating performance metrics for social media influencers. *Social Media + Society*. doi:10.1177/2056305119865475

Gretzel, U. (2017a). Social media activism in tourism. *Journal of Hospitality and Tourism, 15*(2), 1–14.

Gretzel, U. (2017b). The visual turn in social media marketing. *Tourismos, 12*(3), 1–18.

Gretzel, U., & Femenia-Serra, F. (2022). Influence. In D. Buhalis (Ed.), *Encyclopedia of tourism marketing and management*. Northampton, MA: Edward Elgar Publishing.

Gretzel, U., & Hardy, A. (2019). #VanLife: Materiality, makeovers and mobility amongst digital nomads. *E-Review of Tourism Research, 16*(2/3).

Griffith, F. J., & Stein, C. H. (2021). Behind the hashtag: Online disclosure of mental illness and community response on tumblr. *American Journal of Community Psychology, 67*(3–4), 419–432.

Guthrie, S. (2016). The 7 Rs of influencer relations. *The Ketchum Blog*. Retrieved 30 July 2022, from https://www.ketchum.com/the-7-rs-of-influencer-relations/

Hackl, C. (2021). Defining the metaverse today. *Forbes*. Retrieved 15 July 2022, from https://www.forbes.com/sites/cathyhackl/2021/05/02/defining-the-metaverse-today/?sh=35e96c176448

Hahnel, R. (2006). Exploitation: A modern approach. *Review of Radical Political Economics, 38*, 175–192.

Hallinan, B., & Striphas, T. (2016). Recommended for you: The Netflix prize and the production of algorithmic culture. *New Media & Society, 18*(1), 117–137.

Hall, S., & O'Shea, A. (2013). Common-sense neoliberalism. *Soundings, 55*(55), 9–25.

Hall, M., & Tenbarge, K. (2020). How getting 'canceled' can actually prolong a YouTuber's career. *The Insider*. Retrieved 30 March 2022, from https://www.insider.com/cancel-culture-youtube-actually-help-a-youtubers-career-2020-12

Hampton, K. N. (2016). Persistent and pervasive community: New communication technologies and the future of community. *American Behavioral Scientist*, *60*(1), 101–124.

Hartmann, T., & Goldhoorn, C. (2011). Horton and Wohl revisited: Exploring viewers' experience of parasocial interaction. *Journal of Communication*, *61*(6), 1104–1121.

Hazan, E., Kelly, G., Khan, H., Spillecke, D., & Yee, L. (2022). Marketing in the metaverse: An opportunity for innovation and experimentation. *The McKinsey Quarterly*. Retrieved 12 July 2022, from https://www.mckinsey.com/capabilities/growth-marketing-and-sales/our-insights/marketing-in-the-metaverse-an-opportunity-for-innovation-and-experimentation

Hearn, A. (2008). Meat, mask, burden: Probing the contours of the branded self. *Journal of Consumer Culture*, *8*(2), 197–217.

Hedgehog Welfare Society. (2014). African Hedgehog Care Sheet. Retrieved 18 May 2022, from https://hedgehogwelfare.org/Hedgehog_Care_Sheet.pdf

Henley, J. (2020). Finland enlists social influencers in fight against Covid-19. *The Guardian*. Retrieved 30 July 2022, from https://www.theguardian.com/world/2020/apr/01/finland-enlists-social-influencers-in-fight-against-covid-19

Hermann, I., & Paris, C. M. (2020). Digital nomadism: The nexus of remote working and travel mobility. *Information Technology & Tourism*, *22*(3), 329–334.

Hiort, A. (2021a). Prada creates virtual muse named candy. Retrieved 12 July 2022, from https://www.virtualhumans.org/article/prada-creates-first-virtual-muse-candy

Hiort, A. (2021b). Virtual influencers: The future of fashion. Retrieved 12 July 2022, from https://www.virtualhumans.org/article/virtual-influencers-are-the-future-of-fashion

Hochschild, A. R. (1983). Social constructionist and positivist approaches to the sociology of emotions – Comment. *American Journal of Sociology*, *89*(2), 432–434.

Hootsuite. (2022). 16 Key social media metrics to track in 2022. Retrieved 1 August 2022, from https://blog.hootsuite.com/social-media-metrics/

Hopkins, J. (2019). Communication, culture, and governance in Asia. 'We connect with people through stories': Gender and affective labor in momblogging. *International Journal of Communication*, *13*, 4702–4721.

Horton, D., & Wohl, R. (1956). Mass communication and para-social interaction: Observations on intimacy at a distance. *Psychiatry*, *19*(3), 215–229.

Huddleston, T. (2021). How Instagram influencers can fake their way to online fame. *CNBC*. Retrieved 22 June 2022, from https://www.cnbc.com/2021/02/02/hbo-fake-famous-how-instagram-influencers-.html

Huotari, K., & Hamari, J. (2017). A definition for gamification: Anchoring gamification in the service marketing literature. *Electronic Markets*, *27*(1), 21–31.

Hwang, K., & Zhang, Q. (2018). Influence of parasocial relationship between digital celebrities and their followers on followers' purchase and electronic word-of-mouth intentions, and persuasion knowledge. *Computers in Human Behavior*, *87*, 155–173.

HypeAuditor. (2021). The top Instagram virtual influencers 2021. Retrieved 18 May 2022, from https://hypeauditor.com/blog/the-top-instagram-virtual-influencers-in-2021/

Ihlen, Ø. (2005). The power of social capital: Adapting Bourdieu to the study of public relations. *Public Relations Review*, 31(4), 492–496.

Influencer Intelligence. (2022). 7 Influencer marketing trends for 2022. Retrieved 24 July 2022, from https://hello.influencerintelligence.com/influencer-trends-2022/

Influencer Marketing Hub. (2021). What are virtual influencers and how do they work. Retrieved 11 July 2022, from https://influencermarketinghub.com/what-are-virtual-influencers/

Influencer Marketing Hub. (2022a). Influencer [glossary entry]. Retrieved 28 January 2022, from https://influencermarketinghub.com/glossary/influencer/

Influencer Marketing Hub. (2022b). Key influencer marketing statistics you need to know for 2022. Retrieved 9 April 2022, from https://influencermarketinghub.com/influencer-marketing-statistics/

Influencer Marketing Hub. (2022c). How the metaverse will shape the future of business, marketing, and consequently influencer marketing. Retrieved 24 July 2022, from https://influencermarketinghub.com/metaverse-influencer-marketing/

Investing.com. (2022). Metafluence: The first influencer platform connecting influencers, brands and audiences in the metaverse. Retrieved 13 August 2022, from https://www.investing.com/news/cryptocurrency-news/metafluence-the-first-influencer-platform-connecting-influencers-brands-and-audiences-in-the-metaverse-2742112

Izea. (2022). Influencer marketing services. Retrieved 7 August 2022, from https://izea.com/managed-services/

Jarvey, N. (2020). Social media influencers struggle with anxiety amid pressure to create perfectly curated feed. *Hollywood Reporter*. Retrieved 27 March 2022, from https://www.hollywoodreporter.com/lifestyle/lifestyle-news/social-media-influencers-struggle-anxiety-pressure-create-perfectly-curated-feed-1269805/

Jenkins, H. (2006). *Convergence culture: Where old and new media collide*. New York, NY: New York University Press.

Jerslev, A. (2016). Media times| in the time of the microcelebrity: Celebrification and the YouTuber Zoella. *International Journal of Communication*, 10, 5233–5251.

Jerslev, A., & Mortensen, M. (2016). What is the self in the celebrity selfie? Celebrification, phatic communication and performativity. *Celebrity Studies*, 7(2), 249–263.

Jing Daily. (2019). Luxury brands need a proactive plan to navigate China's cancel culture. *Jing Daily*. Retrieved 14 March 2022, from https://jingdaily.com/brands-need-a-proactive-plan-to-navigate-chinas-cancel-culture/

Jing Daily. (2021). The birth of China's cultural opinion leaders. Retrieved 14 August 2022, from https://jingdaily.com/china-cultural-opinion-leaders-influencers/

Jing Daily. (2022). 4 MCNs you need to know in China. Retrieved 10 August 2022, from https://jingdaily.com/4-mcn-china-influencer/

Jin, S. V., & Muqaddam, A. (2019). Product placement 2.0: 'Do brands need influencers, or do influencers need brands?' *Journal of Brand Management*, 26(5), 522–537.

Johnson, A. (2016). Inbound marketing: How influencer marketing attracted 100,000 website clicks to luxury mattress site. *Marketing Sherpa*. Retrieved 18 July 2022, from https://www.marketingsherpa.com/article/case-study/how-influencer-marketing-attracted-website-clicks

Jorge, A., & Pedroni, M. (2021). 'Hey! I'm back after a 24h #DigitalDetox!': Influencers posing disconnection. In A. Chia, A. Jorge, & T. Karppi (Eds.), *Reckoning with social media: Disconnection in the age of the techlash*. Lanham, MD: Rowman & Littlefield.

Just, S. N. (2019). An assemblage of avatars: Digital organization as affective intensification in the GamerGate controversy. *Organization, 26*(5), 716–738.

Kale, P., Singh, H., & Perlmutter, H. (2000). Learning and protection of proprietary assets in strategic alliances: Building relational capital. *Strategic Management Journal, 21*(3), 217–237.

Kalpokas, I. (2021). Problematising reality: The promises and perils of synthetic media. *SN Social Sciences, 1*(1), 1–11.

Karppi, T., Kähkönen, L., Mannevuo, M., Pajala, M., & Sihvonen, T. (2016). Affective capitalism. *Ephemera: Theory and Politics in Organization, 16*(4), 1–13.

Katz, E., & Lazarsfeld, P. F. (1955). *Personal influence. The part played by people in the flow of mass communications*. New York: Free Press.

Keegan, M. (2022). How the world's first virtual influencer with down syndrome was created. *Campaign Asia*. Retrieved 12 July 2022, from https://www.campaignasia.com/article/how-the-worlds-first-virtual-influencer-with-down-syndrome-was-created/477935

Kelman, H. C. (1958). Compliance, identification, and internalization: Three processes of attitude change. *Journal of Conflict Resolution, 2*, 51–60.

Ketcham, C. (2019). How Instagram ruined the great outdoors. *The New Republic*. Retrieved 30 July 2022, from https://newrepublic.com/article/153603/instagram-ruined-great-outdoors

Khamis, S., Ang, L., & Welling, R. (2017). Self-branding, 'micro-celebrity' and the rise of social media influencers. *Celebrity Studies, 8*(2), 191–208.

Kim, J. (2021). Advertising in the metaverse: Research agenda. *Journal of Interactive Advertising, 21*(3), 141–144.

Kircaburun, K., Harris, A., Calado, F., & Griffiths, M. D. (2021). The psychology of mukbang watching: A scoping review of the academic and non-academic literature. *International Journal of Mental Health and Addiction, 19*(4), 1190–1213.

Kitchin, R. (2017). Thinking critically about and researching algorithms. *Information, Communication & Society, 20*(1), 14–29.

Knowles, E. S., & Linn, J. A. (2004). The importance of resistance to persuasion. In E. S. Knowles & J. A. Linn (Eds.), *Resistance and persuasion* (pp. 3–9). Mahwah, NJ: Lawrence Erlbaum.

Kohli, A. K., & Jaworski, B. J. (1990). Market orientation: The construct, research propositions, and managerial implications. *Journal of Marketing, 54*(2), 1–18.

Kozinets, R. V. (2002). The field behind the screen: Using netnography for marketing research in online communities. *Journal of Marketing Research, 39*(1), 61–72.

Kozinets, R. V. (2019). Consuming technocultures: An extended JCR curation. *Journal of Consumer Research, 46*(3), 620–627.

Kozinets, R. V. (2020a). *Netnography: The essential guide to qualitative social media research*. London: SAGE.

Kozinets, R. V. (2020b). #Luxe: Influencers, selfies, and the marketizing of morality. In *Research handbook on luxury branding* (pp. 282–299). Cheltenham: Edward Elgar Publishing.

Kozinets, R. V. (2022). Algorithmic branding through platform assemblages: Core conceptions and research directions for a new era of marketing and service management. *Journal of Service Management*, 33(3), 437–452.

Kozinets, R. V., De Valck, K., Wojnicki, A. C., & Wilner, S. J. (2010). Networked narratives: Understanding word-of-mouth marketing in online communities. *Journal of Marketing*, 74(2), 71–89.

Kozinets, R. V., & Gretzel, U. (2021). Commentary: Artificial intelligence: The marketer's dilemma. *Journal of Marketing*, 85(1), 156–159.

Kozinets, R., Gretzel, U., & Dinhopl, A. (2017a). Self in art/self as art: Museum selfies as identity work. *Frontiers in Psychology*, 8, 731.

Kozinets, R. V., Patterson, A. & Ashman, R. (2017b). Networks of desire: How technology increases our passion to consume. *Journal of Consumer Research*, 43(5), 659–682.

Labrecque, L. I. (2014). Fostering consumer–brand relationships in social media environments: The role of parasocial interaction. *Journal of Interactive Marketing*, 28(2), 134–148.

Laczniak, G. R., & Murphy, P. E. (2006). Normative perspectives for ethical and socially responsible marketing. *Journal of Macromarketing*, 26(2), 154–177.

Laflin, P., Mantzaris, A. V., Ainley, F., Otley, A., Grindrod, P., & Higham, D. J. (2013). Discovering and validating influence in a dynamic online social network. *Social Network Analysis and Mining*, 3(4), 1311–1323.

Lakhani, D. (2005). *Persuasion: The art of getting what you want*. Hoboken, NJ: John Wiley & Sons.

Lam, K. Y. (2016). The Hatsune Miku phenomenon: More than a virtual J-pop diva. *The Journal of Popular Culture*, 49(5), 1107–1124.

Larrison, B. (2022). Digital advertising regulation in 2022: What marketers need to know. *Basis Technologies Blog*. Retrieved 10 August 2022, from https://basis.net/blog/digital-advertising-regulation-in-2022-what-marketers-need-to-know

Lavania, R. (2022). Yam Karkai: The face behind world of women NFT project. *The Crypto Times*. Retrieved 14 July 2022, from https://www.cryptotimes.io/yam-karkai-the-face-behind-world-of-women-nft-project/

Lee, K. M., & Nass, C. (2003). Designing social presence of social actors in human computer interaction. In *Proceedings of the SIGCHI conference on human factors in computing systems* (pp. 289–296).

Lee, K. M., Park, N., & Song, H. (2005). Can a robot be perceived as a developing creature? Effects of a robot's long-term cognitive developments on its social presence and people's social responses toward it. *Human Communication Research*, 31(4), 538–563.

Leighton, H. (2019). What it means for virtual Instagram influencers' popularity rising. *Forbes*. Retrieved 15 July 2022, from https://www.forbes.com/sites/heatherleighton/2019/11/26/what-it-means-for-virtual-instagram-influencers-popularity-rising/?sh=aa6f7ae6e097

Levin, A. (2020). *Influencer marketing for brands: What YouTube and Instagram can teach you about the future of digital advertising*. New York, NY: Springer.

Liederman, E. (2022). How agencies are confronting the influencer pay gap. Retrieved 14 February 2022, from https://www.adweek.com/agencies/how-agencies-are-confronting-the-influencer-pay-gap/

Lloyds Banking Group. (2016). *Reflecting modern Britain: A study into inclusion and diversity in advertising*. Retrieved 8 February 2022, from https://www.lloydsbankinggroup.com/assets/pdfs/who-we-are/responsible-business/inclusion-and-diversity/modern-britain-5.12-single-pages.pdf

Lorenz, T. (2020). Hype house and the Los Angeles TikTok mansion gold rush? *The New York Times*. Retrieved 18 May 2022, from https://www.nytimes.com/2020/01/03/style/hype-house-los-angeles-tik-tok.html

Lorenz, T. (2021a). Jake Paul promised them fame. Was it worth the price? *The New York Times*. Retrieved 9 August 2022, from https://www.nytimes.com/2021/04/22/style/jake-paul-team-10.html

Lorenz, C. (2021b). Young creators are burning out and breaking down. *The New York Times*. Retrieved 28 March 2022, from https://www.nytimes.com/2021/06/08/style/creator-burnout-social-media.html

Lothian-McClean, M. (2021). Inside the influencer pay gap: Why are Black women being paid less for their posts? *Cosmopolitan*. Retrieved 14 February 2022, from https://www.cosmopolitan.com/uk/reports/a35352031/race-inequality-influencer-pay-gap/

Lou, C., & Yuan, S. (2019). Influencer marketing: How message value and credibility affect consumer trust of branded content on social media. *Journal of Interactive Advertising*, *19*(1), 58–73.

Lu, A. (2019). New: Introducing influencer lists 2.0. *Influence*. Retrieved 4 August 2022, from https://influence.bloglovin.com/new-introducing-influencer-lists-2-0-83c5115531a

Lumanu.com. (2022). *A quick guide to influencer whitelisting*. Retrieved 9 August 2022, from https://www.lumanu.com/blog/what-is-influencer-whitelisting

Luthera, N. (2020). The dark side of deepfake artificial intelligence and virtual influencers. *Forbes*. Retrieved 12 July 2022, from https://www.forbes.com/sites/forbesbusinesscouncil/2020/01/16/the-dark-side-of-deepfake-artificial-intelligence-and-virtual-influencers/?sh=bf76c381cd97

Lykousas, N., Casino, F., & Patsakis, C. (2020). Inside the x-rated world of 'premium' social media accounts. In *International conference on social informatics* (pp. 181–191). Berlin: Springer.

Maddox, J. (2021). What do creators and viewers owe each other? Microcelebrity, reciprocity, and transactional tingles in the ASMR YouTube community. *First Monday*, *26*(1). doi:10.5210/fm.v26i1.10804

Mardon, R., Molesworth, M., & Grigore, G. (2018). YouTube Beauty Gurus and the emotional labour of tribal entrepreneurship. *Journal of Business Research*, *92*, 443–454.

Marketing Charts. (2021a). Public trust in advertising practitioners' integrity worsens. Retrieved 27 July 2022, from https://www.marketingcharts.com/business-of-marketing/staffing-116013

Marketing Charts. (2021b). More than 1 in 4 Gen Zers worldwide follow influencers on social media. Retrieved 1 August 2022, from https://www.marketingcharts.com/digital/social-media-117046#:~:text=The%20report%20reveals%20that%2028, ages%2024%2D37%20following%20influencers

Marketing Magazine. (2013). Hamilton Island 'Instameet' roadblocked Instagram's 100m global users. Retrieved 4 February 2022, from https://www.marketingmag. com.au/news-c/hamilton-island-instameet-roadblocked-instagrams-100m-global-users/

Marketingterms.com. (2022). Call to action. Retrieved 25 March 2022, from https://www.marketingterms.com/dictionary/call_to_action/

Marshall, P. D. (2010). The promotion and presentation of the self: Celebrity as marker of presentational media. *Celebrity Studies*, *1*(1), 35–48.

Marwick, A. E. (2013). *Status update: Celebrity, publicity, and branding in the social media age.* New Haven, CT: Yale University Press.

Marwick, A. E. (2015a). Instafame: Luxury selfies in the attention economy. *Public Culture*, *27* (1 (75)), 137–160.

Marwick, A. E. (2015b). You may know me from YouTube (micro-)celebrity in social media. In S. Redmond & P. D. Marshall (Eds.), *A companion to celebrity* (pp. 333–349). Chichester: John Wiley & Sons.

Marwick, A. E., & Boyd, D. (2011). I tweet honestly, I tweet passionately: Twitter users, context collapse, and the imagined audience. *New Media & Society*, *13*(1), 114–133.

Mateer, N., (2021). Looks that quill: The dark side of hedgehog Instagram, *Wired*. Retrieved 3 May 2022, from https://www.wired.com/story/unbearable-cuteness-instagram-hedgehog-influencers/

McBean, S. (2014). Remediating affect: 'Luclyn' and lesbian intimacy on YouTube. *Journal of Lesbian Studies*, *18*(3), 282–297.

McColl-Kennedy, J. R., & Cheung, L. (2018). Value cocreation: Conceptualizations, origins, and developments. In R. F. Lusch & S. L. Vargo (Eds.), *The SAGE handbook of service dominant logic* (pp. 63–79). London: SAGE.

McCracken, G. (1989). Who is the celebrity endorser? Cultural foundations of the endorsement process. *Journal of Consumer Research*, *16*(3), 310–321.

McGrath, L. (2019). Influencer partnerships: How to navigate influencer usage rights and repurpose content. *Marketingprofs.com*. Retrieved 30 July 2022, from https://www.marketingprofs.com/articles/2019/41510/influencer-partnerships-how-to-navigate-influencer-usage-rights-and-repurpose-content

McLachlan, S. (2021). Instagram influencer pricing: How to determine influencer rates in 2022. *Hootsuite Blog*. Retrieved 12 February 2022, from https://blog.hootsuite. com/instagram-influencer-rates/

McLuhan, M. (1964). *Understanding media: The extensions of man*. Cambridge, MA: MIT Press.

McQuarrie, E. F., Miller, J., & Phillips, B. J. (2013). The megaphone effect: Taste and audience in fashion blogging. *Journal of Consumer Research*, *40*(1), 136–158.

Melnick, K. (2022). Snoop Dogg's new video was shot in the metaverse. VR Scout. Retrieved 12 July 2022, from https://vrscout.com/news/snoop-doggs-new-music-video-was-shot-in-the-metaverse/#

Merriam-Webster Dictionary. (2021). *Definition of influencer*. Retrieved from https://www.merriam-webster.com/dictionary/influencer

Merriam-Webster Dictionary. (2022). Data. Retrieved 12 February 2022, from https://www.merriam-webster.com/dictionary/data

Michnik, M. (2022). Light academia in 2022 — Outfits, aesthetics, dashion, quotes. *The Vou*. Retrieved 30 July 2022, from https://thevou.com/fashion/light-academia/

Miller, G. R. (2002). On being persuaded: Some basic distinctions. In J. P. Dillard & M. Pfau (Eds.), *The persuasion handbook: Developments in theory and practice* (pp. 3–16). Thousand Oaks, CA: SAGE.

Miller, V. (2008). New media, networking and phatic culture. *Convergence, 14*(4), 387–400.

Milner, R. M. (2009). Working for the text: Fan labor and the new organization. *International Journal of Cultural Studies, 12*(5), 491–508.

Mitchell, M. (2021). Free ad (vice): Internet influencers and disclosure regulation. *The RAND Journal of Economics, 52*(1), 3–21.

Mobile Marketing Magazine. (2019). 'Influencer' now one of the most popular career aspirations among children. Retrieved 28 March 2022, from https://mobilemarketingmagazine.com/social-media-influencer-youtuber-uk-children-career-aspirations-awin

Moore, J. (2020). Do you need an influencer manager or agent? *Creator Wizard*. Retrieved 8 August 2022, from https://www.creatorwizard.com/post/should-you-hire-an-influencer-manager-or-agent

Moore, K. (2022). 25 Examples of influencer marketing during COVID-19. *Banknotes by #paid*. Retrieved 30 July 2022, from https://hashtagpaid.com/banknotes/25-examples-of-influencer-marketing-during-covid-19

MSL. (2021). *MSL study reveals racial pay gap in influencer marketing*. Retrieved 4 February 2022, from https://mslgroup.com/whats-new-at-msl/msl-study-reveals-racial-pay-gap-influencer-marketing

Murray, D., & Gissen, L. (2022). The fake influencers trying to inspire 'real' change: Kami. *Daily Mail*. Retrieved 12 July 2022, from https://www.dailymail.co.uk/femail/article-10837569/Kami-VIRTUAL-influencer-syndrome-gives-people-disabilities-relate-to.html

Nass, C., Steuer, J., & Tauber, E. R. (1994). Computers are social actors. In *Proceedings of the SIGCHI conference on Human factors in computing systems* (pp. 72–78).

Negri, A., & Hardt, M. (1999). Value and affect. *Boundary 2, 26*(2), 77–88.

Nielsen. (2019). *Global trust in advertising report*. Retrieved 8 February 2022, from https://www.nielsen.com/wp-content/uploads/sites/3/2019/04/global-trust-in-advertising-report-sept-2015-1.pdf

Nobelprize.org. (2014). Malala Yousafzai – Facts. Retrieved 24 April 2022, from https://www.nobelprize.org/prizes/peace/2014/yousafzai/facts/

Norman, D. A. (1988). *The psychology of everyday things*. New York, NY: Basic Books.

NYU News Release. (2020). Kid influencers are promoting junk food brands on YouTube—Garnering more than a billion views. Retrieved 3 August from https://www.nyu.edu/about/news-publications/news/2020/october/kid-influencers-junk-food.html

O'Keefe, D. J. (2015). *Persuasion: Theory and research*. (3rd ed.). Thousand Oaks, CA: SAGE.

Ohanian, R. (1990). Construction and validation of a scale to measure celebrity endorsers' perceived expertise, trustworthiness, and attractiveness. *Journal of Advertising*, *19*(3), 39–52.

Ohlheiser, A. (2022). How aspiring influencers are forced to fight the algorithm. *MIT Technology Review*. Retrieved 17 August 2022, from https://www.technology review.com/2022/07/14/1055906/tiktok-influencers-moderation-bias/

O'Meara, V. (2019). Weapons of the chic: Instagram influencer engagement pods as practices of resistance to Instagram platform labor. *Social Media + Society*, *5*(4). doi:10.1177/2056305119879671

Open Influence team. (2020). Influencer vetting. *Openinfluence.com*. Retrieved 30 July 2022, from https://openinfluence.com/influencer-vetting-a-data-driven-and-human-centered-approach/

Park, G., Nan, D., Park, E., Kim, K. J., Han, J., & del Pobil, A. P. (2021). Computers as social actors? Examining how users perceive and interact with virtual influencers on social media. In *2021 15th international conference on ubiquitous information management and communication (IMCOM)* (pp. 1–6). IEEE.

Pattee, E. (2021). Meet the climate change activists of TikTok. *Wired.com*. Retrieved 17 August 2022, from https://www.wired.com/story/climate-change-tiktok-science-communication/

Pemberton, K., & Takhar, J. (2021). A critical technocultural discourse analysis of Muslim fashion bloggers in France: Charting 'restorative technoscapes'. *Journal of Marketing Management*, *37*(5–6), 387–416.

Perloff, R. M. (2003). *The dynamics of persuasion: Communication and attitudes in the 21st century* (2nd ed.). Mahwah, NJ: Lawrence Erlbaum Associates.

Petty, R. E., & Cacioppo, J. T. (1986). *Communication and persuasion: Central and peripheral routes to attitude change*. New York, NY: Springer.

Pfeffer, J., & Salancik, G. R. (2003). *The external control of organizations: A resource dependence perspective*. Stanford, CA: Stanford University Press.

Pfeiffer, S. (2021). The greater transformation: Digitalization and the transformative power of distributive forces in digital capitalism. *International Critical Thought*, *11*(4), 535–552.

Porsche Newsroom. (2022). Virtual influencers in the automotive industry. Retrieved 10 July 2022, from https://newsroom.porsche.com/it_CH/2022/innovation/porsche-virtual-influencers-ayayi-automotive-industry-imaker-27562.html

PostBeyond Marketing. (2021). What is earned media value? Why is it important? *Postbeyond.com*. Retrieved 30 July 2022, from https://www.postbeyond.com/blog/earned-media-value-employee-advocacy/

Postigo, H. (2016). The socio-technical architecture of digital labor: Converting play into YouTube money. *New Media & Society*, *18*(2), 332–349.

Powers, K. (2019). Virtual influencers are becoming more real — Here's why brands should be cautious. American Marketing Association. Retrieved 10 July 2022, from https://www.ama.org/marketing-news/virtual-influencers-are-becoming-more-real-heres-why-brands-should-be-cautious/

Pöyry, E. I., Pelkonen, M., Naumanen, E., & Laaksonen, S.-M., (2019). A call for authenticity: Audience responses to social media influencer endorsements in strategic communication. *International Journal of Strategic Communication*, *13*(4), 336–351.

Purple Goat Agency. (2022). Retrieved from http://purplegoatagency.com/

Qiu, X. (2022). Meet China's luxury influencer Savi Sui. *Jing Daily*. Retrieved 13 July 2022, from https://jingdaily.com/meet-chinas-luxury-influencer-savi-sui/

Quiroz-Gutierrez, M. (2022). Snoop Dogg caps years of metaverse and NFT investment by dropping a music video set in his own 'Snoopverse'. *Fortune*. Retrieved 12 July 2022, from https://fortune.com/2022/04/04/snoop-dogg-metaverse-music-video-virtual-world-nfts/

Rasmussen, M. (2022). Teflon Sega performs second virtual concert in the metaverse with wave. Retrieved 9 July 2022, from https://www.virtualhumans.org/article/teflon-sega-performs-2nd-virtual-concert-in-the-metaverse-with-wave

Raun, T. (2018). Capitalizing intimacy: New subcultural forms of micro-celebrity strategies and affective labour on YouTube. *Convergence*, *24*(1), 99–113.

Ravindra, S. (2022). How artificial intelligence is transforming influencer marketing. *Single Grain*. Retrieved 1 August 2022, from https://www.singlegrain.com/influencer-marketing/how-artificial-intelligence-is-transforming-influencer-marketing/

Regner, T. (2021). Crowdfunding a monthly income: An analysis of the membership platform Patreon. *Journal of Cultural Economics*, *45*(1), 133–142.

Rogers, E. (1995). *The diffusion of innovations*. London: Springer.

Rokka, J., & Canniford, R. (2016). Heterotopian selfies: How social media destabilizes brand assemblages. *European Journal of Marketing*, *50*(9/10), 1789–1813.

Rubin, R. B., & Rubin, A. M. (2001). Attribution in social and parasocial relationships. In V. Manusov & J. H. Harvey (Eds.), *Attribution, communication behavior, and close relationships* (pp. 320–337). Cambridge, MA: Cambridge University Press.

Russell, A. (2020). *The influencer code: How to unlock the power of influencer marketing*. Hobart, NY: Hatherleigh Press.

Russell, C. A., & Belch, M. (2005). A managerial investigation into the product placement industry. *Journal of Advertising Research*, *45*(1), 73–92.

Sanderson, R. (2019). Chiara Ferragni - The Italian influencer who built a global brand. Glossy. *Financial Times*. Retrieved 10 August 2022, from https://www.ft.com/content/9adce87c-2879-11e9-a5ab-ff8ef2b976c7

Sandler, E. (2020). How Tik Tok hashtag hijacking is impacting beauty campaigns. Glossy. Retrieved 4 August 2022, from https://www.glossy.co/beauty/how-tiktok-hashtag-hijacking-is-impacting-beauty-campaigns/

Santiago, J. K., & Castelo, I. M. (2020). Digital influencers: An exploratory study of influencer marketing campaign process on Instagram. *Online Journal of Applied Knowledge Management (OJAKM)*, *8*(2), 31–52.

Santora, J. (2022). 12 Types of influencers you can use to improve your marketing. *Influencer Marketing Hub*. Retrieved 10 August 2022, from https://influencermarketinghub.com/types-of-influencers/

Saxon, C. (2021). Cottagecore explained. What it is, how it started, why is so popular. *The Vou*. Retrieved 14 July 2022, from https://thevou.com/fashion/cottagecore/

Schaffer, N. (2020). *The age of influence: The power of influencers to elevate your brand*. Nashville, TN: Harper Collins Leadership.

Scharff, C. (2016). The psychic life of neoliberalism: Mapping the contours of entrepreneurial subjectivity. *Theory, Culture & Society*, *33*(6), 107–122.

Schembri, S., & Tichbon, J. (2017). Digital consumers as cultural curators: The irony of vaporwave. *Arts and the Market*, *7*(2), 191–212.

Schouten, A. P., Janssen, L., & Verspaget, M. (2020). Celebrity vs. Influencer endorsements in advertising: The role of identification, credibility, and product-endorser fit. *International Journal of Advertising*, *39*(2), 258–281.

Segraves, M. (2018). DC debates legalizing hedgehogs as pets. *NBCNews*. Retrieved 27 April 2022, from https://www.nbcwashington.com/news/local/dc-debates-legalizing-hedgehogs-as-pets/166841/

Senft, T. M. (2008). *Camgirls: Celebrity and community in the age of social networks*. New York, NY: Peter Lang.

Senft, T. M. (2013). Microcelebrity and the branded self. *A Companion to New Media Dynamics*, *11*, 346–354.

Senft, T. M., & Baym, N. K. (2015). What does the selfie say? Investigating a global phenomenon. *International Journal of Communication*, *9*, 1588–1606.

Sennett, R. (1998). *The corrosion of character: The personal consequences of work in the new capitalism. New York, NY*: WW Norton & Company.

Sheppard, A. (2022). Regulating sponsored influencer marketing. *The Regulatory Review*. Retrieved 10 August 2022, from https://www.theregreview.org/2022/06/01/sheppard-regulating-sponsored-influencer-marketing/

Shipilov, A., & Gawer, A. (2020). Integrating research on interorganizational networks and ecosystems. *Academy of Management Annals*, *14*(1), 92–121.

Shirky, C. (2008). *Here comes everybody: The power of organizing without organizations*. London: Penguin.

Shopify. (2021). 30+ Influencer marketing statistics to have on your radar. Retrieved 26 July 2022, from https://www.shopify.co.uk/blog/influencer-marketing-statistics

Siege Media. (2022). What is a content creator? And how can you become one? *Siege Media*. Retrieved 8 August 2022, from https://www.siegemedia.com/creation/content-creator

Singer, P. W., & Brooking, E. T. (2018). *LikeWar: The weaponization of social media*. Boston, MA: Eamon Dolan Books.

Slone, I. (2020). Escape into cottagecore, calming ethos for our febrile moment. *The New York Times*. Retrieved 14 July 2022, from https://www.nytimes.com/2020/03/10/style/cottagecore.html

Smith, N. C. (1995). Marketing strategies for the ethics era. *MIT Sloan Management Review*, *36*(4), 85.

Smith, R. G. (2015). *Affect and American literature in the age of neoliberalism*. Cambridge, MA: Cambridge University Press.

Sobande, F. (2017). Watching me watching you: Black women in Britain on YouTube. *European Journal of Cultural Studies*, *20*(6), 655–671.

Sobande, F. (2019). Woke-washing: 'Intersectional' femvertising and branding 'woke' bravery, *European Journal of Marketing, 54*(11), 2723–2745.

Sobande, F. (2021a). Spectacularized and branded digital (re) presentations of black people and blackness. *Television & New Media, 22*(2), 131–146.

Sobande, F. (2021b). CGI influencers. When the people we follow on social media aren't human. *The Conversation*. Retrieved 12 July 2022, from https://theconversation.com/cgi-influencers-when-the-people-we-follow-on-social-media-arent-human-165767

Social Day. (2021). *Uncovering the influencer pay gap: What does the research show and how can we tackle it?* Retrieved 17 February 2022, from https://www.socialday.live/features/uncovering-the-influencer-pay-gap

Sokolov, M. (2019). Virtual influencer trends: An overview of the industry. *The Drum*. Retrieved 8 July 2022, from https://www.thedrum.com/opinion/2019/12/05/virtual-influencer-trends-overview-the-industry

Sparks, H. (2022). 1 in 4 pet owners trying to turn furry friends into social media stars, survey says. *New York Post*. Retrieved 10 August 2022, from https://nypost.com/2022/04/04/1-in-4-pet-owners-trying-to-turn-fur-babies-into-social-media-stars/

Sprout Social. (2021). *The future of social media. New data for 2021 & beyond.* Research report. Retrieved 15 July 2022, from https://sproutsocial.com/insights/data/harris-insights-report/

Srnicek, N. (2017a). The challenges of platform capitalism: Understanding the logic of a new business model. *Juncture, 23*(4), 254–257.

Srnicek, N. (2017b). *Platform capitalism*. New York, NY: John Wiley & Sons.

Statista. (2021a). *Influencer marketing worldwide - Statistics & facts*. Retrieved 28 January 2022, from https://www.statista.com/topics/2496/influence-marketing/#dossierKeyfigures

Statista. (2021b). *Leading social media platforms used by marketers worldwide.* Retrieved 18 March 2022, from https://www.statista.com/statistics/259379/social-media-platforms-used-by-marketers-worldwide/

Statista. (2021c). *Petfluencers with the most Instagram followers worldwide 2020.* Retrieved 16 May 2022, from https://www.statista.com/statistics/785972/most-followers-instagram-petfluencers/

Statista. (2022). *Most popular social networks worldwide by number of users.* Retrieved 10 August 2022, from https://www.statista.com/statistics/272014/global-social-networks-ranked-by-number-of-users/

Stoldt, R., Wellman, M., Ekdale, B., & Tully, M. (2019). Professionalizing and profiting: The rise of intermediaries in the social media influencer industry. *Social Media + Society, 5*(1). doi:10.1177/2056305119832587

Stout, P. A., & Leckenby, J. D. (1986). Measuring emotional response to advertising. *Journal of Advertising, 15*(4), 35–42.

Tadajewski, M. (2020). Marketization: Exploring the geographic expansion of market ideology. In H. Roy Chaudhuri & R. Belk (Eds.), *Marketization* (pp. 3–20). Singapore: Springer. doi:10.1007/978-981-15-4514-6_1

Talagala, N. (2022). Data as the new oil is not enough. *Forbes*. Retrieved from https://www.forbes.com/sites/nishatalagala/2022/03/02/data-as-the-new-oil-is-not-enough-four-principles-for-avoiding-data-fires/?sh=625d99e1c208

TalkingInfluence.com. (2021). *WTF series: WTF is metafluence?* Retrieved 3 August 2022, from https://talkinginfluence.com/2021/12/03/wtf-series-wtf-is-metafluence/

Tapinfluence. (2018). Earn 11X ROI with new digital marketing channel. Tapinfluence. Retrieved 9 August 2022, from https://www.tapinfluence.com/tp_resource/influencer-generated-content-can-fit-marketing-strategy/

Taylor, M., Marsh, G., Nicole, D., & Broadbent, P. (2017). *Good work: The Taylor review of modern working practices*. UK Department for Business, Energy & Industrial Strategy. Retrieved 1 March 2018, from https://www.gov.uk/government/publications/good-workthe-taylor-review-of-modern-working-practices

Tedlow, R. S., & Jones, G. G. (Eds.). (2014). *The rise and fall of mass marketing (RLE Marketing)*. London: Routledge.

Tenbarge, K. (2019). A family vlogger who recently built a $10-million mansion said that fans should have to pay to watch his videos and he's getting ripped to shreds. *Insider*. Retrieved 15 March 2022, from https://www.insider.com/austin-mcbroom-ace-family-complains-people-should-pay-youtube-videos-2019-12

Tendo.com. (2022). Content asset. Retrieved 10 August 2022, from https://tendocom.com/glossary/content-asset/#:~:text=A%20content%20asset%20is%20any,audience%2C%20purpose%2C%20and%20goals

The Guardian. (2018). Miquela the 'cyborg' and handbag drones – Milan fashion week's weird vision of the future. Retrieved 20 January 2022, from https://www.theguardian.com/fashion/2018/feb/27/miquela-cyborg-handbag-drones-milan-fashion-week-weird-vision-future

The Guardian. (2020). Kim Kardashian West at 40: How the queen of social media changed the world. Retrieved 4 August 2022, from https://www.theguardian.com/lifeandstyle/2020/oct/21/kim-kardashian-west-at-40-how-the-queen-of-social-media-changed-the-world

Thorsen, D. E. (2010). The neoliberal challenge. What is neoliberalism? *Contemporary Readings in Law and Social Justice, 2*(2), 188–214.

TikTok. (2021). New studies quantify TikTok's growing impact on culture and music. Retrieved 24 May 2022, from https://newsroom.tiktok.com/en-us/new-studies-quantify-tiktoks-growing-impact-on-culture-and-music

Toccoli, A. (2022). La storia di Hatsune Miku: da Vocaloid a Icona Pop in Giappone e nel mondo. *Voyapon*. Retrieved 4 July 2022, from https://voyapon.com/it/hatsune-miku-vocaloid-giappone/

Tomasena, J. M. (2019). Negotiating collaborations: BookTubers, the publishing industry, and YouTube's ecosystem. *Social Media + Society, 5*(4). doi:10.1177/2056305119894004

Tomoson. (2022). Influencer marketing study. *tomoson.com*. Retrieved 28 July 2022, from https://www.tomoson.com/blog/influencer-marketing-study/

Torres, P., Augusto, M., & Matos, M. (2019). Antecedents and outcomes of digital influencer endorsement: An exploratory study. *Psychology & Marketing, 36*(12), 1267–1276.

Travers, C. (2020). What is a virtual influencer? Virtual influencers, defined and explained. Retrieved 10 July 2022, from https://www.virtualhumans.org/article/what-is-a-virtual-influencer-virtual-influencers-defined-and-explained

Truth in Advertising. (2022). Another one: TINA.org calls out DJ Khaled's undisclosed alcohol ads, again. TINA.org. Retrieved 4 August 2022, from https://truthinadvertising.org/articles/another-one-tina-org-calls-out-dj-khaleds-undisclosed-alcohol-ads-again/

Turner, G. (2006). The mass production of celebrity: 'Celetoids', reality TV and the 'demotic turn'. *International Journal of Cultural Studies*, *9*(2), 153–165.

Tybout, A. M., & Sternthal, B. (2012). Developing a compelling brand positioning. In A. M. Tybout & B. J. Calder (Eds.), *Kellogg on marketing* (pp. 73–91). New York, NY: Wiley Online Library.

Urban Paws. (2021). Quirky, cute and cool – Why you should choose an exotic pet influencer! Retrieved 18 May 2022, from https://www.urbanpawsuk.com/2021/10/12/quirky-cute-and-cool-why-you-should-choose-an-exotic-pet-influencer/

Usher, B. (2020). Rethinking microcelebrity: Key points in practice, performance and purpose. *Celebrity Studies*, *11*(2), 171–188.

Uzunoğlu, E., & Kip, S. M. (2014). Brand communication through digital influencers: Leveraging blogger engagement. *International Journal of Information Management*, *34*(5), 592–602.

Vallas, S., & Schor, J. B. (2020). What do platforms do? Understanding the gig economy. *Annual Review of Sociology*, *46*, 273–294.

van Dijck, J. (2013). *The culture of connectivity: A critical history of social media*. Oxford: Oxford University Press.

Venkatesh, A., & Meamber, L. A. (2006). Arts and aesthetics: Marketing and cultural production. *Marketing Theory*, *6*(1), 11–39.

Veresiu, E., & Parmentier, M. A. (2021). Advanced style influencers: Confronting gendered ageism in fashion and beauty markets. *Journal of the Association for Consumer Research*, *6*(2), 263–273.

Vogue Business. (2022). What influencer marketing looks like in the metaverse. Retrieved 29 July 2022, from https://www.voguebusiness.com/technology/what-influencer-marketing-looks-like-in-the-metaverse

von Hippel, E. (1986). Lead users: A source of novel product concepts. *Management Science*, *32*(7), 791–805.

Wang, P., Huang, Q., & Davison, R. M. (2020). How do digital influencers affect social commerce intention? The roles of social power and satisfaction. *Information Technology & People*, *34*(3), 1065–1086.

We Are Social. (2021). In-feed syllabuses. Retrieved 22 April 2022, from https://thinkforward.wearesocial.com/in-feed-syllabuses.html

We Are Social. (2022). All tomorrow's stories. Retrieved 24 April 2022, from https://wearesocial.com/uk/wp-content/uploads/sites/2/2022/02/We-Are-Social-All-Tomorrows-Stories.pdf

Webster, A. (2020). Travis Scott's first Fortnite concert was surreal and spectacular. *The Verge*. Retrieved 18 May 2022, from https://www.theverge.com/2020/4/23/21233637/travis-scott-fortnite-concert-astronomical-live-report

Wellman, M. L., Stoldt, R., Tully, M., & Ekdale, B. (2020). Ethics of authenticity: Social media influencers and the production of sponsored content. *Journal of Media Ethics*, *35*(2), 68–82.

Wiley, D. (2020). Diversity in influencer marketing: Why your brand needs to get it right. *Forbes*. Retrieved 25 February 2022, from https://www.forbes.com/sites/forbesagencycouncil/2020/05/28/diversity-in-influencer-marketing-why-your-brand-needs-to-get-it-right/?sh=54a7aecb5934

Williamson, E. (2022). A child's Tik Tok stardom opens doors. Then, a gunman arrives. *The New York Times*. Retrieved 11 August 2022, from https://www.nytimes.com/2022/02/17/us/politics/tiktok-ava-majury.html

Wiseman, E. (2021). The dark side of wellness: The overlap between spiritual thinking and far-right conspiracies. The Guardian. Retrieved 2 August 2022, from https://www.theguardian.com/lifeandstyle/2021/oct/17/eva-wiseman-conspirituality-the-dark-side-of-wellness-how-it-all-got-so-toxic

Wissinger, E. (2007). Modelling a way of life: Immaterial and affective labour in the fashion modelling industry. *Ephemera: Theory and Politics in Organization*, *7*(1), 250–269.

Wofford, B. (2022). Meet the lobbyist next door. *Wired*. Retrieved 30 July 2022, from https://www.wired.com/story/meet-the-lobbyist-next-door/

Woodcock, J., & Graham, M. (2020). *The gig economy. A critical introduction*. Cambridge: Polity.

Woodcock, J., & Johnson, M. R. (2019). The affective labor and performance of live streaming on Twitch.tv. *Television & New Media*, *20*(8), 813–823.

Wood, A. J., Graham, M., Lehdonvirta, V., & Hjorth, I. (2019). Good gig, bad gig: Autonomy and algorithmic control in the global gig economy. *Work, Employment and Society*, *33*(1), 56–75.

Yankelovich, D., & Meer, D. (2006). Rediscovering market segmentation. *Harvard Business Review*, *84*(2), 122.

Yeboah, S. (2019). By only using white influencers, brands are telling black women we don't belong. *Metro*. Retrieved 5 February 2022, from https://metro.co.uk/2019/06/03/by-only-using-white-influencers-brands-are-telling-black-women-we-dont-belong-9744197/

Yin, Y. (2020). An emergent algorithmic culture: The data-ization of online fandom in China. *International Journal of Cultural Studies*, *23*(4), 475–492.

Yong, D. L., Fam, S. D., & Lum, S. (2011). Reel conservation: Can big screen animations save tropical biodiversity? *Tropical Conservation Science*, *4*(3), 244–253.

Zhou, W. (2022). China further tightens rules on livestream hosts with new regulation. *Technode.com*. Retrieved 24 July 2022, from https://technode.com/2022/06/23/china-further-tightens-rules-on-livestream-hosts-with-new-regulation/

Zuboff, S. (2009). *The age of surveillance capitalism*. London: Profile Books.

Zuckerman, E. (2012). An idea worth at least 40 nanoKardashians of your attention. Retrieved 4 August 2022, from https://ethanzuckerman.com/2012/05/02/an-idea-worth-at-least-40-nanokardashians-of-your-attention/

Zwick, D., Bonsu, S. K., & Darmody, A. (2008). Putting consumers to work: Co-creation and new marketing govern-mentality. *Journal of Consumer Culture*, *8*(2), 163–196.

INDEX

A

Aanam C, 101

Accessibility, influencer culture, 165

Activist influencers, 204, 205

Aden, Halima, 276, 276 (figure)

Advertising, 5, 57–62

Advertising agencies, 102–103

Advertising measurement, 294–295

   awareness, 295

   conversion, 295

   digital components, 296

   impressions, 295

   reach, 295

Affective labour, 176

Affiliate marketing, 70–71

Affordance, 31 (figure), 35–36

Affordance theory, 35–36

Ageism, 146

Algorithms, 36–37

   algorithmic branding, 67

   algorithmic culture, 45–46

Alice, Tiffany, 116

Alizadeh, Madeleine Darya, 15

Amazon's Associates Program, 71

Angiolini, Ambra, 244

Apex Legends game, 6

Appadurai, Arjun, 87

Aristotle, 128

Artificial intelligence (AI), 251, 324–325

Aspirational labour, 44

Attention economy, 42–43, 104

Attitude, 123

Audiences, 104–105

Authenticity, 14, 40, 126, 159 (figure), 166–167

Autobiographical storytelling, 164

Autopreneurs, 38–39, 169

Avatar economy, 334–336

Ayayi, 94

B

Bailon, Adrienne, 208

Banbo Kitty, 332

Barbie, 93, 332

Base and superstructure, influencer system, 30–32, 31 (figure)

Behavioural targeting, 72

Benati, Nima, 244

Bernstein, Danielle, 7

Bhabie, Bhad, 172

Bieber, Justin, 12

Bilton, Nick, 188

Black Girl Magic, 250

Blevins, Richard Tyler, "Ninja", 4–6, 36

Blogger-based strategies, 6

Bloomberg, Michael, 276

Body positivity, 146

Brand ambassadors, 7, 13–14, 19, 18–19, 19 (figure), 60, 93, 114, 179, 248, 331

Brand Desire Spiral, 69–70, 70 (figure), 73, 79

Brand safety, 251–252

Branded content, 60. See also native advertising

Branding, 56, 58, 64, 296–297

Brands, 58, 100–101

Brandwashing, 280

Bravura, Jess, 4

Brossy Meowington, 92

Bruce Wayne & Co., 216

Business ecosystem, 87

Business team, 89 (figure), 95

Business-to-business (B2B) influencers, 12–13, 90

Business-to-consumer (B2C) influencers, 12, 90

C

Calls to Action (CTAs), 129–131, 130 (table), 298–299

Camilleri, Léa, 311

Campaign, influencer marketing, 220

Campaign brief, 259

Campaign design, 236

Campaign execution and management, 274–275, 277–284. See also influencer campaigns

content approval, 280–281
content co-development, 277–278
dos and don'ts, 287, 288 (figure)
implementation, 284–286
internal coordination, 281–282
monitoring, 220 (figure), 232, 277, 282–283,
283 (figure)
types of, 275
Campaign process, influencer marketing,
220–221, 220 (figure)
planning, 222–223
partnering, 241–267
execution, 271–289
evaluation, 294–312
Cancel culture, 45, 178–179
Candy, virtual influencer, 93
Cardi B, 208
Carrillo-Bucaram, Kristina, 12
Cassell, Tom, 4
Castells, Manuel, 119
Celebrity, 13, 19, 19 (figure)
endorsement, 62
Celebrity influencers, 88, 94–95
Charles, James, 99, 161–162, 162 (figure),
173, 253
Cialdini, Robert, 129–131, 130 (table)
Clydeo, 332
Coercion, social influence, 114, 122
Co-creation, 219
Coercive power, 114 (figure), 115
Collabs, 101
Colonel Sanders, 78
Commercialisation, 175–176
Commodification, 160, 169–175
Community building, 74–75
Compensation, influencer, 265, 311–312
Compliance, social influence, 120
Consumer subcultures, 322–323, 327–328
Conspirituality influencers, 119
Content, 10
amplification, 58, 234
approval, 264
asset, 225
branding, see Social media content
branding
censorship, 204
co-creation, see Content co-development
commercialisation, see Commercialisation
commodification, 170
curation, 174–175
monetisation, 31(figure), 36, 41, 48,
169–177
problematic content, 199
professionalisation, see Professionalisation

Content co-development, 277–280
Content creation-focused campaign, 224
Content creators, see Creators
Contract, 262–263, 264 (table)–266 (table),
266
Cost per mille (CPM), 298
Cottagecore aesthetics, 322–323, 323 (figure)
COVID-19 coronavirus pandemic and
influencers, 6–7, 318–319
Creation culture, 76
Creative brief, 258
Creative team, 89 (figure), 90, 92, 95, 219
Creator economy, 47–48, 76
Creators, 15–19, 16 (figure), 19 (figure)
Beeple-Crap, 17, 18 (figure)
definition, 58
vs. influencers, 15–17, 16 (figure)
sWooZie, 18
types of, 90
Crowd learning, 77
Culpo, Olivia, 180
Cultural normalisation, 331

D
D'Amelio, Charli, 9–10, 99
Daisy Yoox, 93
Darnell, Nicole, 208
Data, 37–38
privacy regulation, 207
Davis, Kelvin, 138–139, 146, 152
Deepfakes, 325–326
De Jager, Nikkie, 149, 166
Demotic turn, 160
Destination Marketing Organisation (DMO),
310–311
Diffusion of innovations, 321
Digital economy, 30
Digital agencies, 102–103
Digital marketers, 14–15, 18–19, 19 (figure)
Disclosure guidelines, 201–203
Diversity, 139–142
types of, 140, 140 (figure)
structural barriers to, 144–145
Women in Influencer Marketing (WIIM), 141
DJ Khaled, 201
Dobrik, David, 194
Doja Cat, 238
Dolly Pawton, 92
Donelij, Chris, 194
Doug the Pug, 10
Down syndrome, 331
Drake, 4
Dramageddon 2.0, 161–162, 162 (figure), 173
Dramatisation, 159, 160, 163

Dunbar's Number, 117
Dunham, Lena, 276

E
#Eachversionofyou campaign, 244–245, 245
    (figure), 246 (figure)
Earned media, 61, *see also* PESO model
Earned media value (EMV), 302
Ecosystem, 86. *See also* Influencer and
    creator ecosystem
Eguavoen, Valerie, 139
Elaboration Likelihood Model (ELM), 124–125
Emotional labour, 176–177
Engagement, 255, 261, 263, 294, 303–307,
    305 (figure)
Engagement pods, 91, 256
EnkyBoys, 302
Entrepreneurship, 38–39, 47
Eos campaign, 286–287
Equity, 142–143
    structural barriers, 144–145
E-sports, 4, 233, 322, 338
Ethical influencer marketing, 190–193
    decision-making, 189–190
    rule-bound ethical principles, 191
    rules, types, 191
    situational ethical principles, 191
    situational marketing ethics, 192–194
Eugene the Egg, 10–11
Exotic animal influencers, 194–196
Expedia, 72
Expert power, 115–116
Exploitation, 144
Extremisation, 168–169

F
Fake followers, 188, 199
Fan labour, 39–40
Fedez, 86, 99
Ferragni, Chiara, 13, 86, 99
Fishbach, Mark, 4
Fitness influencers, 118
Foer, Drusilla, 244–245
FOMO and social comparison, 179–180
Fraudulent influencers, 199
Free market economy, 48
FTC Act, United States, 196, 199, 203
Fujita, Saki, 328
Funnel, *see* Marketing funnel

G
Gadot, Gal, 325
Galaxia, 103
Gamification, 174

Gig economy, 43–44
Government censorship, 204
Government-sponsored influencer
    campaigns, COVID-19, 217
Grahn, Sofia, 147, 152
Grande, Ariana, 12
Granovetter, Mark, 117, 173
Guggimon, 10, 331

H
Hannigan, Christina, 196
Hardball culture, 192
Harris, Calvin, 12
Hashtag hijacking, 168–169
Hatsune Miku, 327–328, 328 (figure)
Hawkins, Nina, 93
Hayden, Chloé, 148
Hellyer, Caitlin, 140
Herbee the hedgehog, 195
Hiltz, Nikki, 14
Hinish, Sheri, 13
Humby, Clive, 37
Hustle culture, 171
Hype House, 91
Hyperrealism, 326–327
Hyptertextuality, 169

I
Identification, social influence, 120
Ideology, 32–33, 47–48
Iggy Joey, 216
Imani, Blair, 150–152, 151 (figure)
Imma, 326
Inclusion
    advocacy, 147–148
    and exclusion, 145–146
Influence, 112–113
Influencer, *see* Influencers
Influencer activists, 204, 206–207
Influencer advertising, 21
Influencer and creator ecosystem, 89 (figure)
    media ecosystem, 87
Influencer campaigns
    budgeting, 227–228, 228 (table)
    campaign planning, 222–223
    campaign types, 231–232, 231 (figure)
    design, 236
    influencer type and quantity selection,
        230–231
    goal characteristics, 226–227
    goals, types of, 223–224, 223 (figure)
    influencer platform selection, 229–230
    process, 220–221, 220 (figure)
    target audience identification, 228–229

influencer collectives, 91
Influencer communication process, 122, 122 (figure)
Influencer compensation, 144, 220 (figure), 222, 228, 311–312
Influencer culture, 159–181
  loss of privacy and threats to safety, 181
  marketisation and, 160
  personal branding, 170
  selfie culture, 163
  forces and effects of, 159, 159 (figure)
Influencer debrief, 311–312
Influencer equity, 251–252
influencer identification, 247, 251
Influencer intelligence, 147
Influencer marketing, 21–23, 151–152
  vs. influencer advertising, 21, 23 (figure)
  vs. influencer relations, 20–21, 23 (figure)
Influencer marketing measurement
  promo codes, 310–311
  qualitative data, 304
  short-term sales, 296–297
  goals for, 299–300
Influencer marketing platforms, 90, 103–104
Influencer marketing tools, 221–222
influencer outreach, 256–258, 258 (figure)
Influencer-owned brands, 101–102
Influencer pay gap, 143–144, 143 (figure)
Influencer relations, 22–23, 23 (figure)
Influencer takeover, see social media takeover
Influencers,
  characteristics and roles, 18–20
  definition, 8, 8 (table)
  qualities of, 9–11
  revenue streams, 6
  types of, 88
  what an influencer is not, 11–13
Influencer vetting, 252–254
Informational power, 116
Innanen, Jack, 180
Instagram effect, 200
Instruments of production, 31 (figure), 34–38
Intensification, 159, 161–163, 162 (figure)
Internalisation, social influence, 120
Intersectional influencers, 149–150
Intersectionality, 149–151
Intimacy, 166

J
James, Lebron, 138
Jenkins, Henry, 39
Jenner, Kendall, 10
Jenner, Kris, 95

Jenner, Kylie, 12
Jerrard, Meg, 15
Johansson, Scarlett, 325
JOMO, 179
Joy, Carly, 286–287

K
Kaito, 327
Kami, 331
Kardashian, Kim, 12, 112, 117, 231
Karkai, Yam, 336
Katebi, Hoda, 168
Kattan, Huda, 321
Katz, Elihu, 14
Kelman, Herbert, 120
Key opinion customers (KOCs), 14
Key opinion leader (KOL), 14
Key performance indicators (KPIs), 237, 246, 298, 305, 305 (figure)
Kjellberg, Felix, "PewDiePie", 180, 193–194

L
Labour markets, 43
Lady Gaga, 166, 327
Laissez-faire capitalism, 48
Lazarsfeld, Paul, 14
Lead users, 321–322
Leesa Mattress, 294
Legitimate power, 115
Leong, Lydia, 90
LGBTQ+ influencers, 148–149
Lierac Italia, 244–245, 245 (figure), 246 (figure)
Lilian brand, 308–309
Lil Miquela, 61–62
Lithunium Snow, 127
Livestreaming, 234
Lonelygirl15, 190
Lorna Jane influencer campaign, 233
Lu do Magalu, 11

M
Macro influencers, 88, 94–95
Majury, Ava, 158, 181
Managers, 94–95
Manipulation, social influence, 114
Marketing, 56–66. See also Branding, Influencer marketing
  definition, 57
  ethics, 191–194
  vs. public relations, 20–21
Marketing funnel, 65–66, 66 (figure)
Marketing mix, 57
Marketisation, 177–181
Marx, Karl, 30

Matthews, Alexa, 131
Mattsson, Moa, 101
McKeen, Summer, 179–180
McLaughlin, Sean William, 4
McLuhan, Marshall, 127
MCN, *see* Multichannel networks
Media
    earned media, 61
    owned media, 61
    paid media, 61
    PESO model, 59–60, 60 (figure)
    shared media, 61
    social media, 58, 61
Mega influencers, 88, 94–95
Meiko, 327
Mental health education and influencers,
    147–148
Messi, Lionel, 333
Metafluence, 333
Metaverse, 332–338
Micro influencers, 88
Mills, Elle, 180
Minnie Mouse, 331
Momfluencer, 19, 30, 39
Monetisation, 11–12, 41–42, 177
Mongeau, Tana, 172
Monty Happiness, 207
Morality, 194
Mr. Bag, 101
Mr. Pokee, 195
Mukbang, 67–69, 69 (figure)
Multichannel networks (MCN), 95–96

N

Nano influencers, 88
Native advertising, 61, 70–71, 73, 105,
    198–199, 234
Negotiation, 260–262
Neoliberalism, 47–48
Network power, 120
Neubauer, Luisa, 167
Neufluence, 141–142
Neutrogena, 72
Nicole, Darnell, 208
Ninja, 4–7, 36
Nobody Sausage, 332
Non-fungible tokens (NFTS), 333–334
Non-human influencers, 194–195
Normative social influence, 121
Notoriously Dapper, 138–139, 146, 152

O

Obama, Barack, 167, 325
Ohanian model of source credibility model,
    126, 126 (figure)

Ole Henriksen campaign, 278–280, 279 (table)
OnlyFans, 172
Opinion leaders, 14, 19, 19 (figure)
Organic reach, 59
Oscar the Corgi, 92
Owned media, 60–61, *see also* PESO model

P

Paid media, 21, 60, 71, *see also* PESO model
Pandora campaign, 237
Parasocial relationship, 172
Partnering, 252–267
Parton, Dolly, 232
Paul, Jake, 91, 99
Paul, Logan, 7, 194
Pay gap, equity, 143–144, 143 (figure)
Pelosi, Nancy, 325
Pick, Tom, 221
Personal brand, 170
Personal branding, 9–11
Persuasion,
    channel and message characteristics,
        127–129
    Cialdini's principles of, 129–131, 130 (figure)
    definition, 122
    persuasion knowledge, 5–6
    receiver characteristics, 123–125
    source characteristics, 126–127, 126
        (figure)
PESO model, 59–60, 60 (figure), 60 (table)
Pet influencers, 91–92
PewDiePie, *see* Kjellberg, Felix
Phatic culture, 173
Phatic exchange, 173
Platforms, *see* Social media platforms
Porsche-iMaker collaboration, 93–94
Positioning, 64–65
Post-truth, 193–194
Potter Box, 192
Power
    definition, 33
    instruments, 34–35
    resource-based theory, 33
    social media platform power, 34–38
    sources of social influence power, 114–115
        (table)
Prada influencer takeover, 61–62
Predictions, influencers in the future, 336–338
Prince William, 167
Privacy and threats to personal safety, 181
Problematic content, 199
Product placement, 62
Product seeding, 220 (figure), 231, 232, 267,
    303

Professionalisation, 159, 174–175
Public relations, 20–22, 57
  agencies, 90, 102–103
  vs. marketing, 20–22

Q
Quang Tran, 67–69, 69 (figure)
Quest Nutrition, 248–251
Quiroa, Marimar, 140–141

R
Ratcliffe, Amy, 12
Real Qai Qai, 332
Reciprocity strategies, 131
Referent power, 115
Regulation, 196-203
  disclosure guidelines, 201–203
  fake followers, 199
  fraudulent influencers, 199
Regulators, see Regulatory agencies
Regulatory agencies, 105–106
Reif, Pamela, 101
Relational capital, 41–42
Relations of production, 31 (figure), 38–42
Remarketing, 72
Remix the Dog, 216
Renner, Brittany, 208
Reputation economy, 44–45
Resource-based theory of power, 33
Retargeting, 72
Return on investment (ROI), 247, 300–303,
  301 (figure)
Reward power, 115
Rhetorical triangle, 128
Riccobono, Eva, 244
Rock, Bretman, 278–280, 279 (figure)
Rock, Chris, 178
Rogers, Everett, 320, 321
ROI, see Return on investment
Ronaldo, Cristiano, 12
Rose, Jessica, 190
Rose, Julie, 10
Rubens, Eric, 24
Russell, Amanda, 254, 275, 306, 309

S
Schaffer, Neal, 221
Schemer's schema, 5, 7
Scott, Travis, 4, 335
Search engine marketing (SEM), 73–74
Search engine optimization (SEO), 73
Sears, JP, 119
Segmentation, 63–64
Selfies, 163-164, 175

Selfie culture, 163
Self-presentation, 170
Selters, Jen, 12
Shared media, 61, see also PESO model
Shelesh, Alia Marie, 4
Shopify, 216
Shudu, 103, 329–331
Sibley, Martyn, 140
Simpson, Jessica, 117
Sina Weibo, 40
Singh, Lilly, 180
Situational marketing ethics, 192–194
Skin positivity, 147
SMART goals, 226
Smith, Will, 178
Smith-Schuster, JuJu, 4
Snoop Dogg, 166, 336
Social- and self-comparison effects, 179
Social capital, 41–42
Social influence,
  network structure, 116–118
  as power, 118
  outcomes of, 113
  reactions to, 120–122
  sources of, 114–116, 114 (table)–115 (table)
Social justice, 151
Social media, 4–9, 12, 40, 204, 336–338
  platforms, 97
Social media content branding, 17
Social media platform power, 34
Social media takeover, 61
Social power, 118
Societal base, 31
Societal superstructure, 31
Solares, Jenny, 302
Source credibility, 126
Sparks, Jordin, 208
Specialised media platform, 99
Sphere of influence, 113
Star, Jeffree, 161–162, 321–322
Strategic communication, 218–219
Stream of consciousness, 164
Sugg, Zoe, "Zoella", 167
Sui, Savi, 260
Surveillance capitalism, 46–47
Synthetic media, 142, 325

T
Tahmasian, Lilian, 308–309
Talent agencies, 96–97
Target audience, 229
Targeting, 64
Taylor, Natalia, 198
Team 10, 91

Technoculture, 42
Technocultural superstructure, 31 (figure), 42–47
Technological drivers of change, 324–327
Technological scrutiny, 46
Teddy the Poodle, 216
Teflon Sega, 332–333, 335
The ACE family, 165–166
The Bucket List Family, 10
The Good Advice Cupcake, 332
The Kardashians, 78, 98
Thorne, Adande, "sWooZie", 18
Thunberg, Greta, 11
TikTok, 75
    algorithm, 45
    challenge, 61
Traditional mass media, 98–99
Trajectories, see Predictions, influencers in the future
Trump, Donald, 119–120
Trust, 285–286
Truth-in-advertising, 105–106, 201–203
Twitch, 4, 98
Two-step flow theory, 14
Tyler, Ziggy, 45

U
Uncanny valley, 327
UNICEF campaign, 276, 276 (figure)
User-generated content (UGC), 87–88

V
Van Vu, Julie, 149, 175
Van Vucht, Jelle, 4
Vanity metrics, 297

Video game streamers, 4, 5 (table)
Virality, 58
Virtual influencers, 93-94, 103, 127, 131, 142, 325–327, 335, 337
    ethical challenges of, 329–330
Vulnerable audiences, 199–200

W
Wanzi, Xiao, 329
WeChat, 90, 329
Westbrook, Tati, 161–162
Whitelisting, 234–236
Willis, Bruce, 325
Wilson, Cameron-James, 330
Winkelmann, Michael Joseph, 15–18, 18 (figure)
Wisbiski, Sabrina, 43
Woke-washing, 330
Wolfe, David, 119
Women in Influencer Marketing (WIIM), 141
Word of mouth, 59

X
Xiaxue, 194

Y
Yeboah, Stephanie, 139
Yeyush and Renzo, 216
Yousafzai, Malala, 205–206
YouTube, 36

Z
Zoella, see Sugg, Zoe
Zozoliina, 171
Zuckerman, Ethan, 112